ECONOMICS

CFA® Program Curriculum
2025 • LEVEL I • VOLUME 2

©2024 by CFA Institute. All rights reserved. This copyright covers material written expressly for this volume by the editor/s as well as the compilation itself. It does not cover the individual selections herein that first appeared elsewhere. Permission to reprint these has been obtained by CFA Institute for this edition only. Further reproductions by any means, electronic or mechanical, including photocopying and recording, or by any information storage or retrieval systems, must be arranged with the individual copyright holders noted.

CFA®, Chartered Financial Analyst®, AIMR-PPS®, and GIPS® are just a few of the trademarks owned by CFA Institute. To view a list of CFA Institute trademarks and the Guide for Use of CFA Institute Marks, please visit our website at www.cfainstitute.org.

This publication is designed to provide accurate and authoritative information in regard to the subject matter covered. It is sold with the understanding that the publisher is not engaged in rendering legal, accounting, or other professional service. If legal advice or other expert assistance is required, the services of a competent professional should be sought.

All trademarks, service marks, registered trademarks, and registered service marks are the property of their respective owners and are used herein for identification purposes only.

ISBN 9781953337993 (paper)
ISBN 9781961409118 (ebook)
May 2024

SKY908977EE-5A53-4BA6-8E54-5AC0DE1408F5_032624

Please visit our website at
www.WileyGlobalFinance.com.

CONTENTS

How to Use the CFA Program Curriculum   vii
    CFA Institute Learning Ecosystem (LES)   vii
    Designing Your Personal Study Program   vii
    Errata   viii
    Other Feedback   viii

Economics

Learning Module 1   **The Firm and Market Structures**   3
    Introduction   3
    Profit Maximization: Production Breakeven, Shutdown and Economies of Scale   6
        Profit-Maximization, Breakeven, and Shutdown Points of Production   7
        Breakeven Analysis and Shutdown Decision   9
        The Shutdown Decision   10
        Economies and Diseconomies of Scale with Short-Run and Long-Run Cost Analysis   14
    Introduction to Market Structures   20
        Analysis of Market Structures   20
    Monopolistic Competition   25
        Demand Analysis in Monopolistically Competitive Markets   26
        Supply Analysis in Monopolistically Competitive Markets   27
        Optimal Price and Output in Monopolistically Competitive Markets   27
        Long-Run Equilibrium in Monopolistic Competition   28
    Oligopoly   29
        Oligopoly and Pricing Strategies   29
        Demand Analysis and Pricing Strategies in Oligopoly Markets   30
        The Cournot Assumption   32
        The Nash Equilibrium   34
        Oligopoly Markets: Optimal Price, Output, and Long-Run Equilibrium   36
    Determining Market Structure   40
        Econometric Approaches   41
        Simpler Measures   42
    Practice Problems   45
    Solutions   48

Learning Module 2   **Understanding Business Cycles**   49
    Introduction   49
    Overview of the Business Cycle   51
        Phases of the Business Cycle   52
        Leads and Lags in Business and Consumer Decision Making   55
        Market Conditions and Investor Behavior   55
    Credit Cycles   57
        Applications of Credit Cycles   58

	Consequences for Policy	59
	Economic Indicators over the Business Cycle	60
	The Workforce and Company Costs	60
	Fluctuations in Capital Spending	61
	Fluctuations in Inventory Levels	63
	Economic Indicators	65
	Types of Indicators	65
	Composite Indicators	66
	Leading Indicators	66
	Using Economic Indicators	67
	Other Composite Leading Indicators	68
	Surveys	70
	The Use of Big Data in Economic Indicators	70
	Nowcasting	70
	GDPNow	71
	Practice Problems	*74*
	Solutions	*77*
Learning Module 3	**Fiscal Policy**	**79**
	Introduction	79
	Introduction to Monetary and Fiscal Policy	80
	Roles and Objectives of Fiscal Policy	83
	Roles and Objectives of Fiscal Policy	83
	Deficits and the National Debt	88
	Fiscal Policy Tools	92
	The Advantages and Disadvantages of Different Fiscal Policy Tools	95
	Modeling the Impact of Taxes and Government Spending: The Fiscal Multiplier	96
	The Balanced Budget Multiplier	97
	Fiscal Policy Implementation	98
	Deficits and the Fiscal Stance	99
	Difficulties in Executing Fiscal Policy	100
	Practice Problems	*103*
	Solutions	*104*
Learning Module 4	**Monetary Policy**	**105**
	Introduction	105
	Role of Central Banks	106
	Roles of Central Banks and Objectives of Monetary Policy	107
	The Objectives of Monetary Policy	109
	Monetary Policy Tools and Monetary Transmission	111
	Open Market Operations	112
	The Central Bank's Policy Rate	112
	Reserve Requirements	113
	The Transmission Mechanism	113
	Monetary Policy Objectives	116
	Inflation Targeting	116
	Central Bank Independence	117

Contents

Credibility	117
Transparency	118
The Bank of Japan	121
The US Federal Reserve System	121
Exchange Rate Targeting	123
Contractionary and Expansionary Monetary Policies and Their Limitations	125
What's the Source of the Shock to the Inflation Rate?	126
Limitations of Monetary Policy	126
Interaction of Monetary and Fiscal Policy	132
The Relationship Between Monetary and Fiscal Policy	132
Practice Problems	*137*
Solutions	*139*

Learning Module 5 Introduction to Geopolitics 141

Introduction	141
National Governments and Political Cooperation	144
State and Non-State Actors	144
Features of Political Cooperation	145
Resource Endowment, Standardization, and Soft Power	147
The Role of Institutions	148
Hierarchy of Interests and Costs of Cooperation	149
Power of the Decision Maker	150
Political Non-Cooperation	150
Forces of Globalization	152
Features of Globalization	154
Motivations for Globalization	156
Costs of Globalization and Threats of Rollback	157
Threats of Rollback of Globalization	159
International Trade Organizations	160
Role of the International Monetary Fund	161
World Bank Group and Developing Countries	163
World Trade Organization and Global Trade	164
Assessing Geopolitical Actors and Risk	167
Archetypes of Country Behavior	167
The Tools of Geopolitics	173
The Tools of Geopolitics	173
Multifaceted Approaches	177
Geopolitical Risk and Comparative Advantage	178
Geopolitical Risk and the Investment Process	179
Types of Geopolitical Risk	179
Assessing Geopolitical Threats	182
Impact of Geopolitical Risk	184
Tracking Risks According to Signposts	185
Manifestations of Geopolitical Risk	186
Acting on Geopolitical Risk	188
Practice Problems	*190*
Solutions	*192*

Learning Module 6	**International Trade**	**195**
	Introduction	195
	Benefits and Costs of Trade	196
	Benefits and Costs of International Trade	197
	Trade Restrictions and Agreements—Tariffs, Quotas, and Export Subsidies	199
	Tariffs	200
	Quotas	202
	Export Subsidies	203
	Trading Blocs and Regional Integration	205
	Types Of Trading Blocs	206
	Regional Integration	207
	Practice Problems	*211*
	Solutions	*213*
Learning Module 7	**Capital Flows and the FX Market**	**215**
	Introduction	215
	The Foreign Exchange Market and Exchange Rates	216
	Introduction and the Foreign Exchange Market	216
	Market Participants	223
	Market Composition	226
	Exchange Rate Quotations	229
	Exchange Rate Regimes: Ideals and Historical Perspective	233
	The Ideal Currency Regime	233
	Historical Perspective on Currency Regimes	234
	A Taxonomy of Currency Regimes	237
	Exchange Rates and the Trade Balance: Introduction	245
	Capital Restrictions	246
	Practice Problems	*250*
	Solutions	*251*
Learning Module 8	**Exchange Rate Calculations**	**253**
	Introduction	253
	Cross-Rate Calculations	254
	Forward Rate Calculations	258
	Arbitrage Relationships	259
	Forward Discounts and Premiums	262
	Practice Problems	*266*
	Solutions	*268*
	Glossary	**G-1**

How to Use the CFA Program Curriculum

The CFA® Program exams measure your mastery of the core knowledge, skills, and abilities required to succeed as an investment professional. These core competencies are the basis for the Candidate Body of Knowledge (CBOK™). The CBOK consists of four components:

> A broad outline that lists the major CFA Program topic areas (www.cfainstitute.org/programs/cfa/curriculum/cbok/cbok)

> Topic area weights that indicate the relative exam weightings of the top-level topic areas (www.cfainstitute.org/en/programs/cfa/curriculum)

> Learning outcome statements (LOS) that advise candidates about the specific knowledge, skills, and abilities they should acquire from curriculum content covering a topic area: LOS are provided at the beginning of each block of related content and the specific lesson that covers them. We encourage you to review the information about the LOS on our website (www.cfainstitute.org/programs/cfa/curriculum/study-sessions), including the descriptions of LOS "command words" on the candidate resources page at www.cfainstitute.org/-/media/documents/support/programs/cfa-and-cipm-los-command-words.ashx.

> The CFA Program curriculum that candidates receive access to upon exam registration

Therefore, the key to your success on the CFA exams is studying and understanding the CBOK. You can learn more about the CBOK on our website: www.cfainstitute.org/programs/cfa/curriculum/cbok.

The curriculum, including the practice questions, is the basis for all exam questions. The curriculum is selected or developed specifically to provide candidates with the knowledge, skills, and abilities reflected in the CBOK.

CFA INSTITUTE LEARNING ECOSYSTEM (LES)

Your exam registration fee includes access to the CFA Institute Learning Ecosystem (LES). This digital learning platform provides access, even offline, to all the curriculum content and practice questions. The LES is organized as a series of learning modules consisting of short online lessons and associated practice questions. This tool is your source for all study materials, including practice questions and mock exams. The LES is the primary method by which CFA Institute delivers your curriculum experience. Here, candidates will find additional practice questions to test their knowledge. Some questions in the LES provide a unique interactive experience.

DESIGNING YOUR PERSONAL STUDY PROGRAM

An orderly, systematic approach to exam preparation is critical. You should dedicate a consistent block of time every week to reading and studying. Review the LOS both before and after you study curriculum content to ensure you can demonstrate the knowledge, skills, and abilities described by the LOS and the assigned reading. Use the LOS as a self-check to track your progress and highlight areas of weakness for later review.

Successful candidates report an average of more than 300 hours preparing for each exam. Your preparation time will vary based on your prior education and experience, and you will likely spend more time on some topics than on others.

ERRATA

The curriculum development process is rigorous and involves multiple rounds of reviews by content experts. Despite our efforts to produce a curriculum that is free of errors, in some instances, we must make corrections. Curriculum errata are periodically updated and posted by exam level and test date on the Curriculum Errata webpage (www.cfainstitute.org/en/programs/submit-errata). If you believe you have found an error in the curriculum, you can submit your concerns through our curriculum errata reporting process found at the bottom of the Curriculum Errata webpage.

OTHER FEEDBACK

Please send any comments or suggestions to info@cfainstitute.org, and we will review your feedback thoughtfully.

Economics

LEARNING MODULE 1

The Firm and Market Structures

by Gary L. Arbogast, PhD, CFA, Richard V. Eastin, PhD, Fritz Richard, PhD, and Gambera Michele, PhD, CFA.

Gary L. Arbogast, PhD, CFA (USA). Richard V. Eastin, PhD, is at the University of Southern California (USA). Richard Fritz, PhD, is at the School of Economics at Georgia Institute of Technology (USA). Michele Gambera, PhD, CFA, is at UBS Asset Management and the University of Illinois at Urbana-Champaign (USA).

LEARNING OUTCOMES

Mastery	The candidate should be able to:
☐	determine and interpret breakeven and shutdown points of production, as well as how economies and diseconomies of scale affect costs under perfect and imperfect competition
☐	describe characteristics of perfect competition, monopolistic competition, oligopoly, and pure monopoly
☐	explain supply and demand relationships under monopolistic competition, including the optimal price and output for firms as well as pricing strategy
☐	explain supply and demand relationships under oligopoly, including the optimal price and output for firms as well as pricing strategy
☐	identify the type of market structure within which a firm operates and describe the use and limitations of concentration measures

INTRODUCTION

This learning module addresses several important concepts that extend the basic market model of demand and supply to the assessment of a firm's breakeven and shutdown points of production. Demand concepts covered include own-price elasticity of demand, cross-price elasticity of demand, and income elasticity of demand. Supply concepts covered include total, average, and marginal product of labor; total, variable, and marginal cost of labor; and total and marginal revenue. These concepts are used to calculate the breakeven and shutdown points of production.

This learning module surveys how economists classify market structures. We analyze distinctions between the different structures that are important for understanding demand and supply relations, optimal price and output, and the factors affecting long-run profitability. We also provide guidelines for identifying market structure in practice.

> **LEARNING MODULE OVERVIEW**
>
> - Firms under conditions of perfect competition have no pricing power and, therefore, face a perfectly horizontal demand curve at the market price. For firms under conditions of perfect competition, price is identical to marginal revenue (MR).
> - Firms under conditions of imperfect competition face a negatively sloped demand curve and have pricing power. For firms under conditions of imperfect competition, MR is less than price.
> - Economic profit equals total revenue (TR) minus total economic cost, whereas accounting profit equals TR minus total accounting cost.
> - Economic cost considers the total opportunity cost of all factors of production.
> - Opportunity cost is the next best alternative use of a resource forgone in making a decision.
> - Maximum economic profit requires that (1) MR equals marginal cost (MC) and (2) MC not be falling with output.
> - The breakeven point occurs when TR equals total cost (TC), otherwise stated as the output quantity at which average total cost (ATC) equals price.
> - Shutdown occurs when a firm is better off not operating than continuing to operate.
> - If all fixed costs are sunk costs, then shutdown occurs when the market price falls below the minimum average variable cost. After shutdown, the firm incurs only fixed costs and loses less money than it would operating at a price that does not cover variable costs.
> - In the short run, it may be rational for a firm to continue to operate while earning negative economic profit if some unavoidable fixed costs are covered.
> - Economies of scale is defined as decreasing long-run cost per unit as output increases. Diseconomies of scale is defined as increasing long-run cost per unit as output increases.
> - Long-run ATC is the cost of production per unit of output under conditions in which all inputs are variable.
> - Specialization efficiencies and bargaining power in input price can lead to economies of scale.
> - Bureaucratic and communication breakdowns and bottlenecks that raise input prices can lead to diseconomies of scale.
> - The minimum point on the long-run ATC curve defines the minimum efficient scale for the firm.
> - Economic market structures can be grouped into four categories: perfect competition, monopolistic competition, oligopoly, and monopoly.

- The categories of economic market structures differ because of the following characteristics: The number of producers is many in perfect and monopolistic competition, few in oligopoly, and one in monopoly. The degree of product differentiation, the pricing power of the producer, the barriers to entry of new producers, and the level of non-price competition (e.g., advertising) are all low in perfect competition, moderate in monopolistic competition, high in oligopoly, and generally highest in monopoly.

- A financial analyst must understand the characteristics of market structures to better forecast a firm's future profit stream.

- The optimal MR equals MC. Only in perfect competition, however, does the MR equal price. In the remaining structures, price generally exceeds MR because a firm can sell more units only by reducing the per unit price.

- The quantity sold is highest in perfect competition. The price in perfect competition is usually lowest, but this depends on factors such as demand elasticity and increasing returns to scale (which may reduce the producer's MC). Monopolists, oligopolists, and producers in monopolistic competition attempt to differentiate their products so that they can charge higher prices.

- Typically, monopolists sell a smaller quantity at a higher price. Investors may benefit from being shareholders of monopolistic firms that have large margins and substantial positive cash flows.

- In perfect competition, firms do not earn economic profit. The market will compensate for the rental of capital and of management services, but the lack of pricing power implies that there will be no extra margins.

- In the short run, firms in any market structure can have economic profits, the more competitive a market is and the lower the barriers to entry, the faster the extra profits will fade. In the long run, new entrants shrink margins and push the least efficient firms out of the market.

- Oligopoly is characterized by the importance of strategic behavior. Firms can change the price, quantity, quality, and advertisement of the product to gain an advantage over their competitors. Several types of equilibrium (e.g., Nash, Cournot, kinked demand curve) may occur that affect the likelihood of each of the incumbents (and potential entrants in the long run) having economic profits. Price wars may be started to force weaker competitors to abandon the market.

- Measuring market power is complicated. Ideally, econometric estimates of the elasticity of demand and supply should be computed. However, because of the lack of reliable data and the fact that elasticity changes over time (so that past data may not apply to the current situation), regulators and economists often use simpler measures. The concentration ratio is simple, but the Herfindahl-Hirschman index (HHI), with a little more computation required, often produces a better figure for decision making.

2   PROFIT MAXIMIZATION: PRODUCTION BREAKEVEN, SHUTDOWN AND ECONOMIES OF SCALE

☐ determine and interpret breakeven and shutdown points of production, as well as how economies and diseconomies of scale affect costs under perfect and imperfect competition

Firms generally can be classified as operating in either a perfectly competitive or an imperfectly competitive environment. The difference between the two manifests in the slope of the demand curve facing the firm. If the environment of the firm is perfectly competitive, it must take the market price of its output as given, so it faces a perfectly elastic, horizontal demand curve. In this case, the firm's marginal revenue (MR) and the price of its product are identical. Additionally, the firm's **average revenue** (AR), or revenue per unit, is also equal to price per unit. A firm that faces a negatively sloped demand curve, however, must lower its price to sell an additional unit, so its MR is less than price (P).

These characteristics of MR are also applicable to the total revenue (TR) functions. Under conditions of perfect competition, TR (as always) is equal to price times quantity: $TR = (P)(Q)$. But under conditions of perfect competition, price is dictated by the market; the firm has no control over price. As the firm sells one more unit, its TR rises by the exact amount of price per unit.

Under conditions of imperfect competition, price is a variable under the firm's control, and therefore price is a function of quantity: $P = f(Q)$, and $TR = f(Q) \times Q$. For simplicity, suppose the firm is monopolistic and faces the market demand curve, which we will assume is linear and negatively sloped. Because the monopolist is the only seller, its TR is identical to the total expenditure of all buyers in the market. When price is reduced and quantity sold increases in this environment, a decrease in price initially increases total expenditure by buyers and TR to the firm because the decrease in price is outweighed by the increase in units sold. But as price continues to fall, the decrease in price overshadows the increase in quantity, and total expenditure (revenue) falls. We can now depict the demand and TR functions for firms under conditions of perfect and imperfect competition, as shown in Exhibit 1.

Exhibit 1: Demand and Total Revenue Functions for Firms under Conditions of Perfect and Imperfect Competition

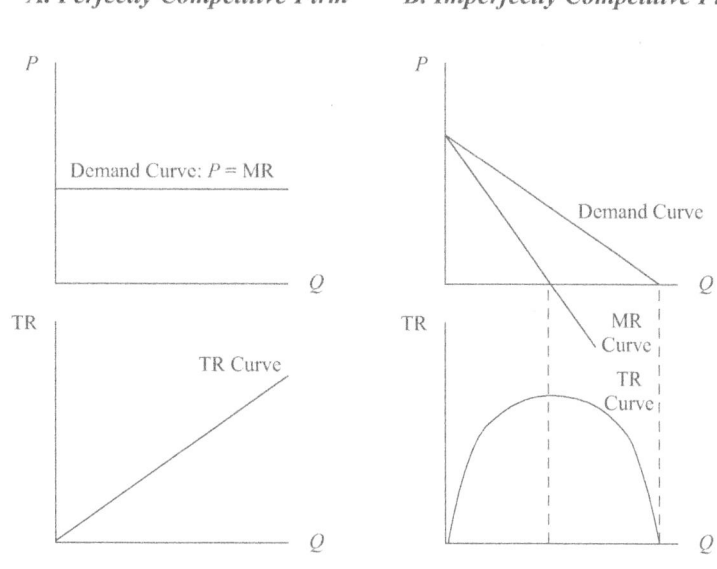

Panel A of Exhibit 1 depicts the demand curve (upper graph) and total revenue curve (lower graph) for the firm under conditions of perfect competition. Notice that the vertical axis in the upper graph is price per unit (e.g., GBP/bushel), whereas TR is measured on the vertical axis in the lower graph (e.g., GBP/week). The same is true for the respective axes in Panel B, which depicts the demand and total revenue curves for the monopolist. The TR curve for the firm under conditions of perfect competition is linear, with a slope equal to price per unit. The TR curve for the monopolist first rises (in the range where MR is positive and demand is elastic) and then falls (in the range where MR is negative and demand is inelastic) with output.

Profit-Maximization, Breakeven, and Shutdown Points of Production

We can now combine the firm's short-run TC curves with its TR curves to represent profit maximization in the cases of perfect competition and imperfect competition. Exhibit 2 shows both the AR and average cost curves in one graph for the firm under conditions of perfect competition.

Exhibit 2: Demand and Average and Marginal Cost Curves for the Firm under Conditions of Perfect Competition

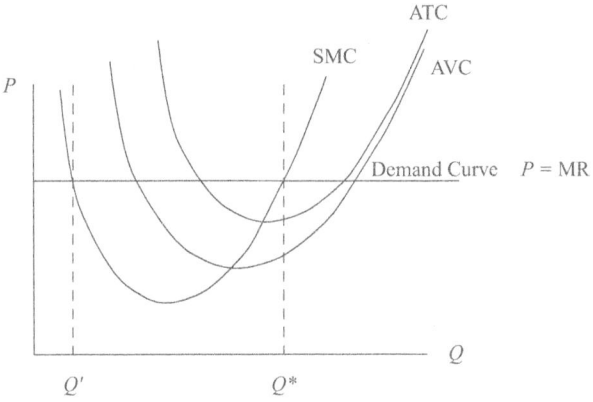

The firm is maximizing profit by producing Q^*, where price is equal to short-run marginal cost (SMC) and SMC is rising. Note at another output level, Q', where $P =$ SMC, SMC is still falling, so this cannot be a profit-maximizing solution. If market price were to rise, the firm's demand and MR curve would simply shift upward, and the firm would reach a new profit-maximizing output level to the right of Q^*. If, however, market price were to fall, the firm's demand and MR curve would shift downward, resulting in a new and lower level of profit-maximizing output. As depicted, this firm is currently earning a positive economic profit because market price exceeds average total cost (ATC), at output level Q^*. This profit is possible in the short run, but in the long run, competitors would enter the market to capture some of those profits and would drive the market price down to a level equal to each firm's ATC.

Exhibit 3 depicts the cost and revenue curves for the monopolist that is facing a negatively sloped market demand curve. The MR and demand curves are not identical for this firm. But the profit-maximizing rule is still the same: Find the level of Q that equates SMC, to MR—in this case, Q^*. Once that level of output is determined, the optimal price to charge is given by the firm's demand curve at P^*. This monopolist is earning positive economic profit because its price exceeds its ATC. The barriers to entry that give this firm its monopolistic power mean that outside competitors would not be able to compete away this firm's profits.

Exhibit 3: Demand and Average and Marginal Cost Curves for the Monopolistic Firm

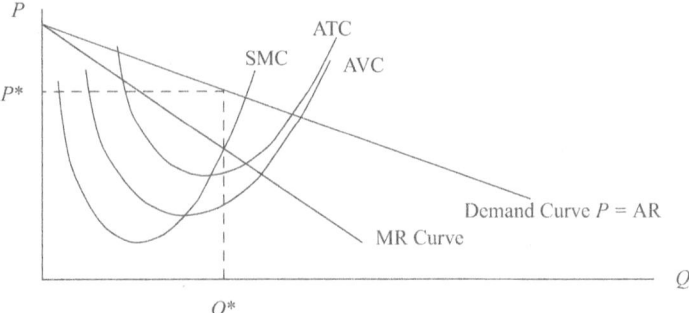

Breakeven Analysis and Shutdown Decision

A firm is said to break even if its TR is equal to its TC. It also can be said that a firm breaks even if its price (AR) is exactly equal to its ATC, which is true under conditions of perfect and imperfect competition. Of course, the goal of management is not just to breakeven but to maximize profit. However, perhaps the best the firm can do is cover all of its economic costs. Economic costs are the sum of total accounting costs and implicit opportunity costs. A firm whose revenue is equal to its economic costs is covering the opportunity cost of all of its factors of production, including capital. Economists would say that such a firm is earning normal profit, but not positive economic profit. It is earning a rate of return on capital just equal to the rate of return that an investor could expect to earn in an equivalently risky alternative investment (opportunity cost). Firms that are operating in a competitive environment with no barriers to entry from other competitors can expect, in the long run, to be unable to earn a positive economic profit; the excess rate of return would attract entrants who would produce more output and ultimately drive the market price down to the level at which each firm is, at best, just earning a normal profit. This situation, of course, does not imply that the firm is earning zero accounting profit.

Exhibit 4 depicts the condition for both a firm under conditions of perfect competition (Panel A) and a monopolist (Panel B) in which the best each firm can do is to break even. Note that at the level of output at which SMC is equal to MR, price is equal to ATC. Hence, economic profit is zero, and the firms are breaking even.

Exhibit 4: Examples of Firms under Perfect Competition and Monopolistic Firms That Can, at Best, Break Even

A. Perfect Competition

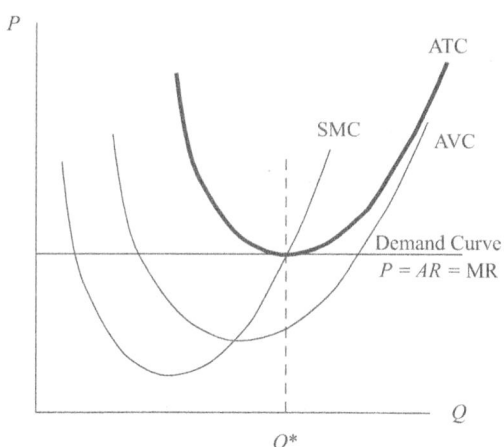

B. Monopolist

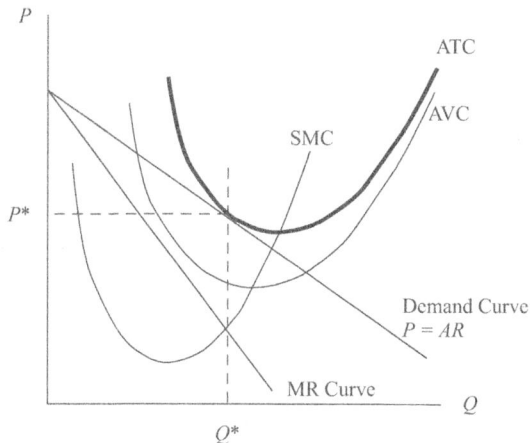

The Shutdown Decision

In the long run, if a firm cannot earn at least a zero economic profit, it will not operate because it is not covering the opportunity cost of all of its factors of production, labor, and capital. In the short run, however, a firm might find it advantageous to continue to operate even if it is not earning at least a zero economic profit. The discussion that follows addresses the decision to continue to operate and earn negative profit or shut down operations.

Recall that typically some or all of a firm's fixed costs are incurred regardless of whether the firm operates. The firm might have a lease on its building that it cannot avoid paying until the lease expires. In that case, the lease payment is a sunk cost: It cannot be avoided, no matter what the firm does. Sunk costs must be ignored in the decision to continue to operate in the short run. As long as the firm's revenues cover at least its variable cost, the firm is better off continuing to operate. If price is greater than average variable cost (AVC), the firm is covering not only all of its variable cost but also a portion of fixed cost.

In the long run, unless market price increases, this firm would exit the industry. But in the short run, it will continue to operate at a loss. Exhibit 5 depicts a firm under conditions of perfect competition facing three alternative market price ranges for its output. At any price above P_1, the firm can earn a positive profit and clearly should continue to operate. At a price below P_2, the minimum AVC, the firm could not even cover its variable cost and should shut down. At prices between P_2 and P_1, the firm should continue to operate in the short run because it is able to cover all of its variable cost and contribute something toward its unavoidable fixed costs. Economists refer to the minimum AVC point as the **shutdown point** and the minimum ATC point as the **breakeven point**.

Exhibit 5: A Firm under Conditions of Perfect Competition Will Choose to Shut Down If Market Price Is Less Than Minimum AVC

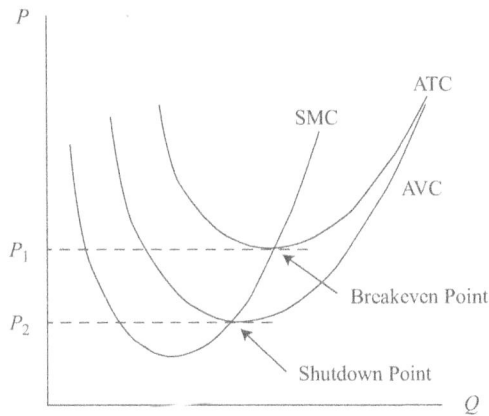

EXAMPLE 1

Breakeven Analysis and Profit Maximization When the Firm Faces a Negatively Sloped Demand Curve under Imperfect Competition

Revenue and cost information for a future period including all opportunity costs is presented in Exhibit 6 for WR International, a newly formed corporation that engages in the manufacturing of low-cost, prefabricated dwelling units for urban housing markets in emerging economies. (Note that quantity increments are in blocks of 10 for a 250 change in price.) The firm has few competitors in a market setting of imperfect competition.

Exhibit 6: Revenue and Cost Information for WR International

Quantity (Q)	Price (P)	Total Revenue (TR)	Total Cost (TC)[a]	Profit
0	10,000	0	100,000	−100,000
10	9,750	97,500	170,000	−72,500

Quantity (Q)	Price (P)	Total Revenue (TR)	Total Cost (TC)[a]	Profit
20	9,500	190,000	240,000	−50,000
30	9,250	277,500	300,000	−22,500
40	9,000	360,000	360,000	0
50	8,750	437,500	420,000	17,500
60	8,500	510,000	480,000	30,000
70	8,250	577,500	550,000	27,500
80	8,000	640,000	640,000	0
90	7,750	697,500	710,000	−12,500
100	7,500	750,000	800,000	−50,000

[a] *Includes all opportunity costs*

1. How many units must WR International sell to initially break even?

   Solution:

   WR International will initially break even at 40 units of production, where TR and TC equal 360,000.

2. Where is the region of profitability?

   Solution:

   The region of profitability will range from greater than 40 units to less than 80 units. Any production quantity of less than 40 units and any quantity greater than 80 units will result in an economic loss.

3. At what point will the firm maximize profit? At what points are there economic losses?

   Solution:

   Maximum profit of 30,000 will occur at 60 units. Lower profit will occur at any output level that is higher or lower than 60 units. From 0 units to less than 40 units and for quantities greater than 80 units, economic losses occur.

Given the relationships between TR, total variable costs (TVC), and total fixed costs (TFC), Exhibit 7 summarizes the decisions to operate, shut down production, or exit the market in both the short run and the long run. The firm must cover its variable cost to remain in business in the short run; if TR cannot cover TVC, the firm shuts down production to minimize loss. The loss would be equal to the amount of fixed cost. If TVC exceeds TR in the long run, the firm will exit the market to avoid the loss associated with fixed cost at zero production. By exiting the market, the firm's investors do not suffer the erosion of their equity capital from economic losses. When TR is enough to cover TVC but not all of TFC, the firm can continue to produce in the short run but will not be able to maintain financial solvency in the long run.

Exhibit 7: Short-Run and Long-Run Decisions to Operate or Not

Revenue–Cost Relationship	Short-Run Decision	Long-Term Decision
TR = TC	Stay in market	Stay in market
TR = TVC but < TC	Stay in market	Exit market
TR < TVC	Shut down production	Exit market

EXAMPLE 2

Shutdown Analysis

For the most recent financial reporting period, a London-based business has revenue of GBP2 million and TC of GBP2.5 million, which are or can be broken down into TFC of GBP1 million and TVC of GBP1.5 million. The net loss on the firm's income statement is reported as GBP500,000 (ignoring tax implications). In prior periods, the firm had reported profits on its operations.

1. What decision should the firm make regarding operations over the short term?

   Solution:

   In the short run, the firm is able to cover all of its TVC but only half of its GBP1 million in TFC. If the business ceases to operate, its loss would be GBP1 million, the amount of TFC, whereas the net loss by operating would be minimized at GBP500,000. The firm should attempt to operate by negotiating special arrangements with creditors to buy time to return operations back to profitability.

2. What decision should the firm make regarding operations over the long term?

   Solution:

   If the revenue shortfall is expected to persist over time, the firm should cease operations, liquidate assets, and pay debts to the extent possible. Any residual for shareholders would decrease the longer the firm is allowed to operate unprofitably.

3. Assume the same business scenario except that revenue is now GBP1.3 million, which creates a net loss of GBP1.2 million. What decision should the firm make regarding operations in this case?

   Solution:

   The firm would minimize loss at GBP1 million of TFC by shutting down. If the firm decided to continue to do business, the loss would increase to GBP1.2 million. Shareholders would save GBP200,000 in equity value by pursuing this option. Unquestionably, the business would have a rather short life expectancy if this loss situation were to continue.

When evaluating profitability, particularly of start-up firms and businesses using turnaround strategies, analysts should consider highlighting breakeven and shutdown points in their financial research. Identifying the unit sales levels at which the firm enters or leaves the production range for profitability and at which the firm can no longer function as a viable business entity provides invaluable insight when making investment decisions.

Economies and Diseconomies of Scale with Short-Run and Long-Run Cost Analysis

Rational behavior dictates that the firm select an operating size or scale that maximizes profit over any time frame. The time frame that defines the short run and long run for any firm is based on the ability of the firm to adjust the quantities of the fixed resources it uses. The short run is the time period during which at least one of the factors of production, such as technology, physical capital, and plant size, is fixed. The long run is defined as the time period during which all factors of production are variable. Additionally, in the long run, firms can enter or exit the market based on decisions regarding profitability. The long run is often referred to as the "planning horizon" in which the firm can choose the short-run position or optimal operating size that maximizes profit over time. The firm is always operating in the short run but planning in the long run.

The time required for long-run adjustments varies by industry. For example, the long run for a small business using very little technology and physical capital may be less than a year, whereas for a capital-intensive firm, the long run may be more than a decade. Given enough time, however, all production factors are variable, which allows the firm to choose an operating size or plant capacity based on different technologies and physical capital. In this regard, costs and profits will differ between the short run and the long run.

Short- and Long-Run Cost Curves

Recall that when we addressed the short-run cost curves of the firm, we assumed that the capital input was held constant. That meant that the only way to vary output in the short run was to change the level of the variable input—in our case, labor. If the capital input—namely, plant and equipment—were to change, however, we would have an entirely new set of short-run cost curves, one for each level of capital input.

The short-run total cost includes all the inputs—labor and capital—the firm is using to produce output. For reasons discussed earlier, the typical short-run total cost (STC) curve might rise with output, first at a decreasing rate because of specialization economies and then at an increasing rate, reflecting the law of diminishing marginal returns to labor. TFC, the quantity of capital input multiplied by the rental rate on capital, determines the vertical intercept of the STC curve. At higher levels of fixed input, TFC is greater, but the production capacity of the firm is also greater. Exhibit 8 shows three different STC curves for the same technology but using three distinct levels of capital input—points 1, 2, and 3 on the vertical axis.

Exhibit 8: Short-Run Total Cost Curves for Various Plant Sizes

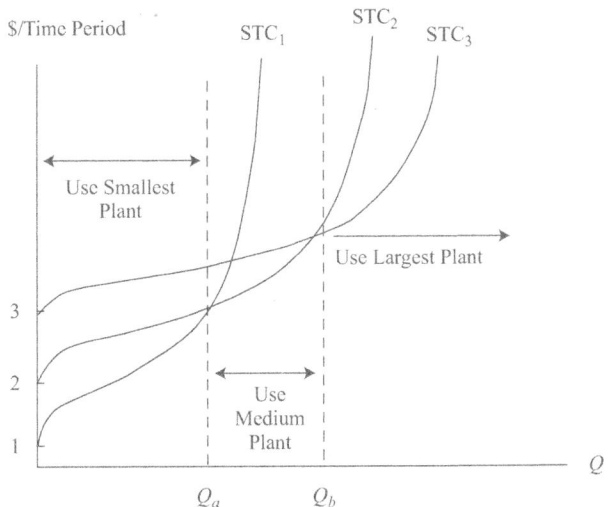

Plant Size 1 is the smallest and, of course, has the lowest fixed cost; hence, its STC_1 curve has the lowest vertical intercept. Note that STC_1 begins to rise more steeply with output, reflecting the lower plant capacity. Plant Size 3 is the largest of the three and reflects that size with both a higher fixed cost and a lower slope at any level of output. If a firm decided to produce an output between zero and Q_a, it would plan on building Plant Size 1 because for any output level in that range, its cost would be less than it would be for Plant Size 2 or 3. Accordingly, if the firm were planning to produce output greater than Q_b, it would choose Plant Size 3 because its cost for any of those levels of output would be lower than it would be for Plant Size 1 or 2. Of course, Plant Size 2 would be chosen for output levels between Q_a and Q_b. The long-run total cost curve is derived from the lowest level of STC for each level of output because in the long run, the firm is free to choose which plant size it will operate. This curve is called an "envelope curve." In essence, this curve envelopes—encompasses—all possible combinations of technology, plant size, and physical capital.

For each STC curve, there is also a corresponding **short-run average total cost** (SATC) curve and a corresponding **long-run average total cost** (LRAC) curve, the envelope curve of all possible short-run average total cost curves. The shape of the LRAC curve reflects an important concept called **economies of scale** and **diseconomies of scale**.

Defining Economies of Scale and Diseconomies of Scale

When a firm increases all of its inputs to increase its level of output (obviously, a long-run concept), it is said to *scale up* its production. *Scaling down* is the reverse—decreasing all of its inputs to produce less in the long run. Economies of scale occur if, as the firm increases its output, cost per unit of production falls. Graphically, this definition translates into an LRAC curve with a negative slope. Exhibit 9 depicts several SATC curves, one for each plant size, and the LRAC curve representing economies of scale.

Exhibit 9: Short-Run Average Total Cost Curves for Various Plant Sizes and Their Envelope Curve, LRAC: Economies of Scale

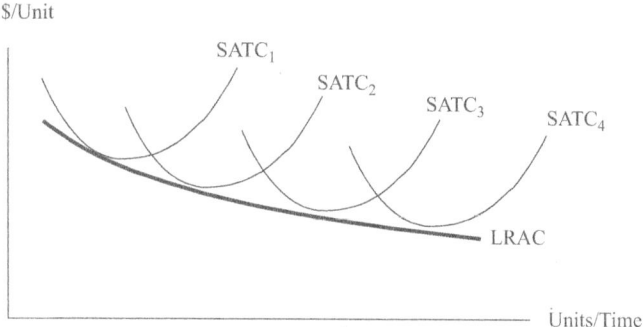

Diseconomies of scale occur if cost per unit rises as output increases. Graphically, diseconomies of scale translate into an LRAC curve with a positive slope. Exhibit 10 depicts several SATC curves, one for each plant size, and their envelope curve, the LRAC curve, representing diseconomies of scale.

Exhibit 10: Short-Run Average Total Cost Curves for Various Plant Sizes and Their Envelope Curve, LRAC: Diseconomies of Scale

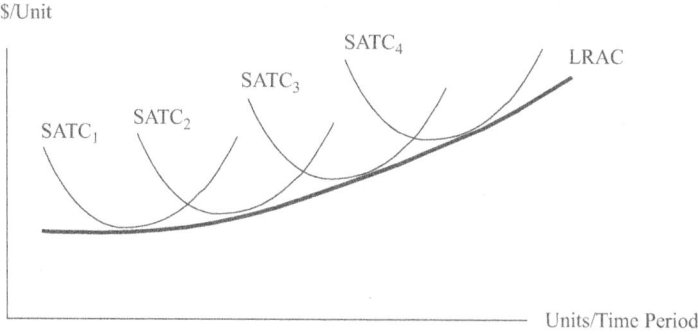

As the firm grows in size, economies of scale and a lower ATC can result from the following factors:

- Achieving **increasing returns to scale** when a production process allows for increases in output that are proportionately larger than the increase in inputs.
- Having a division of labor and management in a large firm with numerous workers, which allows each worker to specialize in one task rather than perform many duties, as in the case of a small business (as such, workers in a large firm become more proficient at their jobs).
- Being able to afford more expensive, yet more efficient equipment and to adapt the latest in technology that increases productivity.
- Effectively reducing waste and lowering costs through marketable by-products, less energy consumption, and enhanced quality control.
- Making better use of market information and knowledge for more effective managerial decision making.

- Obtaining discounted prices on resources when buying in larger quantities.

A classic example of a business that realizes economies of scale through greater physical capital investment is an electric utility. By expanding output capacity to accommodate a larger customer base, the utility company's per-unit cost will decline. Economies of scale help explain why electric utilities have naturally evolved from localized entities to regional and multiregional enterprises. Walmart is an example of a business that has used its bulk purchasing power to obtain deep discounts from suppliers to keep costs and prices low. Walmart also uses the latest technology to monitor point-of-sale transactions to gather timely market information to respond to changes in customer buying behavior, which leads to economies of scale through lower distribution and inventory costs.

Factors that can lead to diseconomies of scale, inefficiencies, and rising costs when a firm increases in size include the following:

- Realizing **decreasing returns to scale** when a production process leads to increases in output that are proportionately smaller than the increase in inputs.
- Being so large that it cannot be properly managed.
- Overlapping and duplicating business functions and product lines.[
- Experiencing higher resource prices because of supply constraints when buying inputs in large quantities.

Before its restructuring, General Motors (GM) was an example of a business that had realized diseconomies of scale by becoming too large. Scale diseconomies occurred through product overlap and duplication (i.e., similar or identical automobile models), and the fixed cost for these models was not spread over a large volume of output. In 2009, GM decided to discontinue three brands (Saturn, Pontiac, and Hummer) and also to drop various low-volume product models that overlapped with others. GM had numerous manufacturing plants around the world and sold vehicles in more than a hundred countries. Given this geographic dispersion in production and sales, the company had communication and management coordination problems, which resulted in higher costs. In 2017, GM sold its European arm, Opel, to Groupe PSA, the maker of Peugeot and Citroën. GM also had significantly higher labor costs than its competitors. As the largest producer in the market, it had been a target of labor unions for higher compensation and benefits packages relative to other firms.

Economies and diseconomies of scale can occur at the same time; the impact on LRAC depends on which dominates. If economies of scale dominate, LRAC decreases with increases in output. The reverse holds true when diseconomies of scale prevail. LRAC may fall (economies of scale) over a range of output and then LRAC might remain constant over another range, which could be followed by a range over which diseconomies of scale prevail, as depicted in Exhibit 11.

The minimum point on the LRAC curve is referred to as the **minimum efficient scale**. The minimum efficient scale is the optimal firm size under perfect competition over the long run. Theoretically, perfect competition forces the firm to operate at the minimum point on the LRAC curve because the market price will be established at this level over the long run. If the firm is not operating at this least-cost point, its long-term viability will be threatened.

Exhibit 11: LRAC Can Exhibit Economies and Diseconomies of Scale

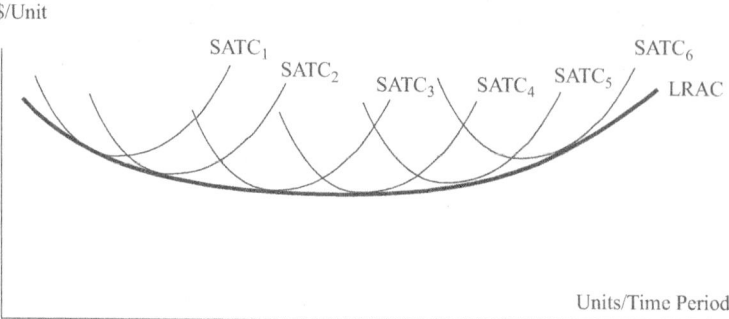

EXAMPLE 3

Long-Run Average Total Cost Curve

Exhibit 12 displays the long-run average total cost curve ($LRAC_{US}$) and the short-run average total cost curves for three hypothetical US-based automobile manufacturers—Starr Vehicles (Starr), Rocket Sports Cars (Rocket), and General Auto (GenAuto). The LRAC curve for foreign-owned automobile companies that compete in the US auto market ($LRAC_{foreign}$) is also indicated in the graph. (The market structure implicit in the exhibit is imperfect competition.)

1. To what extent are the cost relationships depicted in Exhibit 12 useful for an economic and financial analysis of the three US-based auto firms?

Exhibit 12: Long-Run Average Total Cost Curves for Three Auto Manufacturers

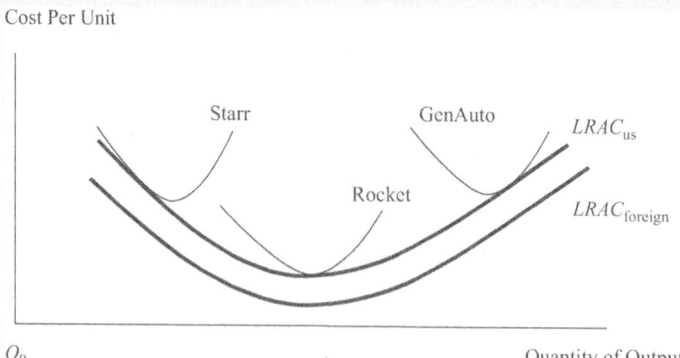

Solution:

First, it is observable that the foreign auto companies have a lower LRAC compared with that of the US automobile manufacturers. This competitive position places the US firms at a cost—and possibly, pricing—disadvantage in the market, with the potential to lose market share to the lower-cost foreign competitors. Second, only Rocket operates at the minimum point of the $LRAC_{US}$, whereas GenAuto is situated in the region of diseconomies of scale and Starr is positioned in the economies of scale portion of the curve. To become more efficient and competitive, GenAuto needs to downsize and restructure, which means moving down the $LRAC_{US}$ curve to a smaller

Profit Maximization: Production Breakeven, Shutdown and Economies of Scale

yet lower-cost production volume. In contrast, Starr has to grow in size to become more efficient and competitive by lowering per-unit costs.

From a long-term investment prospective and given its cost advantage, Rocket has the potential to create more investment value relative to GenAuto and Starr. Over the long run, if GenAuto and Starr can lower their ATC, they will become more attractive to investors. But if any of the three US auto companies cannot match the cost competitiveness of the foreign firms, they may be driven from the market. In the long run, the lower-cost foreign automakers pose a severe competitive challenge to the survival of the US manufacturers and their ability to maintain and grow shareholders' wealth.

QUESTION SET

1. An agricultural firm operating in a perfectly competitive market supplies wheat to manufacturers of consumer food products and animal feeds. If the firm were able to expand its production and unit sales by 10%, the *most likely* result would be:

   A. a 10% increase in total revenue.

   B. a 10% increase in average revenue.

   C. a less than 10% increase in total revenue.

   Solution:

   A is correct. In a perfectly competitive market, an increase in supply by a single firm will not affect price. Therefore, an increase in units sold by the firm will be matched proportionately by an increase in revenue.

2. The marginal revenue per unit sold for a firm doing business under conditions of perfect competition will *most likely* be:

   A. equal to average revenue.

   B. less than average revenue.

   C. greater than average revenue.

   Solution:

   A is correct. Under perfect competition, a firm is a price taker at any quantity supplied to the market, and AR = MR = Price.

3. A profit maximum is *least likely* to occur when:

   A. average total cost is minimized.

   B. marginal revenue is equal to marginal cost.

   C. the difference between total revenue and total cost is maximized.

   Solution:

   A is correct. The quantity at which average total cost is minimized does not necessarily correspond to a profit maximum.

4. The short-term breakeven point of production for a firm operating under perfect competition will *most likely* occur when:

   A. price is equal to average total cost.

   B. marginal revenue is equal to marginal cost.

> **C.** marginal revenue is equal to average variable costs.
>
> **Solution:**
>
> A is correct. Under perfect competition, price is equal to marginal revenue. A firm breaks even when marginal revenue equals average total cost.

3. INTRODUCTION TO MARKET STRUCTURES

☐ describe characteristics of perfect competition, monopolistic competition, oligopoly, and pure monopoly

Different market structures result in different sets of choices facing a firm's decision makers. Thus, an understanding of market structure is a powerful tool in analyzing issues, such as a firm's pricing of its products and, more broadly, its potential to increase profitability. In the long run, a firm's profitability will be determined by the forces associated with the market structure within which it operates. In a highly competitive market, long-run profits will be driven down by the forces of competition. In less competitive markets, large profits are possible even in the long run; in the short run, any outcome is possible. Therefore, understanding the forces behind the market structure will aid the financial analyst in determining firms' short- and long-term prospects.

Market structures address questions such as the following: What determines the degree of competition associated with each market structure? Given the degree of competition associated with each market structure, what decisions are left to the management team developing corporate strategy? How does a chosen pricing and output strategy evolve into specific decisions that affect the profitability of the firm? The answers to these questions are related to the forces of the market structure within which the firm operates.

Analysis of Market Structures

Traditionally, economists classify a market into one of four structures: perfect competition, monopolistic competition, oligopoly, and monopoly.

Economists define a market as a group of buyers and sellers that are aware of each other and can agree on a price for the exchange of goods and services. Although internet access has extended a number of markets worldwide, certain markets remain limited by geographic boundaries. For example, the internet search engine Google operates in a worldwide market. In contrast, the market for premixed cement is limited to the area within which a truck can deliver the mushy mix from the plant to a construction site before the compound becomes useless. Thomas L. Friedman's international best seller *The World Is Flat* challenges the concept of the geographic limitations of the market. If the service being provided by the seller can be digitized, its market expands worldwide. For example, a technician can scan your injury in a clinic in Switzerland. That radiographic image can be digitized and sent to a radiologist in India to be read. As a customer (i.e., patient), you may never know that part of the medical service provided to you was the result of a worldwide market.

Some markets are highly concentrated, with the majority of total sales coming from a small number of firms. For example, in the market for internet search, three firms controlled 98.9 percent of the US market (Google 63.5 percent, Microsoft 24 percent, and Oath (formerly Yahoo!) 11.4 percent) as of January 2018. Other markets are fragmented, such as automobile repairs, in which small independent shops often dominate and large chains may or may not exist. New products can lead to market concentration. For example, Apple introduced its first digital audio player (iPod) in 2001 and despite the entry of competitors had a world market share of more than 70 percent among digital audio players in 2009.

THE IMPORTANCE OF MARKET STRUCTURE

Consider the evolution of television broadcasting. As the market environment for television broadcasting evolved, the market structure changed, resulting in a new set of challenges and choices. In the early days, viewers had only one choice: the "free" analog channels that were broadcast over the airwaves. Most countries had one channel, owned and run by the government. In the United States, some of the more populated markets were able to receive more channels because local channels were set up to cover a market with more potential viewers. By the 1970s, new technologies made it possible to broadcast by way of cable connectivity and the choices offered to consumers began to expand rapidly. Cable television challenged the "free" broadcast channels by offering more choice and a better-quality picture. The innovation was expensive for consumers and profitable for the cable companies. By the 1990s, a new alternative began to challenge the existing broadcast and cable systems: satellite television. Satellite providers offered a further expanded set of choices, albeit at a higher price, than the free broadcast and cable alternatives. In the early 2000s, satellite television providers lowered their pricing to compete directly with the cable providers.

Today, cable program providers, satellite television providers, and terrestrial digital broadcasters that offer premium and pay-per-view channels compete for customers who are increasingly finding content on the internet and on their mobile devices. Companies like Netflix, Apple, and Amazon offered alternative ways for consumers to access content. Over time, these companies had moved beyond the repackaging of existing shows to developing their own content, mirroring the evolution of cable channels, such as HBO and ESPN a decade earlier.

This is a simple illustration of the importance of market structure. As the market for television broadcasting became increasingly competitive, managers have had to make decisions regarding product packaging, pricing, advertising, and marketing to survive in the changing environment. In addition, mergers and acquisitions as a response to these competitive pressures have changed the essential structure of the industry.

Market structure can be broken down into four distinct categories: perfect competition, monopolistic competition, oligopoly, and monopoly.

We start with the most competitive environment, **perfect competition**. Unlike some economic concepts, perfect competition is not merely an ideal based on assumptions. Perfect competition is a reality—for example, in several commodities markets, in which sellers and buyers have a strictly homogeneous product and no single producer is large enough to influence market prices. Perfect competition's characteristics are well recognized and its long-run outcome is unavoidable. Profits under the conditions of perfect competition are driven to the required rate of return paid by the entrepreneur to borrow capital from investors (so-called normal profit or rental cost of capital). This does not mean that all perfectly competitive industries are doomed to extinction by a lack of profits. On the contrary, millions of businesses that do very well are living under the pressures of perfect competition.

Monopolistic competition is also highly competitive; however, it is considered a form of imperfect competition. Two economists, Edward H. Chamberlin (United States) and Joan Robinson (United Kingdom), identified this hybrid market and came up with the term because this market structure not only has strong elements of competition but also some monopoly-like conditions. The competitive characteristic is a notably large number of firms, while the monopoly aspect is the result of product differentiation. That is, if the seller can convince consumers that its product is uniquely different from other, similar products, then the seller can exercise some degree of pricing power over the market. A good example is the brand loyalty associated with soft drinks such as Coca-Cola. Many of Coca-Cola's customers believe that their beverages are truly different from and better than all other soft drinks. The same is true for fashion creations and cosmetics.

The **oligopoly** market structure is based on a relatively small number of firms supplying the market. The small number of firms in the market means that each firm must consider what retaliatory strategies the other firms will pursue when prices and production levels change. Consider the pricing behavior of commercial airline companies. Pricing strategies and route scheduling are based on the expected reaction of the other carriers in similar markets. For any given route—say, from Paris, France, to Chennai, India—only a few carriers are in competition. If one of the carriers changes its pricing package, others likely will retaliate. Understanding the market structure of oligopoly markets can help identify a logical pattern of strategic price changes for the competing firms.

Finally, the least competitive market structure is the **monopoly**. In pure monopoly markets, no other good substitutes exist for the given product or service. A single seller, which, if allowed to operate without constraint, exercises considerable power over pricing and output decisions. In most market-based economies around the globe, pure monopolies are regulated by a governmental authority. The most common example of a regulated monopoly is the local electrical power provider. In most cases, the monopoly power provider is allowed to earn a normal return on its investment and prices are set by the regulatory authority to allow that return.

Factors That Determine Market Structure

The following five factors determine market structure:

1. The number and relative size of firms supplying the product;
2. The degree of product differentiation;
3. The power of the seller over pricing decisions;
4. The relative strength of the barriers to market entry and exit; and
5. The degree of non-price competition.

The number and relative size of firms in a market influence market structure. When many firms exist, the degree of competition increases. With fewer firms supplying a good or service, consumers are limited in their market choices. One extreme case is the monopoly market structure, with only one firm supplying a unique good or service. Another extreme is perfect competition, with many firms supplying a similar product. Finally, an example of relative size is the automobile industry, in which a small number of large international producers (e.g., Volkswagen and Toyota) are the leaders in the global market, and a number of small companies either have market power because they are niche players (e.g., Ferrari or McLaren) or have limited market power because of their narrow range of models or limited geographical presence (e.g., Mazda or Stellantis).

In the case of monopolistic competition, many firms are providing products to the market, as with perfect competition. However, one firm's product is differentiated in some way that makes it appear to be better than similar products from other firms. If a firm is successful in differentiating its product, this differentiation will provide pricing leverage. The more dissimilar the product appears, the more the market will resemble the monopoly market structure. A firm can differentiate its product through aggressive advertising campaigns; frequent styling changes; the linking of its product with other complementary products; or a host of other methods.

When the market dictates the price based on aggregate supply and demand conditions, the individual firm has no control over pricing. The typical hog farmer in Nebraska and the milk producer in Bavaria are **price takers**. That is, they must accept whatever price the market dictates. This is the case under the market structure of perfect competition. In the case of monopolistic competition, the success of product differentiation determines the degree with which the firm can influence price. In the case of oligopoly, there are so few firms in the market that price control becomes possible. However, the small number of firms in an oligopoly market invites complex pricing strategies. Collusion, price leadership by dominant firms, and other pricing strategies can result.

The degree to which one market structure can evolve into another and the difference between potential short-run outcomes and long-run equilibrium conditions depend on the strength of the barriers to entry and the possibility that firms fail to recoup their original costs or lose money for an extended period of time and therefore are forced to exit the market. Barriers to entry can result from large capital investment requirements, as in the case of petroleum refining. Barriers may also result from patents, as in the case of some electronic products and drug formulas. Another entry consideration is the possibility of high exit costs. For example, plants that are specific to a special line of products, such as aluminum smelting plants, are non-redeployable, and exit costs would be high without a liquid market for the firm's assets. High exit costs deter entry and therefore also are considered barriers to entry. In the case of farming, the barriers to entry are low. Production of corn, soybeans, wheat, tomatoes, and other produce is an easy process to replicate; therefore, those are highly competitive markets.

Non-price competition dominates those market structures in which product differentiation is critical. Therefore, monopolistic competition relies on competitive strategies that may not include pricing changes. An example of non-price competition is product differentiation through marketing. In other circumstances, non-price competition may occur because the few firms in the market feel dependent on each other. Each firm fears retaliatory price changes that would reduce total revenue for all of the firms in the market. Because oligopoly industries have so few firms, each firm feels dependent on the pricing strategies of the others. Therefore, non-price competition becomes a dominant strategy.

Characteristics of Market Structure

Exhibit 13: Characteristics of Market Structure

Market Structure	Number of Sellers	Degree of Product Differentiation	Barriers to Entry	Pricing Power of Firm	Non-Price Competition
Perfect competition	Many	Homogeneous/ Standardized	Very Low	None	None
Monopolistic competition	Many	Differentiated	Low	Some	Advertising and Product Differentiation
Oligopoly	Few	Homogeneous/ Standardized	High	Some or Considerable	Advertising and Product Differentiation
Monopoly	One	Unique Product	Very High	Considerable	Advertising

From the perspective of the owners of the firm, the most desirable market structure is that with the most control over price, because this control can lead to large profits (Exhibit 13). Monopoly and oligopoly markets offer the greatest potential control over price; monopolistic competition offers less control. Firms operating under perfectly competitive market conditions have no control over price. From the consumers' perspective, the most desirable market structure is that with the greatest degree of competition because prices are generally lower. Thus, consumers would prefer as many goods and services as possible to be offered in competitive markets.

As often happens in economics, there is a trade-off. While perfect competition gives the largest quantity of a good at the lowest price, other market forms may spur more innovation. Specifically, firms may incur high costs in researching a new product, and they will incur such costs only if they expect to earn an attractive return on their research investment. This is the case often made for medical innovations, for example—the cost of clinical trials and experiments to create new medicines would bankrupt perfectly competitive firms but may be acceptable in an oligopoly market structure. Therefore, consumers can benefit from less-than-perfectly-competitive markets.

PORTER'S FIVE FORCES AND MARKET STRUCTURE

A financial analyst aiming to establish market conditions and consequent profitability of incumbent firms should start with the questions posed earlier: How many sellers are there? Is the product differentiated? Moreover, in the case of monopolies and quasi-monopolies, the analyst should evaluate the legislative and regulatory framework: Can the company set prices freely, or are there governmental controls? Finally, the analyst should consider the threat of competition from potential entrants.

This analysis is often summarized by students of corporate strategy as "Porter's five forces," named after Harvard Business School professor Michael E. Porter. His book, *Competitive Strategy*, presented a systematic analysis of the practice of market strategy. Porter identified the five forces as follows:

- Threat of entry;
- Power of suppliers;
- Power of buyers (customers);
- Threat of substitutes; and
- Rivalry among existing competitors.

It is easy to note the parallels between four of these five forces and the questions posed earlier. The only "orphan" is the power of suppliers, which is not at the core of the theoretical economic analysis of competition, but which has substantial weight in the practical analysis of competition and profitability.

Some stock analysts use the term "economic moat" to suggest that some of the factors protecting the profitability of a firm are similar to the moats (ditches full of water) that were used to protect some medieval castles. A deep moat means that there is little or no threat of entry by invaders (i.e., competitors). It also means that customers are locked in because of high switching costs.

> **QUESTION SET**
>
> 1. A market structure characterized by many sellers with each having some pricing power and product differentiation is *best* described as:
>   A. oligopoly.
>   B. perfect competition.
>   C. monopolistic competition.
>
>   **Solution:**
>
>   C is correct. Monopolistic competition is characterized by many sellers, differentiated products, and some pricing power.
>
> 2. A market structure with relatively few sellers of a homogeneous or standardized product is *best* described as:
>   A. oligopoly.
>   B. monopoly.
>   C. perfect competition.
>
>   **Solution:**
>
>   A is correct. Few sellers of a homogeneous or standardized product characterizes an oligopoly.

MONOPOLISTIC COMPETITION   4

☐ explain supply and demand relationships under monopolistic competition, including the optimal price and output for firms as well as pricing strategy

Many market structures exhibit characteristics of strong competitive forces; however, other distinct non-competitive factors can also play important roles in the market. As the name implies, monopolistic competition is a hybrid market. *The most distinctive factor in monopolistic competition is product differentiation*. Recall the characteristics outlined earlier:

1. The market has a large number of potential buyers and sellers.
2. The products offered by each seller are close substitutes for the products offered by other firms, and each firm tries to make its product look different.
3. Entry into and exit from the market are possible with fairly low costs.
4. Firms have some pricing power.
5. Suppliers differentiate their products through advertising and other non-price strategies.

While the market is made up of many firms that compose the product group, each producer attempts to distinguish its product from that of the others. Product differentiation is accomplished in a variety of ways. For example, consider the wide variety of communication devices available today. Decades ago, when each communication market was controlled by a regulated single seller (the telephone company), all telephones were alike. In today's deregulated market, the variety of physical styles and colors is extensive. All versions accomplish many of the same tasks.

The communication device manufacturers and providers differentiate their products with different colors, styles, networks, bundled applications, conditional contracts, functionality, and more. Advertising is usually the avenue pursued to convince consumers that the goods in the product group are different. Successful advertising and trademark branding result in customer loyalty. A good example is the brand loyalty associated with Harley-Davidson motorcycles. Harley-Davidson's customers believe that their motorcycles are truly different from and better than all other motorcycles.

The extent to which the producer is successful in product differentiation determines pricing power in the market. Very successful differentiation results in a market structure that resembles the single-seller market (monopoly). Because of relatively low entry and exit costs, competition will, in the long run, drive prices and revenues down toward an equilibrium similar to perfect competition. Thus, the hybrid market displays characteristics found in both perfectly competitive and monopoly markets.

Demand Analysis in Monopolistically Competitive Markets

Because each good sold in the product group is somewhat different from the others, the demand curve for each firm in the monopolistic competition market structure is downward sloping to the right. Price and the quantity demanded are negatively related. Lowering the price will increase the quantity demanded and raising the price will decrease the quantity demanded. There will be ranges of prices within which demand is elastic and (lower) prices at which demand is inelastic. Exhibit 14 illustrates the demand, marginal revenue, and cost structures facing a monopolistically competitive firm in the short run.

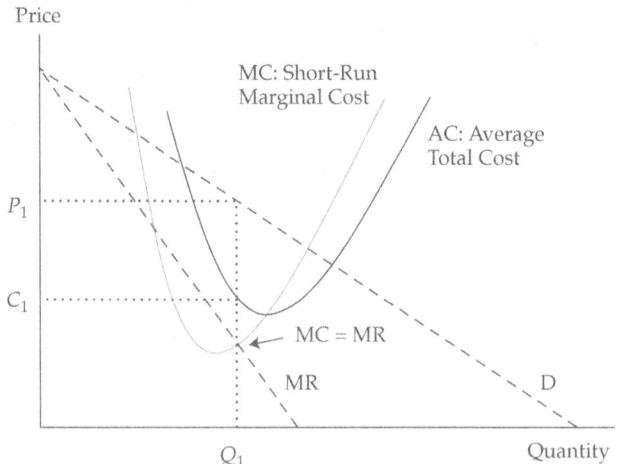

In the short run, the profit-maximizing choice is the level of output at which MR = MC. Because the product is somewhat different from that of the competitors, the firm can charge the price determined by the demand curve. Therefore, in Exhibit 14, Q_1 is the ideal level of output and P_1 is the price consumers are willing to pay to acquire that quantity. Total revenue is the area of the rectangle $P_1 \times Q_1$.

Supply Analysis in Monopolistically Competitive Markets

In perfect competition, the firm's supply schedule is represented by the marginal cost schedule. In monopolistic competition, there is no well-defined supply function. The information used to determine the appropriate level of output is based on the intersection of MC and MR. However, the price that will be charged is based on the market demand schedule. The firm's supply curve should measure the quantity the firm is willing to supply at various prices. That information is not represented by either marginal cost or average cost.

Optimal Price and Output in Monopolistically Competitive Markets

In the short run, the profit-maximizing choice is the level of output at which MR = MC and total revenue is the area of the rectangle $P_1 \times Q_1$ shown in Exhibit 14.

The average cost of producing Q_1 units of the product is C_1, and the total cost is the area of the rectangle $C_1 \times Q_1$. The difference between TR and TC is economic profit. The profit relationship is described as follows:

$\pi = TR - TC$,

where π is total profit, TR is total revenue, and TC is total cost.

> **THE BENEFITS OF IMPERFECT COMPETITION**
>
> Is monopolistic competition indeed imperfect—that is, is it a bad thing? At first, one would say that it is an inefficient market structure because prices are higher and the quantity supplied is less than in perfect competition. At the same time, in the real world, we see more markets characterized by monopolistic competition than markets meeting the strict conditions of perfect competition. If monopolistic competition were that inefficient, one wonders, why would it be so common?
>
> A part of the explanation goes back to Schumpeter. Firms try to differentiate their products to meet the needs of customers. Differentiation provides a profit incentive to innovate, experiment with new products and services, and potentially improve the standard of living.
>
> Moreover, because each customer has differing tastes and preferences, slight variations of each good or service are likely to capture the niche of the market that prefers them. An example is the market for candy, where one can find chocolate, licorice, mint, fruit, and many other flavors.
>
> Another reason why monopolistic competition may be good is that people like variety. Traditional economic theories of international trade suggested that countries should buy products from other countries that they cannot produce domestically. Therefore, Norway should buy bananas from a tropical country and sell crude oil in exchange. But this is not the only kind of exchange that happens in reality: For example, Germany imports Honda, Subaru, and Toyota cars from Japan and sells Volkswagen, Porsche, Mercedes, and BMW cars to Japan. In theory, this should not occur because each of the countries produces good cars domestically and does not need to import them. The truth, however, is that consumers in both countries enjoy variety. Some Japanese drivers prefer to be at the steering wheel of a BMW; others like Hondas, and the same happens in Germany. Variety and product differentiation, therefore, are not necessarily bad things.

Long-Run Equilibrium in Monopolistic Competition

Because total cost includes all costs associated with production, including opportunity cost, economic profit is a signal to the market, and that signal will attract more competition. Just as with the perfectly competitive market structure, with relatively low entry costs, more firms will enter the market and lure some customers away from the firm making an economic profit. The loss of customers to new entrant firms will drive down the demand for all firms producing similar products. In the long run for the monopolistically competitive firm, economic profit will fall to zero. Exhibit 15 illustrates the condition of long-run equilibrium for monopolistic competition.

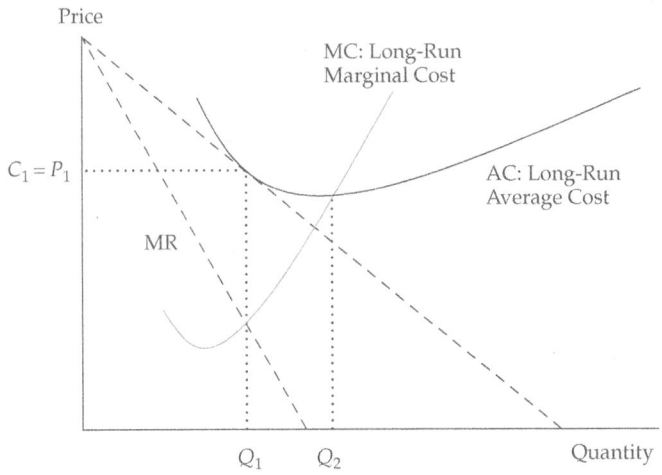

Exhibit 15: Long-Run Equilibrium in Monopolistic Competition

In long-run equilibrium, output is still optimal at the level at which MR = MC, which is Q_1 in Exhibit 15. Again, the price consumers are willing to pay for any amount of the product is determined from the demand curve. That price is P_1 for the quantity Q_1 in Exhibit 15, and total revenue is the area of the rectangle $P_1 \times Q_1$. Notice that unlike long-run equilibrium in perfect competition, in the market of monopolistic competition, the equilibrium position is at a higher level of average cost than the level of output that minimizes average cost. Average cost does not reach its minimum until output level Q_2 is achieved. Total cost in this long-run equilibrium position is the area of the rectangle $C_1 \times Q_1$. Economic profit is total revenue minus total cost. In Exhibit 15, economic profit is zero because total revenue equals total cost: $P_1 \times Q_1 = C_1 \times Q_1$.

In the hybrid market of monopolistic competition, zero economic profit in long-run equilibrium resembles perfect competition. However, the long-run level of output, Q_1, is less than Q_2, which corresponds to the minimum average cost of production and would be the long-run level of output in a perfectly competitive market. In addition, the economic cost in monopolistic competition includes some cost associated with product differentiation, such as advertising. In perfect competition, no costs are associated with advertising or marketing because all products are homogeneous. Prices are lower, but consumers may have little variety.

QUESTION SET

1. A company doing business in a monopolistically competitive market will *most likely* maximize profits when its output quantity is set such that:

   A. average cost is minimized.

   B. marginal revenue is equal to average cost.

   C. marginal revenue is equal to marginal cost.

   Solution:

   C is correct. The profit maximizing choice is the level of output at which marginal revenue equals marginal cost.

OLIGOPOLY 5

☐ explain supply and demand relationships under oligopoly, including the optimal price and output for firms as well as pricing strategy

Oligopoly and Pricing Strategies

An oligopoly market structure is characterized by only a few firms doing business in a relevant market. The products must all be similar and generally are substitutes for one another. In some oligopoly markets, the goods or services may be differentiated by marketing and strong brand recognition, as in the markets for breakfast cereals and for bottled or canned beverages. Other examples of oligopoly markets are made up of homogeneous products with little or no attempt at product differentiation, such as petroleum and cement. *The most distinctive characteristic of oligopoly markets is the small number of firms that dominate the market. There are so few firms in the relevant market that their pricing decisions are interdependent.* That is, each firm's pricing decision is based on the expected retaliation by the other firms. Recall the characteristics of oligopoly markets:

1. There are a small number of potential sellers.
2. The products offered by each seller are close substitutes for the products offered by other firms and may be differentiated by brand or homogeneous and unbranded.
3. Entry into the market is difficult, with fairly high costs and significant barriers to competition.
4. Firms typically have substantial pricing power.
5. Products are often highly differentiated through marketing, features, and other non-price strategies.

Because there are so few firms, each firm can have some degree of pricing power, which can result in substantial profits. Another by-product of the oligopoly market structure is the attractiveness of price collusion. Even without price collusion, a dominant firm may easily become the price maker in the market. Oligopoly markets without collusion typically have the most sophisticated pricing strategies. Perhaps the most well-known oligopoly market with collusion is the Organization of the Petroleum Exporting Countries (OPEC) cartel, which seeks to control prices in the petroleum market by fostering agreements among oil-producing countries.

Demand Analysis and Pricing Strategies in Oligopoly Markets

Oligopoly markets' demand curves depend on the degree of pricing interdependence. In a market in which collusion is present, the aggregate market demand curve is divided by the individual production participants. Under non-colluding market conditions, each firm faces an individual demand curve. Furthermore, non-colluding oligopoly market demand characteristics depend on the pricing strategies adopted by the participating firms. The three basic pricing strategies are pricing interdependence, the Cournot assumption, and the Nash equilibrium.

The first pricing strategy assumes pricing interdependence among the firms in the oligopoly. A good example of this situation is any market in which there are "price wars," such as the commercial airline industry. For example, flying out of their hubs in Atlanta, both Delta Air Lines and AirTran Airways jointly serve several cities. AirTran is a low-cost carrier and typically offers lower fares to destinations out of Atlanta. Delta tends to match the lower fares for those cities also served by AirTran when the departure and arrival times are similar to its own. When Delta offers service to the same cities at different time slots, however, Delta's ticket prices are higher.

The most common pricing strategy assumption in these price war markets is that competitors will match a price reduction and ignore a price increase. The logic is that by lowering its price to match a competitor's price reduction, the firm will not experience a reduction in customer demand. Conversely, by not matching the price increase, the firm stands to attract customers away from the firm that raised its prices. The oligopolist's demand relationship must represent the potential increase in market share when rivals' price increases are not matched and no significant change in market share when rivals' price decreases are matched.

Given a prevailing price, the price elasticity of demand will be much greater if the price is increased and less if the price is decreased. The firm's customers are more responsive to price increases because its rivals have lower prices. Alternatively, the firm's customers are less responsive to price decreases because its rivals will match its price change.

This implies that the oligopolistic firm faces two different demand structures: one associated with price increases and another relating to price reductions. Each demand function will have its own marginal revenue structure as well. Consider the demand and marginal revenue functions in Exhibit 16(A). The functions $D_{P\uparrow}$ and $MR_{P\uparrow}$ represent the demand and marginal revenue schedules associated with higher prices, whereas the functions $D_{P\downarrow}$ and $MR_{P\downarrow}$ represent the lower prices' demand and marginal revenue schedules. The two demand schedules intersect at the prevailing price (i.e., the price at which the price increase and price decrease are both equal to zero).

Oligopoly

Exhibit 16: Kinked Demand Curve in Oligopoly Market

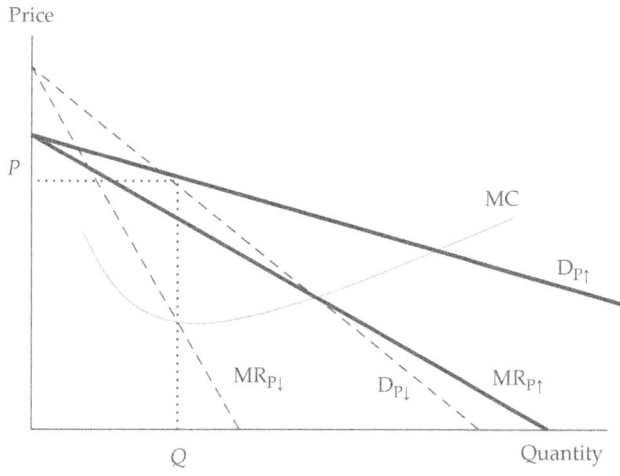

This oligopolistic pricing strategy results in a kinked demand curve, with the two segments representing the different competitor reactions to price changes. The kink in the demand curve also yields a discontinuous marginal revenue structure, with one part associated with the price increase segment of demand and the other relating to the price decrease segment. Therefore, the firm's overall demand equals the relevant portion of $D_{P\uparrow}$ and the relevant portion of $D_{P\downarrow}$. Exhibit 16(B) represents the firm's new demand and marginal revenue schedules. The firm's demand schedule shown in Exhibit 16(B) is segment $D_{P\uparrow}$ and $D_{P\downarrow}$, where overall demand $D = D_{P\uparrow} + D_{P\downarrow}$.

Exhibit 17: Kinked Demand Curve in Oligopoly Market

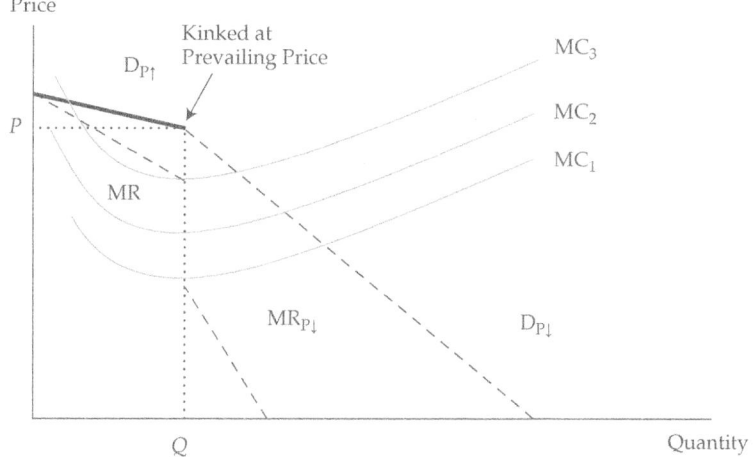

Exhibit 16(B) shows that a wide variety of cost structures are consistent with the prevailing price. If the firm has relatively low marginal costs, MC_1, the profit-maximizing pricing rule established earlier, MR = MC, still holds for the oligopoly firm. Marginal cost can rise to MC_2 and MC_3 before the firm's profitability is challenged. If the marginal cost curve MC_2 passes through the gap in marginal revenue, the most profitable price and output combination remains unchanged at the prevailing price and original level of output.

Criticism of the kinked demand curve analysis focuses on its inability to determine what the prevailing price is from the outset. The kinked demand curve analysis helps explain why stable prices have been observed in oligopoly markets and therefore is a useful tool for analyzing such markets. However, because it cannot determine the original prevailing price, it is considered to be an incomplete pricing analysis.

The Cournot Assumption

The second pricing strategy was first developed by French economist Augustin Cournot in 1838. In the **Cournot assumption**, each firm determines its profit-maximizing production level by assuming that the other firms' output will not change. This assumption simplifies pricing strategy because there is no need to guess what the other firm will do to retaliate. It also provides a useful approach to analyzing real-world behavior in oligopoly markets. Take the most basic oligopoly market situation, a two-firm duopoly market. In equilibrium, neither firm has an incentive to change output, given the other firm's production level. Each firm attempts to maximize its own profits under the assumption that the other firm will continue producing the same level of output in the future. The Cournot strategy assumes that this pattern continues until each firm reaches its long-run equilibrium position. In long-run equilibrium, output and price are stable: No change in price or output will increase profits for either firm.

Consider this example of a duopoly market. Assume that the aggregate market demand has been estimated to as follows:

$$Q_D = 450 - P.$$

The supply function is represented by constant marginal cost $MC = 30$.

The Cournot strategy's solution can be found by setting $Q_D = q_1 + q_2$, where q_1 and q_2 represent the output levels of the two firms. Each firm seeks to maximize profit, and each firm believes the other firm will not change output as it changes its own output (i.e., Cournot's assumption). The firm will maximize profit where MR = MC. Rearranging the aggregate demand function in terms of price, we get:

$$P = 450 - Q_D = 450 - (q_1 + q_2), \text{ and } MC = 30.$$

Total revenue for each of the two firms is found by multiplying price and quantity:

$$TR_1 = Pq_1 = (450 - q_1 - q_2)q_1 = 450q_1 - q_1^2 - q_1q_2,$$

and

$$TR_2 = Pq_2 = (450 - q_1 - q_2)q_2 = 450q_2 - q_2q_1 - q_2^2.$$

Marginal revenue is defined as the change in total revenue, given a change in sales (q_1 or q_2). For the profit-maximizing output, set MR = MC, or

$$450 - 2q_1 - q_2 = 30,$$

and

$$450 - q_1 - 2q_2 = 30.$$

Then find the simultaneous equilibrium for the two firms by solving the two equations with two unknowns:

$$450 - 2q_1 - q_2 = 450 - q_1 - 2q_2.$$

Because $q_2 = q_1$ under Cournot's assumption, insert this solution into the demand function and solve as follows:

$$450 - 2q_1 - q_1 = 450 - 3q_1 = 30.$$

Oligopoly

Therefore, $q_1 = 140$, $q_2 = 140$, and $Q = 280$.

The price is $P = 450 - 280 = 170$.

In the Cournot strategic pricing solution, the market equilibrium price will be 170, and the aggregate output will be 280 units. This result, known as the Cournot equilibrium, differs from the perfectly competitive market equilibrium because the perfectly competitive price will be lower and the perfectly competitive output will be higher. In general, non-competitive markets have higher prices and lower levels of output in equilibrium when compared with perfect competition. In competition, the equilibrium is reached when price equals marginal cost:

$P_C = MR_C = MC$, so $450 - Q = 30$,

where P_C is the competitive firm's equilibrium price.

$Q = 420$, and $P_C = 30$.

Exhibit 17 describes the oligopoly, competitive, and monopoly market equilibrium positions, where P_M is the monopoly optimum price, P_C is the competitive price, and $P_{Cournot}$ is the oligopoly price under the Cournot assumption.

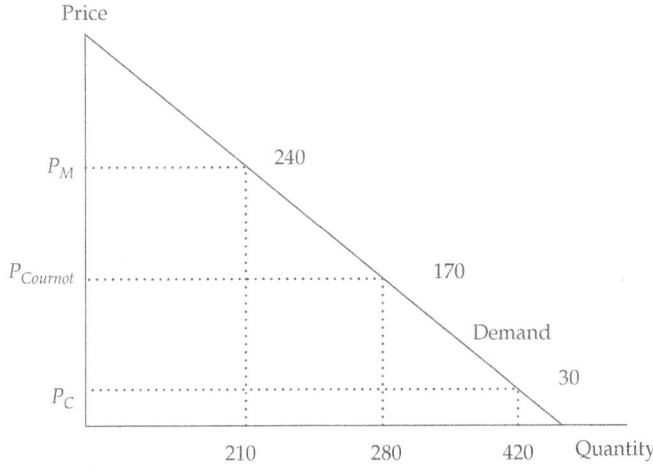

Exhibit 18: Cournot Equilibrium in Duopoly Market

In the later discussion regarding monopoly market structure, equilibrium will be established where MR = MC. That solution is also shown in Exhibit 17. The monopoly firm's demand schedule is the aggregate market demand schedule. Therefore, the solution is

MR = MC.

For the market demand function, total revenue is $P \times Q = 450Q - Q^2$ and $MR = 450 - 2Q$; therefore,

$450 - 2Q = 30$ and $Q = 210$.

From the aggregate demand function, solve for price:

$P_M = 450 - 210 = 240$.

Note that the Cournot solution falls between the competitive equilibrium and the monopoly solution.

As the number of firms increases from two to three, from three to four, and so on, the output and price equilibrium positions move toward the competitive equilibrium solution. Historically, this result has been the theoretical basis for the antitrust policies established in the United States.

The Nash Equilibrium

The third pricing strategy is attributed to one of the 1994 Nobel Prize winners, John Nash, who first developed the general concepts. In the previous analysis, the concept of market equilibrium occurs when firms are achieving their optimum remuneration under the circumstances they face. In this optimum environment, the firm has no motive to change price or output level. Existing firms are earning a normal return (zero economic profit), leaving no motive for entry to or exit from the market. All of the firms in the market are producing at the output level at which price equals the average cost of production.

In **game theory** (the set of tools that decision makers use to consider responses by rival decision makers), the **Nash equilibrium** is present when two or more participants in a non-cooperative game have no incentive to deviate from their respective equilibrium strategies after they have considered and anticipated their opponent's rational choices or strategies. In the context of oligopoly markets, the Nash equilibrium is an equilibrium defined by the characteristic that none of the oligopolists can increase its profits by unilaterally changing its pricing strategy. The assumption is made that each participating firm does the best it can, given the reactions of its rivals. Each firm anticipates that the other firms will react to any change made by competitors by doing the best they can under the altered circumstances. The firms in the oligopoly market have interdependent actions. Their actions are non-cooperative, with each firm making decisions that maximize its own profits. The firms do not collude in an effort to maximize joint profits. The equilibrium is reached when all firms are doing the best they can, given the actions of their rivals.

Exhibit 18 illustrates the duopoly result from the Nash equilibrium. Assume there are two firms in the market, ArcCo and BatCo. ArcCo and BatCo can charge high prices or low prices for the product. The market outcomes are shown in Exhibit 18.

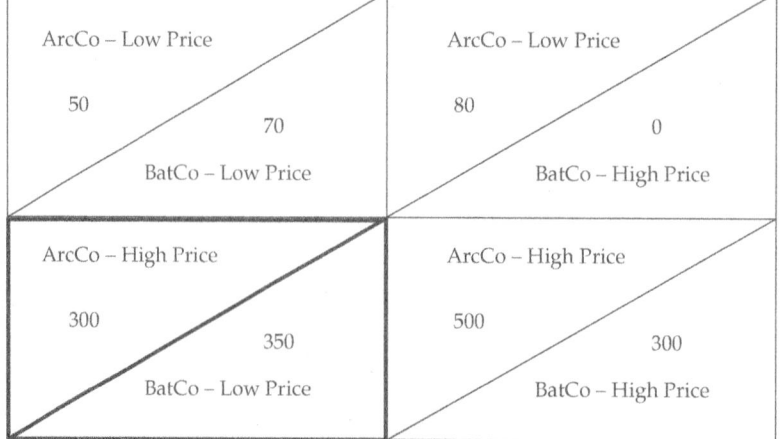

For example, the top left solution indicates that when both ArcCo and BatCo offer the product at low prices, ArcCo earns a profit of 50 and BatCo earns 70. The top right solution shows that if ArcCo offers the product at a low price, BatCo earns zero profits. The solution with the maximum joint profits is the lower right equilibrium, where both firms charge high prices for the product. Joint profits are 800 in this solution.

The Nash equilibrium, however, requires that each firm behaves in its own best interest. BatCo can improve its position by offering the product at low prices when ArcCo is charging high prices. In the lower left solution, BatCo maximizes its profits at 350. Although ArcCo can earn 500 in its best solution, it can do so only if BatCo also agrees to charge high prices. This option is clearly not in BatCo's best interest because it can increase its return from 300 to 350 by charging lower prices.

This scenario brings up the possibility of collusion. If ArcCo agrees to share at least 51 of its 500 when both companies are charging high prices, BatCo should also be willing to charge high prices. In general, such collusion is unlawful in most countries, but it remains a tempting alternative. Clearly, conditions in oligopolistic industries encourage collusion, with a small number of competitors and interdependent pricing behavior. Collusion is motivated by several factors: increased profits, reduced cash flow uncertainty, and improved opportunities to construct barriers to entry.

When collusive agreements are made openly and formally, the firms involved are called a **cartel**. In some cases, collusion is successful; other times, the forces of competition overpower collusive behavior. The following six major factors affect the chances of successful collusion:

1. *The number and size distribution of sellers.* Successful collusion is more likely if the number of firms is small or if one firm is dominant. Collusion becomes more difficult as the number of firms increases or if the few firms have similar market shares. When the firms have similar market shares, the competitive forces tend to overshadow the benefits of collusion.

2. *The similarity of the products.* When the products are homogeneous, collusion is more successful. The more differentiated the products, the less likely it is that collusion will succeed.

3. *Cost structure.* The more similar the firms' cost structures, the more likely it is that collusion will succeed.

4. *Order size and frequency.* Successful collusion is more likely when orders are frequent, received on a regular basis, and relatively small. Frequent small orders, received regularly, diminish the opportunities and rewards for cheating on the collusive agreement.

5. *The strength and severity of retaliation.* Oligopolists will be less likely to break the collusive agreement if the threat of retaliation by the other firms in the market is severe.

6. *The degree of external competition.* The main reason to enter into the formal collusion is to increase overall profitability of the market, and rising profits attract competition. For example, in 2016 the average extraction cost of a barrel of crude oil from Saudi Arabia was approximately $9, while the average cost from United States shale oil fields was roughly $23.50. The cost of extracting oil from the Canadian tar sands in 2016 was roughly $27 per barrel. It is more likely that crude oil producers in the gulf countries will successfully collude because of the similarity in their cost structures (roughly $9–$10 per barrel). If OPEC had held crude oil prices down below $30 per barrel, there would not have been a viable economic argument to develop US shale oil fields through fracking or expand extraction from Canada's tar

sands. OPEC's successful cartel raised crude oil prices to the point at which outside sources became economically possible and, in doing so, increased the competition the cartel faces.

Other possible oligopoly strategies are associated with decision making based on game theory. The Cournot equilibrium and the Nash equilibrium are examples of specific strategic games. A strategic game is any interdependent behavioral choice employed by individuals or groups that share a common goal (e.g., military units, sports teams, or business decision makers). Another prominent decision-making strategy in oligopolistic markets is the first-mover advantage in the **Stackelberg model**, named after the economist who first conceptualized the strategy. The important difference between the Cournot model and the Stackelberg model is that Cournot assumes that in a duopoly market, decision making is simultaneous, whereas Stackelberg assumes that decisions are made sequentially. In the Stackelberg model, the leader firm chooses its output first and then the follower firm chooses after observing the leader's output. It can be shown that the leader firm has a distinct advantage—that is, being a first mover. In the Stackelberg game, the leader can aggressively overproduce to force the follower to scale back its production or even punish or eliminate the weaker opponent. This approach is sometimes referred to as a "top dog" strategy. The leader earns more than in Cournot's simultaneous game, while the follower earns less. Many other strategic games are possible in oligopoly markets. The important conclusion is that the optimal strategy of the firm depends on what its adversary does. The price and marginal revenue the firm receives for its product depend on both its decisions and its adversary's decisions.

Oligopoly Markets: Optimal Price, Output, and Long-Run Equilibrium

As in monopolistic competition, the oligopolist does not have a well-defined supply function. That is, there is no way to determine the oligopolist's optimal levels of output and price independent of demand conditions and competitor's strategies. However, the oligopolist still has a cost function that determines the optimal level of supply. Therefore, the profit-maximizing rule established earlier is still valid: The level of output that maximizes profit is where MR = MC. The price to charge is determined by what price consumers are willing to pay for that quantity of the product. Therefore, the equilibrium price comes from the demand curve, whereas the output level comes from the relationship between marginal revenue and marginal cost.

Consider an oligopoly market in which one of the firms is dominant and thus able to be the price leader. Dominant firms generally have 40 percent or greater market share. When one firm dominates an oligopoly market, it does so because it has greater capacity, has a lower cost structure, was first to market, or has greater customer loyalty than other firms in the market.

Assuming there is no collusion, the dominant firm becomes the price maker, and therefore its actions are similar to monopoly behavior in its segment of the market. The other firms in the market follow the pricing patterns of the dominant firm. Why wouldn't the price followers attempt to gain market share by undercutting the dominant firm's price? The most common explanation is that the dominant firm's supremacy often stems from a lower cost of production. Usually, the price followers would rather charge a price that is even higher than the dominant firm's price choice. If they attempt to undercut the dominant firm, the followers risk a price war with a lower-cost producer that can threaten their survival. Some believe that one explanation for the price leadership position of the dominant firm is simply convenience. Only one firm has to make the pricing decisions, and the others can simply follow its lead.

Oligopoly

Exhibit 19 establishes the dominant firm's pricing decision. The dominant firm's demand schedule, D_L, is a substantial share of the total market demand, D_T. The low-cost position of the dominant firm is represented by its marginal cost, MC_L. The sum of the marginal costs of the price followers is established as ΣMC_F and represents a higher cost of production than that of the price leader.

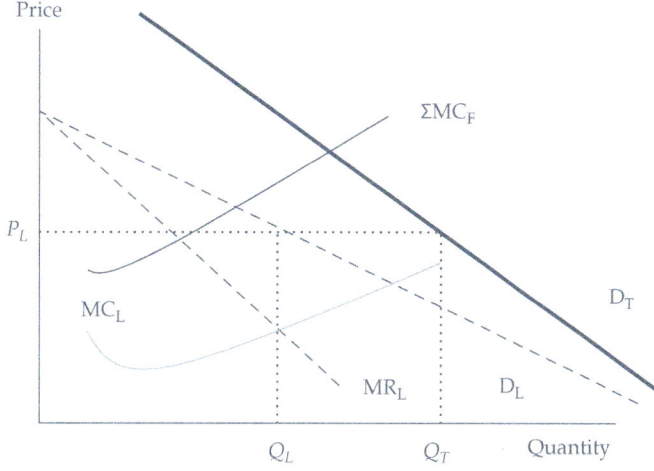

Exhibit 20: Dominant Oligopolist's Price Leadership

An important reason why the total demand curve and the leader demand curve are not parallel is illustrated in Exhibit 19: The leader is the low-cost producer. Therefore, as price decreases, fewer of the smaller suppliers will be able to profitably remain in the market, and several will exit because thwey do not want to sell below cost. Therefore, the leader will have a larger market share as P decreases, which implies that Q_L increases at a low price, exactly as shown by a steeper D_T in the diagram.

The price leader identifies its profit-maximizing output where $MR_L = MC_L$, at output Q_L. This is the quantity it wants to supply; however, the price it will charge is determined by its segment of the total demand function, D_L. At price P_L, the dominant firm will supply quantity Q_L of total demand, D_T. The price followers will supply the difference to the market, $(Q_T - Q_L) = Q_F$. Therefore, neither the dominant firm nor the follower firms have a single functional relationship that determines the quantity supplied at various prices.

Optimal Price and Output in Oligopoly Markets

As this discussion shows, clearly no single optimum price and output analysis fits all oligopoly market situations. The interdependence among the few firms that make up the oligopoly market provides a complex set of pricing alternatives, depending on the circumstances in each market. In the case of the kinked demand curve, the optimum price is the prevailing price at the kink in the demand function. As noted, however, the kinked demand curve analysis does not provide insight into what established the prevailing price in the first place.

Perhaps the case of the dominant firm, with the other firms following the price leader, is the most obvious. In that case, the optimal price is determined at the output level where MR = MC. The profit-maximizing price is then determined by the output position of the segment of the demand function faced by the dominant firm. The price followers have little incentive to change the leader's price. In the case of the Cournot assumption, each firm assumes that the other firms will not alter their output following the dominant firm's selection of its price and output level.

Therefore, again, the optimum price is determined by the output level where MR = MC. In the case of the Nash equilibrium, each firm will react to the circumstances it faces, maximizing its own profit. These adjustments continue until prices and levels of output are stable. Because of the interdependence, the individual firm's price and output level remain uncertain.

Factors Affecting Long-Run Equilibrium in Oligopoly Markets

Long-run economic profits are possible for firms operating in oligopoly markets. History has shown that, however, the market share of the dominant firm declines. Profits attract entry by other firms into the oligopoly market. Over time, the marginal costs of the entrant firms decrease because they adopt more efficient production techniques, the dominant firm's demand and marginal revenue shrink, and the profitability of the dominant firm declines. In the early 1900s, J.P. Morgan, Elbert Gary, Andrew Carnegie, and Charles M. Schwab created the United States Steel Corporation (US Steel). When it was first formed in 1901, US Steel controlled 66 percent of the market. By 1920, US Steel's market share had declined to 46 percent, and by 1925 its market share was 42 percent.

In the long run, optimal pricing strategy must include the reactions of rival firms. History has proven that pricing wars should be avoided because any gains in market share are temporary. Decreasing prices to drive away competitors lowers total revenue to all participants in the oligopoly market. Innovation may be a way—though sometimes an uneconomical one—to maintain market leadership.

OLIGOPOLIES: APPEARANCE VERSUS BEHAVIOR

When is an oligopoly not an oligopoly? There are two extreme cases of this situation. A normal oligopoly has a few firms producing a differentiated good, and this differentiation gives them pricing power.

At one end of the spectrum, we have the oligopoly with a credible threat of entry. In practice, if the oligopolists are producing a good or service that can be easily replicated, has limited economies of scale, and is not protected by brand recognition or patents, they will not be able to charge high prices. The easier it is for a new supplier to enter the market, the lower the margins. In practice, this oligopoly will behave very much like a perfectly competitive market.

At the opposite end of the spectrum, we have the case of the cartel. Here, the oligopolists collude and act as if they were a single firm. In practice, a very effective cartel enacts a cooperative strategy. Instead of going to a Nash equilibrium, the cartel participants go to the more lucrative (for them) cooperative equilibrium.

A cartel may be explicit (i.e., based on a contract) or implicit (based on signals). An example of signals in a duopoly would be that one of the firms reduces its prices and the other does not. Because the firm not cutting prices refuses to start a price war, the firm that cut prices may interpret this signal as a "suggestion" to raise prices to a higher level than before, so that profits may increase for both.

Oligopoly

QUESTION SET

1. Oligopolistic pricing strategy *most likely* results in a demand curve that is:

   A. kinked.
   B. vertical.
   C. horizontal.

   Solution:

   A is correct. The oligopolist faces two different demand structures, one for price increases and another for price decreases. Competitors will lower prices to match a price reduction, but will not match a price increase. The result is a kinked demand curve.

2. Collusion is *less likely* in a market when:

   A. the product is homogeneous.
   B. companies have similar market shares.
   C. the cost structures of companies are similar.

   Solution:

   B is correct. When companies have similar market shares, competitive forces tend to outweigh the benefits of collusion.

3. In an industry composed of three companies, which are small-scale manufacturers of an easily replicable product unprotected by brand recognition or patents, the *most* representative model of company behavior is:

   A. oligopoly.
   B. perfect competition.
   C. monopolistic competition.

   Solution:

   B is correct. The credible threat of entry holds down prices and multiple incumbents are offering undifferentiated products.

4. Deep River Manufacturing is one of many companies in an industry that makes a food product. Deep River units are identical up to the point they are labeled. Deep River produces its labeled brand, which sells for $2.20 per unit, and "house brands" for seven different grocery chains, which sell for $2.00 per unit. Each grocery chain sells both the Deep River brand and its house brand. The *best* characterization of Deep River's market is:

   A. oligopoly.
   B. perfect competition.
   C. monopolistic competition.

   Solution:

   C is correct. There are many competitors in the market, but some product differentiation exists, as the price differential between Deep River's brand and the house brands indicates.

The following information relates to questions 5 & 6

SigmaSoft and ThetaTech are the dominant makers of computer system software. The market has two components: a large mass-market component in which demand is price sensitive, and a smaller performance-oriented component in which demand is much less price sensitive. SigmaSoft's product is considered to be technically superior. Each company can choose one of two strategies:

Open architecture (Open): Mass market focus allowing other software venders to develop products for its platform.

Proprietary (Prop): Allow only its own software applications to run on its platform.

5. Depending upon the strategy each company selects, their profits would be:

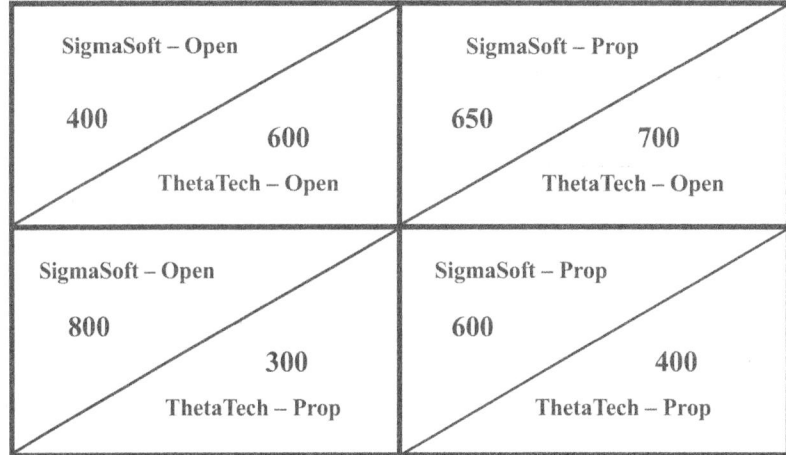

6. The Nash equilibrium for these companies is:

    A. proprietary for SigmaSoft and proprietary for ThetaTech.

    B. open architecture for SigmaSoft and proprietary for ThetaTech.

    C. proprietary for SigmaSoft and open architecture for ThetaTech.

Solution:

C is correct. In the Nash model, each company considers the other's reaction in selecting its strategy. In equilibrium, neither company has an incentive to change its strategy. ThetaTech is better off with open architecture regardless of what SigmaSoft decides. Given this choice, SigmaSoft is better off with a proprietary platform. Neither company will change its decision unilaterally.

6. DETERMINING MARKET STRUCTURE

☐ identify the type of market structure within which a firm operates and describe the use and limitations of concentration measures

Determining Market Structure

Monopoly markets and other situations in which companies have pricing power can be inefficient because producers constrain output to cause an increase in prices. Therefore, less of the good will be consumed, and it will be sold at a higher price, which is generally inefficient for the overall market. As a result, many countries have introduced competition law to regulate the degree of competition in many industries.

Market power in the real world is not always as clear as it is in textbook examples. Governments and regulators often have the difficult task of measuring market power and establishing whether a firm has a dominant position that may resemble a monopoly. A few historical examples of this are as follows:

1. In the 1990s, US regulators prosecuted agricultural corporation Archer Daniels Midland for conspiring with Japanese competitors to fix the price of lysine, an amino acid used as an animal feed additive. The antitrust action resulted in a settlement that involved more than US$100 million in fines paid by the cartel members.

2. In the 1970s, US antitrust authorities broke up the local telephone monopoly, leaving AT&T the long-distance business (and opening that business to competitors), and required AT&T to divest itself of the local telephone companies it owned. This antitrust decision brought competition, innovation, and lower prices to the US telephone market.

3. European regulators (specifically, the European Commission) have affected the mergers and monopoly positions of European corporations (as in the case of the companies Roche, Rhone-Poulenc, and BASF, which were at the center of a vitamin price-fixing case) as well as non-European companies (such as Intel) that do business in Europe. Moreover, the merger between the US company General Electric and the European company Honeywell was denied by the European Commission on grounds of excessive market concentration.

Quantifying excessive market concentration is difficult. Sometimes, regulators need to measure whether something that has not yet occurred might generate excessive market power. For example, a merger between two companies might allow the combined company to be a monopolist or quasi-monopolist in a certain market.

A financial analyst hearing news about a possible merger should always consider the impact of competition law (sometimes called antitrust law)—that is, whether a proposed merger may be blocked by regulators in the interest of preserving a competitive market.

Econometric Approaches

How should one measure market power? The theoretical answer is to estimate the elasticity of demand and supply in a market. If demand is very elastic, the market must be very close to perfect competition. If demand is rigid (inelastic), companies *may* have market power.

From the econometric point of view, this estimation requires some attention. The problem is that observed price and quantity are the equilibrium values of price and quantity and do not represent the value of either supply or demand. Technically, this is called the problem of endogeneity, in the sense that the equilibrium price and quantity are jointly determined by the interaction of demand and supply. Therefore, to have an appropriate estimation of demand and supply, we need to use a model with two equations: an equation of demanded quantity (as a function of price, income of the buyers, and other variables) and an equation of supplied quantity (as a function of price, production costs, and other variables). The estimated parameters will then allow us to compute elasticity.

Regression analysis is useful in computing elasticity but requires a large number of observations. Therefore, one may use a time-series approach and, for example, look at 20 years of quarterly sales data for a market. The market structure may have changed radically over those 20 years, however, and the estimated elasticity may not apply to the current situation. Moreover, the supply curve may change because of a merger among large competitors, and the estimation based on past data may not be informative regarding the future state of the market postmerger.

An alternative approach is a cross-sectional regression analysis. Instead of looking at total sales and average prices in a market over time (the time-series approach mentioned earlier), we can look at sales from different companies in the market during the same year, or even at single transactions from many buyers and companies. Clearly, this approach requires a substantial data-gathering effort, and therefore, this estimation method can be complicated. Moreover, different specifications of the explanatory variables (e.g., using total GDP rather than median household income or per-capita GDP to represent income) may lead to dramatically different estimates.

Simpler Measures

Trying to avoid these drawbacks, analysts often use simpler measures to estimate elasticity. The simplest measure is the concentration ratio, which is the sum of the market shares of the largest N firms. To compute this ratio, one would, for example, add the sales values of the largest 10 firms and divide this figure by total market sales. This number is always between 0 (perfect competition) and 100 percent (monopoly).

The main advantage of the concentration ratio is that it is simple to compute, as shown previously. The disadvantage is that it does not directly quantify market power. In other words, is a high concentration ratio a clear signal of monopoly power? A company may be the only incumbent in a market, but if the barriers to entry are low, the simple presence of a *potential* entrant may be sufficient to convince the incumbent to behave like a firm in perfect competition. For example, a sugar wholesaler may be the only one in a country, but the knowledge that other large wholesalers in the food industry might easily add imported sugar to their range of products should convince the sugar wholesaler to price its product as if it were in perfect competition.

Another disadvantage of the concentration ratio is that it tends to be unaffected by mergers among the top market incumbents. For example, if the largest and second-largest incumbents merge, the pricing power of the combined entity is likely to be larger than that of the two preexisting companies. But the concentration ratio may not change much.

> **CALCULATING THE CONCENTRATION RATIO**
>
> Suppose there are eight producers of a certain good in a market. The largest producer has 35 percent of the market, the second largest has 25 percent, the third has 20 percent, the fourth has 10 percent, and the remaining four have 2.5 percent each. If we computed the concentration ratio of the top three producers, it would be 35 + 25 + 20 = 80 percent, while the concentration ratio of the top four producers would be 35 + 25 + 20 + 10 = 90 percent.
>
> If the two largest companies merged, the new concentration ratio for the top three producers would be 60 (the sum of the market shares of the merged companies) + 20 + 10 = 90 percent, and the concentration ratio for the four top producers would be 92.5 percent. Therefore, this merger affects the concentration ratio very mildly, even though it creates a substantial entity that controls 60 percent of the market.

Determining Market Structure

For example, the effect of consolidation in the US retail gasoline market has resulted in increasing degrees of concentration. In 1992, the top four companies in the US retail gasoline market shared 33 percent of the market. By 2001, the top four companies controlled 78 percent of the market (Exxon Mobil 24 percent, Shell 20 percent, BP/Amoco/Arco 18 percent, and Chevron/Texaco 16 percent).

To avoid the known issues with concentration ratios, economists O. C. Herfindahl and A. O. Hirschman suggested an index in which the market shares of the top N companies are first squared and then added. If one firm controls the whole market (a monopoly), the Herfindahl–Hirschman index (HHI) equals 1. If there are M firms in the industry with equal market shares, then the HHI equals $(1/M)$. This provides a useful gauge for interpreting an HHI. For example, an HHI of 0.20 would be analogous to having the market shared equally by five firms.

The HHI for the top three companies in the example in the box above would be $0.35^2 + 0.25^2 + 0.20^2 = 0.225$ before the merger, whereas after the merger, it would be $0.60^2 + 0.20^2 + 0.10^2 = 0.410$, which is substantially higher than the initial 0.225. The HHI is widely used by competition regulators; however, just like the concentration ratio, the HHI does not take the possibility of entry into account, nor does it consider the elasticity of demand. Therefore, the HHI has limited use for a financial analyst trying to estimate the potential profitability of a company or group of companies.

EXAMPLE 4

The Herfindahl–Hirschman Index

1. Suppose a market has 10 suppliers, each of them with 10 percent of the market. What are the concentration ratio and the HHI of the top four firms?

   A. Concentration ratio 4 percent and HHI 40
   B. Concentration ratio 40 percent and HHI 0.4
   C. Concentration ratio 40 percent and HHI 0.04

   Solution:

   C is correct. The concentration ratio for the top four firms is $10 + 10 + 10 + 10 = 40$ percent, and the HHI is $0.10^2 \times 4 = 0.01 \times 4 = 0.04$.

QUESTION SET

1. An analyst gathers the following market share data for an industry:

Company	Sales (in millions of euros)
ABC	300
Brown	250
Coral	200
Delta	150
Erie	100
All others	50

2. The industry's four-company concentration ratio is *closest* to:

   A. 71%.

B. 86%.

C. 95%.

Solution:

B is correct. The top four companies in the industry account for 86 percent of industry sales: (300 + 250 + 200 + 150)/(300 + 250 + 200 + 150 + 100 + 50) = 900/1050 = 86%.

The following information applies to questions 3 & 4

An analyst gathered the following market share data for an industry composed of five companies:

Company	Market Share (%)
Zeta	35
Yusef	25
Xenon	20
Waters	10
Vlastos	10

3. The industry's three-firm Herfindahl–Hirschman index is *closest* to:

    A. 0.185.

    B. 0.225.

    C. 0.235.

    Solution:

    B is correct. The three-firm Herfindahl–Hirschman index is $0.35^2 + 0.25^2 + 0.20^2 = 0.225$.

4. One disadvantage of the Herfindahl–Hirschman index is that the index:

    A. is difficult to compute.

    B. fails to reflect low barriers to entry.

    C. fails to reflect the effect of mergers in the industry.

    Solution:

    B is correct. The Herfindahl–Hirschman index does not reflect low barriers to entry that may restrict the market power of companies currently in the market.

PRACTICE PROBLEMS

1. The short-term shutdown point of production for a firm operating under perfect competition will *most likely* occur when:
   A. price is equal to average total cost.
   B. marginal revenue is equal to marginal cost.
   C. marginal revenue is equal to average variable costs.

2. Under conditions of perfect competition, a company will break even when market price is equal to the minimum point of the:
   A. average total cost curve.
   B. average variable cost curve.
   C. short-run marginal cost curve.

3. A company will shut down production in the short run if total revenue is less than total:
   A. fixed costs.
   B. variable costs.
   C. opportunity costs.

4. A company has total variable costs of $4 million and fixed costs of $3 million. Based on this information, the company will stay in the market in the long term if total revenue is at least:
   A. $3.0 million.
   B. $4.5 million.
   C. $7.0 million.

5. When total revenue is greater than total variable costs but less than total costs, in the short term, a firm will *most likely*:
   A. exit the market.
   B. stay in the market.
   C. shut down production.

6. Under conditions of perfect competition, in the long run, firms will *most likely* earn:
   A. normal profits.
   B. positive economic profits.
   C. negative economic profits.

7. A firm that increases its quantity produced without any change in per-unit cost is

experiencing:

   A. economies of scale.

   B. diseconomies of scale.

   C. constant returns to scale.

8. A company is experiencing economies of scale when:

   A. cost per unit increases as output increases.

   B. it is operating at a point on the LRAC curve at which the slope is negative.

   C. it is operating beyond the minimum point on the long-run average total cost curve.

9. Diseconomies of scale *most likely* result from:

   A. specialization in the labor force.

   B. overlap of business functions and product lines.

   C. discounted prices on resources when buying in larger quantities.

10. A firm is operating beyond minimum efficient scale in a perfectly competitive industry. To maintain long-term viability, the *most likely* course of action for the firm is to:

    A. operate at the current level of production.

    B. increase its level of production to gain economies of scale.

    C. decrease its level of production to the minimum point on the long-run average total cost curve.

11. Companies *most likely* have a well-defined supply function when the market structure is:

    A. oligopoly.

    B. perfect competition.

    C. monopolistic competition.

12. Aquarius, Inc. is the dominant company and the price leader in its market. One of the other companies in the market attempts to gain market share by undercutting the price set by Aquarius. The market share of Aquarius will *most likely*:

    A. increase.

    B. decrease.

    C. stay the same.

13. Over time, the market share of the dominant company in an oligopolistic market will *most likely*:

    A. increase.

    B. decrease.

C. remain the same.

SOLUTIONS

1. C is correct. The firm should shut down production when marginal revenue is less than or equal to average variable cost.

2. A is correct. A company is said to break even if its total revenue is equal to its total cost. Under conditions of perfect competition, a company will break even when market price is equal to the minimum point of the average total cost curve.

3. B is correct. A company will shut down production in the short run when total revenue is below total variable costs.

4. C is correct. A company will stay in the market in the long term if total revenue is equal to or greater than total cost. Because total costs are $7 million ($4 million variable costs and $3 million fixed costs), the company will stay in the market in the long term if total revenue equals at least $7 million.

5. B is correct. When total revenue is enough to cover variable costs but not total fixed costs in full, the firm can survive in the short run but would not be able to maintain financial solvency in the long run.

6. A is correct. Competition should drive prices down to long-run marginal cost, resulting in only normal profits being earned.

7. C is correct. Output increases in the same proportion as input increases occur at constant returns to scale.

8. B is correct. Economies of scale occur if, as the firm increases output, cost per unit of production falls. Graphically, this definition translates into an LRAC with a negative slope.

9. B is correct. As the firm increases output, diseconomies of scale and higher average total costs can result when business functions and product lines overlap or are duplicated.

10. C is correct. The firm operating at greater than long-run efficient scale is subject to diseconomies of scale. It should plan to decrease its level of production.

11. B is correct. A company in a perfectly competitive market must accept whatever price the market dictates. The marginal cost schedule of a company in a perfectly competitive market determines its supply function.

12. A is correct. As prices decrease, smaller companies will leave the market rather than sell below cost. The market share of Aquarius, the price leader, will increase.

13. B is correct. The dominant company's market share tends to decrease as profits attract entry by other companies.

LEARNING MODULE 2

Understanding Business Cycles

by Gambera Michele, PhD, CFA, Ezrati Milton, and Cao Bolong, PhD, CFA.

Michele Gambera, PhD, CFA, is with UBS Asset Management and the University of Illinois at Urbana-Champaign (USA). Milton Ezrati (USA). Bolong Cao, PhD, CFA, is at Ohio University (USA).

LEARNING OUTCOMES

Mastery	The candidate should be able to:
☐	describe the business cycle and its phases
☐	describe credit cycles
☐	describe how resource use, consumer and business activity, housing sector activity, and external trade sector activity vary over the business cycle and describe their measurement using economic indicators

INTRODUCTION

A typical economy's output of goods and services fluctuates around its long-term path. We now turn our attention to those recurring, cyclical fluctuations in economic output. Some of the factors that influence short-term changes in the economy—such as changes in population, technology, and capital—are the same as those that affect long-term sustainable economic growth. But forces that cause shifts in aggregate demand and aggregate supply curves—such as expectations, political developments, natural disasters, and fiscal and monetary policy decisions—also influence economies, particularly in the short run.

We first describe a typical business cycle and its phases. While each cycle is different, analysts and investors need to be familiar with the typical cycle phases and what they mean for the expectations and decisions of businesses and households that influence the performance of sectors and companies. These behaviors also affect financial conditions and risk appetite, thus affecting the setting of expectations and choices of portfolio exposures to different investment sectors or styles.

In the lessons that follow, we describe credit cycles, introduce several theories of business cycles, and explain how different economic schools of thought interpret the business cycle and their recommendations with respect to it. We also discuss variables that demonstrate predictable relationships with the economy, focusing on those whose movements have value in predicting the future course of the economy. We then proceed to explain measures and features of unemployment and inflation.

> **LEARNING MODULE OVERVIEW**
>
> - Business cycles are recurrent expansions and contractions in economic activity affecting broad segments of the economy.
> - Classical cycle refers to fluctuations in the level of economic activity (e.g., measured by GDP in volume terms).
> - Growth cycle refers to fluctuations in economic activity around the long-term potential or trend growth level.
> - Growth rate cycle refers to fluctuations in the growth rate of economic activity (e.g., GDP growth rate).
> - The overall business cycle can be split into four phases: recovery, expansion, slowdown, and contraction.
> - In the recovery phase of the business cycle, the economy is going through the "trough" of the cycle, where actual output is at its lowest level relative to potential output.
> - In the expansion phase of the business cycle, output increases, and the rate of growth is above average. Actual output rises above potential output, and the economy enters the so-called boom phase.
> - In the slowdown phase of the business cycle, output reaches its highest level relative to potential output (i.e., the largest positive output gap). The growth rate begins to slow relative to potential output growth, and the positive output gap begins to narrow.
> - In the contraction phase of the business cycle, actual economic output falls below potential economic output.
> - Credit cycles describe the changing availability—and pricing—of credit.
> - Strong peaks in credit cycles are closely associated with subsequent systemic banking crises.
> - Economic indicators are variables that provide information on the state of the overall economy.
>   - Leading economic indicators have turning points that usually precede those of the overall economy.
>   - Coincident economic indicators have turning points that usually are close to those of the overall economy.
>   - Lagging economic indicators have turning points that take place later than those of the overall economy.
> - A diffusion index reflects the proportion of a composite index of leading, lagging and coincident indicators that are moving in a pattern consistent with the overall index. Analysts often rely on these diffusion indexes to provide a measure of the breadth of the change in a composite index.

OVERVIEW OF THE BUSINESS CYCLE

☐ describe the business cycle and its phases

Business cycles are recurrent expansions and contractions in economic activity affecting broad segments of the economy. In their 1946 book "Measuring Business Cycles", Burns and Mitchell define the business cycle as follows:

> Business cycles are a type of fluctuation found in the aggregate economic activity of nations that organize their work mainly in business enterprises: a cycle consists of expansions occurring at about the same time in many economic activities, followed by similarly general recessions, contractions, and revivals which merge into the expansion phase of the next cycle; this sequence of events is recurrent but not periodic; in duration, business cycles vary from more than one year to 10 or 12 years.

This definition is rich with important insight. First, business cycles are typical of economies that rely mainly on business enterprises—therefore, not agrarian societies or centrally planned economies. Second, a cycle has an expected sequence of phases, alternating between expansion and contraction, or upswings and downturns. Third, such phases occur at about the same time throughout the economy. Finally, cycles are recurrent; they happen again and again over time but not in a periodic way; they do not all have the exact same intensity and duration. Exhibit 1 provides an illustration of the pattern of economic growth rate in developed markets.

Exhibit 1: Fluctuations of Growth in OECD Countries over Time

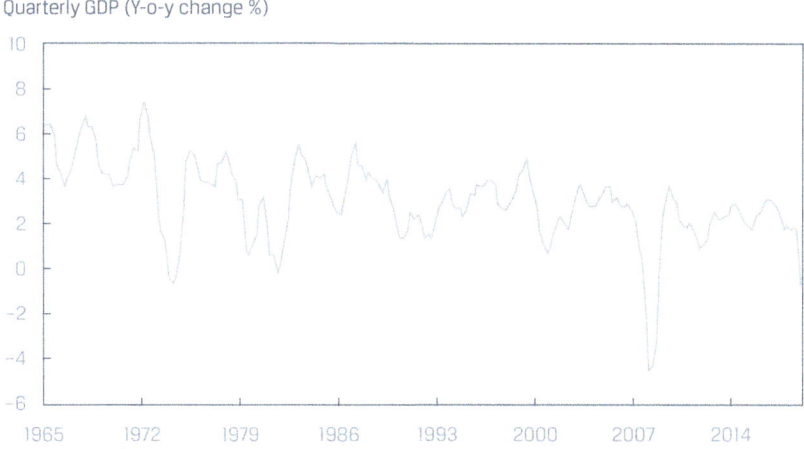

Note: The Organisation for Economic Co-Operation and Development (OECD) includes more than 30 large member countries.

Source: OECD.Stat (https://stats.oecd.org), year-over-year change in quarterly GDP in OECD countries.

Burns and Mitchell's definition remains helpful. History never repeats itself in quite the same way, but it certainly does offer patterns that can be used when analyzing the present and forecasting the future. Business cycle analysis is a wide-ranging topic with conflicting perspectives held by industry participants.

Phases of the Business Cycle

Business cycles are recurring sequences of alternating upswings and downturns. The business cycle can be broken into phases in various ways. The most obvious way is to divide it into two primary segments: the expansion, or the upswing, and the contraction, or the downturn, with two key turning points, or peaks and troughs (see Exhibits 2 and 3). These two periods are fairly easy to identify in retrospect. Subdividing the cycle more finely, however, becomes ambiguous, even in retrospect, because it requires identifying more nuanced changes, such as acceleration or deceleration of growth without a change in its direction. It thus is useful to divide the cycle into several phases distinguished through both economic and financial market characteristics. Our focus is on economic characteristics of the different phases, but we also will highlight their implication for the behavior of different segments of the financial markets.

The timing of these periods will depend on the type of cycle. Before moving on to the description of the four distinct phases to which we will refer in the subsequent sections, we first explain the different cycle concepts that analysts should be aware of given the range of different opinions, interpretations, and descriptions that practitioners use.

Types of Cycles

- **Classical cycle** refers to fluctuations in the level of economic activity (e.g., measured by GDP in volume terms). The contraction phases between peaks and troughs are often short, whereas expansion phases are much longer. Exhibit 2 shows the classical cycle of economic activity. In practice, the classical cycle is not used extensively by academics and practitioners because it does not easily allow the breakdown of movements in GDP between short-term fluctuations and long-run trends. In addition, an absolute decline in activity between peaks and troughs does not occur frequently.

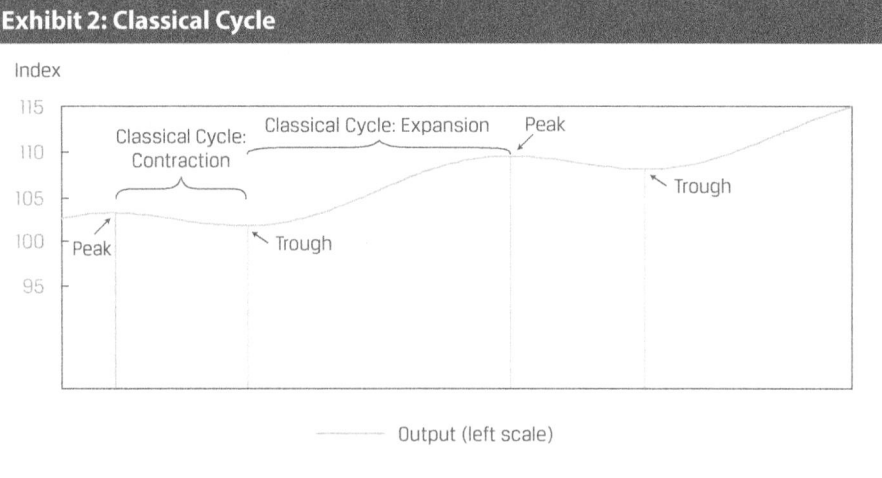

- **Growth cycle** refers to fluctuations in economic activity around the long-term potential or trend growth level. The focus is on how much actual economic activity is below or above trend growth in economic activity. The dashed "wave" in the lower part of Exhibit 3 captures the fluctuation of actual activity from trend growth activity. Exhibit 3 shows "gaps" between actual and trend output. The growth cycle definition comes closest to how mainstream economists think: It dissects overall economic activity into a

Overview of the Business Cycle

part driven by long-run trends and a part reflecting short-run fluctuations. Compared with the classical view of business cycles, peaks generally are reached earlier and troughs later in time. The time periods below and above trend growth are of similar length.

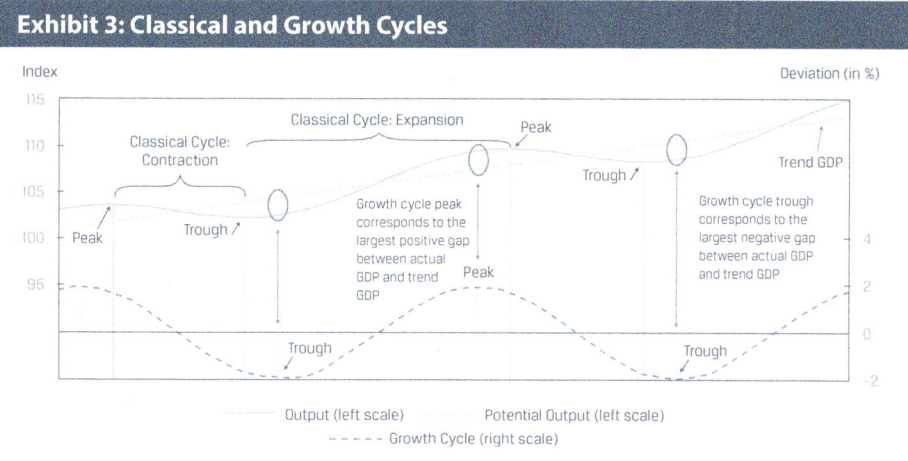

Exhibit 3: Classical and Growth Cycles

- **Growth rate cycle** refers to fluctuations in the growth rate of economic activity (e.g., GDP growth rate). Peaks and troughs are mostly recognized earlier than when using the other two definitions (see Exhibit 4). One advantage of this approach is that it is not necessary to first estimate a long-run growth path. Nevertheless, economists often refer to economic growth being above or below potential growth rate, reflecting upswings or downturns.

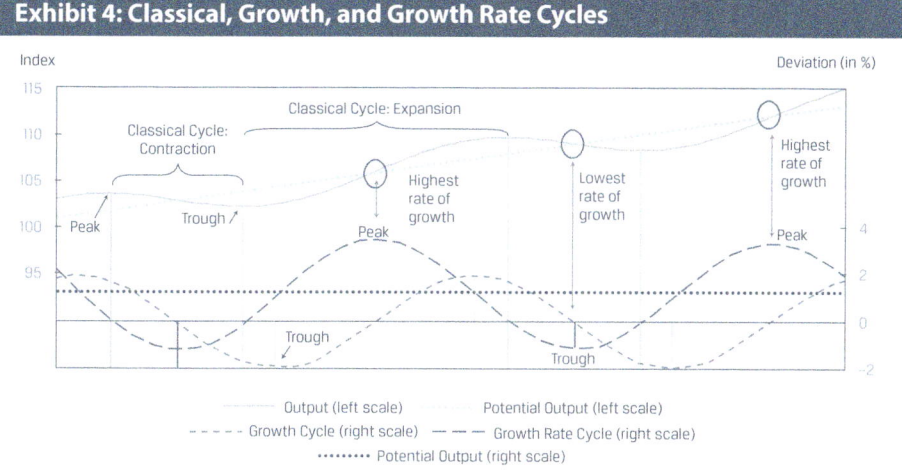

Exhibit 4: Classical, Growth, and Growth Rate Cycles

Notes: The vertical lines indicate troughs and peaks when using either the classical, growth, or growth rate cycle definition of a business cycle. The growth cycle reflects the percentage deviation of output relative to its trend. The growth rates in the growth rate cycle are calculated as annualized month-over-month growth rates.

Practical Issues

In practice, the definitions of a business cycle are used interchangeably, which often causes confusion regarding how one labels the phases and their timing. The classical cycle definition is rarely used. In line with how most economists and practitioners view the cycle, we will generally be using the growth cycle concept in which business cycles can be thought of as fluctuations around potential output (the trend in potential output is shown as the upward sloping dotted line in Exhibit 3).

Four Phases of the Cycle

The overall business cycle can be split into four phases:

Recovery: The economy is going through the "trough" of the cycle, where actual output is at its lowest level relative to potential output. Economic activity, including consumer and business spending, is below potential but is starting to increase, closing the negative output gap.

Expansion: The recovery gathers pace, output increases, and the rate of growth is above average. Actual output rises above potential output, and the economy enters the so-called boom phase. Consumers increase spending, and companies increase production, employment, and investment. Prices and interest rates may start increasing. As the expansion continues, the economy may start to experience shortages in factors of production. Overinvestment in productive capacity may lead companies to reduce further investment spending.

Slowdown: Output of the economy reaches its highest level relative to potential output (largest positive output gap). The growth rate begins to slow relative to potential output growth, and the positive output gap begins to narrow. Consumers remain optimistic about the economy, but companies may rely on overtime rather than using new hires to meet demand. Inflation slows at some point, and price levels may decrease.

Contraction: Actual economic output falls below potential economic output. Consumer and business confidence declines. Companies reduce costs by eliminating overtime and reducing employment. The economy may experience declines in absolute economic activity; a recession; or if the fall in activity is particularly large, a depression. If the decline is moderate, this phase tends to be shorter than the expansion phase.

Exhibit 5 provides a summary of the key characteristics of each phase and describes how several important economic variables evolve through the course of a business cycle.

Exhibit 5: Business Cycle Phase Characteristics

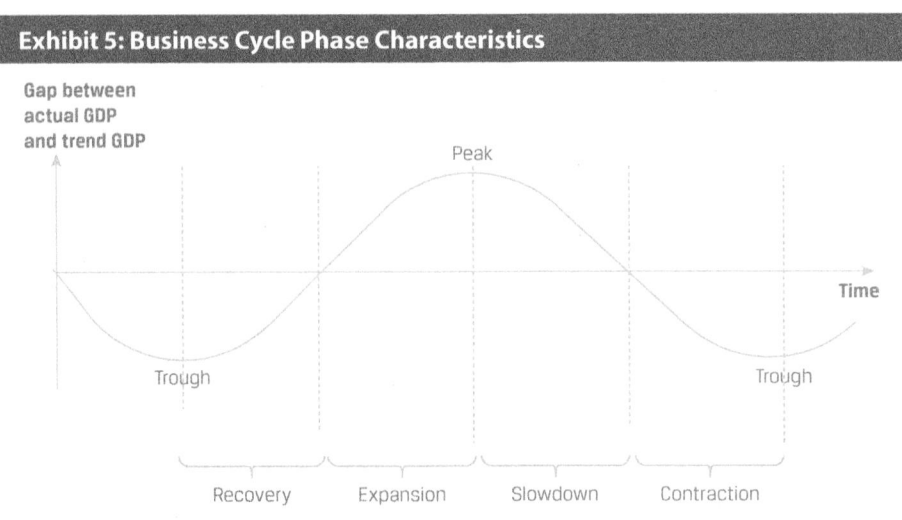

Phase	Recovery	Expansion	Slowdown	Contraction
Description	Economy going through a trough. Negative output gap starts to narrow.	Economy enjoying an upswing. Positive output gap opens.	Economy going through a peak. Positive output gap starts to narrow.	Economy weakens and may go into a recession. Negative output gap opens.
Activity levels: consumers and businesses	Activity levels are below potential but start to increase.	Activity measures show above-average growth rates.	Activity measures are above average but decelerating. Moving to below-average rates of growth.	Activity measures are below potential. Growth is lower than normal.
Employment	Layoffs slow. Businesses rely on overtime before moving to hiring. Unemployment remains higher than average.	Businesses move from using overtime and temporary employees to hiring. Unemployment rate stabilizes and starts falling.	Business continue hiring but at a slower pace. Unemployment rate continues to fall but at decreasing rates.	Businesses first cut hours, eliminate overtime, and freeze hiring, followed by outright layoffs. Unemployment rate starts to rise.
Inflation	Inflation remains moderate.	Inflation picks up modestly.	Inflation further accelerates.	Inflation decelerates but with a lag.

Leads and Lags in Business and Consumer Decision Making

The behavior of businesses and households is key to the cycle and frequently incorporates leads and lags relative to what are established as turning points. For example, at the beginning of an expansion phase, companies may want to fully use their existing workforce and wait to hire new employees until they are sure that the economy is indeed growing. However, gradually all economic variables are going to revert toward their normal range of values (e.g., GDP growth will be close to potential, or average, growth).

Market Conditions and Investor Behavior

Many economic variables and sectors of the economy have distinctive cyclical patterns. Knowledge of these patterns can offer insight into likely cyclical directions overall, or it can be particularly applicable to an investment strategy that requires more specific rather than general cyclical insights for investment success.

Recovery Phase

When asset markets expect the end of a recession and the beginning of an expansion phase, risky assets will be repriced upward. When an expansion is expected, the markets will start incorporating higher profit expectations into the prices of corporate bonds and stocks. Typically, equity markets will hit a trough about three to six months before the economy bottoms out and well before the economic indicators turn up. Indeed, as we will see later, the equity market is classified as a leading indicator of the economy.

Expansion Phase

When an economy's expansion is well-established, a later part of an expansion, referred to as a "**boom**," often follows. The boom is an expansionary phase characterized by economic growth "testing the limits" of the economy, strong confidence, profit, and credit growth. For example, companies may expand so much that they have difficulty finding qualified workers and will compete with other prospective employers by raising wages and continuing to expand capacity, relying on strong cash flows and borrowing. The government or central bank may step in if it is concerned about the economy overheating.

Slowdown Phase

During the boom, the riskiest assets will often have substantial price increases. Safe assets, such as government bonds that were more highly prized during recession, may have lower prices and thus higher yields. In addition, investors may fear higher inflation, which also contributes to higher nominal yields.

Contraction Phase

During contraction, investors place relatively high values on such safer assets as government securities and shares of companies with steady (or growing) positive cash flows, such as utilities and producers of staple goods. Such preferences reflect the fact that the marginal utility of a safe income stream increases in periods when employment is insecure or declining.

WHEN DO RECESSIONS BEGIN AND END?

A simple and commonly referred to rule is the following: A recession has started when a country or region experiences two consecutive quarters of negative real GDP growth. Real GDP growth is a measure of the "real" or "inflation-adjusted" growth of the overall economy. This rule can be misleading because it does not indicate a recession if real GDP growth is negative in one quarter, slightly positive the next quarter, and again negative in the next quarter. Many analysts question this result. This issue is why some countries have statistical and economic committees that apply the principles stated by Burns and Mitchell to several macroeconomic variables—not just real GDP growth—as a basis to identify business cycle peaks and troughs. The National Bureau of Economic Research (NBER) is an organization that dates business cycles in the United States. Interestingly, the economists and statisticians on NBER's Business Cycle Dating Committee analyze numerous time series of data focusing on employment, industrial production, and sales. Because the data are available with a delay (preliminary data releases can be revised even several years after the period they refer to), it also means that the Committee's determinations may take place well after the business cycle turning points have occurred. As we will see later in the reading, practical indicators may help economists understand in advance if a cyclical turning point is about to happen.

1. Which of the following rules is *most likely* to be used to determine whether the economy is in a recession?

    A. The central bank has run out of foreign reserves.

    B. Real GDP has two consecutive quarters of negative growth.

    C. Economic activity experiences a significant decline in two business sectors.

    Solution:

    B is correct. GDP is a measure of economic activity for the whole economy. Changes in foreign reserves or a limited number of sectors may not have a material impact on the whole economy.

2. Suppose you are interested in forecasting earnings growth for a company active in a country where no official business cycle dating committee (such

as the NBER) exists. The variables you are *most likely* to consider to identify peaks and troughs of a country's business cycle are:

A. inflation, interest rates, and unemployment.

B. stock market values and money supply.

C. unemployment, GDP growth, industrial production, and inflation.

Solution:

C is correct. Unemployment, GDP growth, industrial production, and inflation are measures of economic activity. The discount rate, the monetary base, and stock market indexes are not direct measures of economic activities. The first two are determined by monetary policy, which react to economic activities, whereas the stock market indexes tend to be forward looking or leading indicators of the economy.

QUESTION SET

1. The characteristic business cycle patterns of trough, expansion, peak, and contraction are:

    A. periodic.

    B. recurrent.

    C. of similar duration.

    Solution:

    B is correct. The stages of the business cycle occur repeatedly over time.

2. During the contraction phase of a business cycle, it is *most likely* that:

    A. inflation indicators are stable.

    B. aggregate economic activity relative to potential output is decreasing.

    C. investor preference for government securities declines.

    Solution:

    B is correct. The net trend during contraction is negative.

3. An economic peak is *most* closely associated with:

    A. accelerating inflation.

    B. stable unemployment.

    C. declining capital spending.

    Solution:

    A is correct. Inflation is rising at peaks.

CREDIT CYCLES

3

describe credit cycles

Whereas business cycles mostly use GDP as a measure of economic activity, a body of literature has emerged in which cyclical developments of financial variables are analyzed separately. This is most commonly done in terms of credit and property prices. Credit cycles describe the changing availability—and pricing—of credit. They describe growth in private sector credit (availability and usage of loans), which is essential for business investments and household purchases of real estate. Therefore, they are connected to real economic activity captured by business cycles that describe fluctuations in real GDP.

When the economy is strong or improving, the willingness of lenders to extend credit, and on favorable terms, is high. Conversely, when the economy is weak or weakening, lenders pull back, or "tighten" credit, by making it less available and more expensive. This frequently contributes to the decline of such asset values as real estate, causing further economic weakness and higher defaults. This is because of the importance of credit in the financing of construction and the purchase of property. Credit cycles are a subset of a wider family of so-called financial cycles, a topic that goes beyond the scope of our coverage.

Applications of Credit Cycles

Financial factors were for a long time not prominent on the radar screens of macroeconomists. Monetary and financial phenomena were largely seen as a veil that could be ignored when trying to understand the economy. But loose private sector credit is considered to have contributed to several financial crises, such as the Latam crisis of the 1980s; the Mexican, Brazilian, and Russian crises of the 1990s; the Asian crisis of 1997–1998; and the Global Financial Crisis of 2008–2009. Expansive credit conditions often lead to asset price and real estate bubbles that burst when capital market outflows and drawdowns occur mostly because of weaker fundamentals.

It is recognized that in a world with financial frictions, business cycles can be amplified, with deeper recessions and more extensive expansions because of changes in access to external financing. In line with this belief, it is found that the duration and magnitude of recessions and recoveries are often shaped by linkages between business and credit cycles. In particular, recessions accompanied by financial disruption episodes (notably, house and equity price busts), tend to be longer and deeper. Recoveries combined with rapid growth in credit, risk-taking, and house prices tend to be stronger.

Financial variables tend to co-vary closely with each other and can often help explain the size of an economic expansion or contraction, but they are not always synchronized with the traditional business cycle. Credit cycles tend to be longer, deeper, and sharper than business cycles. Although the length of a business cycle varies from peak to trough, the average length of a credit cycle is mostly found to be longer than that of the business cycle. Exhibit 6 illustrates how credit cycles can be visualized.

> **VISUALIZING FINANCIAL CYCLES**
>
> In an October 2019 working paper titled "Predicting Recessions: Financial Cycle versus Term Spread," the Bank for International Settlements (BIS) provided a visual presentation of credit cycles, which is reproduced in Exhibit 6. It shows that such cycles tend to boom before recessions.

Exhibit 6: BIS Visualization of Financial Cycles

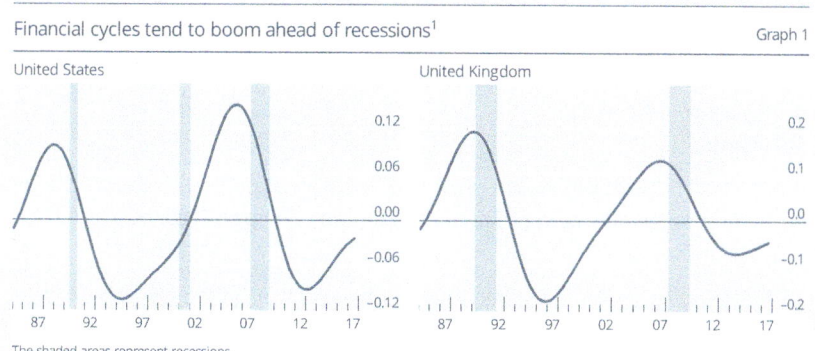

Financial cycles tend to boom ahead of recessions[1]   Graph 1

The shaded areas represent recessions.

[1] Financial cycles are measured by the composite financial cycle proxy calculated from frequency-based (bandpass) filters capturing medium-term cycles in real credit, the credit-to-GDP ratio and real house prices.

Notes: Credit cycles are measured by a (composite) proxy calculated from variables that include credit-to-GDP ratio and real house prices. The axis on the right shows the year-on-year change in the proxy.

Source: Bank for International Settlement (BIS) Material (available on the BIS website: www.bis.org).

Consequences for Policy

Investors pay attention to the stage in the credit cycle because (1) it helps them understand developments in the housing and construction markets; (2) it helps them assess the extent of business cycle expansions as well as contractions, particularly the severity of a recession if it coincides with the contraction phase of the credit cycle; and (3) it helps them better anticipate policy makers' actions. Whereas monetary and fiscal policy traditionally concentrate on reducing the volatility of business cycles, macroprudential stabilization policies that aim to dampen financial booms have gained importance. This is further stressed by findings that strong peaks in credit cycles are closely associated with subsequent systemic banking crises.

QUESTION SET

1. A senior portfolio manager at Carnara Asset Management explains her analysis of business cycles to a junior analyst. She makes two statements:

   Statement 1   Business cycles measure activity by GDP, whereas credit cycles combine a range of financial variables, such as the amount of and pricing of credit.

   Statement 2   Credit cycles and business cycles are unrelated and serve different purposes.

   A. Only Statement 1 is true.
   B. Only Statement 2 is true.
   C. Both statements are true.
   Solution:

   A is correct. Only Statement 1 is true. Statement 2 is not true because researchers have found linkages between financial and business cycles that help explain the magnitude of business cycle expansions and contractions depending on the state of the credit cycle.

2. With which sector of the economy would analysts most commonly associate credit cycles?

   A. Exports
   B. Construction and purchases of property
   C. Food retail

   Solution:

   B is correct. Credit cycles are associated with availability of credit, which is important in the financing of construction and the purchase of property.

3. The reason analysts follow developments in the availability of credit is that:

   A. loose private sector credit may contribute to the extent of asset price and real estate bubbles and subsequent crises.
   B. loose credit helps reduce the extent of asset price and real estate bubbles.
   C. credit cycles are of same length and depth as business cycles.

   Solution:

   A is correct. Studies have shown that loose credit conditions contribute to the extent of asset price and real estate bubbles that tend to be followed by crises.

4 ECONOMIC INDICATORS OVER THE BUSINESS CYCLE

☐ describe how resource use, consumer and business activity, housing sector activity, and external trade sector activity vary over the business cycle and describe their measurement using economic indicators

This lesson provides a broad overview of how the use of resources needed to produce goods and services typically evolves during a business cycle. We start by focusing on circumstances of firms and explore some of the links between fluctuations in inventory, employment, and investment in physical capital with economic fluctuations.

The Workforce and Company Costs

The pattern of hiring and employment is shown in Exhibit 7. When the economy enters contraction, companies reduce costs and eliminate overtime. They may try to retain workers rather than reduce employment only to increase it later. Finding and training new workers is costly, and it may be more cost efficient to keep workers on the payroll even if they are not fully utilized. Companies may also benefit from an implicit bond of loyalty between a company and its workers, boosting productivity in the process. In prolonged contractions, companies will start reducing costs more aggressively—terminating consultants, advertising campaigns, and workers beyond the strict minimum. Capacity utilization will be low, and few companies will invest in new equipment. Companies will try to liquidate their inventories of unsold products. In addition, banks will be reluctant to lend because bankruptcy risks are perceived to be higher, adding to the weakness in the economy.

Decreases in aggregate demand are likely to depress wages or wage growth as well as prices of inputs and capital goods. After a while, all of these input prices will be relatively low. In addition, interest rates may be cut to try to revive the economy.

As prices and interest rates decrease, consumers and companies may begin to purchase more and aggregate demand may begin to rise. This stage is the turning point of the business cycle: Aggregate demand starts to increase and economic activity increases.

Exhibit 7: Business Cycle Phases—Levels of Employment

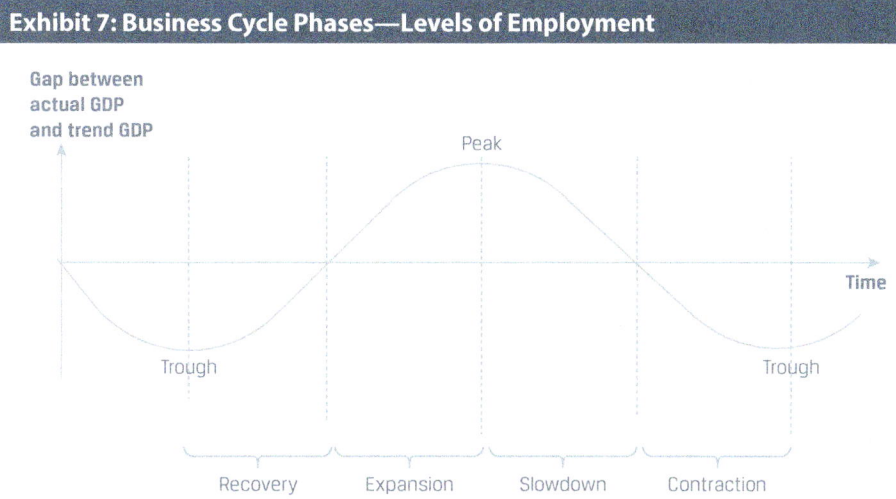

Phase	Recovery	Expansion	Slowdown	Contraction
Description of activity levels	Economy starts at trough and output below potential. Activity picks up, and gap starts to close.	Economy enjoys an upswing, with activity measures showing above-average growth rates.	Economy at peak. Activity above average but decelerating. The economy may experience shortages of factors of production as demand may exceed supply.	Economy goes into a contraction, (recession, if severe). Activity measures are below potential. Growth is lower than normal.
Employment	Layoffs slow. Businesses rely on overtime before moving to hiring. Unemployment remains higher than average.	Businesses move from using overtime and temporary employees to hiring. Unemployment rate stabilizes and starts falling.	Businesses continue hiring but at a slower pace. Unemployment rate continues to fall but at slowly decreasing rates.	Businesses first cut hours, eliminate overtime, and freeze hiring, followed by outright layoffs. Unemployment rate starts to rise.

Levels of employment lag the cycle

Fluctuations in Capital Spending

Capital spending—spending on tangible goods, such as property, plant, and equipment—typically fluctuates with the business cycle. Because business profits and cash flows are sensitive to changes in economic activity, capital spending is also highly sensitive to changes in economic activity. In fact, investment is one of the most procyclical and volatile components of GDP. Company spending decisions are driven by business conditions, expectations, and levels of capacity utilization, all of which fluctuate over the cycle. With regard to efficiency, firms will run "lean production" to generate maximum output with the fewest number of workers at the end of contractions. Exhibit 8 provides a description of capital spending over the cycle. Note that new orders statistics include orders that will be delivered over several years. For example, it is common for airlines to order 40 airplanes to be delivered over five years. Where relevant, analysts use "core" orders that exclude defense and aircrafts for a better understanding of the economy's trend.

Exhibit 8: Capital Spending during the Economic Cycle

Phase of the Cycle	Business conditions and expectations	Capital spending	Examples
Recovery	Excess capacity during trough, low utilization, little need for capacity expansion. Interest rates tend to be low—supporting investment.	Low but increasing as companies start to enjoy better conditions. Capex focus on efficiency rather than capacity. Upturn most pronounced in orders for light producer equipment. Typically, the orders initially reinstated are for equipment with a high rate of obsolescence, such as software, systems, and technological hardware.	Software, systems, and hardware (high rates of obsolescence) orders placed or re-instated first.
Expansion	Companies enjoy favorable conditions. Capacity utilization increases from low levels. Over time, productive capacity may begin to limit ability to respond to demand. Growth in earnings and cash flow gives businesses the financial ability to increase investment spending.	Customer orders and capacity utilization increase. Companies start to focus on capacity expansion. The composition of the economy's capacity may not be optimal for the current structure of demand, necessitating spending on new types of equipment. Orders precede actual shipments, so orders for capital equipment are a widely watched indicator of the future direction of capital spending.	Heavy and complex equipment, warehouses, and factories. A company may need warehouse space in locations different from where existing facilities are located.
Slowdown	Business conditions at peak, with healthy cash flow. Interest rates tend to be higher—aimed at reducing overheating and encouraging investment slowdown.	New orders intended to increase capacity may be an early indicator of the late stage of the expansion phase. Companies continue to place new orders as they operate at or near capacity.	Fiber-optic overinvestment in the late 1990s that peaked with the "technology, media, telecoms bubble."
Contraction	Companies experience fall in demand, profits, and cash flows.	New orders halted, and some existing orders canceled (no need to expand). Initial cutbacks may be sharp and exaggerate the economy's downturn. As the general cyclical bust matures, cutbacks in spending on heavy equipment further intensify the contraction. Maintenance scaled back.	Technology and light equipment with short lead times get cut first. Cuts in construction and heavy equipment follow.

Economic Indicators over the Business Cycle

EXAMPLE 1

Capital Spending

1. Levels of capacity utilization are one of the factors that determine companies' aggregate need for additional capital expenditure. Which of the following is another factor that affects the capital expenditure decision?

   A. The rate of unemployment

   B. The composition of the economy's capacity in relation to how it can satisfy demand

   C. The ability to reinstate orders canceled during the contraction stage

   Solution:

   B is correct. The composition of the current productive capacity may not be optimal of the current structure of demand. C is incorrect because the ability to re-instate canceled orders is a matter that is relevant once the decision to increase capital expenditure is made.

2. Orders for technology and light equipment decline before construction projects in a contraction because:

   A. businesses are uncertain about cyclical directions.

   B. equipment orders are easier to cancel than large construction projects.

   C. businesses value light equipment less than structures and heavy machinery.

   Solution:

   B is correct. Because it usually takes much longer to plan and complete large construction projects than it takes to plan and complete equipment orders, construction projects may be less influenced by business cycles.

Fluctuations in Inventory Levels

The aggregate size of inventories is small relative to the size of the economy, but their accumulation and cutbacks by businesses can occur with substantial speed and frequency. Changing inventories reflect differences between the growth (or decline) in sales and the growth (or decline) in production. A key indicator in this area is the inventory–sales ratio that measures the inventories available for sale to the level of sales. Analysts pay attention to inventories to gauge the position of the economy in the cycle. Exhibit 9 shows how production, sales, and inventories typically move through the phases of a cycle.

Exhibit 9: Inventories throughout the Cycle

Phase of the Cycle	Recovery	Expansion	Slowdown	Contraction
Sales and production	Decline in sales slows. Sales subsequently recover. Production upturn follows but lags behind sales growth. Over time, production approaches normal levels as excess inventories from the downturn are cleared.	Sales increase. Production rises fast to keep up with sales growth and to replenish inventories of finished products. This increases the demand for intermediate products. "Inventory rebuilding or restocking stage."	Sales slow faster than production; inventories increase. Economic slowdown leads to production cutbacks and order cancellations.	Businesses produce at rates below the sales volumes necessary to dispose of unwanted inventories.
Inventory–sales ratio	Begins to fall as sales recovery outpaces production.	Ratio stable.	Ratio increases. Signals weakening economy.	Ratio begins to fall back to normal.

EXAMPLE 2

Inventory Fluctuation

1. Although a small part of the overall economy, changes in inventories can influence economic growth measures significantly because they:

   A. reflect general business sentiment.

   B. tend to move forcefully up or down.

   C. determine the availability of goods for sale.

   Solution:

   B is correct. Inventory levels can fluctuate dramatically over the business cycle.

2. Inventories tend to rise when:

   A. inventory–sales ratios are low.

   B. inventory–sales ratios are high.

   C. economic activity begins to rebound.

   Solution:

   A is correct. When the economy starts to recover, sales of inventories can outpace production, which results in low inventory–sales ratios. Companies then need to accumulate more inventories to restore the ratio to normal level. C is incorrect because in the early stages of a recovery, inventories are likely to fall as sales increase faster than production.

3. Inventories will often fall early in a recovery because:

   A. businesses need profit.

   B. sales outstrip production.

   C. businesses ramp up production because of increased economic activity.

   Solution:

   B is correct. The companies are slow to increase production in the early recovery phase because they first want to confirm the recession is over. Increasing output also takes time after the downsizing during the recession.

4. In a recession, companies are *most likely* to adjust their stock of physical capital by:

    A. selling it at fire sale prices.

    B. not maintaining equipment.

    C. quickly canceling orders for new construction equipment.

    B is correct. Physical capital adjustments to downturns come through aging of equipment plus lack of maintenance.

5. The inventory–sales ratio is *most likely* to be rising:

    A. as a contraction unfolds.

    B. partially into a recovery.

    C. near the top of an economic cycle.

    C is correct. Near the top of a cycle, sales begin to slow before production is cut, leading to an increase in inventories relative to sales.

Economic Indicators

Economic indicators are variables that provide information on the state of the overall economy. They are statistics or data readings that reflect economic circumstances of a country, group of countries, region, or sector. Economic indicators are used by policy makers and analysts to understand and assess the existing condition of the economy and its position in the cycle. They also can be used to help predict or confirm the turning points in the cycle. Such knowledge allows analysts to better predict the financial and market performance of stocks and bonds of issuers operating in different sectors of the economy with different sensitivity to the economic cycle.

Types of Indicators

Economic indicators are often classified according to whether they lag, lead, or coincide with changes in an economy's growth.

- **Leading economic indicators** have turning points that usually precede those of the overall economy. They are believed to have value for predicting the economy's future state, usually near term.

- **Coincident economic indicators** have turning points that are usually close to those of the overall economy. They are believed to have value for identifying the economy's present state.

- **Lagging economic indicators** have turning points that take place later than those of the overall economy. They are believed to have value in identifying the economy's past condition and only change after a trend has been established.

Exhibit 10 provides an illustration of several leading, lagging, and coincident indicators. The leading indicators observed at a point in time labeled as time "1" indicate the direction of the of the activity (output) at a future point in time, such as time "2." The lagging indicators, released around time "3," refer to and help confirm what the state of the economy was at time "2."

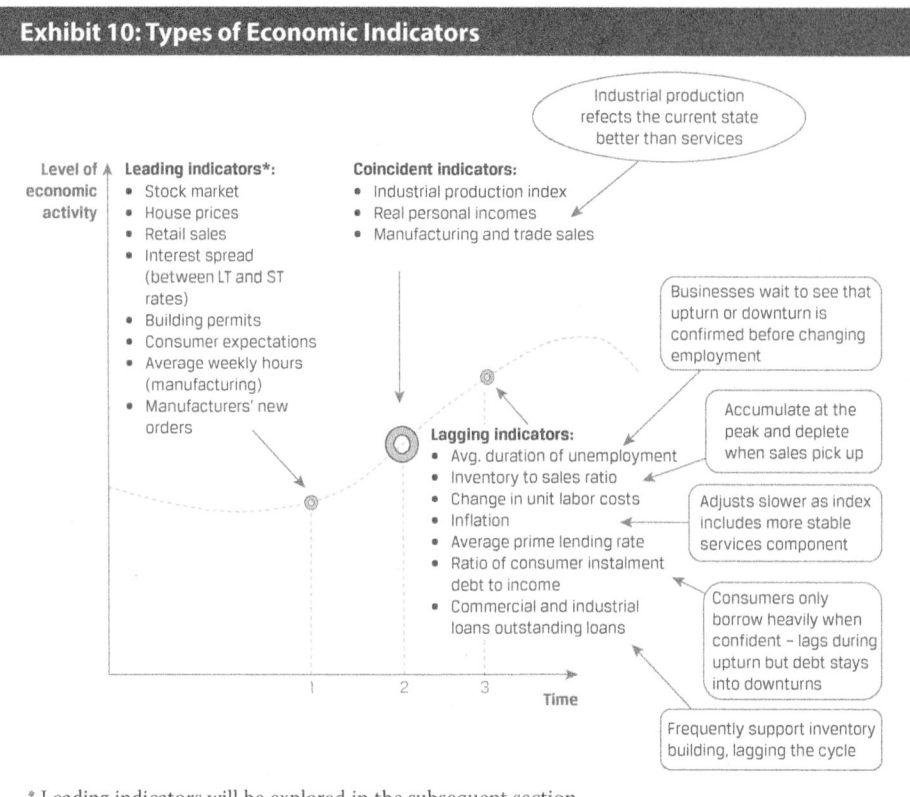

*Leading indicators will be explored in the subsequent section.

Composite Indicators

An economic indicator either consists of a single variable, like industrial production or the total value of outstanding building permits, or can be a composite of different variables that all tend to move together. The latter are regularly labeled composite indicators. Traditionally, most composite indicators to measure the cyclical state of the economy consist of up to a dozen handpicked variables published by organizations like the OECD or national research institutes. The exact variables combined into these composites vary from one economy to the other. In each case, however, they bring together various economic and financial measures that have displayed a consistently leading, coincident, or lagging relationship to that economy's general cycle.

Leading Indicators

The Conference Board, a US industry research organization, publishes a composite leading indicator known as The Conference Board Leading Economic Index (LEI), which consists of 10 component parts (it uses the classical business cycle as the underlying concept). Exhibit 11 presents the 10 components used in the LEI. In addition to naming the indicators, it offers a general description of why each measure is leading the business cycle.

Economic Indicators over the Business Cycle

Exhibit 11: Index of Leading Economic Indicators, United States

Leading indicators	Reason for use
Average weekly hours, manufacturing	Businesses will cut overtime before laying off workers in a downturn and increase it before rehiring in a cyclical upturn. Moves up and down before the general economy.
Average weekly initial claims for unemployment insurance	A very sensitive test of initial layoffs and rehiring.
Manufacturers' new orders for consumer goods and materials	Businesses cannot wait too long to meet demand without ordering. Orders tend to lead at upturns and downturns & captures business sentiment.
ISM new order index *(Survey based)*	Reflects the month on month change in new orders for final sales. Decline of new orders can signal weak demand and can lead to recession.
Manufacturers' new orders for non-defense capital goods excluding aircraft	Captures business expectations and offers first signal of movement up or down. Important sector.
Building permits for new private housing units	Signals new construction activity as permits required before new building can begin.
S&P 500 Index	Stocks tends to anticipate economic turning points; useful early signal.
Leading Credit Index	A vulnerable financial system can amplify the effects of negative shocks, causing widespread recessions.
Interest rate spread between 10-year treasury yields and overnight borrowing rates (federal funds rate)	LT (10 or 30 year) bond yields express market expectations about the direction of short-term interest rates. As rates ultimately follow the economic cycle up and down, a wider spread, by anticipating short rate increases, also anticipates an economic upswing and vice versa.
Average consumer expectations for business conditions *(Survey based)*	Optimism tends to increase spending. Provides early insight into the direction ahead for the whole economy.

Notes:
- *The Institute of Supply Management (ISM) polls its members to build indexes of manufacturing orders, output, employment, pricing, and comparable gauges for services.*
- *A diffusion index usually measures the percentage of components in a series that are rising in the same period. It indicates how widespread a particular movement in the trend is among the individual components.*
- *Aggregates the information from six leading financial indicators, which reflect the strength of the financial system to endure stress.*
- *Inversion of the yield curve occurs when ST interest rate exceed LT rates – meaning that ST rates are expected to fall and activity is expected to weaken.*

Using Economic Indicators

Exhibit 12 shows a simplified process that an analyst could use to identify business cycle phases. The conclusions then can be used to make investment decisions—for example, to decide in what sectors companies are likely to see improving or deteriorating cash flows, which could affect the investment performance of the equity and debt securities issued by the companies. Note that the order of the steps does not have to follow this particular sequence.

> **Exhibit 12: Use of Statistics to Identify Business Cycle Phase**
>
> Step 1
>
> - Data release: Analyst notes an increase in the reported level of consumer instalment debt to income.
> - Analysis: The above indicator normally lags cyclical upturns.
> - Possible conclusion: Initial evidence that an upturn has been underway.
>
> Step 2
>
> - Data release: Industrial Production Index and non-farm payrolls (employees on non-agricultural payrolls) are moving higher.
> - Analysis: These coincident indicators suggest activity is picking up.
> - Possible conclusion: Further evidence that expansion is underway.
>
> Step 3
>
> - Observation: Equity market index has been trending higher. Equity index is a leading indicator. Analyst checks the aggregate LEI Index.
> - Analysis: If the aggregate LEI is moving higher too, evidence suggests that recovery is underway. Confirmation that output is moving higher.
>
> Or
>
> - If aggregate LEI is not moving higher, analyst cannot draw conclusions about recovery.

Other Composite Leading Indicators

For about 30 countries and several aggregates, such as the EU and G–7, the OECD calculates OECD Composite Leading Indicator (CLI), which gauges the state of the business cycle in the economy using the growth cycle concept. One of the interesting features of OECD CLI is that the underlying methodology is consistent across several countries. Therefore, it can be compared more easily to see how each region is faring. Exhibit 13 shows the eight components of CLI used by the OECD. As is usually the case with leading indicators, some data are based on surveys whereas others are based on reported market or economic data.

Economic Indicators over the Business Cycle

Exhibit 13: OECD Euro Area CLI Components

The parallels that can be drawn between many of these components and those used in the United States are clear, but the Euro area includes a services component in its business activity measures that the United States lacks. Additionally, the Euro area forgoes many of the overtime and employment gauges that the United States includes. The OECD CLI for Japan is again similar, but it does include labor market indicators (unlike the Euro area) and it adds a measure of business failures not included in the other two.

GERMANY: THE IFO SURVEY

The German ifo survey is a widely used index capturing business climate in Germany and is published monthly. Exhibit 14 shows how the index moved ahead of quarterly-reported year-over-year changes in German GDP. It also shows an uptick in 2018 despite the GDP growth downturn. These indicators are useful, but they are not foolproof.

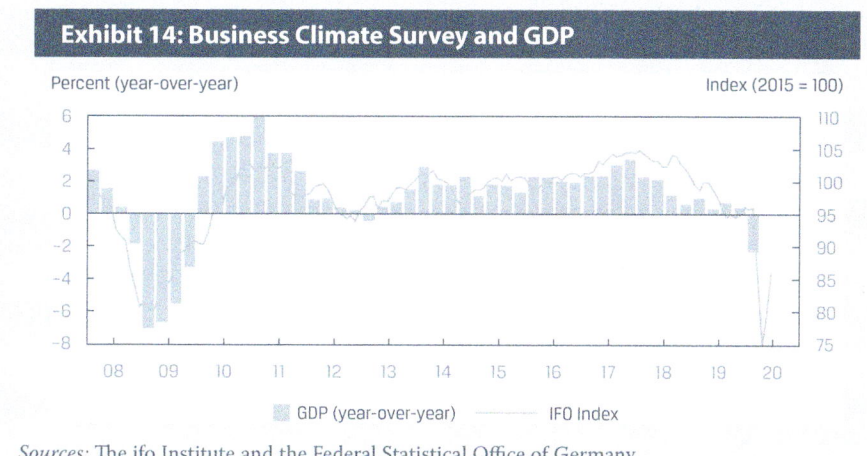

Exhibit 14: Business Climate Survey and GDP

Sources: The ifo Institute and the Federal Statistical Office of Germany.

Surveys

The composite indicators for region- or country-specific business cycles often make use of economic tendency surveys. These monthly or quarterly surveys carried out by central banks, research institutes, statistical offices, and trade associations are conducted among either businesses, consumers, or experts. The mostly qualitative questions posed are often on the state of their finances, level of activity, and confidence in the future.

CIRET (a forum for leading economists and institutions that conducts and analyzes business and consumer survey data), the United Nations, the OECD, and the European Commission operate at different regional levels to harmonize and exchange knowledge regarding these business tendency and consumer surveys. The Directorate-General for Economic and Financial Affairs (DG ECFIN) publishes fully harmonized results for different sectors of the EU member and applicant economies. The Bank of Japan carries out similar surveys and releases the findings in what is called the "Tankan Report." These diverse sources multiply within and across economies. Over the past decade, so-called purchasing managers indexes along similar lines, albeit with often much smaller survey samples, have been introduced in a wide range of countries and regions, including Europe and China.

These economic tendency surveys are often aggregated into or are a part of composite indicators. IHS Markit publishes a global Purchasing Managers' Index (PMI) indicator using results of its national business surveys (see Exhibit 13). A global consumer confidence indicator is published by The Conference Board. Some other institutions collect national survey data and calculate supranational results. For example, the OECD publishes a business confidence indicator and a consumer confidence indicator for the OECD aggregate in its report "Main Economic Indicators." In addition, the European Commission calculates various survey-based indicators for the EU, reflecting the situation in Europe. Based on economic tendency surveys and using the growth rate cycle concept, the Swiss Economic Institute (*Konjunkturforschungsstelle* or KOF) and *Fundação Getúlio Vargas* (FGV), based in Rio de Janeiro, Brazil, publish a coincident and a leading indicator for the world economy called the Global Economic Barometers. These barometers incorporate hundreds of survey variables from around the world.

The Use of Big Data in Economic Indicators

The vast increase in this information and academic developments regarding the use of big(ger) data have in recent years increased the number of variables that go into these composite indicators. For instance, using a statistical technique called principal components analysis, the Federal Reserve Bank of Chicago computes the Chicago Fed National Activity Index (CFNAI) using 85 monthly macroeconomic series. These series cover industrial production, personal income, capital utilization, employment by sectors, housing starts, retail sales, and so on. Principal components analysis extracts the underlying trend that is common to most of these variables, thus distilling the essence of the US business cycle. Similarly, the Bank of Italy in conjunction with the Centre for Economic Policy Research (CEPR) produces the EuroCOIN statistic, which is also based on principal component analysis. More than 100 macroeconomic series are included in EuroCOIN. EuroCOIN also includes data derived from surveys, interest rates, and other financial variables.

Nowcasting

Policy makers and market practitioners use real-time monitoring of economic and financial variables to continuously assess current conditions. To overcome the publication delays (e.g., GDP numbers are published with a substantial delay) and forecast the "present," they make use of a large variety of data—such as financial market transactions, data from the usage of the large amounts of timely internet searches, and electronic payment data—to provide estimates for key low-frequency (monthly or quarterly) economic indicators. This process produces a nowcast, which is an estimate of the current state, and we refer to the process of producing such an estimate as nowcasting. It can be applied to various macroeconomic variables of interest, such as GDP growth, inflation, or unemployment.

GDPNow

Nowcasts are produced by a number of entities in investment banking and asset management for their internal or client use, but they are also published by institutions, such as the Atlanta Fed (the Federal Reserve Bank of Atlanta, one of the 12 Federal Reserve Banks in the United States). According to the Atlanta Fed, "GDPNow" is "best viewed as a running estimate of real GDP growth based on available data for the current measured quarter." The objective is to forecast GDP for the current quarter (which will not be released until after quarter-end) in real time based on data as they are released throughout the quarter. To do this, the Atlanta Fed attempts to use the same methodology and data as will be used by the US Bureau of Economic Analysis (BEA) to estimate GDP, replacing data that have not yet been released with forecasts based on the data already observed. As the quarter progresses, more of the actual data will have been observed. GDPNow should, at least on average, converge to what will be released by the BEA as their "advance" estimate of quarterly GDP about four weeks after quarter-end.

> **DIFFUSION INDEX OF ECONOMIC INDICATORS**
>
> In the United States, The Conference Board also compiles a monthly diffusion index of the leading, lagging, and coincident indicators. The **diffusion index** reflects the proportion of the index's components that are moving in a pattern consistent with the overall index. Analysts often rely on these diffusion indexes to provide a measure of the breadth of the change in a composite index.
>
> For example, The Conference Board tracks the growth of each of the 10 constituents of its LEI, assigning a value of 1.0 to each indicator that rises by more than 0.05 percent during the monthly measurement period, a value of 0.5 for each component indicator that changes by less than 0.05 percent, and a value of 0 for each component indicator that falls by more than 0.05 percent. These assigned values, which of course differ in other indexes in other countries, are then summed and divided by 10 (the number of components). To make the overall measure resemble the more familiar indexes, the Board multiplies the result by 100.
>
> A simple numerical example will help explain. Say, for ease of exposition, the indicator has only four component parts: stock prices, money growth, orders, and consumer confidence. In one month, stock prices rise 2.0 percent, money growth rises 1.0 percent, orders are flat, and consumer confidence falls by 0.6 percent. Using The Conference Board's assigned values, these would contribute respectively: 1.0 + 1.0 + 0.5 + 0 to create a numerator of 2.5. When divided by four (the number of components) and multiplied by 100, it generates an indicator of 62.5 for that month.
>
> Assume that the following month stock prices fall 0.8 percent, money grows by 0.5 percent, orders pick up 0.5 percent, and consumer confidence grows 3.5 percent. Applying the appropriate values, the components would add to 0 + 1.0 + 1.0 + 1.0 = 3.0. Divided by the number of components and multiplied by

100, it yields an index value of 75. The 20.0 percent increase in the index value means more components of the composite index are rising. Given this result, an analyst can be more confident that the higher composite index value actually represents broader movements in the economy. In general, a diffusion index does not reflect outliers in any component (like a straight arithmetic mean would do) but instead tries to capture the overall change common to all components.

QUESTION SET

1. Leading, lagging, and coincident indicators are:

   A. the same worldwide.

   B. based on historical cyclical observations.

   C. based on Keynesian or Monetarist theory.

   Solution:

   B is correct. The recognition of economic indicators is based on empirical observations for an economy.

2. A diffusion index:

   A. measures growth.

   B. reflects the consensus change in economic indicators.

   C. is roughly analogous to the indexes used to measure industrial production.

   Solution:

   B is correct. The diffusion indexes are constructed to reflect the common trends embedded in the movements of all the indicators included in such an index.

3. In the morning business news, a financial analyst, Kevin Durbin, learned that average hourly earnings had increased last month. The most appropriate action for Durbin is to:

   A. call his clients to inform them of a good trading opportunity today.

   B. examine other leading indicators to see any confirmation of a possible turning point for the economy.

   C. use the news in his research report as a confirmation for his belief that the economy has recovered from a recession.

   Solution:

   B is correct. Financial analysts need to synthesize the information from various indicators in order to gather a reliable reading of the economic trends.

4. The following table shows the trends in various economic indicators in the two most recent quarters:

Economic Indicator	Trend
Interest rate spread between long-term government bonds and overnight borrowing rate	Narrowing
New orders for capital goods	Declining
Residential building permits	Declining

Economic Indicators over the Business Cycle

Economic Indicator	Trend
Employees on non-agricultural payrolls	Turned from rising to falling
Manufacturing and trade sales	Stable
Average duration of unemployment	Small decline
Change in unit labor costs	Rising

Given the information, this economy is *most likely* experiencing a:

A. continuing recession.

B. peak in the business cycle.

C. strong recovery out of a trough.

Solution:

B is correct. The first three indicators are leading indicators, and all of them are indicating an impending recession, which means the economy has reached the peak in this cycle. Non-agricultural payrolls and manufacturing and trade sales are coincident indicators. The trends in these two variables further indicate that the economy may begin to decline. The trends in the last two indicators—both lagging indicators—indicate that the economy may either continue to grow or it may be close to a peak. Aggregating the signals given by all three groups of economic indicators, it appears the economy may be near the peak of a business cycle.

PRACTICE PROBLEMS

1. Based on typical labor utilization patterns across the business cycle, productivity (output per hours worked) is *most likely* to be highest:
   A. at the peak of a boom.
   B. into a maturing expansion.
   C. at the bottom of a recession.

2. As the expansion phase of the business cycle advances from early stage to late stage, businesses *most likely* experience a decrease in:
   A. labor costs.
   B. capital investment.
   C. availability of qualified workers.

3. An analyst writes in an economic report that the current phase of the business cycle is characterized by accelerating inflationary pressures and borrowing by companies. The analyst is *most likely* referring to the:
   A. peak of the business cycle.
   B. contraction phase of the business cycle.
   C. early expansion phase of the business cycle.

4. The indicator indexes created by various organizations or research agencies:
   A. include only leading indicators to compute their value.
   B. are highly reliable signals on the phase of business cycles.
   C. evolve over time in terms of composition and computation formula.

5. Which one of the following trends in various economic indicators is *most* consistent with a recovery from a recession?
   A. A declining inventory–sales ratio and stable industrial production index
   B. A rising broad stock market index and unit labor costs turning from increasing to decreasing
   C. A decrease in average weekly initial claims for unemployment insurance and an increase in aggregate real personal income

6. Which of the following statements gives the *best* description of nowcasting?
   A. This method is used to forecast future trends in economic variables based on their past and current values.
   B. This method is used for real-time monitoring of economic and financial variables to continuously assess current conditions and provide an estimate of the current state.

Practice Problems

    C. This method is used to study past relationships between variables to determine which ones have explained the path of a particular variable of interest.

7. Which of the following statements is the *best* description of the characteristics of economic indicators?

    A. Leading indicators are important because they track the entire economy.

    B. Lagging indicators, in measuring past conditions, do not require revisions.

    C. A combination of leading and coincident indicators can offer effective forecasts.

8. When the spread between 10-year US Treasury yields and the short-term federal funds rate narrows and at the same time the prime rate stays unchanged, this mix of indicators *most likely* forecasts future economic:

    A. growth.

    B. decline.

    C. stability.

9. Current economic statistics indicating little change in services inflation, rising residential building permits, and increasing average duration of unemployment are *best* interpreted as:

    A. conflicting evidence about the direction of the economy.

    B. evidence that a cyclical upturn is expected to occur in the future.

    C. evidence that a cyclical downturn is expected to occur in the future.

10. If relative to prior values of their respective indicators, the inventory–sales ratio has risen, unit labor cost is stable, and real personal income has decreased, it is *most likely* that a peak in the business cycle:

    A. has occurred.

    B. is just about to occur.

    C. will occur sometime in the future.

11. When aggregate real personal income, industrial output, and the S&P 500 Index all increase in a given period, it is *most accurate* to conclude that a cyclical upturn is:

    A. occurring.

    B. about to end.

    C. about to begin.

12. Which of the following is *most likely* to increase after an increase in aggregate real personal income?

    A. Equity prices

    B. Building permits for new private housing units

C. The ratio of consumer installment debt to income

13. Which of the following indicators is *most* appropriate in predicting a turning point in the economy?

    A. The Industrial Production Index

    B. The average bank prime lending rate

    C. Average weekly hours, manufacturing

14. The unemployment rate is considered a lagging indicator because:

    A. new job types must be defined to count their workers.

    B. multiworker households change jobs at a slower pace.

    C. businesses are slow to hire and fire due to related costs.

15. During an economic recovery, a lagging unemployment rate is *most likely* attributable to:

    A. businesses quickly rehiring workers.

    B. new job seekers entering the labor force.

    C. underemployed workers transitioning to higher-paying jobs.

SOLUTIONS

1. C is correct. At the end of a recession, firms will run "lean production" to generate maximum output with the fewest number of workers.

2. C is correct. When an economy's expansion is well established, businesses often have difficulty finding qualified workers.

3. A is correct. Accelerating inflation and rapidly expanding capital expenditures typically characterize the peak of the business cycle. During such times, many businesses finance their capital expenditures with debt to expand their production capacity.

4. C is correct. The indicator indexes are constantly updated for their composition and methodology based on the accumulation of empirical knowledge, and they can certainly include more than just leading indicators.

5. C is correct. The improving leading indicator, average weekly initial claims for unemployment insurance, and the improving coincident indicator, aggregate real personal income, are most consistent with an economic recovery. Even though a declining inventory-to-sales ratio, a lagging indicator, is consistent with an early recovery, the coincident indicator, the stable industrial production index, does not support that conclusion. Although a rising stock market index can signal economic expansion, the lagging indicator, the unit labor costs, has peaked, which is more consistent with a recession.

6. B is correct. Nowcasting involves the use of techniques to estimate the present state. A is incorrect because nowcasting aims to estimate the present, not forecast the future. C is incorrect because the focus of nowcasting is to estimate the current, present value of a variable, such as GDP.

7. C is correct. Although no single indicator is definitive, a mix of them—which can be affected by various economic determinants—can offer the strongest signal of performance.

8. B is correct. The narrowing spread of this leading indicator foretells a drop in short-term rates and a fall in economic activity. The prime rate is a lagging indicator and typically moves after the economy turns.

9. B is correct. Rising building permits—a leading indicator—indicate that an upturn is expected to occur or continue. Increasing average duration of unemployment—a lagging indicator—indicates that a downturn has occurred, whereas the lack of any change in services inflation—also a lagging indicator—is neither negative nor positive for the direction of the economy. Taken together, these statistics indicate that a cyclical upturn may be expected to occur.

10. A is correct. Both inventory–sales and unit labor costs are lagging indicators that decline somewhat after a peak. Real personal income is a coincident indicator that, by its decline, shows a slowdown in business activity.

11. A is correct. Aggregate real personal income and industrial output are coincident indicators, whereas the S&P 500 is a leading indicator. An increase in aggregate personal income and industrial output signals that an expansion is occurring, whereas an increase in the S&P 500 signals that an expansion will occur or is expected to continue. Taken together, these statistics indicate that a cyclical upturn is occurring.

12. C is correct. Aggregate real personal income is a coincident indicator of the business cycle, and the ratio of consumer installment debt to income is a lagging indicator. Increases in the ratio of consumer installment debt follow increases in average aggregate income during the typical business cycle.

13. C is correct. Leading economic indicators have turning points that usually precede those of the overall economy. Average weekly hours, manufacturing is a leading economic indicator. The Industrial Production Index is a coincident economic indicator, and the average bank prime lending rate is a lagging economic indicator.

14. C is correct. This effect makes unemployment rise more slowly as recessions start and fall more slowly as recoveries begin.

15. B is correct. In an economic recovery, new job seekers return to the labor force, and because they seldom find work immediately, their return may initially raise the unemployment rate.

LEARNING MODULE 3

Fiscal Policy

by Andrew Clare, PhD, and Stephen Thomas, PhD.

Andrew Clare, PhD, and Stephen Thomas, PhD, are at Cass Business School (UK).

LEARNING OUTCOMES

Mastery	The candidate should be able to:
☐	compare monetary and fiscal policy
☐	describe roles and objectives of fiscal policy as well as arguments as to whether the size of a national debt relative to GDP matters
☐	describe tools of fiscal policy, including their advantages and disadvantages
☐	explain the implementation of fiscal policy and difficulties of implementation as well as whether a fiscal policy is expansionary or contractionary

INTRODUCTION

Fiscal policy refers to the government's decisions about taxation and spending, whereas **monetary policy** refers to central bank activities that are directed toward influencing the quantity of money and credit in an economy. Fiscal policy involves the use of government spending and changing tax revenue to affect certain aspects of the economy, such as the overall level of aggregate demand. Government deficits are the difference between government revenues and expenditures over a period of calendar time. The fiscal tools available to a government include transfer payments, current government spending, capital expenditures, and taxes. Economists often examine the **structural budget deficit** as an indicator of a government's fiscal stance.

LEARNING MODULE OVERVIEW

- Fiscal policy refers to the government's decisions about taxation and spending.
- Monetary policy refers to central bank activities that are directed toward influencing the quantity of money and credit in an economy.

- The primary goal of both monetary and fiscal policy is the creation of an economic environment in which growth is stable and positive, and inflation is stable and low.
- Fiscal policy involves the use of government spending and changing tax revenue to affect certain aspects of the economy, including the level of economic activity in an economy, the distribution of income and wealth among different segments of the population, and the allocation of resources between different sectors and economic agents.
- The **budget surplus/deficit** is the difference between government revenue and expenditure for a fixed period of time, such as a fiscal or calendar year.
- There are several strong arguments both for and against being concerned about national debt relative to GDP.
- The fiscal tools available to a government include transfer payments, current government spending, capital expenditures, direct taxes, and indirect taxes.
- Taxes can be justified both in terms of raising revenues to finance expenditures and in terms of income and wealth redistribution policies.
- Fiscal policy tools seek to achieve or maintain an economy on a path of positive, stable growth with low inflation.
- Economists assess the structural (or cyclically adjusted) budget deficit as an indicator of the government's fiscal stance, which is defined as the deficit that would exist if the economy was at full employment.
- Actual government deficits may not be a good measure of fiscal stance because of the distinction between real and nominal interest rates and the role of inflation adjustment when applied to budget deficits.
- Fiscal policy cannot stabilize aggregate demand completely because the difficulties in executing fiscal policy cannot be completely overcome.

2. INTRODUCTION TO MONETARY AND FISCAL POLICY

☐ compare monetary and fiscal policy

The economic decisions of households can have a significant impact on an economy. For example, a decision on the part of households to consume more and to save less can lead to an increase in employment, investment, and ultimately profits. Equally, the investment decisions made by corporations can have an important impact on the real economy and on corporate profits. But individual corporations can rarely affect large economies on their own; the decisions of a single household concerning consumption will have a negligible impact on the wider economy.

By contrast, the decisions made by governments can have an enormous impact on even the largest and most developed of economies for two main reasons. First, the public sectors of most developed economies normally employ a significant proportion of the population, and they usually are responsible for a significant proportion

Introduction to Monetary and Fiscal Policy

of spending in an economy. Second, governments are also the largest borrowers in world debt markets. Exhibit 1 gives some idea of the scale of government borrowing and spending.

Scale of Government Borrowing and Spending

Panel A. Central Government Debt to GDP, 2017

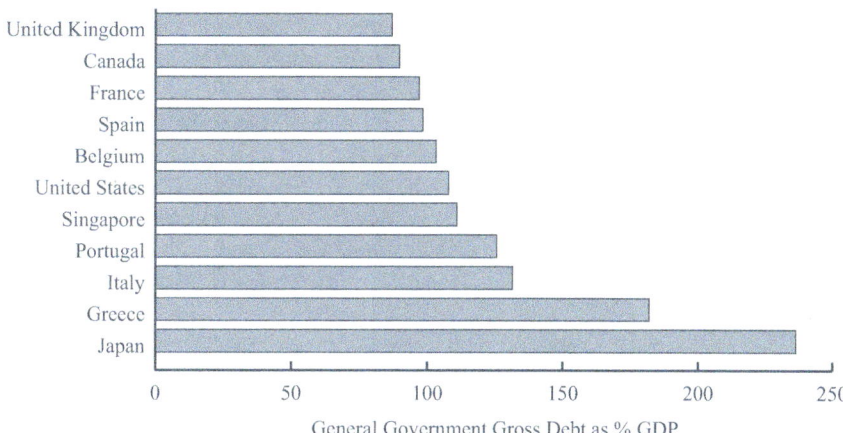

Panel B. Public Sector Spending to GDP, 2017

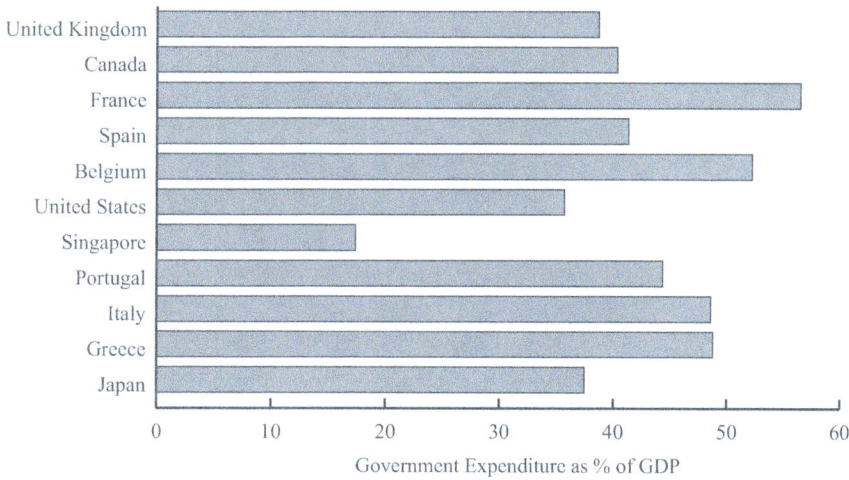

Source: IMF, World Economic Outlook Database, April 2018.

Government policy is ultimately expressed through its borrowing and spending activities. In this reading, we identify and discuss two types of government policy that can affect the macroeconomy and financial markets: monetary policy and fiscal policy.

Monetary policy refers to central bank activities that are directed toward influencing the quantity of money and credit in an economy. Central banks can implement monetary policy almost completely independent of government interference and influence at one end of the scale or may simply act as the agent of the government at the other end of the scale.

By contrast, fiscal policy refers to the government's decisions about taxation and spending. Both monetary and fiscal policies are used to regulate economic activity over time. They can be used to accelerate growth when an economy starts to slow or to moderate growth and activity when an economy starts to overheat. In addition, fiscal policy can be used to redistribute income and wealth.

The overarching goal of both monetary and fiscal policy is normally the creation of an economic environment in which growth is stable and positive and inflation is stable and low. Crucially, the aim is to steer the underlying economy so that it does not experience economic booms that may be followed by extended periods of low or negative growth and high levels of unemployment. In such a stable economic environment, households can feel secure in their consumption and saving decisions, while corporations can concentrate on their investment decisions, on making their regular coupon payments to their bond holders, and on making profits for their shareholders.

The challenges to achieving this overarching goal are many. Economies frequently are buffeted by shocks (such as oil price jumps), and some economists believe that natural cycles in the economy also exist. Moreover, we can find plenty of examples from history in which government policies—either monetary, fiscal, or both—have exacerbated an economic expansion that eventually led to damaging consequences for the real economy, for financial markets, and for investors.

QUESTION SET

1. Which of the following statements *best* describes monetary policy? Monetary policy:

    A. involves the setting of medium-term targets for broad money aggregates.

    B. involves the manipulation by a central bank of the government's budget deficit.

    C. seeks to influence the macroeconomy by influencing the quantity of money and credit in the economy.

    Solution:

    C is correct, as monetary policy involves central bank activities directed toward influencing the quantity of money and credit. Choice A is incorrect because, although the setting of targets for monetary aggregates is a possible *tool* of monetary policy, monetary policy itself is concerned with influencing the overall, or macro, economy.

2. Which of the following statements *best* describes fiscal policy? Fiscal policy:

    A. is used by governments to redistribute wealth and incomes.

    B. is the attempt by governments to balance their budgets from one year to the next.

    C. involves the use of government spending and taxation to influence economy activity.

    Solution:

    C is correct. Note that governments may wish to use fiscal policy to redistribute income and balance their budgets, but the overriding goal of fiscal policy is usually to influence a broader range of economic activity.

ROLES AND OBJECTIVES OF FISCAL POLICY

☐ describe roles and objectives of fiscal policy as well as arguments as to whether the size of a national debt relative to GDP matters

Fiscal policy involves the use of government spending and changing tax revenue to affect a number of aspects of the economy:

- Overall level of aggregate demand in an economy and hence the level of economic activity.
- Distribution of income and wealth among different segments of the population.
- Allocation of resources between different sectors and economic agents.

The discussion of fiscal policy often focuses on the impact of changes in the difference between government spending and revenue on the aggregate economy, rather than on the actual levels of spending and revenue themselves.

Roles and Objectives of Fiscal Policy

A primary aim for fiscal policy is to help manage the economy through its influence on aggregate national output, that is, real GDP.

Fiscal Policy and Aggregate Demand

Aggregate demand is the amount companies and households plan to spend. We can consider a number of ways that fiscal policy can influence aggregate demand. For example, an **expansionary** policy could take one or more of the following forms:

- Cuts in personal income tax raise disposable income with the objective of boosting aggregate demand.
- Cuts in sales (indirect) taxes to lower prices raise real incomes with the objective of raising consumer demand.
- Cuts in corporation (company) taxes to boost business profits may raise capital spending.
- Cuts in tax rates on personal savings to raise disposable income for those with savings, with the objective of raising consumer demand.
- New public spending on social goods and infrastructure, such as hospitals and schools, boost personal incomes with the objective of raising aggregate demand.

We must stress, however, that the reliability and magnitude of these relationships will vary over time and from country to country. For example, in a recession with rising unemployment, it is not always the case that cuts in income taxes will raise consumer spending because consumers may wish to raise their precautionary (rainy day) saving in anticipation of further deterioration in the economy. Indeed, in very general terms, economists are often divided into two camps regarding the workings of fiscal policy. **Keynesians** believe that fiscal policy can have powerful effects on aggregate demand, output, and employment when there is substantial spare capacity in an economy. **Monetarists** believe that fiscal changes only have a temporary effect on aggregate demand and that monetary policy is a more effective tool for restraining or boosting inflationary pressures. Monetarists tend not to advocate using monetary policy for countercyclical adjustment of aggregate demand. This intellectual division naturally will be reflected in economists' divergent views on the efficacy of the large fiscal expansions observed in many countries following the 2008–2009 Global Financial Crisis, along with differing views on the possible impact of quantitative easing.

Government Receipts and Expenditure in Major Economies

In Exhibit 1, we present the total government revenues as a percentage of GDP for some major economies. This is the share of a country's output that is gathered by the government through taxes and such related items as fees, charges, fines, and capital transfers. It is often considered as a summary measure of the extent to which a government is involved both directly and indirectly in the economic activity of a country.

Taxes are formally defined as compulsory, unrequited payments to the general government (they are unrequited in the sense that benefits provided by a government to taxpayers usually are not related to payments). Exhibit 1 contains taxes on incomes and profits, social security contributions, indirect taxes on goods and services, employment taxes, and taxes on the ownership and transfer of property.

Exhibit 1: General Government Revenues as Percent of GDP

	1995	2000	2005	2008	2010	2015
Australia	34.5	36.1	36.5	35.3	32.4	34.9
Germany	45.1	46.4	43.6	43.8	43.0	44.5
Japan	31.2	31.4	31.7	34.4	30.6	35.7
United Kingdom	38.2	40.3	40.8	42.2	38.2	38.0
United States	33.8	35.4	33.0	32.3	30.9	33.4
OECD	37.9	39.0	37.7	37.9	39.8	40.9

Source: Organisation for Economic Co-Operation and Development (OECD).

Taxes on income and profits have been fairly constant for the member countries of the Organisation for Economic Co-operation and Development (OECD) at around 12.5–13 percent of GDP since the mid-1990s, while taxes on goods and services have been steady at about 11 percent of GDP for that period. Variations between countries can be substantial; taxes on goods and services are around 5 percent of GDP for the United States and Japan but are more than 16 percent for Denmark.

Exhibit 2 shows the percentage of GDP represented by government expenditure in a variety of major economies over time. Generally, these have been fairly constant since 1995, although Germany had a particularly high number at the start of the period because of reunification costs. The impacts of governments' fiscal stimulus programs in the face of the 2008–2009 financial crisis show up as significant increases in government expenditures in Exhibit 2 and increases in government deficits between 2008 and 2010 are evident in Exhibit 3.

Exhibit 2: General Government Expenditures as Percent of GDP

	1995	2000	2005	2008	2010	2015
Australia	38.2	35.2	34.8	34.3	34.4	36.2
Germany	54.8	45.1	46.9	43.8	47.3	43.9
Japan	36.0	39.0	38.4	37.1	39.6	39.4
United Kingdom	44.1	36.6	44.0	47.5	47.6	42.2

	1995	2000	2005	2008	2010	2015
United States	37.1	33.9	36.2	38.8	42.9	37.6
OECD	42.7	38.7	40.5	41.4	45.2	41.8

Source: OECD.

Clearly, the possibility that fiscal policy can influence output means that it may be an important tool for **economic stabilization**. In a recession, governments can raise spending (**expansionary fiscal policy**) in an attempt to raise employment and output. In boom times—when an economy has full employment and wages and prices are rising too fast—government spending may be reduced and taxes raised (**contractionary fiscal policy**).

Hence, a key concept is the budget surplus or deficit, which is the positive or negative difference between government revenue and expenditure for a fixed period of time, such as a fiscal or calendar year. Government revenue includes tax revenues net of transfer payments; government spending includes interest payments on the government debt. Analysts often focus on changes in the budget surplus or deficit from year to year as indicators of whether the fiscal policy is getting tighter or looser. An increase in a budget surplus would be associated with contractionary fiscal policy, while a rise in a deficit is an expansionary fiscal policy. Of course, over the course of a business cycle, the budget surplus will vary automatically in a countercyclical way. For example, as an economy slows and unemployment rises, government spending on social insurance and unemployment benefits will also rise and add to aggregate demand. This is known as an **automatic stabilizer**. Similarly, if boom conditions ensue and employment and incomes are high, then progressive income and profit taxes are rising and also act as automatic stabilizers increasing budget surplus or reducing budget deficit. The great advantage of automatic stabilizers is that they are automatic and do not require the identification of shocks to which policy makers must consider a response. By reducing the responsiveness of the economy to shocks, these automatic stabilizers reduce output fluctuations. Automatic stabilizers should be distinguished from discretionary fiscal policies, such as changes in government spending or tax rates, which are actively used to stabilize aggregate demand. If government spending and revenues are equal, then the budget is **balanced**.

Exhibit 3: General Government Net Borrowing or Lending as Percent of GDP

	1995	2000	2005	2008	2010	2015
Australia	−3.7	0.9	1.7	−3.8	−4.4	−2.2
Germany	−9.7	1.3	−3.3	−0.2	−4.2	0.8
Japan	−4.7	−7.6	−6.7	−4.1	−9.1	−3.6
United Kingdom	−5.8	3.7	−3.3	−5.1	−9.4	−4.2
United States	−3.3	1.5	−3.3	−7.0	−12.0	−4.2
OECD	−4.8	0.2	−2.7	−1.5	−5.1	−1.9

Source: OECD.

EXAMPLE 1

Sources and Uses of Government Cash Flows: The Case of the United Kingdom

The precise components of revenue and expenditure will of course vary over time and between countries. But, as an example of the breakdown of expenditure and revenue, in Exhibit 4 and Exhibit 5 we have presented the budget projections of the United Kingdom for 2018/2019. The budget projected that total spending would come to GBP808 billion, whereas total revenue would be only GBP769 billion. The government was therefore forecasting a budget shortfall of GBP39 billion for the fiscal year, meaning that it had an associated need to borrow GBP39 billion from the private sector in the United Kingdom or the private and public sectors of other economies.

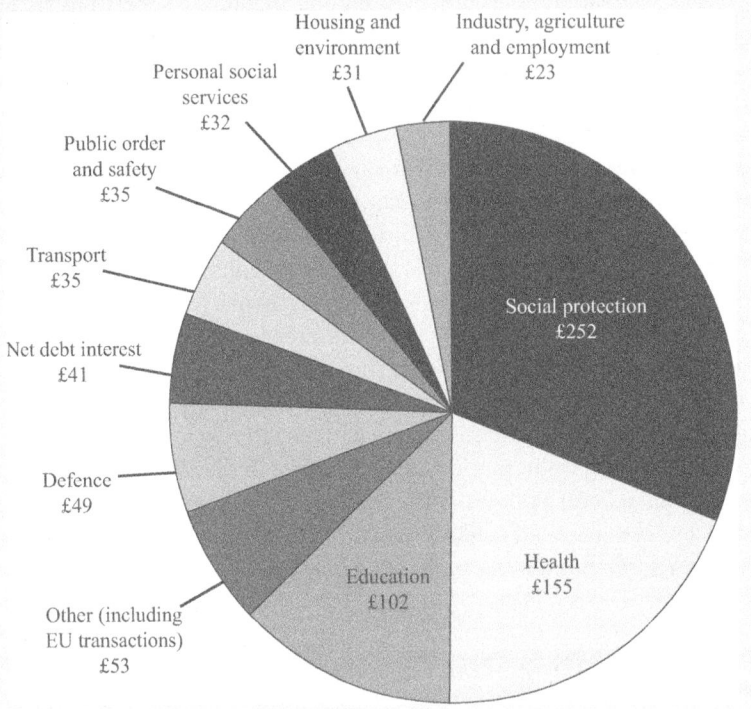

Exhibit 4: Where Does the Money Go? United Kingdom, 2018–2019

Note: All values are in billions of pounds.

Source: HM Treasury, United Kingdom.

Roles and Objectives of Fiscal Policy

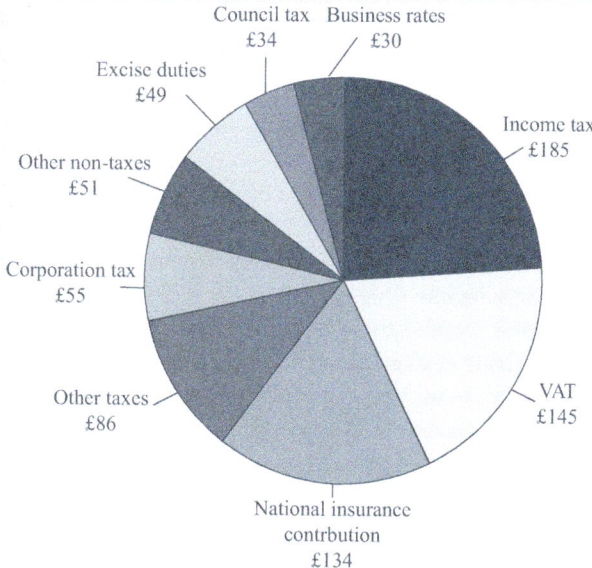

Exhibit 5: Where Does the Money Come From? United Kingdom, 2018–2019

- Council tax £34
- Business rates £30
- Excise duties £49
- Income tax £185
- Other non-taxes £51
- Corporation tax £55
- Other taxes £86
- VAT £145
- National insurance contrbution £134

Note: All values are in billions of pounds.

Source: HM Treasury, United Kingdom.

QUESTION SET

1. The *least likely* goal of a government's fiscal policy is to:

   A. redistribute income and wealth.

   B. influence aggregate national output.

   C. ensure the stability of the purchasing power of its currency.

   Solution:

   C is correct. Ensuring stable purchasing power is a goal of monetary rather than fiscal policy. Fiscal policy involves the use of government spending and tax revenue to affect the overall level of aggregate demand in an economy and hence the level of economic activity.

2. Which of the following *best* represents a contractionary fiscal policy?

   A. Temporary suspension of payroll taxes

   B. Public spending on a high-speed railway

   C. Freeze in discretionary government spending

   Solution:

   C is correct. A freeze in discretionary government spending is an example of a contractionary fiscal policy.

3. A "pay-as-you-go" rule, which requires that any tax cut or increase in entitlement spending be offset by an increase in other taxes or reduction in other entitlement spending, is an example of which fiscal policy stance?

   A. Neutral

B. Expansionary

C. Contractionary

Solution:

A is correct. A "pay-as-you-go" rule is a neutral policy because any increases in spending or reductions in revenues would be offset. Accordingly, there would be no net impact on the budget deficit/surplus.

Deficits and the National Debt

Government deficits are the difference between government revenues and expenditures over a period of calendar time, usually a year. Government (or national) debt is the accumulation over time of these deficits. Government deficits are financed by borrowing from the private sector, often through private pension and insurance fund portfolio investments. We read that governments are more likely to have deficits than surpluses over long periods of time. As a result, a large stock of outstanding government debt may be owned by the private sector. This will vary as the business cycle ebbs and flows. Exhibit 6 shows the time path of the ratio of public debt to GDP for the United Kingdom over several hundred years. It can be clearly seen that the major cause of fluctuations in that ratio through history has been the financing of wars, in particular the Napoleonic Wars of 1799–1815 and the First and Second World Wars of 1914–1918 and 1939–1945.

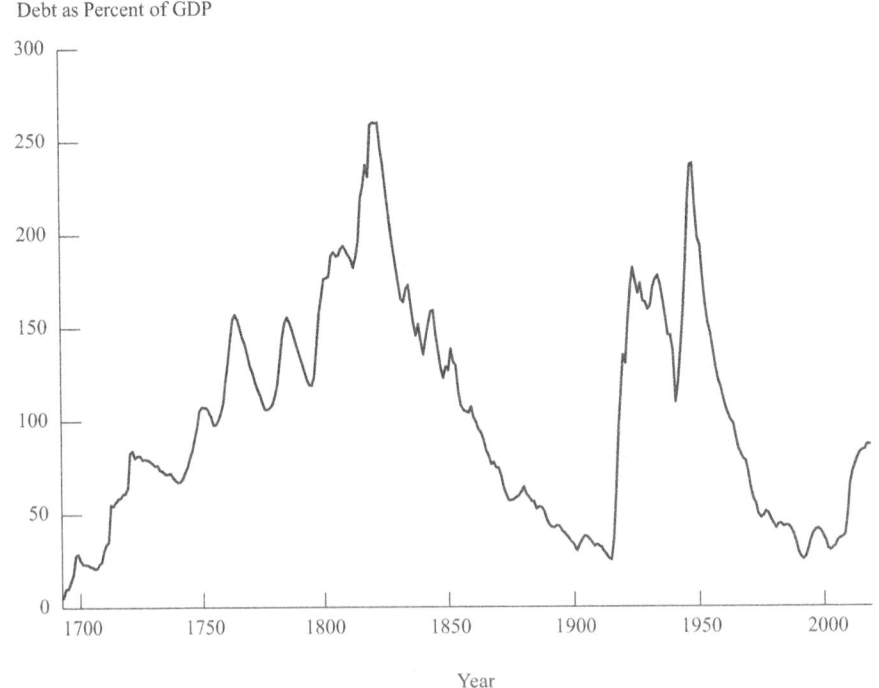

Exhibit 6: UK National Debt as Percent of GDP, 1692–2018

Source: http://ukpublicspending.co.uk.

With the onset of the credit crisis of 2008, governments actively sought to stimulate their economies through increased expenditures without raising taxes and revenues. This led to increased borrowing, shown in Exhibit 7, which became a concern in the financial markets in 2010 for such countries as Greece. Indeed, between 2008 and 2009, according to the OECD, central government debt rose from USD1.2 trillion to USD1.6 trillion in the United Kingdom and from USD5.8 trillion to USD7.5 trillion for the United States. The fiscal expansion by governments in the face of the financial crisis seems to have significantly raised the general government debt-to-GDP ratio over the long term for many countries, as illustrated in Exhibit 7.

Exhibit 7: General Government Debt as Percent of GDP

	1995	2000	2005	2008	2010	2015
Australia	57.3	41.1	30.0	30.0	41.9	64.1
Germany	54.1	59.5	70.1	68.1	84.5	78.9
Japan	94.7	142.6	176.2	181.6	207.5	237.4
United Kingdom	51.4	48.7	51.3	63.3	88.8	111.7
United States	83.2	61.7	79.0	93.2	117.0	125.3
OECD	65.8	59.9	59.5	60.8	73.0	85.3

Source: www.oecd.org.

Ultimately, if the ratio of debt to GDP rises beyond a certain unknown point, then the solvency of the country comes into question. An additional indicator for potential insolvency is the ratio of interest rate payments to GDP, which is shown for some major economies in Exhibit 8. These represent payments required of governments to service their debts as a percentage of national output and, as such, reflect both the size of debts and the interest charged on them.

Exhibit 8: General Government Net Debt Interest Payments as Percent of GDP

	1995	2000	2005	2008	2010	2015
Australia	3.5	1.7	1.0	−0.5	0.0	0.3
Germany	2.9	2.7	2.4	2.3	2.1	0.9
Japan	1.3	1.5	0.8	0.3	0.6	0.4
United Kingdom	3.1	2.4	1.8	1.7	2.6	2.0
United States	3.5	2.5	1.8	2.6	2.9	2.8
OECD	3.6	2.5	1.8	1.9	2.1	1.9

Source: OECD.

Government spending was far in excess of revenues following the credit crisis of 2007–2010 as governments tried to stimulate their economies; this level of spending raised concerns in some quarters about the scale of governmental debt accumulation. Exhibit 7 shows that government debt relative to GDP for the OECD countries overall rose from 59.5 percent in 2005 to 85.3 percent in 2015. In Japan, where fiscal spending has been used to stimulate the economy from the early 1990s, the ratio has risen from 94.7 percent in 1995 to 237.4 percent in 2015. If an economy grows in real terms, so do the real tax revenues and hence the ability to service a growing real debt at constant tax rate levels. If, however, the real growth in the economy is lower than the real interest rate on the debt, then the debt ratio will worsen even though the economy is growing because the debt burden (i.e., the real interest rate times the debt) grows faster than the economy. Hence, an important issue for governments and their creditors is whether their additional spending leads to sufficiently higher tax revenues to pay the interest on the debt used to finance the extra spending.

However, within a national economy, the real value of the outstanding debt will fall if the overall price level rises (i.e., inflation, and hence a rise in nominal GDP even if real GDP is static) and thus the ratio of debt to GDP may not be rising. If the general price level falls (i.e., deflation), then the ratio may stay elevated for longer. If net interest payments rise rapidly and investors lose confidence in a government's ability to honor its debts, then financing costs may escalate even more quickly and make the situation unstable.

Should we be concerned about the size of a national debt (relative to GDP)? There are strong arguments both for and against:

- The arguments against being concerned about national debt (relative to GDP) are as follows:

    - The scale of the problem may be overstated because the debt is owed internally to fellow citizens. This is certainly the case in Japan and South Korea, where 93 percent is owned by local residents. Canada is similar with 90 percent of debt is owned by residents. However, other countries have a much lower percentage owned internally. According to data from the Bank for International Settlements (BIS) and International Monetary Fund (IMF), the figures are 53 percent and 73 percent in the United States and United Kingdom, respectively, whereas in Italy, only 46 percent is owned by local residents.
    - A proportion of the money borrowed may have been used for capital investment projects or to enhance human capital (e.g., training, education); these should lead to raised future output and tax revenues.
    - Large fiscal deficits require tax changes that actually may reduce distortions caused by existing tax structures.
    - Deficits may have no net impact because the private sector may act to offset fiscal deficits by increasing saving in anticipation of future increased taxes. This argument is known as "Ricardian equivalence" and is discussed in more detail later.
    - If there is unemployment in an economy, then the debt is not diverting activity away from productive uses (and indeed the debt could be associated with an increase in employment).

- The arguments in favor of being concerned about national debt are as follows:

    - High levels of debt to GDP may lead to higher tax rates in the search for higher tax revenues. This may lead to disincentives to economic activity as the higher marginal tax rates reduce labor effort and entrepreneurial activity, leading to lower growth in the long run.
    - If markets lose confidence in a government, then the central bank may have to print money to finance a government deficit. This ultimately may lead to high inflation, as evidenced by the economic history of Germany in the 1920s and more recently in Zimbabwe.
    - Government borrowing may divert private sector investment from taking place (an effect known as crowding out); if there is a limited amount of savings to be spent on investment, then larger government demands will lead to higher interest rates and lower private sector investing.

Roles and Objectives of Fiscal Policy

An important distinction to make is between long- and short-run effects. Over short periods of time (say, a few years), crowding out may have little effect. If it lasts for a longer time, however, then capital accumulation in an economy may be damaged. Similarly, tax distortions may not be too serious over the short term but will have a more substantial impact over many years.

QUESTION SET

1. Which of the following is *not* associated with an expansionary fiscal policy?

    A. Rise in capital gains taxes

    B. Cuts in personal income taxes

    C. New capital spending by the government on road building

    Solution:

    A is correct. A rise in capital gains taxes reduces income available for spending and hence reduces aggregate demand, other things being equal. Cutting income tax raises disposable income, while new road building raises employment and incomes; in both cases, aggregate demand rises and hence policy is expansionary.

2. Fiscal expansions will *most likely* have the greatest impact on aggregate output when the economy is in which of the following states?

    A. Full employment

    B. Near full employment

    C. Considerable unemployment

    Solution:

    C is correct. When an economy is close to full employment, a fiscal expansion raising aggregate demand can have little impact on output because there are few spare unused resources (e.g., labor or idle factories); instead, there will be upward pressure on prices (i.e., inflation). The greatest impact on aggregate output will occur when there is considerable unemployment.

3. Which one of the following is *most likely* a reason to *not* use fiscal deficits as an expansionary tool?

    A. They may crowd out private investment.

    B. They may facilitate tax changes to reduce distortions in an economy.

    C. They may stimulate employment when there is substantial unemployment in an economy.

    Solution:

    A is correct. A frequent argument against raises in fiscal deficits is that the additional borrowing to fund the deficit in financial markets will displace private sector borrowing for investment (i.e., crowding out).

4. The *most likely* argument against high national debt levels is that:

    A. the debt is owed internally to fellow citizens.

    B. they create disincentives for economic activity.

C. they may finance investment in physical and human capital.
   Solution:
   B is correct. The belief is that high levels of debt to GDP may lead to higher future tax rates, which may lead to disincentives to economic activity.

5. Which statement regarding fiscal deficits is *most* accurate?
   A. According to the Ricardian equivalence, deficits have a multiplicative effect on consumer spending.
   B. Higher government spending may lead to higher interest rates and lower private sector investing.
   C. Central bank actions that grow the money supply to address deflationary conditions decrease fiscal deficits.
   Solution:
   B is correct. Government borrowing may compete with private sector borrowing for investment purposes.

4   FISCAL POLICY TOOLS

☐ describe tools of fiscal policy, including their advantages and disadvantages

We now look at the nature of the fiscal tools available to a government. Government spending can take a variety of forms:

- **Transfer payments** are welfare payments made through the social security system and, depending on the country, include payments for state pensions, housing benefits, tax credits and income support for poorer families, child benefits, unemployment benefits, and job search allowances. Transfer payments exist to provide a basic minimum level of income for low-income households, and they also provide a means by which a government can change the overall income distribution in a society. Note that these payments are not included in the definition of GDP because they do not reflect a reward to a factor of production for economic activity. Also, they are not considered to be part of general government spending on goods and services.
- **Current government spending** involves spending on goods and services that are provided on a regular, recurring basis—including health, education, and defense. Clearly, such spending will have a big impact on a country's skill level and overall labor productivity.
- **Capital expenditure** includes infrastructure spending on roads, hospitals, prisons, and schools. This investment spending will add to a nation's capital stock and affect productive potential for an economy.

Government spending can be justified on both economic and social grounds:

- To provide such services as defense that benefit all citizens equally.
- For infrastructure capital spending (e.g., roads) to help a country's economic growth.

- To guarantee a minimum level of income for poorer people and hence redistribute income and wealth (e.g., welfare and related benefits).
- To influence a government's economic objectives of low inflation and high employment and growth (e.g., management of aggregate demand).
- To subsidize the development of innovative and high-risk new products or markets (e.g., alternative energy sources).

Government revenues can take several forms:

- **Direct taxes** are levied on income, wealth, and corporate profits and include capital gains taxes, national insurance (or labor) taxes, and corporate taxes. They also may include a local income or property tax for both individuals and businesses. Inheritance tax on a deceased's estate will have both revenue-raising and wealth-redistribution aspects.
- **Indirect taxes** are taxes on spending on a variety of goods and services in an economy—such as the excise duties on fuel, alcohol, and tobacco as well as sales (or value-added tax)—and often exclude health and education products on social grounds. In addition, taxes on gambling may be considered to have a social aspect in deterring such activity, while fuel duties will serve an environmental purpose by making fuel consumption and hence travel more expensive.

Taxes can be justified both in terms of raising revenues to finance expenditures and in terms of income and wealth redistribution policies. Economists typically consider four desirable attributes of a tax policy:

- Simplicity: This refers to ease of compliance by the taxpayer and enforcement by the revenue authorities. The final liability should be certain and not easily manipulated.
- Efficiency: Taxation should interfere as little as possible in the choices individuals make in the marketplace. Taxes affect behavior and should, in general, discourage work and investment as little as possible. A major philosophical issue among economists is whether tax policy should deliberately deviate from efficiency to promote "good" economic activities, such as savings, and discourage harmful ones, such as tobacco consumption. Although most would accept a limited role in guiding consumer choices, some will question if policy makers are equipped to decide on such objectives and whether there will be unwanted ancillary effects, such as giving tax breaks for saving among people who already save and whose behavior does not change.
- Fairness: This refers to the fact that people in similar situations should pay the same taxes ("horizontal equity") and that richer people should pay more taxes ("vertical equity"). Of course, the concept of fairness is really subjective. Still, most would agree that income tax rates should be progressive—that is, that households and corporations should pay proportionately more as their incomes rise. However, some people advocate "flat" tax rates, whereby all should pay the same proportion of taxable income.
- Revenue sufficiency: Although revenue sufficiency may seem obvious as a criterion for tax policy, there may be a conflict with fairness and efficiency. For example, one may believe that increasing income tax rates to reduce fiscal deficits reduces labor effort and that tax rate increases are thus an inefficient policy tool.

SOME ISSUES WITH TAX POLICY

1. **Incentives.** Some economists believe that income taxes reduce the incentive to work, save, and invest and that the overall tax burden has become excessive. These ideas are often associated with supply-side economics and the US economist Arthur Laffer. A variety of income tax cuts and simplifications have taken place in the United States since 1981, and despite substantial controversy, some claim that work effort did rise (although tax cuts had little impact on savings). Similarly, some found that business investment did rise, while others claimed it was independent of such cuts.

2. **Fairness.** How do we judge the fairness of the tax system? One way is to calibrate the tax burden falling on different groups of people ranked by their income and to assess how changes in taxes affect these groups. Of course, this imposes huge data demands on investigators and must be considered incomplete. In the United States, the federal system is indeed highly progressive. Many countries use such methods to analyze the impact of tax changes on different income groups when they announce their annual fiscal policy plans.

3. **Tax reform.** There is continuous debate on reforming tax policy. Should there be a flat-rate tax on labor income? Should all investment be immediately deducted for corporate taxes? Should more revenue be sourced from consumption taxes? Should taxes be indexed to inflation? Should dividends be taxed when profits have already been subject to tax? Should estates be taxed at all? Many of these issues are raised in the context of their impact on economic growth.

QUESTION SET

1. Which of the following is *not* a tool of fiscal policy?
    A. A rise in social transfer payments
    B. The purchase of new equipment for the armed forces
    C. An increase in deposit requirements for the buying of houses

Solution:

C is correct. Rises in deposit requirements for house purchases are intended to reduce the demand for credit for house purchases and hence would be considered a tool of monetary policy. This is a policy used actively in several countries and is under consideration by regulators in other countries to constrain house price inflation.

2. Which of the following is *not* an indirect tax?
    A. Excise duty
    B. Value-added tax
    C. Employment taxes

Solution:

C is correct. Both excise duty and value-added tax (VAT) are applied to prices, whereas taxes on employment apply to labor income and hence are not indirect taxes.

> 3. Which of the following statements is *most* accurate?
>   A. Direct taxes are useful for discouraging alcohol consumption.
>   B. Because indirect taxes cannot be changed quickly, they are of no use in fiscal policy.
>   C. Government capital spending decisions are slow to plan, implement, and execute and hence are of little use for short-term economic stabilization.
>
> **Solution**:
>
> C is correct. Capital spending is much slower to implement than changes in indirect taxes; and indirect taxes affect alcohol consumption more directly than direct taxes.

The Advantages and Disadvantages of Different Fiscal Policy Tools

The different tools used to expedite fiscal policy as a means to try to put or keep an economy on a path of positive, stable growth with low inflation have both advantages and disadvantages:

Advantages

- Indirect taxes can be adjusted almost immediately after they are announced and can influence spending behavior instantly and generate revenue for the government at little or no cost to the government.
- Social policies, such as discouraging alcohol or tobacco use, can be adjusted almost instantly by raising such taxes.

Disadvantages

- Direct taxes are more difficult to change without considerable notice, often many months, because payroll computer systems will have to be adjusted (although the announcement may well have a powerful effect on spending behavior more immediately). The same may be said for welfare and other social transfers.
- Capital spending plans take longer to formulate and implement, typically over a period of years. For example, building a road or hospital requires detailed planning, legal permissions, and implementation. This is often a valid criticism of an active fiscal policy and was widely heard during the US fiscal stimulus in 2009–2010. Such policies, however, do add to the productive potential of an economy, unlike a change in personal or indirect taxes. Of course, the slower the impact of a fiscal change, the more likely other exogenous changes will already be influencing the economy before the fiscal change kicks in.

These tools may have expectational effects at least as powerful as the direct effects. The announcement of future income tax rises a year ahead potentially could lead to reduced consumption immediately. Such delayed tax rises were a feature of the UK fiscal policy of 2009–2010; however, the evidence is anecdotal because spending behavior changed little until the delayed tax changes actually came into force.

We may also consider the relative potency of the different fiscal tools. Direct government spending has a far bigger impact on aggregate spending and output than income tax cuts or transfer increases; however, if the latter are directed at the poorest in society (basically, those who spend all their income), then this will give a relatively strong boost. Further discussion and examples of these comparisons are given in the section on the interaction between monetary and fiscal policy.

Modeling the Impact of Taxes and Government Spending: The Fiscal Multiplier

The conventional macroeconomic model has government spending, G, adding directly to aggregate demand, AD, and reducing it via taxes, T; these include both indirect taxes on expenditures and direct taxes on factor incomes. Further government spending is increased through the payment of transfer benefits, B, such as social security payments. Hence, the net impact of the government sector on aggregate demand is as follows:

$G - T + B$ = Budget surplus OR deficit.

Net taxes (NT; taxes less transfers) reduce disposable income (YD) available to individuals relative to national income or output (Y) as follows:

$YD = Y - NT = (1 - t) Y$,

where t is the **net tax rate**. Net taxes are often assumed to be proportional to national income, Y, and hence total tax revenue from net taxes is tY. If t = 20% or 0.2, then for every USD1 rise in national income, net tax revenue will rise by USD0.20 and household disposable income will rise by USD0.80.

The **fiscal multiplier** is important in macroeconomics because it tells us how much output changes as exogenous changes occur in government spending or taxation. The recipients of the increase in government spending will typically save a proportion $(1 - c)$ of each additional dollar of disposable income, where c is the **marginal propensity to consume** (MPC) this additional income. Ignoring income taxes, we can see that $\$c$ will, in turn, be spent by these recipients on more goods and services. The recipients of this $\$c$ also will spend a proportion c of this additional income (i.e., $\$c \times c$, or c-squared). This process continues with income and spending growing at a constant rate of c as it passes from hand to hand through the economy. This is the familiar geometric progression with constant factor c, where $0 < c < 1$. The sum of this geometric series is $1/(1 - c)$.

We define s as the **marginal propensity to save** (MPS), the amount saved out of an additional dollar of disposable income. Because $c + s = 1$, $s = 1 - c$.

Exhibit 9: Disposable Income, Saving, and the MPC

Income	Income Tax	Disposable Income	Consumption	Saving
USD100	USD20	USD80	USD72	USD8

In Exhibit 9, the MPC out of disposable income is 90 percent or 0.9 (72/80). The MPS is therefore 1 − 0.9 or 0.1.

For every dollar of new (additional) spending, total incomes and spending rises by USD$1/(1 - c)$. And because $0 < c < 1$, this must be > 1; this is the multiplier. If c = 0.9 (or individuals spend 90 percent of additions to income), then the multiplier = $1/(1 − 0.9) = 10$.

A formal definition of the multiplier would be the ratio of the change in equilibrium output to the change in autonomous spending that caused the change. This is a monetary measure, but because prices are assumed to be constant in this analysis, real and monetary amounts are identical. Given that fiscal policy is about changes

Fiscal Policy Tools

in government spending, G, net taxes, NT, and tax rates, t, we can see that the multiplier is an important tool for calibrating the possible impact of policy changes on output. How can we introduce tax changes into the multiplier concept? We do this by introducing the idea of disposable income, YD, defined as income less income taxes net of transfers, $Y - NT$.

Households spend a proportion c of disposable income, YD, that is, cYD or $c(Y - NT)$ or $c(1 - t)Y$. The marginal propensity to consume in the presence of taxes is then $c(1 - t)$. If the government increases spending, say on road building, by an amount, G, then disposable income rises by $(1 - t)G$ and consumer spending by $c(1 - t)G$. Provided there are unused sources of capital and labor in the economy, this leads to a rise in aggregate demand and output; the recipients of this extra consumption spending will have $(1 - t)c(1 - t)G$ extra disposable income available and will spend c of it. This cumulative extra spending and income will continue to spread through the economy at a decreasing rate as $0 < c(1 - t) < 1$. The overall final impact on aggregate demand and output will effectively be the sum of this decreasing geometric series with the common ratio $c(1 - t)$, which sums to $1/[1 - c(1 - t)]$. This is known as the fiscal multiplier and is relevant to studies of fiscal policy as changes in G or tax rates will affect output in an economy through the value of the multiplier.

For example, if the tax rate is 20 percent, or 0.2, and the marginal propensity to consume is 90 percent, or 0.9, then the fiscal multiplier will be as follows: $1/[1 - 0.9(1 - 0.2)]$ or $1/0.28 = 3.57$. In other words, if the government raises G by USD1 billion, total incomes and spending rise by USD3.57 billion.

Discretionary fiscal policy will involve changes in these variables with a view to influencing Y.

The Balanced Budget Multiplier

If a government increases G by the same amount as it raises taxes, the aggregate output actually rises. Why is this?

Because the marginal propensity to consume out of disposable income is less than 1, for every dollar less in YD, spending falls only c. Hence, aggregate spending falls less than the tax rise by a factor of c. A balanced budget leads to a rise in output, which in turn leads to further rises in output and incomes through the multiplier effect.

Suppose an economy has an equilibrium output or income level of USD1,000 consisting of USD900 of consumption and USD100 of investment spending, which is fixed and not related to income. If government spending is set at USD200, financed by a tax rate of 20 percent (giving tax revenue of USD200), what will happen to output? First, additional government spending of USD200 will raise output by that amount. But taxes of USD200 will not reduce output by a similar amount if the MPC is less than 1. Suppose it is 0.9, and hence spending will fall only by 90 percent of USD200, or USD180. The initial impact of the balanced fiscal package on aggregate demand will be to raise it by USD200 - USD180 = USD20. This additional output, in turn, will lead to further increases in income and output through the multiplier effect.

Even though this policy involved a combination of government spending and tax increases that initially left the government's budget deficit/surplus unchanged, the induced rise in output will lead to further tax revenue increases and a further change in the budget position. Could the government adjust the initial change in spending to offset exactly the eventual total change in tax revenues? The answer is "yes," and we can ask what the effect will be on output of this genuinely balanced budget change. This balanced budget multiplier always takes the value unity.

EXAMPLE 1

Government Debt, Deficits, and Ricardo Equivalence

The total stock of government debt is the outstanding stock of IOUs issued by a government and not yet repaid. They are issued when the government has insufficient tax revenues to meet expenditures and has to borrow from the public. The size of the outstanding debt equals the cumulative quantity of net borrowing it has done, and the fiscal or budget deficit is added in the current period to the outstanding stock of debt. If the outstanding stock of debt falls, we have a negative deficit or a surplus.

If a government reduces taxation by USD10 billion one year and replaces that revenue with borrowing of USD10 billion from the public, will it have any real impact on the economy? The important issue is how people perceive that action: Do they recognize what will happen over time as interest and bond principal have to be repaid out of future taxes? If so, they may think of the bond finance as equivalent to delayed taxation finance; thus, the reduction in current taxation will have no impact on spending because individuals save more in anticipation of higher future taxes to repay the bond. This is called **Ricardian equivalence** after the economist David Ricardo. If people do not correctly anticipate all the future taxes required to repay the additional government debt, then they feel wealthier when the debt is issued and may increase their spending, adding to aggregate demand.

Whether Ricardian equivalence holds in practice is ultimately an empirical issue and is difficult to calibrate conclusively given the number of factors that are changing at any time in a modern economy.

QUESTION SET

1. Which of the following is the *most likely* example of a tool of fiscal policy?

   A. Public financing of a power plant
   B. Regulation of the payment system
   C. Central bank's purchase of government bonds

   Solution:

   A is correct. Public financing of a power plant could be described as a fiscal policy tool to stimulate investment.

---

5 FISCAL POLICY IMPLEMENTATION

☐ explain the implementation of fiscal policy and difficulties of implementation as well as whether a fiscal policy is expansionary or contractionary

We next discuss major issues in fiscal policy implementation.

Deficits and the Fiscal Stance

An important question is the extent to which the budget is a useful measure of the government's fiscal stance. Does the size of the deficit actually indicate whether fiscal policy is expansionary or contractionary? Clearly, such a question is important for economic policy makers insofar as the deficit can change for reasons unrelated to actual fiscal policy changes. For example, the automatic stabilizers mentioned earlier will lead to changes in the budget deficit unrelated to fiscal policy changes; a recession will cause tax revenues to fall and the budget deficit to rise. An observer may conclude that fiscal policy has been loosened and is expansionary and that no further government action is required.

To this end, economists often look at the structural budget deficit as an indicator of the fiscal stance. This is defined as the deficit that would exist *if the economy was at full employment (or full potential output)*. Hence, if we consider a period of relatively high unemployment, such as 2009–2010 with around 9–10 percent of the workforce out of work in the United States and Europe, then the budget deficits in those countries would be expected to be reduced substantially if the economies returned to full employment. At this level, tax revenues would be higher and social transfers lower. Historical data for major countries are given in Exhibit 10, where negative numbers refer to deficits and positive numbers are surpluses.

Exhibit 10: General Government Cyclically Adjusted Balances as Percent of GDP

	1995	2000	2005	2008	2010	2015
Australia	−3.1	0.9	2.0	−0.4	−3.8	−0.1
Germany	−9.5	0.9	−2.6	−0.8	−3.3	0.7
Japan	−4.6	−6.4	−4.1	−4.0	−8.2	−3.6
United Kingdom	−5.6	0.8	−4.5	−5.6	−7.6	−4.3
United States	−2.9	−0.4	−5.4	−7.1	−10.0	−3.5
OECD	−4.6	−1.2	−3.6	−4.5	−6.9	−2.0

Source: OECD Economic Outlook, Volume 2018 Issue 1.

Another reason why actual government deficits may *not* be a good measure of fiscal stance is the distinction between real and nominal interest rates and the role of inflation adjustment when applied to budget deficits. Although national economic statistics treat the cash interest payments on debt as government expenditure, it makes more sense to consider only the inflation-adjusted (or real) interest payments because the real value of the outstanding debt is being eroded by inflation. Automatic stabilizers—such as income tax, VAT, and social benefits—are important because as output and employment fall and reduce tax revenues, *net* tax revenues also fall as unemployment benefits rise. This acts as a fiscal stimulus and serves to reduce the size of the multiplier, dampening the output response of whatever caused the fall in output in the first place. By their very nature, automatic stabilizers do not require policy changes; no policy maker has to decide that an economic shock has occurred and how to respond. Hence, the responsiveness of the economy to shocks is automatically reduced, as are movements in employment and output.

In addition to these automatic adjustments, governments also use discretionary fiscal adjustments to influence aggregate demand. These will involve tax changes and/or spending cuts or increases usually with the aim of stabilizing the economy. A natural question is why fiscal policy cannot stabilize aggregate demand completely, hence ensuring full employment at all times.

Difficulties in Executing Fiscal Policy

Fiscal policy cannot stabilize aggregate demand completely because the difficulties in executing fiscal policy cannot be completely overcome.

First, the policy maker does not have complete information about how the economy functions. It may take several months for policy makers to realize that an economy is slowing, because data appear with a considerable time lag and even then are subject to substantial revision. This is often called the **recognition lag** and has been likened to the problem of driving while looking in the rearview mirror. Then, when policy changes are finally decided on, they may take many months to implement. This is the **action lag**. If a government decides to raise spending on capital projects to increase employment and incomes, for example, these may take many months to plan and put into action. Finally, the result of these actions on the economy will take additional time to become evident; this is the **impact lag**. These types of policy lags also occur in the case of discretionary monetary policy.

A second aspect of time in this process is the uncertainty of where the economy is heading independently of these policy changes. For example, a stimulus may occur simultaneously with a surprise rise in investment spending or in the demand for a country's exports just as discretionary government spending starts to rise. Macroeconomic forecasting models generally do not have a good track record for accuracy and hence cannot be relied on to aid the policy-making process in this context. In addition, when discretionary fiscal adjustments are announced (or are already underway), private sector behavior may well change, leading to rises in consumption or investment, both of which will reinforce the effects of a rise in government expenditure. Again, this will make it difficult to calibrate the required fiscal adjustment to secure full employment.

The following wider macroeconomic issues also are involved:

- If the government is concerned with both unemployment *and* inflation in an economy, then raising aggregate demand toward the full employment level may also lead to a tightening labor market and rising wages and prices. The policy maker may be reluctant to further fine-tune fiscal policy in an uncertain world because it might induce inflation.

- If the budget deficit is already large relative to GDP and further fiscal stimulus is required, then the necessary increase in the deficit may be considered unacceptable by the financial markets when government funding is raised, leading to higher interest rates on government debt and political pressure to tackle the deficit.

- Of course, all this presupposes that we know the level of full employment, which is difficult to measure accurately. Fiscal expansion raises demand, but what if we are already at full employment, which will be changing as productive capacity changes and workers' willingness to work at various wage levels changes?

- If unused resources reflect a low supply of labor or other factors rather than a shortage of demand, then discretionary fiscal policy will not add to demand and will be ineffective, raising the risk of inflationary pressures in the economy.

Fiscal Policy Implementation

- The issue of crowding out may occur: If the government borrows from a limited pool of savings, the competition for funds with the private sector may crowd out private firms with subsequently less investing and economic growth. In addition, the cost of borrowing may rise, leading to the cancellation of potentially profitable opportunities. This concept is the subject of continuing empirical debate and investigation.

QUESTION SET

1. Which of the following statements is *least* accurate?

    A. The economic data available to policy makers have a considerable time lag.

    B. Economic models always offer an unambiguous guide to the future path of the economy.

    C. Surprise changes in exogenous economic variables make it difficult to use fiscal policy as a stabilization tool.

    Solution:

    B is correct. Economic forecasts from models will always have an element of uncertainty attached to them and thus are not unambiguous or precise in their prescriptions. Once a fiscal policy decision has been made and implemented, unforeseen changes in other variables may affect the economy in ways that would lead to changes in the fiscal policy if we had perfect foresight. Note that it is true that official economic data may be available with substantial time lags, making fiscal judgments more difficult.

2. Which of the following statements is *least* accurate?

    A. Discretionary fiscal changes are aimed at stabilizing an economy.

    B. Automatic fiscal stabilizers include new plans for additional road building by the government.

    C. In the context of implementing fiscal policy, the recognition lag is often referred to as "driving while looking in the rearview mirror."

    Solution:

    B is correct. New plans for road building are discretionary and not automatic.

3. Which of the following statements regarding a fiscal stimulus is *most* accurate?

    A. Accommodative monetary policy reduces the impact of a fiscal stimulus.

    B. Different statistical models will predict different impacts for a fiscal stimulus.

    C. It is always possible to precisely predict the impact of a fiscal stimulus on employment.

    Solution:

    B is correct. Different models embrace differing views on how the economy works, including differing views on the impact of fiscal stimuli.

4. Which of the following statements is *most* accurate?

    A. An increase in the budget deficit is always expansionary.
    B. An increase in government spending is always expansionary.
    C. The structural deficit is always larger than the deficit below full employment.

    Solution:

    A is correct. Note that increases in government spending may be accompanied by even bigger rises in tax receipts and hence may not be expansionary.

PRACTICE PROBLEMS

1. Crowding out refers to a:
   A. fall in interest rates that reduces private investment.
   B. rise in private investment that reduces private consumption.
   C. rise in government borrowing that reduces the ability of the private sector to access investment funds.

2. A contractionary fiscal policy will always involve which of the following?
   A. Balanced budget
   B. Reduction in government spending
   C. Fall in the budget deficit or rise in the surplus

3. Which one of the following statements is *most* accurate?
   A. Ricardian equivalence refers to individuals having no idea of future tax liabilities.
   B. Governments do not allow political pressures to influence fiscal policies but do allow voters to affect monetary policies.
   C. If there is high unemployment in an economy, then easy monetary and fiscal policies should lead to an expansion in aggregate demand.

4. Which statement regarding fiscal policy is *most* accurate?
   A. Cyclically adjusted budget deficits are appropriate indicators of fiscal policy.
   B. To raise business capital spending, personal income taxes should be reduced.
   C. An increase in the budget surplus is associated with expansionary fiscal policy.

5. The *least likely* explanation for why fiscal policy cannot stabilize aggregate demand completely is that:
   A. private sector behavior changes over time.
   B. policy changes are implemented very quickly.
   C. fiscal policy focuses more on inflation than on unemployment.

SOLUTIONS

1. C is correct. A fall in interest rates is likely to lead to a rise in investment. Crowding out refers to government borrowing that reduces the ability of the private sector to invest.

2. C is correct. Note that a reduction in government spending could be accompanied by an even bigger fall in taxation, making it be expansionary.

3. C is correct. Note that governments often allow pressure groups to affect fiscal policy and that Ricardian equivalence involves individuals correctly anticipating future taxes. Thus, A and B are not correct choices.

4. A is correct. Cyclically adjusted budget deficits are appropriate indicators of fiscal policy. These are defined as the deficit that would exist if the economy was at full employment (or full potential output).

5. B is correct. Fiscal policy is subject to recognition, action, and impact lags.

LEARNING MODULE 4

Monetary Policy

LEARNING OUTCOMES

Mastery	The candidate should be able to:
☐	describe the roles and objectives of central banks
☐	describe tools used to implement monetary policy tools and the monetary transmission mechanism, and explain the relationships between monetary policy and economic growth, inflation, interest, and exchange rates
☐	describe qualities of effective central banks; contrast their use of inflation, interest rate, and exchange rate targeting in expansionary or contractionary monetary policy; and describe the limitations of monetary policy
☐	explain the interaction of monetary and fiscal policy

INTRODUCTION

Central banks play several important roles in modern economies. These roles include being the monopoly supplier of the currency, the banker to the government and the bankers' bank, the lender of last resort, the regulator and supervisor of the payments system, the conductor of monetary policy, and the supervisor of the banking system. Central banks have three primary tools available to them: open market operations, the refinancing rate, and reserve requirements. The success of central banks is thought to depend on three key concepts: central bank independence, credibility, and transparency. Both fiscal and monetary policy can alter aggregate demand, but they do so through differing channels with differing impacts on the composition of aggregate demand.

LEARNING MODULE OVERVIEW

- Central banks are the sole supplier of domestic currency, the banker to the government and the bankers' bank, the lender of last resort, the regulator and supervisor of the payments system, the conductor of monetary policy, and the supervisor of the banking system.

- The highest profile role that central banks assume is the operation of a country's monetary policy, which refers to central bank activities that are directed toward influencing the quantity of money and credit in an economy.
- The overarching goal of most central banks in maintaining price stability is the associated goal of controlling inflation.
- Central banks can manipulate the money supply in one of three ways: open market operations, its official policy rate and associated actions in the repo market, and manipulation of official reserve requirements.
- The central bank target **interest rate** (or **policy rate**) is used to influence short- and long-term interest rates and, ultimately, real economic activity.
- The central bank's policy rate works through the economy via the following interconnected channels: short-term interest rates, changes in the values of key asset prices, the exchange rate, and the expectations of economic agents.
- The success of inflation-targeting by central banks depends on three key characteristics: central bank independence, credibility, and transparency.
- Many emerging market economies choose to operate monetary policy by targeting their currency's exchange rate, rather than an explicit level of domestic inflation.
- A major problem for central banks as they try to manage the money supply to influence the real economy is that they cannot control the amount of money that households and corporations put in banks on deposit, nor can they easily control the willingness of banks to create money by expanding credit.
- Both fiscal and monetary policy can alter aggregate demand, but they do so through differing channels with differing impacts on the composition of aggregate demand.
- Both fiscal and monetary policies suffer from a lack of precise current knowledge of the economy, because periodic economic data are released with a time lag and are subject to revision.
- The interaction between monetary and fiscal policies is evident in the Ricardian equivalence because if tax cuts have no impact on private spending due to higher expected future taxes, then this may lead policy makers to favor monetary tools.

2

ROLE OF CENTRAL BANKS

☐ describe the roles and objectives of central banks

Roles of Central Banks and Objectives of Monetary Policy

Central banks play several key roles in modern economies. Generally, a central bank is the sole supplier of the domestic currency, the banker to the government and the bankers' bank, the lender of last resort, the regulator and supervisor of the payments system, the conductor of monetary policy, and the supervisor of the banking system. Let us examine these roles in turn.

In its earliest form, money could be exchanged for a prespecified precious commodity, usually gold, and promissory notes were issued by many private banks. Today, however, state-owned institutions—usually central banks—are designated in law as being the monopoly suppliers of a currency. Initially, these monopolists supplied money that could be converted into a prespecified amount of gold; they adhered to a **gold standard**. For example, until 1931, bank notes issued by Britain's central bank, the Bank of England, could be redeemed at the bank for a prespecified amount of gold. But Britain, like most other major economies, abandoned this convertibility principle in the first half of the twentieth century. Money in all major economies today is not convertible by law into anything else, but it is, in law, **legal tender**. This means that it must be accepted when offered in exchange for goods and services. Money that is not convertible into any other commodity is known as **fiat money**. Fiat money derives its value through government decree and because people accept it for payment of goods and services and for debt repayment.

As long as fiat money is acceptable to everyone as a medium of exchange, and it holds its value over time, then it also will be able to serve as a unit of account. However, once an economy has moved to a system of fiat money, the role of the supplier of that money becomes even more crucial because they could, for example, expand the supply of this money indefinitely should they wish to do so. Central banks, therefore, play a crucial role in modern economies as the suppliers and guardians of the value of their fiat currencies and as institutions charged with the role of maintaining confidence in their currencies. As the sole suppliers of domestic currency, central banks are at the center of economic life. As such, they assume other roles in addition to being the suppliers and guardians of the value of their currencies.

Most central banks act as the banker to the government and to other banks. They also act as a **lender of last resort** to banks. Because the central bank effectively has the capacity to print money, it is in the position to be able to supply the funds to banks that are facing crisis. The facts that economic agents know that the central bank stands ready to provide the liquidity required by any of the banks under its jurisdiction and that they trust government bank deposit insurance help to prevent bank runs in the first place. However, the recent financial crisis has shown that this knowledge is not always sufficient to deter a bank run.

EXAMPLE 1

The Northern Rock Bank Run

In the latter part of the summer of 2007, the fall in US house prices and the related implosion of the US sub-prime mortgage market became the catalyst for a global liquidity crisis. Banks began to hoard cash and refused to lend to other banks at anything other than extremely punitive interest rates through the interbank market. This caused severe difficulties for a UK mortgage bank, Northern Rock. Northern Rock's mortgage book had expanded rapidly in the preceding years as it borrowed aggressively from the money markets. It is now clear that this expansion was at the expense of loan quality. The then–UK regulatory authority, the Financial Services Authority (FSA), later reported in 2008 that Northern Rock's lending practices did not pay due regard to either the credit quality of the mortgagees or the values of the properties on which the mortgages were secured. Being at the worst end of banking practice and relying heavily on international capital markets for its funding, Northern Rock was therefore susceptible to a global reduction in liquidity. As the liquidity crisis took hold, Northern Rock found that it could not replace its maturing money market borrowings. On 12 September 2007, in desperate need of liquidity, Northern Rock's board approached the UK central bank to ask for the necessary funds.

However, the news of Northern Rock's perilous liquidity position became known by the public and, more pertinently, by Northern Rock's retail depositors. On 14 September, having heard the news, queues began to form outside Northern Rock branches as depositors tried to withdraw their savings. On that day, it was estimated that Northern Rock depositors withdrew around GBP1 billion, representing 5 percent of Northern Rock's deposits. Further panic ensued as investors in "internet-only" Northern Rock accounts could not withdraw their money because of the collapse of Northern Rock's website. A further GBP1 billion was withdrawn over the next two days.

Northern Rock's share price dropped rapidly, as did the share prices of other similar UK banks. The crisis therefore threatened to engulf more than one bank. To prevent contagion, the chancellor of the exchequer announced on 17 September that the UK government would guarantee all Northern Rock deposits. This announcement was enough to stabilize the situation and given that lending to Northern Rock was now just like lending to the government, deposits actually started to rise again.

Eventually Northern Rock was nationalized by the UK government, with the hope that at some time in the future it could be privatized once its balance sheet had been repaired.

Central banks often are charged by the government to supervise the banking system, or at least to supervise those banks that they license to accept deposits. In some countries, this role is undertaken by a separate authority. In other countries, the central bank can be jointly responsible with another body for the supervision of its banks.

Exhibit 1 lists the banking supervisors in the G–10 countries; central banks are underlined. As the exhibit shows, most but not all bank systems have a single supervisor, which is not necessarily a central bank. A few countries, such as Germany and the United States, have more than one supervisor.

Exhibit 1: Banking Supervision in the G–10

Country	Institutions
Belgium	Banking and Finance Commission
Canada	Office of the Superintendent of Financial Institutions
France	Commission Bancaire
Germany	Federal Banking Supervisory Office; Deutsche Bundesbank
Italy	Bank of Italy
Japan	Financial Services Agency
Netherlands	Bank of Netherlands
Sweden	Swedish Financial Supervisory Authority
Switzerland	Federal Commission
United Kingdom	Bank of England
United States	Office of the Comptroller of the Currency; Federal Reserve; Federal Deposit Insurance Corporation

The United Kingdom is an interesting case study in this regard. Until May 1997, the Bank of England had statutory responsibility for banking supervision in the United Kingdom. In May 1997, banking supervision was removed from the Bank of England and assigned to a new agency, the Financial Services Authority (FSA). However, the removal of responsibility for banking supervision from the central bank was seen by some as being a contributory factor in the run on the mortgage bank Northern Rock, and generally as a contributory factor in the recent banking crisis. Because of this perceived weakness in the separation of the central bank from banking supervision, the Bank of England regained responsibility for banking supervision and regulation in 2013.

Perhaps the least appreciated role of a central bank is its role in the **payments system**. Central banks are usually asked to oversee, regulate, and set standards for a country's payments system. For the system to work properly, procedures must be robust and standardized. The central bank will usually oversee the payments system and will also be responsible for the successful introduction of any new processes. Given the international nature of finance, the central bank will also be responsible for coordinating payments systems internationally with other central banks.

Most central banks are responsible for managing their country's **foreign currency reserves** as well as its gold reserves. With regard to the latter, even though countries abandoned the gold standard in the early part of the twentieth century, the world's central bankers still hold large quantities of gold. As such, if central banks were to decide to sell significant proportions of their gold reserves, it could potentially depress gold prices.

Finally, central banks are usually responsible for the operation of a country's **monetary policy**. This is arguably the highest profile role that these important organizations assume. Recall that monetary policy refers to central bank activities that are directed toward influencing the quantity of money and credit in an economy. As the sole supplier of a country's domestic currency, central banks are in the ideal position to implement and determine monetary policy.

To summarize, central banks assume a range of roles and responsibilities. They do not all assume responsibility for the supervision of the banks, but all of the following roles normally are assumed by the central bank:

- Monopoly supplier of the currency;
- Banker to the government and the bankers' bank;
- Lender of last resort;
- Regulator and supervisor of the payments system;
- Conductor of monetary policy; and
- Supervisor of the banking system.

The Objectives of Monetary Policy

Central banks fulfill a variety of important roles, but for what overarching purpose? A perusal of the websites of the world's central banks will reveal a wide range of explanations of their objectives. Their objectives are clearly related to their roles, and so there is frequent mention of objectives related to the stability of the financial system and to the payments systems. Some central banks are charged with doing all they can to maintain full employment and output. Some also have related but less tangible roles, such as *maintaining confidence in the financial system*, or even to *promote understanding of the financial sector*. Most seem to acknowledge explicitly one overarching objective—the objective of maintaining **price stability**.

So, although central banks usually have to perform many roles, most specify an overarching objective. Exhibit 2 lists what we might call the primary objectives of a number of central banks, from both developed market and emerging market economies.

Exhibit 2: The Objectives of Central Banks

The Central Bank of Brazil

Its institutional mission is to "ensure the stability of the currency's purchasing power and a solid and efficient financial system."

The European Central Bank

"[T]o maintain price stability is the primary objective of the Euro system and of the single monetary policy for which it is responsible. This is laid down in the Treaty on the Functioning of the European Union, Article 127 (1)."

"Without prejudice to the objective of price stability", the euro system will also "support the general economic policies in the Community with a view to contributing to the achievement of the objectives of the Community." These include a "high level of employment" and "sustainable and non-inflationary growth."

The US Federal Reserve

"The Federal Reserve sets the nation's monetary policy to promote the objectives of maximum employment, stable prices, and moderate long-term interest rates."

The Reserve Bank of Australia

"It is the duty of the Reserve Bank Board, within the limits of its powers, to ensure that the monetary and banking policy of the Bank is directed to the greatest advantage of the people of Australia and that the powers of the Bank ... are exercised in such a manner as, in the opinion of the Reserve Bank Board, will best contribute to:

a. the stability of the currency of Australia;
b. the maintenance of full employment in Australia; and
c. the economic prosperity and welfare of the people of Australia."

The Bank of Korea

"The primary purpose of the Bank, as prescribed by the Bank of Korea Act of 1962, is the pursuit of price stability."

Source: "Central Bank and Monetary Authority Websites," Bank for International Settlements, http://www.bis.org/cbanks.htm.

QUESTION SET

1. A central bank is normally *not* the:
    A. lender of last resort.
    B. banker to the government and banks.

> **C.** body that sets tax rates on interest on savings.
>
> **Solution:**
>
> C is correct. A central bank is normally the lender of last resort and the banker to the banks and government, but the determination of all tax rates is normally the preserve of the government and is a fiscal policy issue.
>
> 2. Which of the following *best* describes the overarching, long-run objective of most central banks?
>
>   **A.** Price stability
>
>   **B.** Fast economic growth
>
>   **C.** Current account surplus
>
>   **Solution:**
>
>   A is correct. Central banks normally have a variety of objectives, but the overriding one is nearly always price stability.
>
> 3. Which role is a central bank *least likely* to assume?
>
>   **A.** Lender of last resort
>
>   **B.** Supplier of the currency
>
>   **C.** Sole supervisor of banks
>
>   **Solution:**
>
>   C is correct. The supervision of banks is not a role that all central banks assume. When it is a central bank's role, responsibility may be shared with one or more entities.

As we have discussed, one of the essential features of a monetary system is that the medium of exchange should have a relatively stable value from one period to the next. Arguably then, the overarching goal of most central banks in maintaining price stability is the associated goal of controlling inflation. Before we explore the tools central banks use to control inflation, we should first consider the potential costs of inflation. In other words, we should ask why it is that central bankers believe that it is so important to control a nominal variable.

MONETARY POLICY TOOLS AND MONETARY TRANSMISSION

3

☐ describe tools used to implement monetary policy tools and the monetary transmission mechanism, and explain the relationships between monetary policy and economic growth, inflation, interest, and exchange rates

Central banks have three primary tools available to them: open market operations, the refinancing rate, and reserve requirements.

Open Market Operations

One of the most direct ways for a central bank to increase or reduce the amount of money in circulation is through **open market operations**. Open market operations involve the purchase and sale of government bonds from and to commercial banks or designated market makers. For example, when the central bank buys government bonds from commercial banks, this increases the reserves of private sector banks on the asset side of their balance sheets. If banks then use these surplus reserves by increasing lending to corporations and households, then broad money growth expands through the money multiplier process. Similarly, the central bank can sell government bonds to commercial banks. In so doing, the reserves of commercial banks decline, reducing their capacity to make loans (i.e., create credit) to households and corporations and thus causing broad money growth to decline through the money multiplier mechanism. In using open market operations, the central bank may target a desired level of commercial bank reserves or a desired interest rate for these reserves.

The Central Bank's Policy Rate

The most obvious expression of a central bank's intentions and views comes through the interest rate it sets. The name of the **official interest rate** (or **official policy rate** or just **policy rate**) varies from central bank to central bank, but its purpose is to influence short- and long-term interest rates and ultimately real economic activity.

The interest rate that a central bank sets and that it announces publicly is normally the rate at which it is willing to lend money to the commercial banks (although practices do vary from country to country). This policy rate can be achieved by using short-term collateralized lending rates, known as repo rates. For example, if the central bank wishes to increase the supply of money, it might buy bonds (usually government bonds) from the banks, with an agreement to sell them back at some time in the future. This transaction is known as a **repurchase agreement**. Normally, the maturity of repo agreements ranges from overnight to two weeks. In effect, this represents a secured loan to the banks, and the lender (in this case the central bank) earns the repo rate.

Suppose that a central bank announces an increase in its official interest rate. Commercial banks normally would increase their **base rates** at the same time. A commercial bank's base rate is the reference rate on which it bases lending rates to all other customers. For example, large corporate clients might pay the base rate plus 1 percent on their borrowing from a bank, whereas the same bank might lend money to a small corporate client at the base rate plus 3 percent. But why would commercial banks immediately increase their base or reference rates just because the central bank's refinancing rate had increased?

The answer is that commercial banks do not want to lend at a rate of interest below that which they are charged by the central bank. Effectively, the central bank can force commercial banks to borrow from it at this rate because it can conduct open market operations that create a shortage of money, forcing the banks to sell bonds to it with an agreed-upon repurchase price (i.e., a repurchase agreement). The repo rate would be such that the central bank earned the official refinancing rate on the transactions.

The name of each central bank's official refinancing rate varies. The Bank of England's refinancing rate is the **two-week repo rate**. In other words, the Bank of England fixes the rate at which it is willing to lend two-week money to the banking sector. The European Central Bank's (ECB's) official policy rate is known as the **refinancing rate**, which defines the rate at which the ECB is willing to lend short-term money to the Euro area banking sector.

The corresponding rate in the United States is the discount rate, which is the rate for member banks borrowing directly from the Federal Reserve System. The most important interest rate used in US monetary policy is the **federal funds rate**. The federal

Monetary Policy Tools and Monetary Transmission

funds rate (or **fed funds rate**) is the interbank lending rate on overnight borrowings of reserves. The Federal Open Market Committee (FOMC) seeks to move this rate to a target level by reducing or adding reserves to the banking system by means of open market operations. The level of the rate is reviewed by the FOMC at its meetings held every six weeks (although the target can be changed between meetings, if necessary).

Through the setting of a policy rate, a central bank can manipulate the amount of money in the money markets. Generally speaking, the higher the policy rate, the higher the potential penalty that banks will have to pay to the central bank if they run short of liquidity, the greater their willingness will be to reduce lending, and the more likely it will be that broad money growth will shrink.

Reserve Requirements

The third primary way in which central banks can limit or increase the supply of money in an economy is through the **reserve requirement**. We already have seen that the money creation process is more powerful the lower the percentage reserve requirement of banks. So, a central bank could restrict money creation by raising the reserve requirements of banks. However, this policy tool is not used much today in developed market economies. Indeed, some central banks, such as the Bank of England, no longer even set minimum reserve requirements for the banks under their jurisdiction. Changing reserve requirements frequently is disruptive for banks. For example, if a central bank increased the reserve requirements, a bank that was short on reserves might have to cease its lending activities until it had built up the necessary reserves, because deposits would be unlikely to rise quickly enough for the bank to build its reserves in this way. However, reserve requirements are still actively used in many emerging market countries to control lending and remain a potential policy tool for those central banks that do not currently use it.

To summarize, central banks can manipulate the money supply in one of three ways:

- open market operations;
- official policy rates and associated actions in the repo market; and
- manipulation of official reserve requirements.

The Transmission Mechanism

The overarching goal of a central bank is to maintain price stability. We have demonstrated how a central bank can manipulate the money supply and growth of the money supply. We also indicated how policy rates set and targeted by the central banks are usually very short term in nature; often they target overnight interest rates. However, most businesses and individuals in the real economy borrow and lend over much longer time frames than this. It may not be obvious, then, how changing short-term interest rates can influence the real economy, particularly if money neutrality holds in the long run. The fact that central bankers believe that they can affect real economic variables, in particular economic growth, by influencing broad money growth suggests that they believe that money is not neutral—at least not in the short run.

Exhibit 3 presents a stylized representation of the **monetary transmission mechanism**. This is the process whereby a central bank's interest rate is transmitted through the economy and ultimately affects the rate of increase of prices—that is, inflation.

Exhibit 3: A Stylized Representation of the Monetary Transmission Mechanism

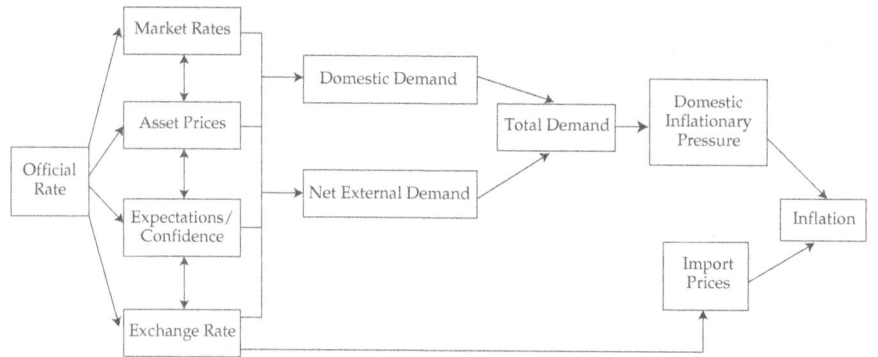

Source: Bank of England, https://www.bankofengland.co.uk/.

Suppose that a central bank announces an increase in its official interest rate. The implementation of the policy may begin to work through the economy via four interrelated channels. Those channels include bank lending rates, asset prices, agents' expectations, and exchange rates. First, as described earlier, the base rates of commercial banks and interbank rates should rise in response to the increase in the official rate. Banks, in turn, would increase the cost of borrowing for individuals and companies over both short- and long-term horizons. Businesses and consumers would then tend to borrow less as interest rates rise. An increase in short-term interest rates could also cause the price of such assets as bonds or the value of capital projects to fall as the discount rate for future cash flows rises.

Market participants would then come to the view that higher interest rates will lead to slower economic growth, reduced profits, and reduced borrowing to finance asset purchases. Exporters' profits might decline if the rise in interest rates causes the country's exchange rate to appreciate, because this would make domestic exports more expensive to overseas buyers and dampen demand to purchase them. The fall in asset prices as well as an increase in prices would reduce household financial wealth and therefore lead to a reduction in consumption growth. Expectations regarding interest rates can play a significant role in the economy. Often companies and individuals will make investment and purchasing decisions based on their interest rate expectations, extrapolated from recent events. If the central bank's interest rate move is widely expected to be followed by other interest rate increases, investors and companies will act accordingly. Consumption, borrowing, and asset prices may all decline as a result of the revision in expectations.

A rise in the central bank's policy rate can reduce real domestic demand and net external demand (that is, the difference between export and import consumption) through a wide range of interconnected ways. Weaker total demand would tend to put downward pressure on the rate of domestic inflation—as would a stronger currency, which would reduce the prices of imports. Taken together, these factors might begin to put downward pressure on the overall measure of inflation.

To summarize, the central bank's policy rate works through the economy via one or more of the following interconnected channels:

- Short-term interest rates;
- Changes in the values of key asset prices;
- The exchange rate; and
- The expectations of economic agents.

QUESTION SET

1. Which of the following variables are *most likely* to be affected by a change in a central bank's policy rate?

   A. Asset prices only
   B. Expectations about future interest rates only
   C. Both asset prices and expectations about future interest rates

   Solution:

   C is correct. The price of equities, for example, might be affected by the expectation of future policy interest rate changes. In other words, a rate change may be taken as a signal of the future stance of monetary policy—contractionary or expansionary.

2. Which of the following does a central bank seek to influence directly via the setting of its official interest rate?

   A. Import prices
   B. Domestic inflation
   C. Inflation expectations

   Solution:

   C is correct. By setting its official interest rate, a central bank could expect to have a direct influence on inflation expectations—as well as on other market interest rates, asset prices, and the exchange rate (where this is freely floating). If it can influence these factors, it might ultimately hope to influence import prices (via changes in the exchange rate) and also domestically generated inflation (via its impact on domestic or external demand). The problem is that the workings of the transmission mechanism—from the official interest rate to inflation—are complex and can change over time.

3. Monetary policy is *least likely* to include:

   A. setting an inflation rate target.
   B. changing an official interest rate.
   C. enacting a transfer payment program.

   Solution:

   C is correct. Transfer payment programs represent fiscal, not monetary policy.

4. Which is the *most* accurate statement regarding central banks and monetary policy?

   A. Central bank activities are typically intended to maintain price stability.
   B. Monetary policies work through the economy via four independent channels.

> C. Commercial and interbank interest rates move inversely to official interest rates.
>
> **Solution:**
>
> A is correct. Central bank activities are typically intended to maintain price stability. B is not correct because the transmission channels of monetary policy are not independent.

4. MONETARY POLICY OBJECTIVES

> describe qualities of effective central banks; contrast their use of inflation, interest rate, and exchange rate targeting in expansionary or contractionary monetary policy; and describe the limitations of monetary policy

Inflation Targeting

Throughout the 1990s, a consensus began to build among both central bankers and politicians that the best way to control inflation and thereby maintain price stability was to target a certain level of inflation and to ensure that this target was met by monitoring a wide range of monetary, financial, and real economic variables. Today, inflation-targeting frameworks are the cornerstone of monetary policy and macroeconomic policy in many economies. Exhibit 4 shows the growth in the number of inflation-targeting monetary policy regimes over time.

The inflation-targeting framework that is now commonly practiced was pioneered in New Zealand. In 1988, the New Zealand Minister of Finance, Roger Douglas, announced that economic policy would focus on bringing inflation down from the prevailing level of around 6 percent to a target range of 0 to 2 percent. This goal was given legal status by the Reserve Bank of New Zealand Act 1989. As part of the Act, the Reserve Bank of New Zealand (RBNZ) was given the role of pursuing this target. The bank was given **operational independence**; it was free to set interest rates in the way that it thought would best meet the inflation target. Although the RBNZ had independent control of monetary policy, it was still accountable to the government and was charged with communicating its decisions in a clear and transparent way. As Exhibit 4 shows, the New Zealand model was widely copied.

Exhibit 4: The Progressive Adoption of Inflation Targeting by Central Banks

1989	New Zealand			
1990	Chile	Canada		
1991	Israel	United Kingdom		
1992	Sweden	Finland	Australia	
1995	Spain			
1998	Czech Republic	South Korea	Poland	
1999	Mexico	Brazil	Colombia	ECB
2000	South Africa	Thailand		

2001	Iceland	Norway	Hungary	Peru	Philippines
2005	Guatemala	Indonesia	Romania		
2006	Turkey	Serbia			
2007	Ghana				

Note: Spain and Finland later joined the EMU.
Sources: For 2001 and earlier, Truman (2003). For 2002 to 2007, Roger (2010).

Although these inflation-targeting regimes vary a little from economy to economy, their success is thought to depend on three key concepts: central bank independence, credibility, and transparency.

Central Bank Independence

In most cases, the central bank that is charged with targeting inflation has a degree of independence from its government. This independence is thought to be important. It is conceivable that politicians could announce an inflation target and direct the central bank to set interest rates accordingly. Indeed, this was the process adopted in the United Kingdom between 1994 and 1997. But politicians have a constant eye on reelection and might be tempted, for example, to keep rates "too low" in the lead-up to an election in the hope that this might help their reelection prospects. As a consequence, this might lead to higher inflation. Thus, it is now widely believed that monetary policy decisions should rest in the hands of an organization that is remote from the electoral process. The central bank is the natural candidate to be the monopoly supplier of a currency.

However, there are degrees of independence. For example, the head of the central bank is nearly always chosen by government officials. The chair of the US Federal Reserve's Board of Governors is appointed by the president of the United States of America; the head of the ECB is chosen by the committee of Euro area finance ministers; and the governor of the Bank of England is chosen by the chancellor of the exchequer. So, in practice, separating control from political influence completely is probably an impossible (although a desirable) goal.

There are further degrees of independence. Some central banks are both operationally and **target independent**. This means that they not only decide the level of interest rates but also determine the definition of inflation that they target, the rate of inflation that they target, and the horizon over which the target is to be achieved. The ECB has independence of this kind. By contrast, other central banks—including those in New Zealand, Sweden, and the United Kingdom—are tasked to hit a definition and level of inflation determined by the government. Therefore, these central banks are only operationally independent.

Credibility

The independence of the central bank and public confidence in it are key in the design of an inflation-targeting regime.

To illustrate the role of credibility, suppose that instead of the central bank, the government assumes the role of targeting inflation, but the government is heavily indebted. Given that higher inflation reduces the real value of debt, the government would have an incentive to avoid reaching the inflation target or to set a high inflation target such that price stability and confidence in the currency could be endangered. As a result, few would believe the government was really intent on controlling inflation; thus, the government would lack credibility. Many governments have very large levels of debt, especially since the 2008–2009 Global Financial Crisis. In such a situation, economic agents might expect a high level of inflation, regardless of the actual, stated target. The target might have little credibility if the organization's likelihood of sticking to it is in doubt.

If a respected central bank assumes the inflation-targeting role and if economic agents believe that the central bank will hit its target, this belief could become self-fulfilling. If everyone believes that the central bank will hit an inflation target of 2 percent next year, this expectation might be built into wage claims and other nominal contracts that would make it hit the 2 percent target. For this reason, central bankers pay a great deal of attention to inflation expectations. If these expectations were to rise rapidly, perhaps following a rapid increase in oil prices, unchecked expectations could get embedded into wage claims and eventually cause inflation to rise.

Transparency

One way to establish credibility is for a central bank to be transparent in its decision making. Many, if not all, independent inflation-targeting central banks produce a quarterly assessment of their economies. These **inflation reports**, as they are usually known, give central banks' views on the range of indicators that they watch when they come to their (usually) monthly interest rate decision. They will consider and outline their views on the following subjects, usually in this order:

- Broad money aggregates and credit conditions;
- Conditions in financial markets;
- Developments in the real economy (e.g., the labor market); and
- Evolution of prices.

Consideration of all of these important components of an economy is then usually followed by a forecast of growth and inflation over a medium-term horizon, usually two years.

By explaining their views on the economy and by being transparent in decision making, the independent, inflation-targeting central banks seek to gain reputation and credibility, making it easier to influence inflation expectations and hence ultimately easier to meet the inflation target.

The Target

Whether the target is set by the central bank or by the government for the central bank to hit, the level of the target and the horizon over which the target is to be hit is a crucial consideration in all inflation-targeting frameworks.

Exhibit 5: A Range of Inflation Targets

Country/Region	
Australia	Australian Federal Reserve's target is inflation between 2% and 3%.
Canada	Bank of Canada's target is CPI inflation within the 1% to 3% range.
Euro area	ECB's target is CPI inflation close to, but below, a ceiling of 2%.
South Korea	Bank of Korea's target since 2019 has been CPI inflation of 2%.
New Zealand	The Reserve Bank of New Zealand's target is to keep future inflation between 1% and 3% with a focus on the average future inflation rate near 2%.

Country/Region	
Sweden	Riksbank's target is CPI inflation within ±1.0 percentage point of 2%.
United Kingdom	Bank of England's target is CPI inflation within ±1.0 percentage point of 2%.

Note: CPI, consumer price index.
Source: Central bank websites (http://www.bis.org/cbanks.htm).

Exhibit 5 shows that many central banks in developed economies target an inflation rate of 2 percent based on a consumer price index (CPI). Given that the operation of monetary policy is both art and science, the banks are normally allowed a range around the central target of +1 percent or −1 percent. For example, with a 2 percent target, they would be tasked to keep inflation between 1 percent and 3 percent. But why target 2 percent and not 0 percent?

The answer is that aiming to hit 0 percent could result in negative inflation, known as **deflation**. One of the limitations of monetary policy that we will discuss is its ability or inability to deal with periods of deflation. If deflation is something to be avoided, why not target 10 percent? The answer to this question is that levels of inflation that high would not be consistent with price stability; such a high inflation rate would further tend to be associated with high inflation volatility and uncertainty. Central bankers seem to agree that 2 percent is far enough away from the risks of deflation and low enough not to lead to destabilizing inflation shocks.

Finally, we should keep in mind that the headline inflation rate that is announced in most economies every month, and which is the central bank's target, is a measure of how much a basket of goods and services has risen over the previous twelve months. It is history. Furthermore, interest rate changes made today will take some time to have their full effect on the real economy as they make their way through the monetary transmission mechanism. It is for these two reasons that inflation targeters do not target current inflation but instead usually focus on inflation two years ahead.

Although inflation-targeting mandates may vary from country to country, they have common elements: the specification of an explicit inflation target, with permissible bounds, and a requirement that the central bank should be transparent in its objectives and policy actions. This is all usually laid out in legislation that imposes statutory obligations on the central bank. As mentioned earlier, New Zealand pioneered the inflation-targeting approach to monetary policy that has since been copied widely. New Zealand's Policy Targets Agreement, which specifies the inflation-targeting mandate of its central bank, the RBNZ, is included in Example 2.

EXAMPLE 2

New Zealand's Policy Targets Agreement

"This agreement between the Minister of Finance and the Governor of the Reserve Bank of New Zealand (the Bank) is made under section 9 of the Reserve Bank of New Zealand Act 1989 (the Act). The Minister and the Governor agree as follows:

Price stability

a. Under Section 8 of the Act the Reserve Bank is required to conduct monetary policy with the goal of maintaining a stable general level of prices.

b. The Government's economic objective is to promote a growing, open and competitive economy as the best means of delivering permanently higher incomes and living standards for New Zealanders. Price stability plays an important part in supporting this objective.

Policy target

a. In pursuing the objective of a stable general level of prices, the Bank shall monitor prices as measured by a range of price indexes. The price stability target will be defined in terms of the All Groups Consumers Price Index (CPI), as published by Statistics New Zealand.

b. For the purpose of this agreement, the policy target shall be to keep future CPI inflation outcomes between 1 per cent and 3 per cent on average over the medium term.

Inflation variations around target

a. For a variety of reasons, the actual annual rate of CPI inflation will vary around the medium-term trend of inflation, which is the focus of the policy target. Amongst these reasons, there is a range of events whose impact would normally be temporary. Such events include, for example, shifts in the aggregate price level as a result of exceptional movements in the prices of commodities traded in world markets, changes in indirect taxes,[9] significant government policy changes that directly affect prices, or a natural disaster affecting a major part of the economy.

b. When disturbances of the kind described in clause 3(a) arise, the Bank will respond consistent with meeting its medium-term target.

Communication, implementation, and accountability

a. On occasions when the annual rate of inflation is outside the medium-term target range, or when such occasions are projected, the Bank shall explain in Policy Statements made under section 15 of the Act why such outcomes have occurred, or are projected to occur, and what measures it has taken, or proposes to take, to ensure that inflation outcomes remain consistent with the medium-term target.

b. In pursuing its price stability objective, the Bank shall implement monetary policy in a sustainable, consistent, and transparent manner and shall seek to avoid unnecessary instability in output, interest rates and the exchange rate.

c. The Bank shall be fully accountable for its judgments and actions in implementing monetary policy."

Source: Reserve Bank of New Zealand, http://www.rbnz.govt.nz/.

To summarize, an inflation-targeting framework normally has the following features:

- An independent and credible central bank;
- A commitment to transparency;
- A decision-making framework that considers a wide range of economic and financial market indicators; and
- A clear, symmetric, and forward-looking medium-term inflation target, sufficiently above 0 percent to avoid the risk of deflation but low enough to ensure a significant degree of price stability.

Indeed, independence, credibility, and transparency are arguably the crucial ingredients for an effective central bank, whether or not they target inflation.

The Main Exceptions to the Inflation-Targeting Rule

Although the practice of inflation targeting is widespread, two prominent central banks have not adopted a formal inflation target along the lines of the New Zealand model: the Bank of Japan (BoJ) and the US Federal Reserve System.

The Bank of Japan

Japan's central bank, the BoJ, does not target an explicit measure of inflation. Japan's government and its monetary authorities have been trying to combat deflation for much of the past two decades. However, despite their efforts—including the outright printing of money—inflation has remained very weak. Inflation targeting is seen very much as a way of combating and controlling inflation; as such, it would seem to have no place in an economy that suffers from persistent deflation.

Some economists have argued, however, that an inflation target is exactly what the Japanese economy needs. By announcing that positive inflation of say 3 percent is desired by the central bank, this might become a self-fulfilling prophecy if Japanese consumers and companies factor this target into nominal wage and price contracts. But for economic agents to believe that the target will be achieved, they have to believe that the central bank is capable of achieving it. Given that the BoJ has failed to engineer persistent, positive inflation, it is debatable how much credibility Japanese households and corporations would afford such an inflation-targeting policy.

The US Federal Reserve System

It is perhaps rather ironic that the world's most influential central bank, the US Federal Reserve, which controls the supply of the world's de facto reserve currency, the US dollar, does not have an explicit inflation target. However, it is felt that the single-minded pursuit of inflation might not be compatible with the Fed's statutory goal as laid out in the Federal Reserve Act, which charges the Fed's board to: "promote effectively the goals of maximum employment, stable prices, and moderate long-term interest rates."

In other words, it has been argued that inflation targeting might compromise the goal of "maximum employment." In practice, however, the Fed has indicated that it sees core inflation measured by the personal consumption expenditure (PCE) deflator of about, or just below, 2 percent as being compatible with "stable prices." Financial markets therefore watch this US inflation gauge very carefully to anticipate the rate actions of the Fed.

Monetary Policy in Developing Countries

Developing economies often face significant impediments to the successful operation of any monetary policy—that is, the achievement of price stability. These include:

- the absence of a sufficiently liquid government bond market and developed interbank market through which monetary policy can be conducted;
- a rapidly changing economy, making it difficult to understand what the neutral rate might be and what the equilibrium relationship between monetary aggregates and the real economy might be;
- rapid financial innovation that frequently changes the definition of the money supply;
- a poor track record in controlling inflation in the past, making monetary policy intentions less credible; and

- an unwillingness of governments to grant genuine independence to the central bank.

Taken together, any or all of these impediments might call into question the effectiveness of any developing economy's monetary policy framework, making any related monetary policy goals difficult to achieve.

QUESTION SET

1. The reason some inflation-targeting banks may target low inflation and not zero percent inflation is *best* described by which of the following statements?

   A. Some inflation is viewed as being good for an economy.

   B. It is very difficult to eliminate all inflation from a modern economy.

   C. Targeting zero percent inflation runs a higher risk of a deflationary outcome.

   Solution:

   C is correct. Inflation targeting is art, not science. Sometimes inflation will be above target and sometimes below. Were central banks to target zero percent, then inflation would almost certainly be negative on some occasions. If a deflationary mindset then sets in among economic agents, it might be difficult for the central bank to respond to this because they cannot cut interest rates much below zero.

2. The degree of credibility that a central bank is afforded by economic agents is important because:

   A. they are the lender of last resort.

   B. they set targets that can become self-fulfilling prophecies.

   C. they are the monopolistic suppliers of the currency.

   Solution:

   B is correct. If a central bank operates within an inflation-targeting regime and if economic agents believe that it will achieve its target, this expectation will become embedded into wage negotiations, for example, and become a self-fulfilling prophecy. Also, banks need to be confident that the central bank will lend them money when all other sources are closed to them; otherwise, they might curtail their lending drastically, leading to a commensurate reduction in money and economic activity.

3. A central bank that decides the desired levels of interest rates and inflation and the horizon over which the inflation objective is to be achieved is *most* accurately described as being:

   A. target independent and operationally independent.

   B. target independent but not operationally independent.

   C. operationally independent but not target independent.

   Solution:

   A is correct. The central bank described is target independent because it set its own targets (e.g., the target inflation rate) and operationally independent because it decides how to achieve its targets (e.g., the time horizon).

Exchange Rate Targeting

Many developing economies choose to operate monetary policy by targeting their currency's exchange rate, rather than an explicit level of domestic inflation. Such targeting involves setting a fixed level or band of values for the exchange rate against a major currency, with the central bank supporting the target by buying and selling the national currency in foreign exchange markets. There are recent examples of developed economies using such an approach. In the 1980s, following the failure of its policy of trying to control UK inflation by setting medium-term goals for money supply growth, the UK government decided to operate monetary policy such that the sterling's exchange rate equaled a predetermined value in terms of German deutschemarks. The basic idea is that by tying a domestic economy's currency to that of an economy with a credible policy of maintaining low inflation, the domestic economy would effectively "import" the inflation experience of the low-inflation economy.

Suppose that a developing country wished to maintain the value of its currency against the US dollar. The government or central bank would announce the currency exchange rate that they wished to target. To simplify matters, let us assume that the domestic inflation rates are very similar in both countries and that the monetary authorities of the developing economy have set an exchange rate target that is consistent with relative price levels in the two economies. Under these (admittedly unlikely) circumstances, in the absence of shocks, there would be no reason for the exchange rate to deviate significantly from this target level. As long as domestic inflation closely mirrors US inflation, the exchange rate should remain close to its target (or within a target band). It is in this sense that a successful exchange rate policy imports the inflation of the foreign economy.

Now suppose that economic activity in the developing economy starts to rise rapidly and that domestic inflation in the developing economy rises above the level in the United States. With a freely floating exchange rate regime, the currency of the developing economy would start to fall against the dollar. To arrest this fall, and to protect the exchange rate target, the developing economy's monetary authority sells foreign currency reserves and buys its own currency. This has the effect of reducing the domestic money supply and increasing short-term interest rates. The developing economy experiences a monetary policy tightening that, if expected to bring down inflation, will cause its exchange rate to rise against the dollar.

By contrast, in a scenario in which inflation in the developing country fell relative to the United States, the central bank would need to sell the domestic currency to support the target, tending to increase the domestic money supply and reduce the rate of interest.

In practice, the interventions of the developing economy central bank will simply stabilize the value of its currency, with many frequent adjustments. But this simplistic example should demonstrate one very important fact: *When the central bank or monetary authority chooses to target an exchange rate, interest rates and conditions in the domestic economy must adapt to accommodate this target and domestic interest rates and money supply can become more volatile.*

The monetary authority's commitment to and ability to support the exchange rate target must be credible for exchange rate targeting to be successful. If that is not the case, then speculators may trade against the monetary authority. Speculative attacks forced sterling out of the European Exchange Rate Mechanism in 1992. The fixed exchange rate regime was abandoned, and the United Kingdom allowed its currency to float freely. Eventually, the UK government adopted a formal inflation target in 1997. Similarly, in the Asian financial crisis of 1997–1998, Thailand's central bank tried to defend the Thai baht against speculative attacks for much of the first half of 1997 but then revealed at the beginning of July that it had no reserves left. The subsequent devaluation triggered a debt crisis for banks and companies that had borrowed in foreign currency, and contagion spread throughout Asia.

Despite these risks, many currencies are pegged to other currencies, most notably the US dollar. Exhibit 6 shows a list of some of the currencies that were pegged to (fixed against) the US dollar at the end of 2018. Other currencies operate under a "managed exchange rate policy," where they are allowed to fluctuate within a range that is maintained by a monetary authority through market intervention. Dollarization occurs when a country adopts the US dollar as their functional currency. This is stronger than pegging to the dollar because under dollarization, the US dollar replaces the previous national currency. Exhibit 6 breaks out countries that peg their currency to the dollar and those that have adopted the US dollar as their currency.

Exhibit 6: Select Currencies Pegged to the US Dollar, as of December 2018

Pegged to USD

- Bermuda
- Bahamas
- Lebanon
- Hong Kong SAR
- Saudi Arabia
- Qatar
- United Arab Emirates

Dollarized

- Panama (1904)
- Ecuador (2000)
- East Timor (2001)
- El Salvador (2000)
- Caribbean Netherlands (2011)

QUESTION SET

1. When the central bank chooses to target a specific value for its exchange rate:
    - **A.** it must also target domestic inflation.
    - **B.** it must also set targets for broad money growth.
    - **C.** conditions in the domestic economy must adapt to accommodate this target.

   Solution:

   C is correct. The adoption of an exchange rate target requires that the central bank set interest rates to achieve this target. If the target comes under pressure, domestic interest rates may have to rise, regardless of domestic conditions. It may have a "target" level of inflation in mind as well as "targets" for broad money growth, but as long as it targets the exchange rate, domestic inflation and broad money trends must simply be allowed to evolve.

2. With regard to monetary policy, what is the expected benefit of adopting an exchange rate target?
    - **A.** Freedom to pursue redistributive fiscal policy
    - **B.** Freedom to set interest rates according to domestic conditions

> C. Ability to "import" the inflation experience of the economy whose currency is being targeted
>
> **Solution:**
>
> C is correct. Note that interest rates have to be set to achieve this target and are therefore subordinate to the exchange rate target and partially dependent on economic conditions in the foreign economy.
>
> 3. Which of the following is *least* likely to be an impediment to the successful implementation of monetary policy in developing economies?
>
>   A. Fiscal deficits
>   B. Rapid financial innovation
>   C. Absence of a liquid government bond market
>
>   **Solution:**
>
>   A is correct. Note that the absence of a liquid government bond market through which a central bank can enact open market operations and/or repo transactions will inhibit the implementation of monetary policy—as would rapid financial innovation because such innovation can change the relationship between money and economic activity. In contrast, fiscal deficits are not normally an impediment to the implementation of monetary policy, although they could be if they were perceived to be unsustainable.
>
> 4. A country that maintains a target exchange rate is *most likely* to have which outcome when its inflation rate rises above the level of the inflation rate in the target country?
>
>   A. Increase in short-term interest rates
>   B. Increase in the domestic money supply
>   C. Increase in its foreign currency reserves
>
>   **Solution:**
>
>   A is correct. Interest rates are expected to rise to protect the exchange rate target.

Contractionary and Expansionary Monetary Policies and Their Limitations

Most central banks will adjust liquidity conditions by adjusting their official policy rate. When they believe that economic activity is likely to lead to an increase in inflation, they might increase interest rates, thereby reducing liquidity. In these cases, market analysts describe such actions as **contractionary** because the policy is designed to cause the rate of growth of the money supply and the real economy to contract (see Exhibit 3 for the possible transmission mechanism). Conversely, when the economy is slowing and inflation and monetary trends are weakening, central banks may increase liquidity by cutting their target rate. In these circumstances, monetary policy is said to be **expansionary**.

Thus, when policy rates are high, monetary policy may be described as contractionary; when low, it may be described as expansionary. But what are they "high" and "low" in comparison to?

The **neutral rate of interest** is often taken as the point of comparison. One way of characterizing the neutral rate is to say that it is that rate of interest that neither spurs on nor slows down the underlying economy. As such, when policy rates are above the neutral rate, monetary policy is contractionary; when they are below the neutral rate, monetary policy is expansionary. The neutral rate should correspond to the average policy rate over a business cycle.

However, economists' views of the neutral rate for any given economy might differ, and therefore, their view of whether monetary policy is contractionary, neutral, or expansionary might differ too. What economists do agree on is that the neutral policy rate for any economy has two components:

- Real trend rate of growth of the underlying economy, and
- Long-run expected inflation.

The real trend rate of growth of an economy is also difficult to discern, but it corresponds to that rate of economic growth that is achievable in the long run that gives rise to stable inflation. If we are thinking about an economy with a credible inflation-targeting regime, where the inflation target is, say, 2 percent per year and where an analyst believes that the economy can grow sustainably over the long term at a rate of 2.5 percent per year, then they might also estimate the neutral rate to be:

Neutral rate = Trend growth + Inflation target = 2.5% + 2.0% = 4.5%

The analyst would therefore describe the central bank's monetary policy as being contractionary when its policy rate is above 4.5 percent and expansionary when it is below this level.

In practice, central banks often indicate what they believe to be the neutral rate of interest for their economy too. But determining this "neutral rate" is more art than science. For example, many analysts have recently revised down their estimates of trend growth for many western countries following the collapse of the credit bubble, because in many cases, the governments and private individuals of these economies are now being forced to reduce consumption levels and pay down their debts.

What's the Source of the Shock to the Inflation Rate?

An important aspect of monetary policy for those charged with its conduct is the determination of the source of any shock to the inflation rate. Suppose that the monetary authority sees that inflation is rising beyond its target, or simply in a way that threatens price stability. If this rise was caused by an increase in the confidence of consumers and business leaders, which in turn has led to increases in consumption and investment growth rates, then we could think of it as being a **demand shock**. In this instance, it might be appropriate to tighten monetary policy to bring the inflationary pressures generated by these domestic demand pressures under control.

However, suppose instead that the rise in inflation was caused by a rise in the price of oil (for the sake of argument). In this case, the economy is facing a **supply shock**, and raising interest rates might make a bad situation worse. Consumers are already facing an increase in the cost of fuel prices that might cause profits and consumption to fall and eventually unemployment to rise. Putting up interest rates in this instance might simply exacerbate the oil price-induced downturn, which ultimately might cause inflation to fall sharply.

It is important, then, for the monetary authority to try to identify the source of the shock before engineering a contractionary or expansionary monetary policy phase.

Limitations of Monetary Policy

The limitations of monetary policy include problems in the transmission mechanism and the relative ineffectiveness of interest rate adjustment as a policy tool in deflationary environments.

Problems in the Monetary Transmission Mechanism

In Exhibit 3, we presented a stylized representation of the monetary policy transmission mechanism, including the channels of bank lending rates, asset prices, expectations, and exchange rates. The implication of the diagram is that there are channels through which the actions of the central bank or monetary authority are transmitted to both the nominal and real economy. In some occasions, however, the will of the monetary authority is not transmitted seamlessly through the economy.

Suppose that a central bank raises interest rates because it is concerned about the strength of underlying inflationary pressures. Long-term interest rates are influenced by the path of expected short-term interest rates, so the outcome of the rate hike will depend on market expectations. Suppose that bond market participants think that short-term rates are already too high, that the monetary authorities are risking a recession, and that the central bank will likely undershoot its inflation target. This fall in inflation expectations could cause long-term interest rates to fall. That would make long-term borrowing cheaper for companies and households, which could in turn stimulate economic activity rather than cause it to contract.

Arguably, the more credible the monetary authority, the more stable the long end of the yield curve; moreover, the monetary authority will be more confident that its "policy message" will be transmitted throughout the economy. A term recently used in the marketplace is **bond market vigilantes**. These "vigilantes" are bond market participants who might reduce their demand for long-term bonds, thus pushing up their yields, if they believe that the monetary authority is losing its grip on inflation. That yield increase could act as a brake on any loose monetary policy stance. Conversely, the vigilantes may push long-term rates down by increasing their demand for long-dated government bonds if they expect that tight monetary policy is likely to cause a sharp slowdown in the economy, thereby loosening monetary conditions for long-term borrowers in the economy.

A credible monetary policy framework and authority will tend not to require the vigilantes to do the work for it.

In very extreme instances, there may be occasions in which the demand for money becomes infinitely elastic—that is, where the demand curve is horizontal and individuals are willing to hold additional money balances without any change in the interest rate—so that further injections of money into the economy will not serve to further lower interest rates or affect real activity. This is known as a **liquidity trap**. In this extreme circumstance, monetary policy can become completely ineffective. The economic conditions for a liquidity trap are associated with the phenomenon of deflation.

Interest Rate Adjustment in a Deflationary Environment and Quantitative Easing as a Response

Deflation is a pervasive and persistent fall in a general price index and is more difficult for conventional monetary policy to deal with than inflation. This is because cutting nominal interest rates much below zero to stimulate the economy is difficult. For example, policy interest rates were cut below zero in several European countries in 2014 and subsequently in Japan in 2016. At this point, the economic conditions for a liquidity trap arise.

Deflation raises the real value of debt, while the persistent fall in prices can encourage consumers to put off consumption today, leading to a fall in demand that leads to further deflationary pressure. Thus a deflationary "trap" can develop, which is characterized by weak consumption growth, falling prices, and increases in real debt levels. Japan eventually found itself in such a position following the collapse of its property bubble in the early 1990s.

If conventional monetary policy—the adjustment of short-term interest rates—is no longer capable of stimulating the economy once the zero or even negative nominal interest rate bound has been reached, is monetary policy useless?

In the aftermath of the collapse of the high-tech bubble in November 2002, Federal Reserve Governor Ben Bernanke gave a speech entitled "Deflation: Making Sure 'It' Doesn't Happen Here." In this speech, Bernanke stated that inflation was always and everywhere a monetary phenomenon, and he expressed great confidence that by expanding the money supply by various means (including dropping it out of a helicopter on the population below), the Federal Reserve as the sole supplier of money could always engineer positive inflation in the US economy. He said:

> I am confident that the Fed would take whatever means necessary to prevent significant deflation in the United States and, moreover, that the US central bank, in cooperation with other parts of the government as needed, has sufficient policy instruments to ensure that any deflation that might occur would be both mild and brief.

Following the 2008–2009 Global Financial Crisis, a number of governments along with their central banks cut rates to (near) zero, including those in the United States and the United Kingdom. However, there was concern that the underlying economies might not respond to this drastic monetary medicine, mainly because the related banking crisis had caused banks to reduce their lending drastically. To kick-start the process, both the Federal Reserve and the Bank of England effectively printed money and pumped it into their respective economies. This "unconventional" approach to monetary policy, known as **quantitative easing** (QE), is operationally similar to open market purchase operations but is conducted on a much larger scale.

The additional reserves created by central banks in a policy of quantitative easing can be used to buy any assets. The Bank of England chose to buy **gilts** (bonds issued by the UK government), where the focus was on gilts with three to five years maturity. The idea was that this additional reserve would kick-start lending, causing broad money growth to expand, which would eventually lead to an increase in real economic activity. But there is no guarantee that banks will respond in this way. In a difficult economic climate, it may be better to hold excess reserves rather than to lend to households and businesses that may default.

In the United States, the formal plan for QE mainly involved the purchase of mortgage bonds issued or guaranteed by Freddie Mac and Fannie Mae. Part of the intention was to push down mortgage rates to support the US housing market, as well as to increase the growth rate of broad money. Before implementing this formal program, the Federal Reserve intervened in several other markets that were failing for lack of liquidity, including interbank markets and the commercial paper market. These interventions had a similar effect on the Federal Reserve's balance sheet and the money supply as the later QE program.

This first round of QE by the Federal Reserve was then followed by another round of QE, known as QE2. In November 2010, the Federal Reserve judged that the US economy had not responded sufficiently to the first round of QE (QE1). The Fed announced that it would create $600 billion and use this money to purchase long-dated US Treasuries in equal tranches over the following eight months. The purpose of QE2 was to ensure that long bond yields remained low to encourage businesses and households to borrow for investment and consumption purposes, respectively.

The final round of QE, known as QE3, was implemented in September 2012 to provide $40 billion per month to purchase agency mortgage-backed securities "until the labor market improved substantially." QE3 lasted until December 2013, when the Federal Reserve announced it was tapering back on these purchases. These purchases, and quantitative easing, ended 10 months later in October 2014.

Monetary Policy Objectives

As long as central banks have the appropriate authority from the government, they can purchase any assets in a quantitative easing program. But the risks involved in purchasing assets with credit risk should be clear. In the end, the central bank is just a special bank. If it accumulates bad assets that then turn out to create losses, it could face a fatal loss of confidence in its main product: fiat money.

Limitations of Monetary Policy: Summary

The ultimate problem for monetary authorities as they try to manipulate the supply of money to influence the real economy is that they cannot control the amount of money that households and corporations put in banks on deposit, nor can they easily control the willingness of banks to create money by expanding credit. Taken together, this also means that they cannot always control the money supply. Therefore, there are definite limits to the power of monetary policy.

EXAMPLE 3

The Limits of Monetary Policy: The Case of Japan

The Background

Between the 1950s and 1980s, Japan's economy achieved faster real growth than any other G–7 economy. But the terrific success of the economy sowed the seeds of the problems that were to follow. The very high real growth rates achieved by Japan over four decades became built into asset prices, particularly equity and commercial property prices. Toward the end of the 1980s, asset prices rose to even higher levels when the BoJ followed a very easy monetary policy as it tried to prevent the Japanese yen from appreciating too much against the US dollar. However, when interest rates went up in 1989–1990 and the economy slowed, investors eventually came to believe that the growth assumptions that were built into asset prices and other aspects of the Japanese economy were unrealistic. This realization caused Japanese asset prices to collapse. For example, the Nikkei 225 stock market index reached 38,915 in 1989; by the end of March 2003, it had fallen by 80 percent to 7,972. The collapse in asset prices caused wealth to decline dramatically. Consumer confidence understandably fell sharply too, and consumption growth slowed. Corporate spending also fell, while bank lending contracted sharply in the weak economic climate. Although many of these phenomena are apparent in all recessions, the situation was made worse when deflation set in. In an environment when prices are falling, consumers may put off discretionary spending today until tomorrow; by doing this, however, they exacerbate the deflationary environment. Deflation also raises the real value of debts; as deflation takes hold, borrowers find the real value of their debts rising and may try to increase their savings accordingly. Once again, such actions exacerbate the recessionary conditions.

The Monetary Policy Response

Faced with such a downturn, the conventional monetary policy response is to cut interest rates to try to stimulate real economic activity. The Japanese central bank, the BoJ, cut rates from 8 percent in 1990 to 1 percent by 1996. By February 2001, the Japanese policy rate was cut to zero where it stayed.

Once rates are at or near zero, there are two broad approaches suggested by theory, though the two are usually complementary. First, the central bank can try to convince markets that interest rates will remain low for a long time, even after the economy and inflation pick up. This will tend to lower interest rates along the yield curve. Second, the central bank can try to increase the money supply by purchasing assets from the private sector, so-called quantitative easing. The BoJ did both in 2001. It embarked on a program of quantitative easing supplemented by an explicit promise not to raise short-term interest rates until deflation had given way to inflation.

Quantitative easing simply involves the printing of money by the central bank. In practice, this involved the BoJ using open market operations to add reserves to the banking system through the direct purchase of government securities in the open market.

The reserve levels became the new target. The BoJ's monetary policy committee determined the level of reserves and the quantity of bond purchases that should be undertaken, rather than voting on the policy rate.

The success of this policy is difficult to judge. As Exhibit 7 shows, although deflation turned to inflation for a while, it returned to deflation in 2008–2009 when the Japanese economy suffered a sharp recession along with much of the rest of the world. At that time, having reversed its QE policy during 2004–2008 by reducing its bond holdings, the BoJ began to buy again.

The BoJ ramped up its asset purchases starting in 2013, when other central banks began to unwind their QE programs. At the beginning of 2013, BoJ Assets to Japanese GDP were approximately 30 percent, but rose to more than 170 percent in 2020. Economists debate the point, but arguably, even the BoJ's much larger program of QE has not been able to eliminate deflation. The Japanese experience suggests that there may be limits to the power of monetary policy.

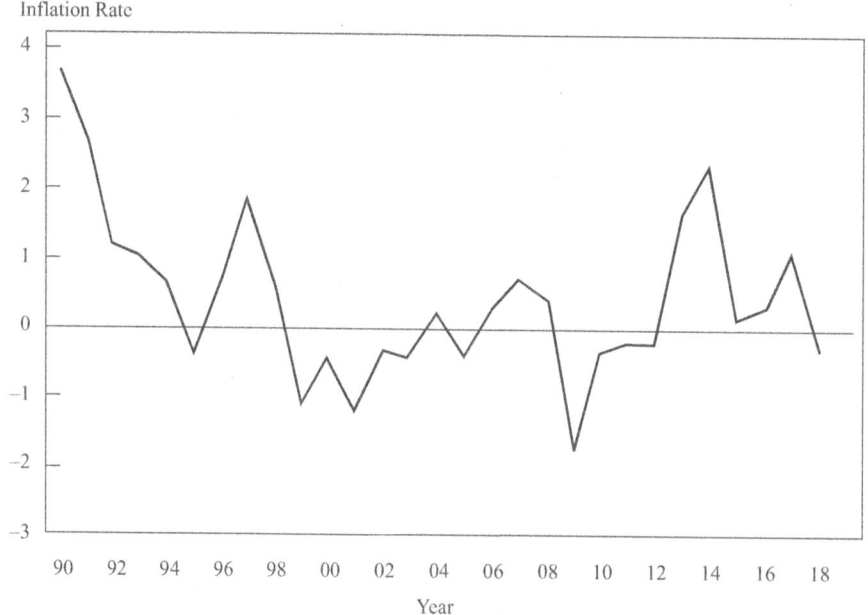

Exhibit 7: Inflation and Deflation in Japan

Source: "Japan Annual and Monthly Inflation Tables," StatBureau, www.statbureau.org/en/japan/inflation-tables.

Monetary Policy Objectives

QUESTION SET

1. If an economy's trend GDP growth rate is 3 percent and its central bank has a 2 percent inflation target, which policy rate is *most consistent* with an expansionary monetary policy?

   A. 4 percent
   B. 5 percent
   C. 6 percent

   Solution:

   A is correct. The neutral rate of interest, which in this example is 5 percent, is considered to be that rate of interest that neither spurs on nor slows down the underlying economy. As such, when policy rates are above the neutral rate, monetary policy is contractionary; when they are below the neutral rate, monetary policy is expansionary. It has two components: the real trend rate of growth of the underlying economy (in this example, 3 percent) and long-run expected inflation (in this example, 2 percent).

2. An increase in a central bank's policy rate might be expected to reduce inflationary pressures by:

   A. reducing consumer demand.
   B. reducing the foreign exchange value of the currency.
   C. driving up asset prices leading to an increase in personal sector wealth.

   Solution:

   A is correct. If an increase in the central bank's policy rate is successfully transmitted through the money markets to other parts of the financial sector, consumer demand might decline as the rate of interest on mortgages and other credit rises. This decline in consumer demand should, all other things being equal and among other affects, lead to a reduction in upward pressure on consumer prices.

3. Which of the following statements *best* describes a fundamental limitation of monetary policy? Monetary policy is limited because central bankers:

   A. cannot control the inflation rate perfectly.
   B. are appointed by politicians and are therefore never truly independent.
   C. cannot control the amount of money that economic agents put in banks, nor the willingness of banks to make loans.

   Solution:

   C is correct. Central bankers do not control the decisions of individuals and banks that can influence the money creation process.

4. In theory, setting the policy rate equal to the neutral interest rate should promote:

   A. stable inflation.
   B. balanced budgets.

> C. greater employment.
>
> **Solution:**
>
> A is correct. The neutral rate of interest is that rate of interest that neither stimulates nor slows down the underlying economy. The neutral rate should be consistent with stable long-run inflation.

5. INTERACTION OF MONETARY AND FISCAL POLICY

☐ explain the interaction of monetary and fiscal policy

The Relationship Between Monetary and Fiscal Policy

Both monetary and fiscal policies can be used to try to influence the macroeconomy. But the impact of monetary policy on aggregate demand may differ depending on the fiscal policy stance. Conversely, the impact of fiscal policy might vary under various alternative monetary policy conditions. Clearly, policy makers need to understand this interaction. For example, they need to consider the impact of changes to the budget when monetary policy is accommodative as opposed to when it is restrictive: Can we expect the same impact on aggregate demand in both situations?

Although both fiscal and monetary policy can alter aggregate demand, they do so through differing channels with differing impact on the composition of aggregate demand. The two policies are not interchangeable. Consider the following cases in which the assumption is made that *wages and prices are rigid*:

- *Easy fiscal policy/tight monetary policy*: If taxes are cut or government spending rises, the expansionary fiscal policy will lead to a rise in aggregate output. If this is accompanied by a reduction in money supply to offset the fiscal expansion, then interest rates will rise and have a negative effect on private sector demand. We have higher output and higher interest rates, and government spending will be a larger proportion of overall national income.

- *Tight fiscal policy/easy monetary policy*: If a fiscal contraction is accompanied by expansionary monetary policy and low interest rates, then the private sector will be stimulated and will rise as a share of GDP, while the public sector will shrink.

- *Easy monetary policy/easy fiscal policy*: If both fiscal and monetary policy are easy, then the joint impact will be highly expansionary—leading to a rise in aggregate demand, lower interest rates (at least if the monetary impact is larger), and growing private and public sectors.

- *Tight monetary policy/tight fiscal policy*: Interest rates rise (at least if the monetary impact on interest rates is larger) and reduce private demand. At the same time, higher taxes and falling government spending lead to a drop in aggregate demand from both public and private sectors.

Factors Influencing the Mix of Fiscal and Monetary Policy

Although governments are concerned about stabilizing the level of aggregate demand at close to the full employment level, they are also concerned with the growth of potential output. To this end, encouraging private investment will be important. It may best be achieved by accommodative monetary policy with low interest rates and a tight fiscal policy to ensure free resources for a growing private sector.

At other times, the lack of a good quality, trained workforce—or perhaps a modern capital infrastructure—will be seen as an impediment to growth; thus, an expansion in government spending in these areas may be seen as a high priority. If taxes are not raised to pay for this, then the fiscal stance will be expansionary. If a loose monetary policy is chosen to accompany this expansionary spending, then it is *possible* that inflation may be induced. Of course, it is an open question as to whether policy makers can judge the appropriate levels of interest rates or fiscal spending levels.

Clearly, the mix of policies will be heavily influenced by the political context. A weak government may raise spending to accommodate the demands of competing vested interests (e.g., subsidies to particular sectors, such as agriculture in the EU), and thus a restrictive monetary policy may be needed to hold back the possibly inflationary growth in aggregate demand through raised interest rates and less credit availability.

Both fiscal and monetary policies suffer from the lack of precise knowledge of where the economy is today, because data initially appear to be subject to revision and to have a time lag. However, fiscal policy suffers from two further issues with regard to its use in the short run.

As we saw earlier, it is difficult to implement quickly because spending on capital projects takes time to plan, procure, and put into practice. In addition, it is politically easier to loosen fiscal policy than to tighten it; in many cases, automatic stabilizers are the source of fiscal tightening, because tax rates are not changing and political opposition is muted. Similarly, the independence of many central banks means that decisions on raising interest rates are outside the hands of politicians and thus can be taken more easily.

The interaction between monetary and fiscal policies was implicit in our discussion of Ricardian equivalence because if tax cuts have no impact on private spending as individuals anticipate future higher taxes, then clearly this may lead policy makers to favor monetary tools.

Ultimately, the interaction of monetary and fiscal policies in practice is an empirical question, which we also touched on earlier. In their detailed research paper using the International Monetary Fund's (IMF'S) Global Integrated Monetary and Fiscal Model, IMF researchers examined four forms of coordinated global fiscal loosening over a two-year period, which will be reversed gradually after the two years are completed. These are:

- an increase in social transfers to all households,
- a decrease in tax on labor income,
- a rise in government investment expenditure, and
- a rise in transfers to the poorest in society.

The two types of monetary policy responses considered are:

- no monetary accommodation, so rising aggregate demand leads to higher interest rates immediately; or
- interest rates are kept unchanged (accommodative policy) for the two years.

The following important policy conclusions from this study emphasize the role of policy interactions:

- *No monetary accommodation*: Government spending increases have a much bigger effect (six times bigger) on GDP than similar size social transfers because the latter are not considered to be permanent, although real interest rates rise as monetary authorities react to rises in aggregate demand and inflation. Targeted social transfers to the poorest citizens have double the effect of the non-targeted transfers, while labor tax reductions have a slightly bigger impact than the latter.

- *Monetary accommodation:* Except for the case of the cut in labor taxes, fiscal multipliers are now much larger than when there is no monetary accommodation. The cumulative multiplier (i.e., the cumulative effect on real GDP over the two years divided by the percentage of GDP, which is a fiscal stimulus) is now 3.9 for government expenditure compared with 1.6 with no monetary accommodation. The corresponding numbers for targeted social transfer payments are 0.5 without monetary accommodation and 1.7 with it. The larger multiplier effects with monetary accommodation result from rises in aggregate demand and inflation, leading to falls in real interest rates and additional private sector spending (e.g., on investment goods). Labor tax cuts are less positive.

Quantitative Easing and Policy Interaction

What about the scenario of zero interest rates and deflation? Fiscal stimulus should still raise demand and inflation, lowering real interest rates and stimulating private sector demand. We saw earlier that quantitative easing was a feature of major economies following the 2008–2009 Global Financial Crisis. This involved the purchase of government or private securities by the central bank from individuals, institutions, or banks and substituting central bank balances for those securities. The ultimate aim was for recipients to subsequently increase expenditures, lending or borrowing in the face of raised cash balances and lower interest rates.

If the central bank purchases government securities on a large scale, it is effectively funding the budget deficit and the independence of monetary policy is an illusion. This so-called printing of money is feared by many economists as the monetization of the government deficit. Note that it is unrelated to the conventional inflation target of central banks, such as the Bank of England. Some economists question whether an independent central bank should engage in such activity.

The Importance of Credibility and Commitment

The IMF model implies that if governments run persistently high budget deficits, real interest rates rise and crowd out private investment, reducing each country's productive potential. As individuals realize that deficits will persist, inflation expectations and long-term interest rates rise: This reduces the effect of the stimulus by half.

Further, if there is a real lack of commitment to fiscal discipline over the longer term, (e.g., because of aging populations) and the ratio of government debt to GDP rose by 10 percentage points permanently in the United States alone, then world real interest rates would rise by 0.14 percent—leading to a 0.6 percent permanent fall in world GDP.

Interaction of Monetary and Fiscal Policy

QUESTION SET

1. In a world in which Ricardian equivalence holds, governments would *most likely* prefer to use monetary rather than fiscal policy because under Ricardian equivalence:

   A. real interest rates have a more powerful effect on the real economy.

   B. the transmission mechanism of monetary policy is better understood.

   C. the future impact of fiscal policy changes are fully discounted by economic agents.

   Solution:

   C is correct. If Ricardian equivalence holds, then economic agents anticipate that the consequence of any current tax cut will be future tax rises, which leads them to increase their saving in anticipation of this so that the tax cut has little effect on consumption and investment decisions. Governments would be forced to use monetary policy to affect the real economy on the assumption that money neutrality did not hold in the short term.

2. If fiscal policy is easy and monetary policy tight, then:

   A. interest rates would tend to fall, reinforcing the fiscal policy stance.

   B. the government sector would tend to shrink as a proportion of total GDP.

   C. the government sector would tend to expand as a proportion of total GDP.

   Solution:

   C is correct. With a tight monetary policy, real interest rates should rise and reduce private sector activity, which could be at least partially offset by an expansion in government activity via the loosening of fiscal policy. The net effect, however, would be an expansion in the size of the public sector relative to the private sector.

3. Which of the following has the greatest impact on aggregate demand according to an IMF study? 1 percent of GDP stimulus in:

   A. government spending

   B. rise in transfer benefits

   C. cut in labor income tax across all income levels

   Solution:

   A is correct. The study clearly showed that direct spending by the government leads to a larger impact on GDP than changes in taxes or benefits.

4. Given an independent central bank, monetary policy actions are *more likely* than fiscal policy actions to be:

   A. implementable quickly.

   B. effective when a specific group is targeted.

   C. effective when combating a deflationary economy.

   Solution:

   A is correct. Monetary actions may face fewer delays to taking action than fiscal policy, especially when the central bank is independent.

5. Which policy alternative is *most likely* to be effective for growing both the public and private sectors?

   A. Easy fiscal/easy monetary policy
   B. Easy fiscal/tight monetary policy
   C. Tight fiscal/tight monetary policy

   Solution:

   A is correct. If both fiscal and monetary policies are "easy," then the joint impact will be highly expansionary, leading to a rise in aggregate demand, low interest rates, and growing private and public sectors.

PRACTICE PROBLEMS

1. When a central bank announces a decrease in its official policy rate, the desired impact is an increase in:

   A. investment.

   B. interbank borrowing rates.

   C. the national currency's value in exchange for other currencies.

2. Which action is a central bank *least likely* to take if it wants to encourage businesses and households to borrow for investment and consumption purposes?

   A. Sell long-dated government securities

   B. Purchase long-dated government treasuries

   C. Purchase mortgage bonds or other securities

3. A central bank's repeated open market purchases of government bonds:

   A. decreases the money supply.

   B. is prohibited in most countries.

   C. is consistent with an expansionary monetary policy.

4. A prolonged period of an official interest rate very close to zero without an increase in economic growth *most likely* suggests:

   A. quantitative easing must be limited to be successful.

   B. the effectiveness of monetary policy may be limited.

   C. targeting reserve levels is more important than targeting interest rates.

5. Raising the reserve requirement is *most likely* an example of which type of monetary policy?

   A. Neutral

   B. Expansionary

   C. Contractionary

6. Which of the following is a limitation on the ability of central banks to stimulate growth in periods of deflation?

   A. Ricardian equivalence

   B. Interaction of monetary and fiscal policy

   C. Interest rates cannot fall significantly below zero

7. The *least likely* limitation to the effectiveness of monetary policy is that central banks cannot:
   accurately determine the neutral rate of interest.

A. regulate the willingness of financial institutions to lend.

B. control amounts that economic agents deposit into banks.

8. Quantitative easing, the purchase of government or private securities by the central banks from individuals or institutions, is an example of which monetary policy stance?

A. Neutral

B. Expansionary

C. Contractionary

SOLUTIONS

1. A is correct. Investment is expected to move inversely with the official policy rate.

2. A is correct. Such action would tend to constrict the money supply and increase interest rates, all else being equal.

3. C is correct. The purchase of government bonds through open market operations increases banking reserves and the money supply; it is consistent with an expansionary monetary policy.

4. B is correct. A central bank would decrease an official interest rate to stimulate the economy. The setting in which an official interest rate is lowered to zero (or even slightly below zero) without stimulating economic growth suggests that there are limits to monetary policy.

5. C is correct. Raising reserve requirements should slow money supply growth.

6. C is correct. Deflation poses a challenge to conventional monetary policy because once the central bank has cut nominal interest rates to zero (or slightly less than zero) to stimulate the economy, they cannot cut them further.

7. A is correct. The inability to determine exactly the neutral rate of interest does not necessarily limit the power of monetary policy.

8. B is correct. Quantitative easing is an example of an expansionary monetary policy stance. It attempts to spur aggregate demand by drastically increasing the money supply.

LEARNING MODULE 5

Introduction to Geopolitics

by Goodwin Lauren, Nair-Reichert Usha, PhD, and Witschi Daniel Rober, PhD.

Lauren Goodwin, CFA, is at New York Life Investments (USA). Usha Nair-Reichert, PhD, is at Georgia Institute of Technology (USA). Daniel Robert Witschi, PhD, CFA, is at Dreyfus Sons & Co Ltd. (Switzerland).

LEARNING OUTCOMES	
Mastery	The candidate should be able to:
☐	describe geopolitics from a cooperation versus competition perspective
☐	describe geopolitics and its relationship with globalization
☐	describe functions and objectives of the international organizations that facilitate trade, including the World Bank, the International Monetary Fund, and the World Trade Organization
☐	describe geopolitical risk
☐	describe tools of geopolitics and their impact on regions and economies
☐	describe the impact of geopolitical risk on investments

INTRODUCTION

Investors study geopolitics and geopolitical risk because they can have a material impact on investment outcomes. These relations affect key drivers of investment performance, including economic growth, business performance, market volatility, and transaction costs. On a portfolio level, geopolitical risk can affect the suitability of a security or strategy for an investor's goals, risk tolerance, and time horizon. In this learning module, we will build a framework by which investors can measure, assess, track, and react to geopolitical risk, with a goal of improving investment outcomes.

LEARNING MODULE OVERVIEW

- Geopolitics is the study of how geography affects politics and international relations. Within the field of geopolitics, analysts study actors—the individuals, organizations, companies, and national governments that carry out political, economic, and financial activities—and how they interact with one another.

- State actors can be cooperative or non-cooperative. A country may want to cooperate with its neighbors or with other state actors for many reasons. These reasons are typically defined by a country's national interest—its goals and ambitions—whether they be military, economic, or cultural.

- The cooperation and engagement among countries is also affected by its resource endowment, standardization of the rules of engagement, and cultural factors and soft power.

- A country's national interest can be viewed as a hierarchy of factors, with those essential for survival at the top of the hierarchy and nice-but-not-essential elements lower in the hierarchy. Governments use the hierarchy of interests to guide their behavior.

- Political cooperation versus non-cooperation is only one lens through which geopolitical actors engage with the world, but it is an important one for understanding countries' priorities.

- Globalization is marked by economic and financial cooperation, including the active trade of goods and services, capital flows, currency exchange, and cultural and information exchange. By contrast, antiglobalization or nationalism is the promotion of a country's own economic interests to the exclusion or detriment of the interests of other nations. Nationalism is marked by limited economic and financial cooperation.

- Globalization provides potential gains, such as:
  - increased profits—through increasing sales and/or reducing costs,
  - access to resources—market access and investment opportunities, and
  - intrinsic gains—an improved quality of life.

- Globalization also has some potential drawbacks, such as:
  - unequal economic and financial gains,
  - interdependence that can lead to supply chain disruption, and
  - possible exploitation of social and environmental resources.

- The International Monetary Fund's (IMF's) main mandate is to ensure the stability of the international monetary system, the system of exchange rates and international payments that enables countries to buy goods and services from each other.

- The World Bank's main objective is to help developing countries fight poverty and enhance environmentally sound economic growth.

- The World Trade Organization (WTO) provides the legal and institutional foundation of the multinational trading system. It regulates cross-border trade relationships among nations on a global scale.

Introduction

- A geopolitical framework for analysis includes four archetypes of country behavior: autarky, hegemony, multilateralism, and bilateralism. Each archetype has its own costs, benefits, and trade-offs with respect to geopolitical risk.

- Geopolitical risk is the risk associated with tensions or actions between actors (state and non-state) that affect the normal and peaceful course of international relations. Geopolitical risk tends to rise when the geographic and political factors underpinning country relations shift.

- The tools of geopolitics may be separated into the following three types:

  - national security tools,
  - economic tools, and
  - financial tools.

- The most extreme example of a national security tool is that of armed conflict. Espionage is an indirect national security tool. Military alliances are often used either to aid in direct conflict or to deter conflict from arising in the first place.

- Economic tools are used to reinforce a cooperative or non-cooperative stance through economic means. Among state actors, economic tools can include multilateral trade agreements or the global harmonization of tariff rules. Economic tools also can be non-cooperative in nature. Nationalization is a non-cooperative approach to asserting economic control.

- Financial tools are the actions used to reinforce a cooperative or non-cooperative stance through financial mechanisms. Examples of cooperative financial tools include the free exchange of currencies across borders and allowing foreign investment. Examples of non-cooperative financial tools include limiting access to local currency markets and restricting foreign investment.

- There are three basic types of geopolitical risk:

  - event risk,
  - exogenous risk, and
  - thematic risk.

- Event risk evolves around set dates known in advance. Political events, for example, often result in changes to investor expectations related to a country's cooperative stance. Brexit is an example of event risk.

- Exogenous risk is a sudden or unanticipated risk that can affect either a country's cooperative stance, the ability of non-state actors to globalize, or both. Examples include sudden uprisings, invasions, or the aftermath of natural disasters.

- Thematic risks are known risks that evolve and expand over time. Climate change, cyber threats, and the ongoing threat of terrorism fall into this category.

- To make an assessment, an investor considers geopolitical risk in terms of the following three areas:

  - likelihood it will occur,

- velocity (speed) of its impact, and
- size and nature of that impact.
- Geopolitical risks seldom develop in linear fashion, making it difficult to monitor and forecast their likelihood, velocity, and size and nature of impact on a portfolio. As a result, many investors deploy an approach that includes scenario building and signposting rather than a single point forecast.
- Investors study geopolitical risk because it has a tangible impact on investment outcomes. On a macroeconomic level, these risks can affect capital markets conditions, such as economic growth, interest rates, and market volatility.
- Changes in capital markets conditions can have an important influence on asset allocation decisions, including an investor's choice of geographic exposures.
- On a portfolio level, geopolitical risk can influence the appropriateness of an investment security or strategy for an investor's goals, risk tolerance, and time horizon.

2. NATIONAL GOVERNMENTS AND POLITICAL COOPERATION

☐ describe geopolitics from a cooperation versus competition perspective

The international environment is constantly evolving. Such trends as the growth of emerging market economies, globalization, and the rise of populism affect the range of opportunities and threats that companies, industries, nations, and regional groups face. **Geopolitics** is the study of how geography affects politics and international relations. Within the field of geopolitics, analysts study actors—the individuals, organizations, companies, and national governments that carry out political, economic, and financial activities—and how they interact with one another. The role of state and non-state actors is discussed in the following section.

State and Non-State Actors

Relationships within and among countries can be complex. To begin, many actors influence international relations, political developments, and economic affairs. In the introduction, we defined actors as the individuals, organizations, companies, and national governments that carry out political, economic, and financial activities. This definition can be divided into two types of actors relevant for geopolitical risk: state actors and non-state actors. **State actors** are typically national governments, political organizations, or country leaders that exert authority over a country's national security and resources. The South African president, sultan of Brunei, Malaysia's parliament, and the British Prime minister are all examples of state actors. **Non-state actors** are those that participate in global political, economic, or financial affairs but do not directly control national security or country resources. Examples of non-state actors are non-governmental organizations (NGOs), multinational companies, charities, and even influential individuals, such as business leaders or cultural icons.

These actors are influenced not only by their relationship with one another but also by factors affecting their other allies and adversaries. For example, if Country A has a cooperative relationship with Country B but Country B attacks Country C, a close ally of Country A, then the relationship between Countries A and B may become strained or even broken. The opposite is also true: A country's cooperation across many political, economic, or financial channels may increase trust over time. As a result, the international system is composed of multifaceted webs of affairs that can shape events and decisions as well as economic and market outcomes. Although a "one-size-fits-all" model does not exist for geopolitical actors, understanding and categorizing the threats and opportunities that a country faces may help us to gauge the likelihood that geopolitical risk will arise.

Countries and their governments are heavily influenced by economic, financial, and national security considerations as well as by social and cultural factors and non-state actors. In fact, economic and financial considerations are inextricably linked with a country's national interest and political dynamic. That said, it is useful to isolate one of these areas—national actors and political cooperation—as a starting point in understanding actors' interwoven goals and the way they may affect geopolitical risk. In the next section, we will develop a sense of state actors and their motivations for cooperation (versus non-cooperation) before adding layers of geopolitical risk analysis.

Features of Political Cooperation

At the highest level, relations between countries or national governments (state actors) can be cooperative or competitive in nature. **Cooperation** is the process by which countries work together toward some shared goal or purpose. These goals may, and often do, vary widely—from strategic or military concerns to economic influence or cultural preferences. Given the expansive nature of country goals and interests, their interactions with one another also may be complex, generating the potential for geopolitical risk to arise.

We begin that framework by exploring one specific type of cooperation—political cooperation—which is the degree to which countries work toward agreements on rules and standardization for the activities and interactions between them. Within this context, a **cooperative country** is one that engages and reciprocates in rules standardization; harmonization of tariffs; and international agreements on trade, immigration, or regulation and that also allows for the free flow of information, including technology transfer. In contrast, a **non-cooperative country** is one with inconsistent and even arbitrary rules; restricted movement of goods, services, people, and capital across borders; retaliation; and limited technology exchange. We show the degree of political cooperation in Exhibit 1

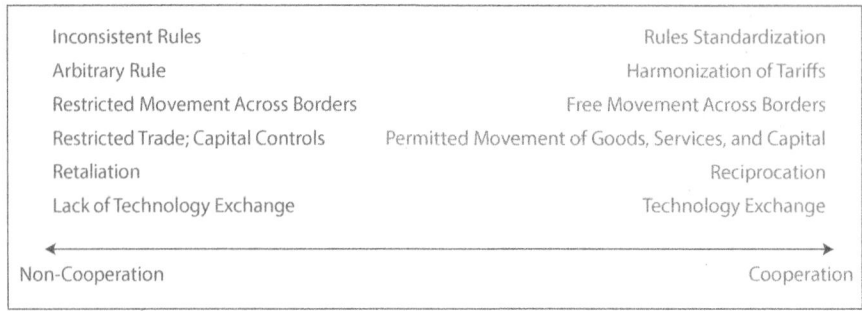

Exhibit 1: Political Cooperation and Non-Cooperation

Inconsistent Rules	Rules Standardization
Arbitrary Rule	Harmonization of Tariffs
Restricted Movement Across Borders	Free Movement Across Borders
Restricted Trade; Capital Controls	Permitted Movement of Goods, Services, and Capital
Retaliation	Reciprocation
Lack of Technology Exchange	Technology Exchange

Non-Cooperation ←——————————————→ Cooperation

A country may want to cooperate with its neighbors or with other state actors for many reasons. These reasons are typically defined by a country's national interest—its goals and ambitions—whether they be military, economic, or cultural.

National Security or Military Interest

National security or national defense involves protecting a country, including its citizens, economy, and institutions, from external threat. These threats may be broad in nature—from military attacks and terrorism, to crime, cybersecurity, and even natural disasters.

Geographic factors play an important role in shaping a country's approach to national security and the extent to which it will choose a cooperative approach. Landlocked countries, such as Switzerland, rely extensively on their neighbors for access to vital resources. This reliance may make cooperation more important for sustaining international access and growth or even for survival. By the same token, countries highly connected to trade routes, such as Singapore, or countries acting as a conduit for trade, such as Panama, may use their geographic location as a lever of power in broader international dynamics.

Economic Interest

Over time, the concept of national security has expanded to include economic factors, including access to such resources as energy, food, or water. On a domestic level, growing national wealth and limiting income inequality can contribute to social stability, another important component of national security. On the international level, the ability of national firms to operate on a global scale is increasingly important as well. In this context, countries that cooperate in support of their economic interest are likely focused on one of two factors: Either they would like to secure essential resources through trade, or they would like to level the global playing field for their companies or industries through standardization.

EXAMPLE 1

Factors Affecting Cooperation

1. True or false: Geographic factors do not influence the extent to which a country will choose a cooperative approach. Explain your reasoning.

    A. True

B. False

Solution:

B is correct. Geographic factors play an important role in shaping a country's approach to national security and the extent to which it will choose a cooperative approach. A country with limited access to resources because of its geographic characteristics might be more inclined to cooperate as it needs access to resources to thrive, whereas a country rich in internal resources might use its resources as leverage to influence international dynamics. Countries with direct access to the sea have an advantage related to trade and transport as well as the natural resources provided by the ocean.

EXAMPLE 2

Factors Affecting Cooperation

1. Fill in the blank: Two factors on which a cooperative country is likely focused include____ and___.

   Solution:

   Two factors on which a cooperative country is likely focused include *trade* and *standardization*.

Resource Endowment, Standardization, and Soft Power

The cooperation and engagement among countries is also affected by its resource endowment, standardization of the rules of engagement, and cultural factors and soft power. These factors are examined in the section that follows.

Geophysical Resource Endowment

At a basic level, **geophysical resource endowment** includes such factors as livable geography and climate as well as access to food and water, which are necessary for sustainable growth. Geophysical resource endowment is highly unequal among countries. Some countries, such as the United States, Russia, Australia, and China, are relatively self-sufficient in their resource use. Others, such as Western Europe, Japan, and Turkey, are highly reliant on others for key factors of production, such as fossil fuels. Still others, such as Saudi Arabia, have a plentiful endowment of fossil fuels but rely on others for many basic needs.

These different starting points create power dynamics that can affect the terms of engagement between states. A country heavily endowed with a resource may find itself with more political leverage when dealing with another country in desperate need of that resource. At the same time, a resource-rich country may become vulnerable if the use or sale of the resource benefits certain groups more than others, therefore contributing to internal political instability.

Standardization

Economic and financial activities may cross borders with or without explicit government support. As they do, governments have more incentive to cooperate with others in standardizing the rules of engagement. **Standardization** is the process of creating protocols for the production, sale, transport, or use of a product or service. Standardization occurs when relevant parties agree to follow these protocols together. It helps support expanded economic and financial activities across borders, such as trade and capital flows, which support higher economic growth and standards of living. Rules standardization can take many forms—from regulatory cooperation, to process standardization, to operational synchronization. Rules standardization may also be driven by non-state entities, such as industry groups or organizations. Exhibit 2 provides examples of standardization.

Exhibit 2: Types of Rules Standardization

	Regulatory Cooperation	Process Standardization	Operational Synchronization
Challenge	As financial cooperation expands, countries need a comprehensive standard for governance and risk management of the banking sector.	Financial transactions across borders faced higher costs and longer wait times, increasing the burden for cross-border activity.	Increasing international trade created supply chain bottlenecks as containers of different sizes and shapes were sent to ports worldwide.
Solution	Basel Committee on Banking Supervision (BCBS)	Society for Worldwide Interbank Financial Telecommunication (SWIFT)	Containerization
Process	The BCBS was established in 1974 by the G–10 banking authorities. Membership has since expanded to the G–20.	SWIFT was established in 1973 to provide a global financial infrastructure.	Standards set for containers of uniform size and shape using multimodal forms of transport (land, sea, air, rail) and port cranes.
Benefit	Allows for more effective supervision of the global banking sector and international capital flows.	Facilitates global payments in more than 200 countries and territories, servicing more than 11,000 institutions worldwide.	Dramatically reduces the time and cost of shipping goods.

Cultural Considerations and Soft Power

Finally, countries may have cultural reasons for cooperating with others. These could be historical in nature, such as long-standing political ties, immigration patterns, shared experiences, or cultural similarities. In other cases, countries may engage in **soft power**, a means of influencing another country's decisions without force or coercion. Soft power can be built over time through such actions as cultural programs, advertisement, travel grants, and university exchange. For example, the European Union (EU) Erasmus+ program provides funding for exchange programs in education and sport to drive social inclusion and participation between participants from different countries and also to promote such priority policies as the EU's green and digital transitions. In another example, countries like South Korea advertise visiting Seoul, the country's capital city, in subway systems globally. These advertisements use popular Korean-made products, musical acts, and actors to encourage interaction with Korean culture and business.

The Role of Institutions

An **institution** is an established organization or practice in a society or culture. An institution can be a formal structure, such as a university, organization, or process backed by law; or, it can be informal, such as customs or behavioral patterns important to a society. Institutions can, but need not be, formed by national governments. Examples of institutions include NGOs, charities, religious customs, family units, the media, political parties, and educational practice.

National Governments and Political Cooperation

Generally, strong institutions contribute to more stable internal and external political forces. That consistency, in turn, gives a country more opportunity to develop cooperative relationships. Countries with strong institutions—including organizations and structures promoting government accountability, rule of law, and property rights—allow them to act with more authority and independence in the international space. Stronger institutions also make cooperative relationships more durable. By integrating a cooperative relationship in multiple layers of society, strong institutions can reduce the likelihood that a country defects from its cooperative roles.

Hierarchy of Interests and Costs of Cooperation

The national interest of a country is its set of goals and ambitions. For some countries, national interest is viewed primarily in geospatial terms—the need for self-determination, survival as a nation state, the need for clear national borders, or expansion of the nation state. For others, national interest incorporates a wide array of interrelated factors, including the economic and social considerations discussed earlier. This broad approach can create conflicts among a country's many important needs, which complicates the assessment of geopolitical actors and their motivations.

We can think of a country's national interest as a hierarchy of factors, with those essential for survival at the top of the hierarchy and nice-but-not-essential elements lower in the hierarchy. Governments use the hierarchy of interests to guide their behavior. They will choose to cooperate where it benefits the nation-state, but when two needs result in conflicting cooperation tactics, those higher on the hierarchy are prioritized. For example, cooperation in the form of tariff harmonization may benefit the country on a stand-alone basis; however, if those countries are in a military conflict, then there is a higher cost to cooperation. In this case, if military determination is higher on the countries' hierarchies, then cooperation may not be in their national interest, despite the potential benefits.

Exhibit 3 shows how countries prioritize their hierarchy of interests. Every country has different resources, goals, and leadership and thus different priorities, as well. In the exhibit, Country A prioritizes access to food and water. In contrast, Country B, prioritizes independence from foreign influence. Additionally, these priorities may shift as political leadership turns over or as global events change. For investors, it is important to understand how these resources, goals, and leadership styles may interact or even conflict with one another over time. When countries' goals misalign or change, it may give rise to geopolitical risk.

Exhibit 3: Hierarchy of Interests

Highest Priority

Example: Country A	Example: Country B	Example: Country C
Access to Food and Water	Independence from Foreign Influence	Economic Stability
Border Security	Government Dominance over Population	Equal Access to Resources Such as Food and Education for all Citizens
Economic Influence	Cultural Homogeneity	
Cultural Ties with Other Countries	Growing Personal or Family Wealth	Regular Transition of Power via Elections

Lowest Priority

Power of the Decision Maker

Some elements on the hierarchy of national interests may appear clear-cut; securing access to food and water may take precedence over funding a cultural program, for example. However, as basic societal needs are met, the hierarchy of national interests can become more subjective. One government may treat the prioritization of some interests—such as military buildup or providing health care—very differently from its predecessor. How governments weigh those issues will determine the depth and nature of political cooperation.

The length of a country's political cycle has an important impact on priority designation. Many countries have political cycles of just a few years, which means that long-term risks like climate change or addressing income inequality can be difficult to prioritize against projects or goals that can be achieved in a short-term horizon. Intrinsic in this reality is that governmental decision makers, whether political parties or individuals, have their own set of influences and needs. Although we will not explore this idea in depth, it is important to acknowledge that, for the purpose of geopolitical risk analysis, decision makers' motivations can affect a country's cooperative and non-cooperative choices. This introduces a factor of psychology and non-predictability into choices along the hierarchy of a nation's needs that can shape geopolitical relationships.

> **EXAMPLE 3**
>
> ### Country's Political Cycle
>
> 1. True or false: The length of a country's political cycle does not affect its priority designation.
>
>   Explain your reasoning.
>
>   **A.** True
>
>   **B.** False
>
> **Solution:**
>
> B is correct. The length of a country's political cycle has an important impact on priority designation as governments with shorter cycles have little incentive to focus on longer-term priorities, even if those priorities would be beneficial for society. Australia, for example, has shorter than average parliamentary terms, which could potentially affect governmental priorities.

Political Non-Cooperation

We consider political cooperation and non-cooperation as existing along a spectrum. While it is in some countries' interest to be highly politically cooperative, for others it is less essential. Over time, most countries cooperate on standardized rules on an international scale. In some instances of extreme non-cooperation, however, countries' political self-determination is more important than the benefits of any cooperative actions. These extreme cases are rare, not least because the importance of cooperation for other state actors may result in attempts to coerce non-cooperative state actors into participation.

National Governments and Political Cooperation

INTERNATIONAL SANCTIONS AGAINST VENEZUELA (2015–)

The United States has had concerns about Venezuelan narcotics trafficking since 2005 and Venezuela's lack of cooperation in combatting terrorism since 2006. With support from Congress and in response to increasing political repression in Venezuela, US President Obama levied additional sanctions for human rights abuses, corruption, and antidemocratic actions. The European Union urged Venezuelan officials to work toward political reconciliation but ultimately joined the United States in targeted sanctions to encourage a credible and meaningful process toward re-starting cooperation.

Throughout this time, sanctions have included targeted restrictions on Venezuelan officials, blocking financial transactions, and an embargo on the oil sector, which is highly important to the country's economy. Some politicians continue to support economic sanctions as a means to pressure the Venezuelan government to meet international standards on human rights and political cooperation. Others are concerned about the increasing humanitarian cost of those sanctions.

Venezuela's non-cooperative stance in the international arena has resulted in it being subject to substantial international sanctions. Imposing sanctions is in itself a non-cooperative approach by the United States and the European Union meant to influence the behavior of a country or its political leadership. Venezuela's non-cooperative stance indicates that its political self-determination is a priority above that of the humanitarian cost being inflicted on its citizens.

Political cooperation versus non-cooperation is only one lens through which geopolitical actors engage with the world, but it is an important one for understanding countries' priorities. Assessing a state actor's hierarchy of needs and how it may change may help us to understand its motivations and priorities. These factors affect not only countries' political and military actions but also their willingness to support economic and financial cooperation, which we will explore next.

QUESTION SET

1. Which of these is likely lowest on a country's hierarchy of interests?

   A. Tariff harmonization

   B. Military determination

   C. Cultural program development

   Solution:

   C is correct. Cultural program development is likely lowest on a country's hierarchy of interests. Military determination (B) is often a primary source of national security and key to a country's national interest. Tariff harmonization (A) may improve economic activity and improve cooperation. Cultural programs are important and influential but likely lower priority compared with A and B.

2. Which of the following actions by a country is *most likely* a form of geopolitical cooperation?

   A. Acting as a conduit for trade

   B. Engaging in rules standardization

C. Opting to use soft power over military retaliation

Solution:

B is correct. Political cooperation is associated with anything related to agreements of rules and standardization, with countries working together toward some shared goal. A cooperative country is one that engages and reciprocates in rules standardization. A is incorrect because acting as a conduit of trade, like Panama, involves non-cooperatively using a country's geographic location as a lever of power in broader international dynamics. C is incorrect because both soft power and military retaliation are examples of non-cooperative behavior, with the former being a less extreme means to influence another country's decisions without force or coercion.

3. Which of the following statements represents an aspect of geopolitical risk?

   A. Modeling geopolitical risk is relatively easy to standardize.

   B. An engaged country can be considered cooperative, even if it does not reciprocate.

   C. The strength of a country's institutions is relevant to the durability of its cooperative relationships.

Solution:

C is correct. The strength of a country's institutions can make cooperative relationships more durable. A is incorrect because modeling geopolitical risk is not easily standardized. B is incorrect because a cooperative country is one that is both engaged and reciprocates.

3   FORCES OF GLOBALIZATION

☐ describe geopolitics and its relationship with globalization

Globalization is the process of interaction and integration among people, companies, and governments worldwide. It is marked by the spread of products, information, jobs, and culture across borders. Indeed, the spread of goods and services across borders has been increasing for decades. The World Bank Openness Index, a key measure of globalization, has risen from 27 percent in 1970 to more than 60 percent in 2019, as shown in Exhibit 4. Since 2008, globalization has experienced headwinds; these include the impact of the Global Financial Crisis, which increased scrutiny of cross-border activity, and the rise in nationalism, which decreased some countries' appetite for using imported products or services. Capacity constraints may also create an important headwind. Global trade cannot make up 100 percent of global economic activity, meaning its expansion may slow even without specific disruptions.

Exhibit 4: Global Trade as Percentage of GDP

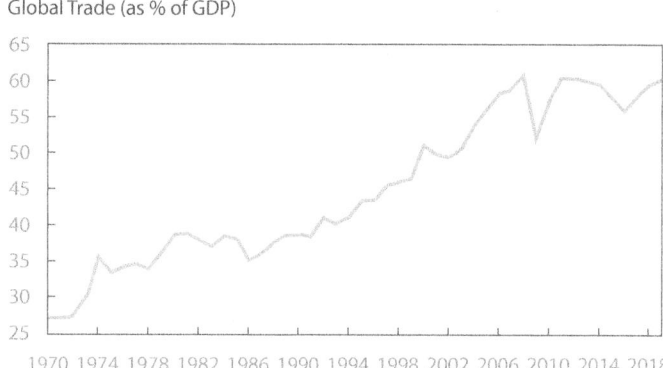

Source: World Bank Open Data, World Bank, https://data.worldbank.org. Trade is defined as imports plus exports in the global economy.

In addition to its macroeconomic impact, globalization is also visible at a microeconomic level. Take, for example, the production of an automobile. A car may be designed in Japan, with electrical parts made in Germany, steering systems designed in the United States, seatbelts manufactured in Sweden, climate system made in Belgium, and vehicles assembled in Mexico. In fact, automobiles are often assembled in one country with parts from all over the world, finished in a second country, and sold in a third (see Exhibit 5). This extensive process provides opportunities for companies to find the best inputs for their product, whether in terms of quality or cost-effectiveness. The process of globalization also opens opportunities for investors worldwide, who may invest in aspects of engineering, production, or even the process of supply chain management and logistics.

Exhibit 5: Production of Automobiles

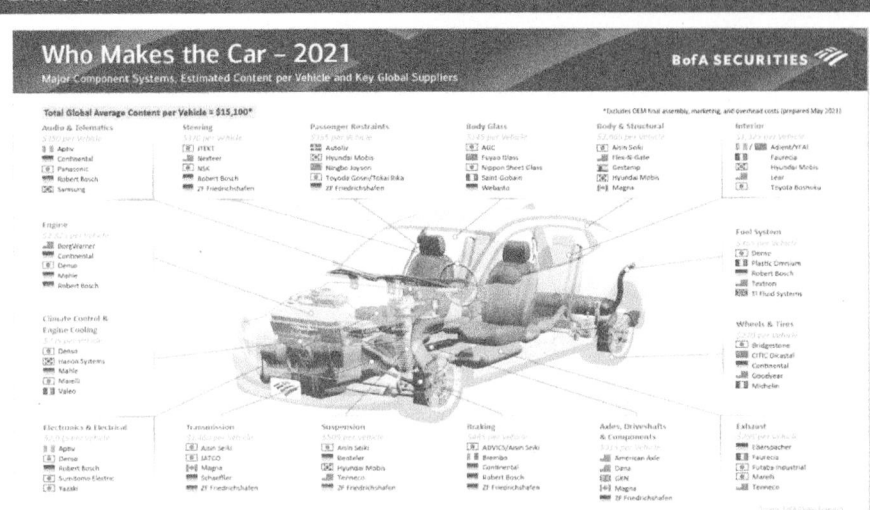

Notes: Reprinted with permission. Copyright © 2021 Bank of America Corporation ("BAC"). The use of the above in no way implies that BAC or any of its affiliates endorses the views or interpretation or the use of such information or acts as any endorsement of the use of such information. The information is provided "as is" and none of BAC or any of its affiliates warrants the accuracy or completeness of the information.

Source: Bank of America Merrill Lynch Global Research.

Globalization also has cultural and communicative features. Although it can be difficult to measure these features, such as the spread of information or culture, it is not difficult to see them in our daily lives. A grocery store in Warsaw may hold Italian cheese, Moroccan spices, Colombian coffee, and Indian sauces. Social media allows users in South Africa to collaborate on dances with a Japanese music group. Faster and more affordable travel has increased interactions between citizens of countries all over the world. Internet usage allows for the near-instantaneous spread of cultural information and context.

Features of Globalization

In the previous section, we considered political cooperation and non-cooperation as one lens through which to consider geopolitical actors—primarily national or state actors. Globalization, by contrast, is the result of economic and financial cooperation. It is carried out mostly by non-state actors, such as corporations, individuals, or organizations.

Globalization is marked by economic and financial cooperation, including the active trade of goods and services, capital flows, currency exchange, and cultural and information exchange. Actors participating in globalization are likely to reach beyond their national borders for access to new markets, talent, or learning. In contrast, anti-globalization or **nationalism** is the promotion of a country's own economic interests to the exclusion or detriment of the interests of other nations. Nationalism is marked by limited economic and financial cooperation. These actors may focus on national production and sales, limited cross-border investment and capital flows, and restricted currency exchange. Exhibit 6 shows a continuum from nationalism to globalization.

Forces of Globalization

Exhibit 6: Globalization: Economic and Financial Cooperation

Globalization and cooperation tend to be correlated, meaning that globalization can be facilitated or accelerated by political cooperation, but globalization is also an independent process. Organic private sector forces can drive the exchange of products or ideas even without government support or harmonized rules.

EXAMPLE 4

Features of Globalization

1. Fill in the blanks using the following words: *government*; *private sector*; *national*; *subnational*.

   Although political cooperation and non-cooperation can be driven by _____ actors, globalization as the result of economic and financial cooperation is carried out mostly by _____ actors, such as corporations, individuals, or organizations. Organic _____ forces can drive the exchange of products or ideas even without _____ support.fill-in-the-blank

   Solution:

   Although political cooperation and non-cooperation can be driven by *national* actors, globalization as the result of economic and financial cooperation is carried out mostly by *subnational* actors, such as corporations, individuals, or organizations. Organic *private* sector forces can drive the exchange of products or ideas even without *government* support.

EXAMPLE 5

Features of Globalization

1. True or False: Globalization is primarily carried out by governmental actors.

   Explain your reasoning.

   A. True

B. False

Solution:

B is correct. Globalization is primarily carried out by non-governmental actors, such as corporations, individuals, or organizations, and is the result of economic and financial cooperation. Multinational corporations, for example, want a competitive advantage leading them to seek new markets, talent, and learning as well as trade, capital, currency, and cultural and information exchange. Corporate outsourcing of talent is an example of globalization.

Motivations for Globalization

Non-state actors, such as companies and investors, who choose to participate in globalization consider three potential gains:

- Increasing profits
- Access to resources and markets
- Intrinsic gain

Increasing Profits

Profit can be increased by two means: increasing sales or reducing costs.

Increasing sales

The opportunity to generate higher profits may motivate companies to globalize. The first way to generate profit is to increase sales. Companies may choose to engage in globalization in order to access new customers for their goods and services. This process may require extensive investment, including acquiring or building property, plant, and equipment in the local market. It may also require hiring workers in new markets and offering training directly benefiting the countries involved.

Reducing costs

Another way to increase profits is to reduce costs. Globalization allows companies to access lower tax-operating environments, reduce labor costs, or seek other supply chain efficiency gains, all of which are cost-reduction measures. Of course, increasing sales and reducing costs can be closely intertwined. The consolidation of the global automobile industry is one instructive example. For capital-intensive production processes, companies experience economies of scale, reducing average costs, by producing more. By consolidating, automakers can benefit from a global sales opportunity while reducing costs per auto sold.

Access to Resources and Markets

In "Motivations for Globalization," we described the economic interest countries may have to cooperate, including access to resources. The same may be true of non-state actors, such as companies, seeking sustainable access to resources, such as talent or raw materials. If those resources are not readily available or affordable in the home country, then the non-state actor may globalize to improve access.

A non-state actor may also seek market access or investment opportunities abroad. For example, a country experiencing low domestic market returns and increasing wealth may experience a higher propensity to accept cross-border risk—a catalyst for seeking returns abroad. For investment professionals, there are two important types of flows. **Portfolio investment flows** are short-term investments in foreign assets, such as stocks or bonds. Alternatively, **foreign direct investments (FDI)** are long-term investments in the productive capacity of a foreign country. These concepts will be covered in more detail elsewhere in the curriculum.

As appetite for cross-border investment has increased, such globalizing actors as companies and organizations (i.e., industry groups, NGOs, or charitable organizations), have established processes for facilitating those needs, including foreign exchange, accounting services, and global investment management services. This globalizing force, while an independent one, has been facilitated and strengthened over time by the harmonization of foreign exchange markets and investment practices.

Intrinsic Gain

Intrinsic gain is a side effect or consequence of an activity that generates a benefit beyond profit itself. It is difficult to measure but contributes to globalization's momentum. It can also be a stabilizing force, increasing empathy between actors and reducing the likelihood that a geopolitical threat is levied. One example of intrinsic gain is the personal growth or education that individuals may receive from expanding their horizons, experiencing new places, or learning new ideas. Another example is accelerated productivity from learning new methods.

Regardless of the motivation for globalization—profit driven or intrinsically driven—these processes and investments can have multiplicative effects. As globalization deepens, companies develop standards and processes to incorporate multiple cultures into their overall corporate culture. They must cooperate with multiple sets of rules, and they may establish standard procedures based on the groups of companies in which they operate.

While these factors provide important motivating forces for globalization, they are not the only benefits of globalization. The process of reducing barriers between global businesses and organization can also provide aggregate economic benefits, such as increased choice, higher quality goods, increased competition among firms, higher efficiency, and increased labor mobility.

Costs of Globalization and Threats of Rollback

While globalization provides many benefits, costs also may be associated with it for individual economies or sectors, depending on how it is implemented. Some of the potential disadvantages of globalization are discussed in the following sections.

Unequal Accrual of Economic and Financial Gains

Economic theory tells us that aggregate economic activity is improved when all actors seek profit maximization and efficiency. However, improvement on the aggregate does not mean improvement for everyone. If a company moves a factory to another country, it creates jobs in the new country but reduces them at home, while firms in the new country may have to compete with the foreign firm for labor. Some actors will benefit from this exchange, but others may suffer.

Lower Environmental, Social, and Governance Standards

Companies operating in lower-cost countries often operate in the local standards of those countries. If standards on environmental protection, social benefits, or corporate governance are lower in one country compared with another, and companies ultimately reduce their standards of production in that context, then globalization can create a drain on human, administrative, and environmental resources. The more measurable corporate profit factor may show a gain, but the overall effect of that activity may be negative. For example, many European countries have stricter standards on carbon emissions than those elsewhere in the world. Imagine that a European-based company decides to produce in a different country with lighter environmental regulations and cheaper labor costs. If the company decides to act according to local standards rather than its home country standards, it may make more profit but reduce environmental quality.

Political Consequences

These two costs can create a third cost of globalization: the political consequences of global expansion. While some individuals may enjoy global exposure, others may fear it. While some countries may benefit from improved labor force utilization, others may lose jobs as a company moves abroad. Therefore, globalization can contribute to income and wealth inequality, as well as differences in opportunity, within and between countries. These dynamics can manifest in countries' local politics, resulting in a force not only for reduced political and economic cooperation but also for a rollback in political cooperation.

Interdependence

Through the process of greater economic and financial cooperation, companies may become dependent on other countries' resources for their supply chains. On aggregate, this can result in the nation becoming dependent on other nations for certain resources. If there is a disruption to the supply chain, including through a moment of political non-cooperation, then firms may not be able to produce the good themselves. Commodities production illustrates this potential risk. Rare earth metals, used for light-emitting diode (LED) lights and most electronic displays, are largely produced in China. Copper, essential for renewable energy construction, is largely produced in Chile. Disruptions to production in these countries, including mining accidents or floods, can disrupt entire industries relying on those resources.

> **THE COVID-19 PANDEMIC AND SUPPLY CHAIN SHORTAGES**
>
> The COVID-19 pandemic, which began in late 2019 and reached global impact in 2020, provides an interesting example of how geopolitical disruptions can impact companies' supply chains and countries' access to important resources. In the early months of 2020, many countries enforced stay-at-home orders in hopes of protecting their citizens against the pandemic's spread. As a result, demand for many goods and services collapsed and manufacturing activity was restricted, resulting in a significant slowdown in production of many goods and services. Even as production resumed, the impact of production slowdown had ripple effects across industries.
>
> Semiconductors were one such product. Semiconductor production is highly concentrated in China and is very important to the automobile industry. The chips are used for fuel-pressure sensors, navigation displays, and speedometers, among other automotive devices. Gradually, as the pandemic wore on, mobility began to improve, but supply remained constrained. The result was a severe shortage of semiconductor supply, which contributed to high and rising prices for new, used, and rental automobiles in many countries across the world. This dependence of a global industry on one country's production illustrates how interconnected supply chains can create important financial risks. Additionally, the effects of the semiconductor shortage soon moved beyond the automobile industry, as other industrial players struggled to secure chips for their devices.

> The experience of the COVID-19 pandemic built upon preexisting challenges to global supply chain management. Supply disruptions revealed the pitfalls of overreliance on any single production location. Corporates found their supply chains were fragile as inputs sourced from foreign countries became unavailable or manufacturing moved offshore suddenly fell victim to lockdown orders.

Threats of Rollback of Globalization

The threat of deglobalization has grabbed headlines since 2018 when the Trump administration began a series of "America first" policies. Rooted in nationalism, isolationism, and concerns for national and economic security, trade wars escalated in fits and starts for several years. Targets evolved to include not only countries traditionally seen as US competitors but also long-standing allies, such as the European Union, through tariffs on imported products, and Canada and Mexico, through a renegotiation of the North America Free Trade Agreement now known as the U.S.-Mexico-Canada Agreement (USMCA). These developments have led investors and policy makers to consider whether globalization is reversing and what it means for the path of geopolitical risk.

Indeed, the impact of political non-cooperation on multinational companies is significant. Global design, manufacturing, and distribution systems are complex, making a change in the rules—such as a restriction on the free movement of goods and services—burdensome, which raises questions about profitability and efficiency. Multinational corporations are accustomed, however, to the political and operational risks of international production. This makes management rightfully slow to change carefully engineered processes over political disputes that eventually may be cleared up.

Despite the deglobalization discussion, completely reversing globalization seems unlikely. Instead, companies are likely to use a combination of the following tactics to fortify their supply chains:

1. *Reshoring the essentials:* Shortages of prescription medication, personal protective equipment, and other essential items during the pandemic highlighted the need for certain "essential" supply chains to be rebuilt domestically for emergency situations. Companies seeking to reduce manufacturing and procurement risk may relocate back to their home countries.

2. *Reglobalizing production:* The same concerns about production disruptions, rising labor costs, or political risk may instead prompt companies to duplicate or fortify their supply chains.

3. *Doubling down on key markets:* China has been the focus of US trade concerns, but the political risk is unlikely to change the need for some globalization. Not all manufacturing would be able to move outside of such key markets as China, Canada, and Mexico, particularly for companies that also seek to sell to those markets. While labor costs in some trading partners have risen over time, so too has the productivity of those workers. Add large market size, physical infrastructure supporting coordination, sophisticated supply chains, and the investment required to rebuild supply chains elsewhere, and some companies may consider doubling down on key markets. Developing production "In country, for the country," in combination with external supply chains, may be required.

> **QUESTION SET**
>
> 1. Which of these actions would do the most to increase geopolitical risk?
>
>   **A.** Increase capital flows
>
>   **B.** Restrict foreign currency exchange
>
>   **C.** Engage in trade of goods and services
>
> **Solution:**
>
> B is correct. Restricted foreign currency exchange—a characteristic of anti-globalization—would likely reduce political and economic cooperation and thus increase geopolitical risk. A is incorrect because an increase in capital flows would reduce geopolitical risk. C is incorrect because an increase in trade would reduce geopolitical risk.

4. INTERNATIONAL TRADE ORGANIZATIONS

> describe functions and objectives of the international organizations that facilitate trade, including the World Bank, the International Monetary Fund, and the World Trade Organization

During the Great Depression in the 1930s, countries attempted to support their failing economies by sharply raising barriers to foreign trade, devaluing their currencies to compete against each other for export markets, and restricting their citizens' freedom to hold foreign exchange. These attempts proved to be self-defeating. World trade declined dramatically and employment and living standards fell sharply in many countries. By the 1940s, it had become a widespread conviction that the world economy needed organizations to help promote international economic cooperation. In July 1944, during the United Nations Monetary and Financial Conference in Bretton Woods, New Hampshire, representatives of 45 governments agreed on a framework for international economic cooperation. Two crucial, multinational organizations emanated from this conference—the World Bank, which was founded during the conference, and the International Monetary Fund (IMF), which came into formal existence in December 1945. Although the IMF was founded with the goal to stabilize exchange rates and assist the reconstruction of the world's international payment system, the World Bank was created to facilitate post-war reconstruction and development.

A third institution, the International Trade Organization (ITO), was to be created to handle the trade side of international economic cooperation, joining the other two Bretton Woods institutions. The draft ITO charter was ambitious, extending beyond world trade regulations to include rules on employment, commodity agreements, restrictive business practices, international investment, and services. The objective was to create the ITO at a United Nations Conference on Trade and Employment in Havana, Cuba in 1947. Meanwhile, 15 countries had begun negotiations in December 1945 to reduce and regulate customs tariffs. With World War II only barely ended, they wanted to give an early boost to trade liberalization and begin to correct the legacy of protectionist measures that had remained in place since the early 1930s. The group had expanded to 23 nations by the time the deal was signed on 30 October

1947 and the General Agreement on Tariffs and Trade (GATT) was born. The Havana conference began on 21 November 1947, less than a month after GATT was signed. The ITO charter was finally approved in Havana in March 1948, but ratification in some national legislatures proved impossible. The most serious opposition was in the US Congress, even though the US government had been one of the driving forces. In 1950, the US government announced that it would not seek congressional ratification of the Havana Charter, and the ITO was effectively dead. As a consequence, the GATT became the only multilateral instrument governing international trade from 1948 until the World Trade Organization (WTO) was officially established in 1995.

Role of the International Monetary Fund

As we saw earlier, current account deficits reflect a shortage of net savings in an economy and can be addressed by policies designed to rein in domestic demand. This approach, however, could have adverse consequences for domestic employment. The IMF stands ready to lend foreign currencies to member countries to assist them during periods of significant external deficits. A pool of gold and currencies contributed by members provides the IMF with the resources required for these lending operations. The funds are lent only under strict conditions and borrowing countries' macroeconomic policies are continually monitored. The IMF's main mandate is to ensure the stability of the international monetary system, the system of exchange rates and international payments that enables countries to buy goods and services from each other. More specifically, the IMF:

- provides a forum for cooperation on international monetary problems;
- facilitates the growth of international trade and promotes employment, economic growth, and poverty reduction;
- supports exchange rate stability and an open system of international payments; and
- lends foreign exchange to members when needed, on a temporary basis and under adequate safeguards, to help them address balance of payments problems.

The 2008–2009 Global Financial Crisis demonstrated that domestic and international financial stability cannot be taken for granted, even in the world's most developed countries. In light of these events, the IMF has redefined and deepened its operations by:

- *enhancing its lending facilities*: The IMF has upgraded its lending facilities to better serve its members. As part of a wide-ranging reform of its lending practices, it also has redefined the way it engages with countries on issues related to structural reform of their economies. In this context, it has doubled member countries' access to fund resources and streamlined its lending approach to reduce the stigma of borrowing for countries in need of financial help.
- *improving the monitoring of global, regional, and country economies*: The IMF has taken several steps to improve economic and financial surveillance, which is its framework for providing advice to member countries on macroeconomic policies and warning member countries of risks and vulnerabilities in their economies.
- *helping resolve global economic imbalances*: The IMF's analysis of global economic developments provides finance ministers and central bank governors with a common framework for discussing the global economy.

- *analyzing capital market developments*: The IMF is devoting more resources to the analysis of global financial markets and their links with macroeconomic policy. It also offers training to country officials on how to manage their financial systems, monetary and exchange regimes, and capital markets.
- *assessing financial sector vulnerabilities*: Resilient, well-regulated financial systems are essential for macroeconomic stability in a world of ever-growing capital flows. The IMF and the World Bank jointly run an assessment program aimed at alerting countries to vulnerabilities and risks in their financial sectors.

From an investment perspective, the IMF helps to keep country-specific market risk and global systemic risk under control. The Greek sovereign debt crisis, which threatened to destabilize the entire European banking system, is an example. In early 2010, the Greek sovereign debt rating was downgraded to non-investment grade by leading rating agencies as a result of serious concerns about the sustainability of Greece's public sector debt load. Yields on Greek government bonds rose substantially following the downgrading and the country's ability to refinance its national debt was seriously questioned in international capital markets. Bonds issued by some other European governments fell and equity markets worldwide declined in response to spreading concerns of a Greek debt default. The downgrading of Greek sovereign debt was the ultimate consequence of persistent and growing budget deficits the Greek government had run before and after the country had joined the European Monetary Union (EMU) in 2001. Most of the budget shortfalls reflected elevated outlays for public-sector jobs, pensions, and other social benefits as well as persistent tax evasion. Reports that the Greek government had consistently and deliberately misreported the country's official economic and budget statistics contributed to further erosion of confidence in Greek government bonds in international financial markets. Facing default, the Greek government requested that a joint European Union/IMF bailout package be activated, and a loan agreement was reached between Greece, the other EMU member countries, and the IMF. The deal consisted of an immediate EUR45 billion in loans to be provided in 2010, with more funds available later. A total of EUR110 billion was agreed depending on strict economic policy conditions that included cuts in wages and benefits, an increase in the retirement age for public-sector employees, limits on public pensions, increases in direct and indirect taxes, and a substantial reduction in state-owned companies. By providing conditional emergency lending facilities to the Greek government and designing a joint program with the European Union on how to achieve fiscal consolidation, the IMF prevented a contagious wave of sovereign debt crises in global capital markets.

Another example of IMF activities is the East Asian Financial Crisis in the late 1990s. It began in July 1997, when Thailand was forced to abandon its currency's peg with the US dollar. Currency devaluation subsequently hit other East Asian countries that had similar balance of payment problems, including South Korea, Malaysia, the Philippines, and Indonesia. They had run persistent and increasing current account deficits, financed mainly with short-term capital imports, in particular, domestic banks borrowing in international financial markets. External financing was popular because of the combination of lower foreign (especially US) interest rates and fixed exchange rates. Easy money obtained from abroad led to imprudent investment, which contributed to overcapacities in several industries and inflated prices on real estate and stock markets. The IMF came to the rescue of the affected countries with considerable loans, accompanied by policies designed to control domestic demand, which included fiscal austerity and tightened monetary reins.

World Bank Group and Developing Countries

The World Bank's main objective is to help developing countries fight poverty and enhance environmentally sound economic growth. For developing countries to grow and attract business, they have to

- strengthen their governments and educate their government officials;
- implement legal and judicial systems that encourage business;
- protect individual and property rights and honor contracts;
- develop financial systems robust enough to support endeavors ranging from micro credit to financing larger corporate ventures; and
- combat corruption.

Given these targets, the World Bank provides funds for a wide range of projects in developing countries worldwide and financial and technical expertise aimed at helping those countries reduce poverty.

The World Bank's two closely affiliated entities—the International Bank for Reconstruction and Development (IBRD) and the International Development Association (IDA)—provide low or no-interest loans and grants to countries that have unfavorable or no access to international credit markets. Unlike private financial institutions, neither the IBRD nor the IDA operates for profit. The IBRD is market-based, and uses its high credit rating to pass the low interest it pays for funds on to its borrowers—developing countries. It pays for its own operating costs because it does not look to outside sources to furnish funds for overhead.

IBRD lending to developing countries is primarily financed by selling AAA-rated bonds in the world's financial markets. Although the IBRD earns a small margin on this lending, the greater proportion of its income comes from lending out its own capital. This capital consists of reserves built up over the years and money paid in from the Bank's 185 member country shareholders. IBRD's income also pays for World Bank operating expenses and has contributed to IDA and debt relief. IDA is the world's largest source of interest-free loans and grant assistance to the poorest countries. IDA's funds are replenished every three years by 40 donor countries. Additional funds are regenerated through repayments of loan principal on 35- to 40-year, no-interest loans, which are then available for relending. At the end of September 2010, the IBRD had net loans outstanding of USD125.5 billion, while its borrowings amounted to USD132 billion.

In addition to acting as a financier, the World Bank also provides analysis, advice, and information to its member countries to enable them to achieve the lasting economic and social improvements their people need. Another core function of the World Bank is to increase the capabilities of its partners, people in developing countries, and its own staff. Links to a wide range of knowledge-sharing networks have been set up by the Bank to address the vast need for information and dialogue about development.

From an investment perspective, the World Bank helps to create the basic economic infrastructure that is essential for the creation of domestic financial markets and a well-functioning financial industry in developing countries. Moreover, the IBRD is one of the most important supranational borrowers in the international capital markets. Because of its strong capital position and its very conservative financial, liquidity, and lending policies, it enjoys the top investment-grade rating from the leading agencies, and investors have confidence in its ability to withstand adverse events. As a result, IBRD bonds denominated in various major currencies are widely held by institutional and private investors.

World Trade Organization and Global Trade

The WTO provides the legal and institutional foundation of the multinational trading system. It is the only international organization that regulates cross-border trade relationships among nations on a global scale. It was founded on 1 January 1995, replacing the General Agreement on Tariffs and Trade (GATT) that had come into existence in 1947. The GATT was the only multilateral body governing international trade from 1947 to 1995. It operated for almost half a century as a quasi-institutionalized, provisional system of multilateral treaties. Several rounds of negotiations took place under the GATT, of which the Tokyo round and the Uruguay round may have been the most far reaching. The Tokyo round was the first major effort to address a wide range of non-tariff trade barriers, whereas the Uruguay round focused on the extension of the world trading system into several new areas, particularly trade in services and intellectual property, but also to reform trade in agricultural products and textiles. The GATT still exists in an updated 1994 version and is the WTO's principal treaty for trade in goods. The GATT and the General Agreement on Trade in Services (GATS) are the major agreements within the WTO's body of treaties that encompasses a total of about 60 agreements, annexes, decisions, and understandings.

In November 2001, the most recent round of negotiations was launched by the WTO in Doha, Qatar. The Doha round was an ambitious effort to enhance globalization by slashing barriers and subsidies in agriculture and addressing a wide range of cross-border services. So far, under GATS, which came into force in January 1995, banks, insurance companies, telecommunication firms, tour operators, hotel chains, and transport companies that want to do business abroad can enjoy the same principles of free and fair trade that previously had applied only to international trade in goods. Although no final agreement was reached in the Doha round, it marked one of the most crucial events in global trade over the past several decades: China's accession to the WTO in December 2001. The inability to reach agreement in the Doha round led to an increasing number of bilateral and multilateral trade agreements, such as the Trans-Pacific Partnership with Japan, Vietnam, and nine other countries.

The WTO's most important functions are the implementation, administration, and operation of individual agreements; acting as a platform for negotiations; and settling disputes. Moreover, the WTO has the mandate to review and propagate its members' trade policies and ensure the coherence and transparency of trade policies through surveillance in a global policy setting. The WTO also provides technical cooperation and training to developing, least-developed, and low-income countries to assist with their adjustment to WTO rules. In addition, the WTO is a major source of economic research and analysis, producing ongoing assessments of global trade in its publications and research reports on special topics. Finally, the WTO works in cooperation with the other two Bretton Woods institutions, the IMF and the World Bank.

From an investment perspective, the WTO's framework of global trade rules provides the major institutional and regulatory base without which today's global multinational corporations would be hard to conceive. Modern financial markets would look different without the large, multinational companies whose stocks and bonds have become key elements in investment portfolios. In the equity universe, for instance, investment considerations focusing on global sectors rather than national markets would make little sense without a critical mass of multinational firms competing with each other in a globally defined business environment.

> **QUESTION SET**
>
> On 10 May 2010, the Greek government officially applied for emergency lending facilities extended by the International Monetary Fund. It sent the following letter to the IMF's Managing Director:

International Trade Organizations

Request for Stand-By Arrangement

This paper was prepared based on the information available at the time it was completed on Monday, May 10, 2010. The views expressed in this document are those of the staff team and do not necessarily reflect the views of the government of Greece or the Executive Board of the IMF. The policy of publication of staff reports and other documents by the IMF allows for the deletion of market-sensitive information.

May 3, 2010
Managing Director
International Monetary Fund
Washington DC

The attached Memorandum of Economic and Financial Policies (MEFP) outlines the economic and financial policies that the Greek government and the Bank of Greece, respectively, will implement during the remainder of 2010 and in the period 2011–2013 to strengthen market confidence and Greece's fiscal and financial position during a difficult transition period toward a more open and competitive economy. The government is fully committed to the policies stipulated in this document and its attachments, to frame tight budgets in the coming years with the aim to reduce the fiscal deficit to below 3 percent in 2014 and achieve a downward trajectory in the public debt-GDP ratio beginning in 2013, to safeguard the stability of the Greek financial system, and to implement structural reforms to boost competitiveness and the economy's capacity to produce, save, and export. (...) The government is strongly determined to lower the fiscal deficit, (...) by achieving higher and more equitable tax collections, and constraining spending in the government wage bill and entitlement outlays, among other items. In view of these efforts and to signal the commitment to effective macroeconomic policies, the Greek government requests that the Fund supports this multi-year program under a Stand-By Arrangement (SBA) for a period of 36 months in an amount equivalent to SDR26.4 billion. (A SDR (special drawing right) is a basket of four leading currencies: Japanese yen (JPY), US dollar (USD), British pound (GBP), and euro (EUR).) A parallel request for financial assistance to euro area countries for a total amount of EUR80 billion has been sent. The implementation of the program will be monitored through quantitative performance criteria and structural benchmarks as described in the attached MEFP and Technical Memorandum of Understanding (TMU). There will be twelve quarterly reviews of the program supported under the SBA by the Fund, (....) to begin with the first review that is expected to be completed in the course of the third calendar quarter of 2010, and then every quarter thereafter until the last quarterly review envisaged to be completed during the second calendar quarter of 2013, to assess progress in implementing the program and reach understandings on any additional measures that may be needed to achieve its objectives. (....) The Greek authorities believe that the policies set forth in the attached memorandum are adequate to achieve the objectives of the economic program, and stand ready to take any further measures that may become appropriate for this purpose. The authorities will consult with the Fund in accordance with its policies on such consultations, (....) and in advance of revisions to the policies contained in the MEFP. All information requested by the Fund (....) to assess implementation of the program will be provided.

(....)
Sincerely,

George Papaconstantinou	George Provopoulos
Minister of Finance	Governor of the Bank of Greece

1. What is the objective of the IMF's emergency lending facilities?

   Solution:

   The program seeks to safeguard the stability of the Greek financial system and to implement structural reforms to boost competitiveness and the economy's capacity to produce, save, and export.

2. What are the macroeconomic policy conditions under which the IMF provides emergency lending to Greece?

   Solution:

   The Greek government has to reduce the country's fiscal deficit by achieving higher and more equitable tax collections as well as constrain spending in the government wage bill and entitlement outlays.

3. What is the amount Greece requests from the IMF as emergency funds?

   Solution:

   Greece applied for a standby arrangement in an amount equivalent to SDR26.4 billion (approximately USD39.5 billion, based on the 10 May 2010 exchange rate).

4. Which of the following international trade organizations regulates cross-border exchange among nations on a global scale?

   A. World Bank Group (World Bank)
   B. World Trade Organization (WTO)
   C. International Monetary Fund (IMF)

   Solution:

   B is correct. The WTO provides the legal and institutional foundation of the multinational trading system and is the only international organization that regulates cross-border trade relations among nations on a global scale. The WTO's mission is to foster free trade by providing a major institutional and regulatory framework of global trade rules. Without such global trading rules, today's global transnational corporations would be hard to conceive.

5. Which of the following international trade organizations has a mission to help developing countries fight poverty and enhance environmentally sound economic growth?

   A. World Bank Group (World Bank)
   B. World Trade Organization (WTO)
   C. International Monetary Fund (IMF)

   Solution:

   A is correct. The World Bank's mission is to help developing countries fight poverty and enhance environmentally sound economic growth. The World Bank helps to create the basic economic infrastructure essential for creation and maintenance of domestic financial markets and a well-functioning financial industry in developing countries.

6. Which of the following organizations helps to keep global systemic risk under control by preventing contagion in scenarios such as the 2010 Greek sovereign debt crisis?

   A. World Bank Group (World Bank)

> **B.** World Trade Organization (WTO)
>
> **C.** International Monetary Fund (IMF)
>
> **Solution:**
>
> C is correct. From an investment perspective, the IMF helps to keep country-specific market risk and global systemic risk under control. The Greek sovereign debt crisis in 2010, which threatened to destabilize the entire European banking system, is a recent example. The IMF's mission is to ensure the stability of the international monetary system—that is, the system of exchange rates and international payments that enables countries to buy goods and services from each other.

> 7. Which of the following international trade bodies was the only multilateral body governing international trade from 1948 to 1995?
>
>   **A.** World Trade Organization (WTO)
>
>   **B.** International Trade Organization (ITO)
>
>   **C.** General Agreement on Tariffs and Trade (GATT)
>
>   **Solution:**
>
>   C is correct. The GATT was the only multilateral body governing international trade from 1948 to 1995. It operated for almost half a century as a quasi-institutionalized, provisional system of multilateral treaties and included several rounds of negotiations.

ASSESSING GEOPOLITICAL ACTORS AND RISK

☐ describe geopolitical risk

Using the two axes we have discussed—political cooperation versus non-cooperation and globalization versus nationalism—investment analysts can assess geopolitical actors and the likelihood of threat to investment outcomes. Where countries stand in that balance shapes their standing compared with other geopolitical actors, the tools of geopolitics they can use, and the threats and opportunities they face. This lesson provides a framework for analyzing a country's geopolitical risk.

Archetypes of Country Behavior

The framework, using the two axes, shown in Exhibit 7 presents four archetypes of country behavior: **autarky**, **hegemony**, **multilateralism**, and **bilateralism**. Each archetype has its own costs, benefits, and trade-offs with respect to geopolitical risk. In general terms, regions, countries, and industries that are more dependent on cross-border goods and capital flows will have growth rates and investment returns that benefit from greater global cooperation. The interdependent nature of their activities may reduce the likelihood that collaborative countries levy economic, financial, or political attacks on one another. That same interdependence often makes cooperative actors more vulnerable to geopolitical risk than those less dependent on cooperation and trade. Diversifying the means of production provides some shield against risk but also provides more touchpoints by which risk can occur. In the remainder of the section, we describe the costs and benefits of each archetype, with some examples of each.

Exhibit 7: Archetypes of Globalization and Cooperation

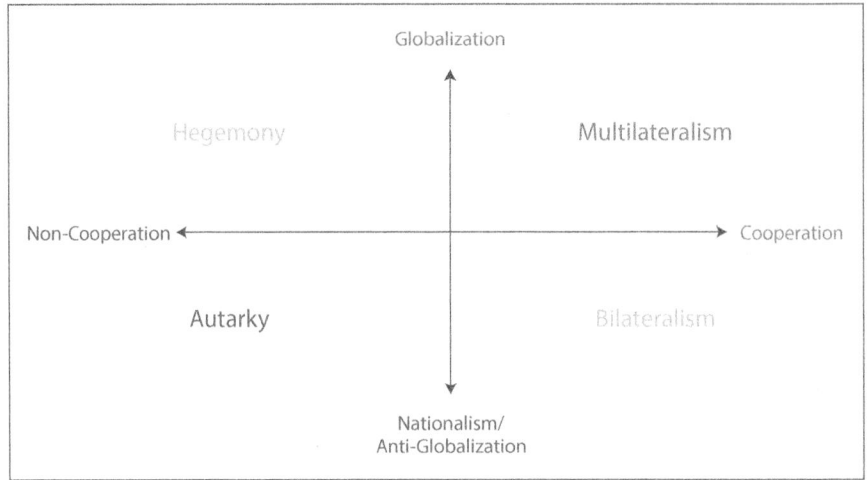

Note that each of the axes explored in this framework—cooperation versus non-cooperation and globalization versus nationalism—represent a spectrum. Rarely do countries represent full extremes of either of these factors. As you can see from the examples provided, a country's place within the framework can be a moving target. As such, the examples provided in no way represent a value judgment of a country's goals or approach.

For geopolitical risk analysis, it matters not only which quadrant a country falls in today but also its stability within that quadrant. A hegemon that is working to build more political cooperation may be less of a threat to investment results than a multilateral actor trying to break them.

The "America first" example given in the section "Threats of Rollback of Globalization" is highly relevant. Adjusting previously agreed-upon rules may be in a country's national interest, but inconsistent application of those rules presents a risk for companies and economic growth. Investors must be aware of actors' movement within the framework to assess the likelihood and impact of geopolitical risk more appropriately.

EXAMPLE 6

Geopolitical Risk Analysis

1. True or false: The relative permanence of geographic factors implies a fundamental stability in geopolitical risk analysis of the involved parties.

   Explain your selection.

   A. True
   B. False

   Solution:

   B is correct. Geopolitical risk analysis is fundamentally dynamic, with analysts needing to be aware of the parties' movement within the relevant framework to assess the likelihood and impact of geopolitical risk. Geopolitical actors face a delicate balance between harnessing the potential intrinsic and profit gains from globalization while managing the many and sometimes unforeseen consequences. Further complicating the picture is the intricate connection between globalization and cooperation. A country's place within the globalization and cooperation framework can be a moving target, and for geopolitical risk analysis, it matters not only which quadrant a company falls in today but also its stability within that quadrant.

Autarky

Autarky describes countries seeking political self-sufficiency with little or no external trade or finance. State-owned enterprises control strategic domestic industries. The self-sufficiency of autarkic countries allows them to be stronger politically, including the ability to exercise complete control over the supply of technology, goods, and services, as well as media and political messaging. In some cases, periods of autarky can provide a country with swifter economic and political development. For example, for much of the 20th century, China could have been described as autarkic, exercising very little political cooperation or globalization. However, China's autarkic stance resulted in substantial poverty alleviation and an eventual move toward more economic and financial cooperation. That said, an autarkic stance does not come without costs. In other cases, such as North Korea and the earlier example of Venezuela, autarky has resulted in a gradual loss of economic and political development within the country.

Hegemony

Hegemonic countries tend to be regional or even global leaders, and they use their political or economic influence of others to control resources. State-owned enterprises tend to control key export markets. A hegemonic system can provide valuable benefits both to the hegemonic countries and to the international system. For the country, economic and political dominance may provide important influence on global affairs. For the global system, countries aligning with the hegemon's rules and standards may enjoy the rewards provided by the leader, including the stabilizing force of monitoring and enforcing the hegemon's standards. That said, there may be costs to hegemonic systems. As hegemons gain or lose influence in the international system, they may become more competitive, increasing the likelihood of geopolitical risk.

CHINA AND TECHNOLOGY TRANSFER

In 2011, China overtook Japan as the world's second largest economy. Having joined the World Trade Organization (WTO) in 2001, China's economy had globalized meaningfully. At the same time, the importance of China's economy gave it important influence on the rules of play in the international stage. One area where China has exerted its political influence is in technology transfer. For many years, China's stance was, in order to integrate into the Chinese production machine, including access to a skilled and plentiful labor supply, some companies would be required to transfer their technology ideas and processes to Chinese partners. For a smaller or less important economy, these rules might be difficult to enforce, but China's size and importance made it possible. These policies may have some globalizing effects. By having Chinese companies adopt more international technological ideas and rules, they become more globalized in their approach. At the same time, they can also create investment risks. If China were to become more restrictive, it could disrupt global supply chains and increase costs for global companies.

RUSSIA AND GAS DISPUTES

Russia's economy, and particularly its oil sector, is well-integrated into global supply chains. However, the country is also largely politically autonomous, which can contribute to geopolitical risk and uncertainty. For example, Russia's control of important natural gas pipelines gives it significant political leverage over other countries, particularly those in Europe that rely on it for fossil fuels. As a result, European countries may be less likely to confront Russia in other areas. Between February and March 2014, Russia annexed Crimea, Ukraine. Other countries condemned the annexation and considered it to be a violation of international law, including such previously politically cooperative agreements as the 1991 Belavezha Accords that established the Commonwealth of Independent States. Still, the annexation continues, in part because many countries are unwilling to disrupt an important economic relationship.

In addition to political uncertainty, the annexation contributed to important economic and market developments affecting investors. In the immediate aftermath of the annexation, the Russian ruble depreciated significantly, contributing to higher market volatility and inflation. Other significant economic impacts followed. For example, countries, including Canada, the United States, and European Union member states, imposed sanctions on Russian officials. Ukraine responded to the annexation by cutting off water to the area, contributing to crop failure.

Multilateralism

Multilateralism describes countries that participate in mutually beneficial trade relationships and extensive rules harmonization. Private firms are fully integrated into global supply chains with multiple trade partners. Examples of multilateral countries include Germany and Singapore.

SINGAPORE AS MULTILATERAL ACTOR

Singapore is ranked as the most open economy in the world by the World Economic Forum, the third least corrupt by Transparency International, and the second most pro-business by the World Bank Doing Business Report. It has low tax rates and the second highest per capita GDP in terms of purchasing power of its citizens. The results are shown In Exhibit 8.

Exhibit 8: Select Global Data

	World Bank Ease of Doing Business Rank (2019)	Corruption Perceptions Index Rank (2020)	Corporate Tax Rate (2021)	GDP (per capita, in international dollars, 2021)
Singapore	2	3	17.00%	95,650
United States	6	25	21.00%	63,594
Germany	22	9	30.00%	53,024
Australia	18	11	30.00%	51,102
United Kingdom	8	11	19.00%	43,839
Japan	29	19	30.60%	41,507

	World Bank Ease of Doing Business Rank (2019)	Corruption Perceptions Index Rank (2020)	Corporate Tax Rate (2021)	GDP (per capita, in international dollars, 2021)
Mexico	60	124	30.00%	18,867
China	31	78	25.00%	17,624
Brazil	124	94	34.00%	14,563
South Africa	82	69	28.00%	11,582
Philippines	95	115	30.00%	8,436

Sources: World Bank (doingbusiness.org), Transparency International (transparency.org), KPMG, International Monetary Fund (imf.org).

What is behind these impressive statistics? For starters, Singapore's factor endowment makes it highly dependent on cooperation and innovation to survive. The country has limited natural resources, including water and arable land, which means the country must rely on agrotechnology parks and reclaimed land for agricultural production as well as trade partners for the inputs to that production.

Geographic factors also contribute to Singapore's economic openness. The country is located at the intersection of many important global trade routes. Its population is highly ethnically and racially diverse, allowing for English as a key language for global business. In addition, its workforce is highly skilled, giving Singapore an important role as a center for trade and innovation throughout Asia.

Politically, Singapore has highly stable institutions. The government is strategically involved in its economic system to allow for consistent prioritization of economic activity and enforcement of business-friendly institutional governance. Singapore's openness has contributed to its attractiveness as a potential partner.

As a result of its location and factor endowments, Singapore is both capable of and highly dependent on international cooperation for its economic growth. The country generates higher economic growth rates because of this greater global cooperation. However, that same cooperation may leave Singapore more vulnerable to geopolitical risk than those countries that are less dependent on cooperation and trade.

EXAMPLE 7

Key Globalization Factors

1. Identify at least two of the factors accounting for Singapore's reliance on globalization to achieve economic success.

   Solution:

   First, Singapore's factor endowment of limited natural resources makes it dependent on cooperation and innovation to survive.
   Second, Singapore's geographic location at the intersection of multiple important global trade routes helps make it an Asian center for world business.
   Third, culturally it has a highly ethnically and racially diverse population fluent in the key global business language of English, enhancing its collaborative capabilities.
   Finally, it has highly stable political institutions with high governmental priorities on promoting economic activity and enforcing business-friendly

institutional governance. These qualities make it an attractive potential business partner and likely sought out for global cooperation.

Bilateralism

Bilateralism is the conduct of political, economic, financial, or cultural cooperation between two countries. Countries engaging in bilateralism may have relations with many different countries, but they are one-at-a-time agreements without multiple partners. Typically, countries exist on a spectrum between bilateralism and multilateralism. In between the two extremes is **regionalism**, in which a group of countries cooperate with one another. Both bilateralism and regionalism can be conducted at the exclusion of other groups. For example, regional blocs may agree to provide trade benefits to one another and increase barriers for those outside of that group.

It is noteworthy that relatively few countries perfectly fit the bilateral mold. Moving toward stronger political cooperation tends to lead organically to globalization; it is common for non-state actors to globalize as long as the path is laid for them. Additionally, innovations, such as the internet and digital transfer, have made it even easier for firms to globalize.

Bilateralism once nicely described Japan; its government engaged in substantial political cooperation for the sake of building a strong export market, but it did not globalize its imports. That said, as the importance of international capital markets has deepened, Japan has been a pioneer of globalizing its equity and bond markets for international players. Today it would be considered a multilateral player.

QUESTION SET

1. For the following contrasting pairs of archetypes of globalization and cooperation, which one reflects the *greatest* differences in country behavior?

    A. Bilateralism versus autarky

    B. Multilateralism versus autarky

    C. Multilateralism versus hegemony

Solution:

B is correct. Multilateralism describes countries that participate in mutually beneficial trade relationships and extensive rules harmonization. Autarky describes countries seeking political self-sufficiency with little or no external trade or finance. In the Exhibit 7 display of these behavior patterns, these choices are most widely separated on both the globalization and cooperation continuums. A is incorrect because bilateral or regional approaches describe those countries leveraging regional trade relationships and may face the world as a group. Bilateralism shares with autarky a bias against globalization. These approaches diverge, however, regarding cooperation, with autarky being more non-cooperative. C is incorrect because multilateralism describes countries that participate in mutually beneficial trade relationships and extensive rules harmonization. Hegemony represents countries exerting political or economic influence of others to control resources. Multilateralism shares with hegemony an inclination toward globalization, as shown in Exhibit 7, but diverges from hegemony regarding cooperation; hegemony is more non-cooperative.

THE TOOLS OF GEOPOLITICS

☐ describe tools of geopolitics and their impact on regions and economies

Now that we understand the characteristics of geopolitical actors, we can examine the tools these actors use to manifest or reinforce their interests with respect to others. The tools an actor uses are ultimately the source of geopolitical risk as it affects investors—shaping the likelihood of risk as well as the speed and size of impact, as we will explore in Lesson 6. As a result, understanding these tools may be just as important as understanding the motivations for using them.

The Tools of Geopolitics

The tools of geopolitics may be separated into three types:

- national security tools,
- economic tools, and
- financial tools.

Among each of these tools, there are choices that reflect or improve cooperation and those that reflect or escalate conflict (non-cooperation). Tools facilitating cooperation are those that increase flows between countries; this can mean an increased flow of goods, services, capital, or labor through treaties, trade agreements, capital provisions, and approved migration. Tools escalating conflict are those that reduce these flows between countries.

We can use the framework provided in the section "Archetypes of Country Behavior" in Lesson 4 to assess the nature of tools used by geopolitical actors and to strengthen our designation of countries within that framework. The extent to which actors use these tools to improve cooperation or escalate conflict influences their position within the framework. As we described earlier, it is important for geopolitical risk analysts to track not only which quadrant best describes an actor but also its stability within that quadrant. Using different national security, economic, or financial tools may indicate that an actor is changing in character, which would increase or decrease geopolitical risk. Exhibit 9 shows how the tools of geopolitics fit in the four archetypes of country behavior (presented in Exhibit 7).

Exhibit 9: Tools of Geopolitics

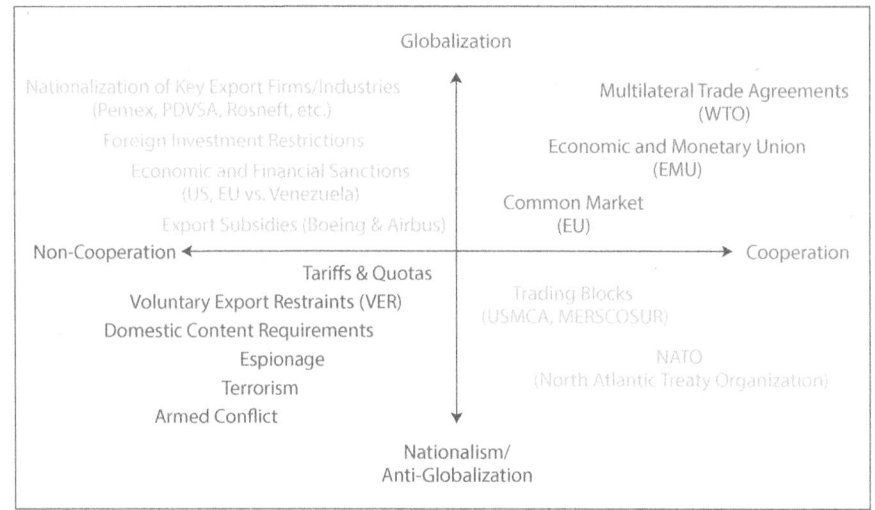

National Security Tools

National security tools are those used to influence or coerce a state actor through direct or indirect impact on the country's resources, people, or borders. National security tools may be active, meaning they are being used at the time of analysis, or threatened, meaning they are not currently used but their use is likely enough to warrant concern.

The most extreme example of a national security tool is that of armed conflict. Armed conflict is a direct and active national security tool. It can be internal or external to a country and has two major impacts. The first is the disruption or destruction of physical infrastructure, which can inflict long-term damage on a country's capital stock and ability to rebuild that stock. The second impact is on migration away from areas of armed conflict, which can reshape international flows of goods, services, capital, and labor. It also can affect neighboring countries and states accepting refugees.

SYRIAN REFUGEE CRISIS (SINCE 2011) AND IMPACTS ON GERMANY

The Syrian refugee crisis began in March 2011 after a violent government crackdown on public demonstrations. Protests turned into an armed rebellion and escalated to civil war. As a result, Syria has experienced extreme deterioration of its physical infrastructure, including buildings transportation, and other structures. As conflict prolonged, more than 6.6 million Syrians have fled the country, with another 6.7 million having been internally displaced. Beyond the tragic human toll of this ongoing conflict, Syria has also experienced negative impact on its current and potential economic growth as a result of the deterioration of its capital and labor stock. According to the International Monetary Fund (IMF), Syria's economy grew by 4.5 percent, on average, from 2000 to 2010. By 2016, the Syrian economy was less than half its size before the war. In investment terms, these developments have contributed to a sustained higher discount rate and lower bond and equity returns.

The majority of refugees have found refuge in neighboring countries, such as Turkey, Lebanon, and Jordan. However, many also made their way, often by dangerous routes, to European countries. The refugee crisis attracted significant international attention in 2015 when German Chancellor Angela Merkel announced that the country would admit 1 million Syrian refugees. In the short-term, the decision was disruptive to domestic politics and international cooperation as not all citizens and neighboring countries were supportive of the approach. The decision also carried economic costs, including constructing housing and establishing resettlement programs. However, in the long-term, Germany appears to be benefiting from the cooperative decision, having attracted a younger and skilled demographic of migrants thus improving the demographic balance of an otherwise-aging country. The resulting improvements in Germany's labor and capital stock may improve Germany's potential economic growth rate. In investment terms, a higher potential economic growth rate contributes to higher expected market returns, all else equal, and may contribute to industry developments or innovations.

Of course, not all tools are used in so direct a nature as armed conflict. For example, espionage, or the practice of using spies to obtain political or military information, is a necessarily indirect national security tool. Military alliances often are used to aid in direct conflict and also to deter conflict from arising in the first place.

Additionally, not all national security tools are used in a non-cooperative way. State actors can combine forces to reduce the likelihood that national security tools are used. For example, the North Atlantic Treaty Organization (NATO), an alliance between the European Union, United States, United Kingdom, and Canada, is used to discuss and deescalate potential conflict among members and between members and outside states. Originally constructed to provide collective security against the Soviet Union, NATO now serves as a collective effort to reduce nuclear proliferation and other common national security goals.

EXAMPLE 8

Tools of Geopolitics

1. True or false: Although geopolitical financial tools can be used for both cooperative and non-cooperative reasons, national security tools are characteristically non-cooperative. Explain your selection.

    A. True

    B. False

    Solution:

    B is correct. National security tools are non-cooperative in cases like armed conflict. But collective security agreements, such as NATO, can also be used cooperatively to reduce the possibility of conflict among members and between members and outside states.

    Financial tools may be cooperative in reducing geopolitical risk if they encourage cooperation in security, economic, or financial arenas. They may also tend to non-cooperation by creating vulnerabilities in the international system. US dominance is one such example, both promoting financial activity and making other countries vulnerable to US monetary policy changes.

Economic Tools

Economic tools are the actions used to reinforce cooperative or non-cooperative stances through economic means. Among state actors, economic tools can include multilateral trade agreements, such as the Southern Common Market (MERCOSUR), which facilitates trade among member countries in South America, or the global harmonization of tariff rules, as facilitated by the World Trade Organization (WTO). Highly cooperative economic tools may also include common markets, like the European Union, or a common currency, like the euro.

By contrast, economic tools can also be non-cooperative in nature. Nationalization, the process of transferring an activity or industry from private to state control, is a non-cooperative approach to asserting economic control. Nationalization is most common in sectors perceived as vital to economic security or competitiveness, such as the energy sector. For example, after a period of privatization, Argentina moved in 2012 to renationalize YPF, the nation's largest energy firm. In addition to controlling an important geophysical resource, Argentina's government looked to secure the sale of fossil fuels as an important source of foreign exchange, a scarcity at the time. Countries can engage in voluntary export restraints, meaning they refuse to trade as much of their goods and services as would meet demand. Countries also can impose domestic content requirements, asserting that a certain proportion or type of domestic input be included in an exported good.

Financial Tools

Financial tools are the actions used to reinforce cooperative or non-cooperative stances through financial mechanisms. Examples of cooperative financial tools include the free exchange of currencies across borders and allowing foreign investment. Examples of non-cooperative financial tools include limiting access to local currency markets and restricting foreign investment. Sanctions, described earlier, provide a useful example of countries using financial tools to influence geopolitical outcomes.

Cooperative financial tools may reduce geopolitical risk if they encourage cooperation in security, economic, or financial arenas. However, the same tools may also create vulnerabilities in the international system. The dominance of the US dollar is one such example. The international interbank market, in which banks borrow and lend to one another, hosts transactions heavily denominated in US dollars. The market provides a tool of cooperation, and the free exchange of currency helps facilitate financial activity and cooperation more broadly. That said, the US dollar's importance to exchange also makes other countries vulnerable to changes in US monetary policy. Specifically, tighter US monetary policy can contribute to liquidity shortages in countries that do not or cannot maintain US dollar reserves.

EXAMPLE 9

Financial Tools of Geopolitics

1. Describe the conditions under which cooperative financial tools may decrease geopolitical risk as well as create vulnerabilities in the international system.

    Solution:

    Cooperative financial tools may reduce geopolitical risk if they encourage cooperation in security, economic, and financial arenas. However, if the system becomes too dependent on a particular financial tool or if the tool becomes too dominant, it may introduce vulnerabilities in the international system that can have far-reaching implications.

Multifaceted Approaches

Just as geopolitics is multifaceted and includes many types of actors and features, so too are the tools of geopolitics. Systems of political, economic, and financial cooperation can be, and often are, intertwined. One interesting example is **cabotage**, or the right to transport passengers or goods within a country by a foreign firm. Many countries, including those with multilateral trade agreements, impose restrictions on cabotage across transportation subsectors—meaning that shippers, airlines, and truck drivers are not allowed to transport goods and services within another country's borders. Allowing cabotage requires coordination on areas like physical security and economic coordination, a highly multilateral process.

International organizations may also make use of multiple tools of geopolitics. For example, the Association of Southeast Asian Nations (ASEAN) is composed of 10 members states and seeks to facilitate economic, political, security, military, educational, and cultural integration between its members. The European Union, which began as a six-country economic bloc, has expanded to include 27 member states (as of 2022) and features substantial financial and national security components. Generally, as actors incorporate more tools of collaboration, they are less likely to initiate conflict or use a non-cooperative tool against associated actors.

EUROPEAN UNION AND BREXIT

As shown in Exhibit 10, one of the most pronounced transitions toward multilateral cooperation and globalization is in the European Union (EU). From 1945 until 2016, European countries exhibited fairly steady progress toward political cooperation—via shared security, free movement of goods and people, and harmonization of rules and regulations—and economic and financial globalization. EU member states offer European citizenship and the right for workers and companies from all EU member states to operate within other EU countries. The strongest manifestation of this multilateralism is exhibited in the creation of the common currency for the euro area, a subset of European countries.

Exhibit 10: Timeline: The Path of European Cooperation and Globalization

1945	World War II Ends
1950	European Coal and Steel Community Begins, Uniting Countries Economically and Politically
1960s	Customs Duties Removed
1970s	Single European Act is Signed Creating "the Single Market"
1970s	EU Regional Policy Begins to Transfer Money to Create Jobs and Infrastructure in Poorer Areas
1990s	Foundational EU Treaties Introduce European Citizenship, Common Foreign and Security Policy, Free Movement of People, and European Parliament
2000s	Countries Continue to Join the EU
2010s	Croatia Becomes 28th EU Member State. United Kingdom Votes to Leave EU

In 2016, the European integration process experienced a marked disruption when the United Kingdom voted to exit the EU. Despite the benefits of cooperation and globalization, the costs became increasingly felt, affecting local politics. The United Kingdom's sudden reversal in some of its multilateral momentum was a surprise to many global actors and investors. This geopolitical risk resulted in near-term market volatility, particularly in financial and currency markets.

> It has also resulted in the dismantling of political cooperation in recent years; the United Kingdom's multilateral approach is, in some areas, shifting toward a bilateral approach.

Geopolitical Risk and Comparative Advantage

The geopolitical tools discussed in this section generate important risks and opportunities for investors, but they do not operate in a vacuum. In fact, geopolitical risk and the tools of geopolitics can shape actors' core priorities. Models of international trade will be explored later in the curriculum. (In this context, we reference them briefly to illustrate how geopolitical tools can shape, destroy, or build upon a country's core approach to other actors.)

In the classic example of international trade, countries are endowed with certain resources, or factors, and technological capabilities. Not every country will be endowed with the same factors and capabilities and thus may benefit from cooperating via trade. For example, Ghana is rich in resources, such as hydrocarbons, gold, agricultural products, and several industrial metals. However, it relies heavily on other countries for both processing and industrial use of those resources. Each country specializes in areas defined by its resources and capabilities and then exchanges with the other in a way that benefits both parties. Through specialization and exchange, industries within each country experience greater economies of scale. Households and firms therefore will have a greater variety of products to choose from. Competition between firms is higher, and resources are allocated more efficiently.

Geopolitical risk and the tools of geopolitics can tilt comparative advantage in one direction or another. For example, countries or regions with limited geopolitical risk exposure may attract more labor and capital. In contrast, those with higher geopolitical risk exposure may suffer a loss of labor and capital. Similarly, a consistent threat of conflict may drive more regular volatility in asset prices, prompting investors to require higher compensation for risk taken (i.e., an increase in the required rate of return or the discount rate used in valuation).

QUESTION SET

1. True or false: Germany's reaction to the Syrian refugee crisis is an example of comparative advantage stemming from geopolitical risk. Explain your selection.

    A. True

    B. False

    Solution:

    A is correct. Countries with a lower geopolitical risk exposure have the ability to attract resources, such as labor and capital. With its strong economic position in the EU and longstanding stability of political leadership, Germany was able to undertake the resettlement of one million Syrian refugees to it while assuming the short-term relocation costs and disruption of its domestic politics. This improves its long-term demographic balance by adding young and talented migrants, with the resulting increase in labor and capital stock potentially increasing Germany's economic growth rate.

---

2. In the following table, match the geopolitical tool with the *most* appropriate example of each tool.

Geopolitical Tool	Example
1. Financial	A. Nationalization
2. Economic	B. Espionage
3. National security	C. Free exchange of currency across borders

Solution:

Option 1 (Financial) matches with C (Free exchange of currency across borders).

Option 2 (Economic) matches with A (Nationalization).

Option 3 (National security) matches with B (Espionage).

GEOPOLITICAL RISK AND THE INVESTMENT PROCESS 7

☐ describe the impact of geopolitical risk on investments

There is no shortage of attention to geopolitical risk in financial market analysis. However, the extent to which investors incorporate geopolitical risk into their decision making will vary widely with their investment objectives and risk tolerance. Some investors may be considered *takers* of geopolitical risk. These investors may incorporate geopolitical risk into their analysis only to the extent that it affects the long-term attractiveness of asset classes or strategies. For other investors, geopolitical risk may be a central component of their investment process. For these portfolios, monitoring dislocations is an achievable and meaningful driver of alpha creation, where focused geopolitical risk analysis can reduce the impact and severity of adverse events and enhance the potential for upside growth. For example, an investor that anticipates an important political transition may enact portfolio hedges to shield against market volatility or may use the market volatility as a buying opportunity—in either case, improving investment outcomes.

What follows is a discussion of the impact of geopolitical risk on the investment environment. We begin with a discussion of types of geopolitical risk, followed by a means of assessing those risks and the ways that they can manifest in a portfolio.

Types of Geopolitical Risk

There are three basic types of geopolitical risk: event risk, exogenous risk, and thematic risk.

Event risk evolves around set dates, such as elections, new legislation, or other date-driven milestones, such as holidays or political anniversaries, known in advance. Political events often result in changes to investor expectations related to a country's cooperative stance. As a result, risk analysts often use political calendars as a starting place for assessing event risk.

One example of event risk is the United Kingdom's referendum on European Union membership (Exhibit 11). This was a known event risk; it was planned for 23 June 2016, well in advance. The stakes of the election were well understood, with many years' worth of politically cooperative steps likely to unwind in the event of a "yes" vote. Most investors expected a "no" vote; when the results proved the opposite, investor expectations related to the United Kingdom's cooperative stance were drastically changed.

Exhibit 11: Market Reaction to Event Risk: United Kingdom's EU Referendum, 2016

	First Day	30 Days	1 Year
FTSE	−3.1%	6.2%	17.1%
GBP	−8.1%	−11.9%	−14.5%
10-year bond yield (Gilt)	−21.0%	−42.0%	−25.0%

The United Kingdom's vote to end its European Union membership came as a surprise to many investors. Several asset classes were immediately affected, including equities, the national currency, and government bonds. In the weeks that followed, investors adjusted to the news but became concerned about what a rollback in political cooperation might mean for long-term economic growth. As a result, equity prices recovered, but the British pound continued on a steady decline. Government bond yields declined precipitously in the month following the vote, recovering somewhat as the year progressed.

It is useful to note that the predictability of an event does not necessarily change its likelihood, its speed of impact, or the size of impact on investors; however, it does give investors more time to prepare a response. We will come back to this example and others in this section when we discuss the assessment of geopolitical threats.

Exogenous risk is a sudden or unanticipated risk that affects either a country's cooperative stance, the ability of non-state actors to globalize, or both (Exhibit 12). Examples include sudden uprisings, invasions, or the aftermath of natural disasters.

Exhibit 12: Market Reaction to Exogenous Risk: Japan's Fukushima Nuclear Disaster, 2011

	First Day	30 Days	1 Year
Nikkei	−6.2%	−5.2%	−3.6%
Yen	−0.3%	3.4%	0.5%
Japanese 10-year bond yield	−3.3%	5.9%	−22.3%

On 11 March 2011, Japan was struck with an earthquake and subsequent tsunami wave, resulting in significant loss of human life, homes, and productive capital. The natural disaster also caused a significant nuclear accident that resulted in further human, property, and environmental damage and also disrupted supply chains. The initial market response reflected market concern: Equities fell, the currency depreciated, and bond prices rose. In the weeks that followed and as the toll of the environmental disaster became more apparent, Japanese equity markets continued to suffer, declining up to 20.4 percent (as of 25 November 2011) from their levels the day of the earthquake.

As the environmental costs of the accident became clear, this event contributed to a shifting stance on political cooperation on environmental issues. Less than three months after the incident, Germany decided to phase out nuclear power entirely by 2022. Belgium confirmed plans to exit nuclear power by 2025, and such countries as Italy, Spain, and Switzerland opted not to reintroduce nuclear energy programs.

Finally, **thematic risks** are known risks that evolve and expand over a period of time. Climate change, pattern migration, the rise of populist forces, and the ongoing threat of terrorism fall into this category.

Cyber threats are another example of thematic risk (Exhibit 13). Cyber risks include any attempt to expose, alter, disable, destroy, steal, or gain information through unauthorized access to or unauthorized use of computer systems. These threats began with the expansion of internet and computer use and have increased in number and scale. Now, the number of records stolen or affected by cyberattacks is in the billions per year. While the basic nature of cyberattacks is consistent, the size, scale, and sophistication of attacks have increased over time.

Exhibit 13: Market Reaction to Thematic Risk: Equifax Data Breach, 2017

	First Day	30 Days	1 Year
Stock price	−13.7%	−22.0%	−4.8%
Financial services industry	0.9%	10.3%	18.6%

In September 2017, the US consumer credit reporting company Equifax announced a data breach that exposed personal information, including names, dates of birth, and personal identification numbers of approximately 147 million people. The initial market reaction was very negative. Equifax's equity price fell by 13.7 percent in one day and by 34.9 percent over the first week, reaching its low on 15 September 2017. Over time, the impact moderated somewhat, but Equifax still underperformed the financial services industry in the year after its data breach.

At first, the data breach affected Equifax the most, including instituting protections and credit monitoring for affected customers, without significant impacts on the broader financial industry.

However, the event also triggered broader impacts over time. Other companies have increased spending on cybersecurity and instituted stronger processes, including software upgrades.

EXAMPLE 10

Geopolitical Risk and the Investor

1. Which of the following types of risks are known in advance? Select all that apply.

    A. Event risk

    B. Exogenous risk

    C. Thematic risk

    Solution:

    A and C are correct.

    Event risk evolves around set dates, and thematic risk is a known risk that evolves and expands over a period of time. Exogenous risk is a sudden or unanticipated risk.

Assessing Geopolitical Threats

Geopolitical risk is always present in the investment environment, and these risks can affects investments in many different ways—from broad macroeconomic levels, to industry impacts, down to individual companies. The question for investors is whether the particular geopolitical risk is relevant for their portfolio management decisions. To make this assessment, an investor considers geopolitical risk in terms of the following three areas:

- *likelihood* it will occur,
- *velocity* (speed) of its impact, and
- size and nature of that *impact*.

Likelihood

The likelihood of a risk is the probability that it will occur. Measuring likelihood is a challenging process. The highly unpredictable nature of many risks—their build over time, the many and conflicting motivations of actors involved—means this exercise can be more art than science. However, we may use the framework from Lesson 4 to assess the basic likelihood of risk occurring. Highly collaborative and globalized countries are, on balance, less likely to experience geopolitical risk because the political, economic, and financial costs of partners inflicting those risks are higher. That same interconnectedness, however, may make multilateral countries more vulnerable to certain risks. Their operation in and cooperation with other countries means a risk posed to any of those countries may also have an impact on itself. Similarly, multiple risk exposures may increase the impact of that risk when it occurs.

Of course, many other factors may increase the likelihood that a risk may occur. Internal political stability, economic need, and the motivations of governmental actors play an important role in increasing the likelihood of disruptive action. In fact, these considerations are so plentiful and intertwined that geopolitical risk monitoring tools have emerged as key components of many research offerings for investors. The numerous scenarios for any given risk make measuring risk likelihood a potentially never-ending task. As a result, investors must balance the time spent on this activity with the relative importance of its input to the investment process.

The examples used in the section "Types of Geopolitical Risk" in Lesson 6, can help us put a finer point on this concept. Of the three risks described, a cyber risk may have been the most likely to occur and to affect a given investment strategy, whereas the United Kingdom's "yes" vote and Russia's annexation of Crimea were less likely at the time in which they occurred. Of course, all three of these risks have different potential impacts on investors. As a result, likelihood should be considered only in conjunction with the velocity and impact of the risk.

Velocity

The **velocity** of geopolitical risk is the pace at which it affects an investor portfolio. For the sake of simplicity, we explore short-term or "high-velocity" impacts, medium-term, and long-term or "low-velocity" impacts (see Exhibit 14).

In the short term, we may see volatility in the markets affecting entire industries or even the entire market. Exogenous or "black swan" events tend to fit into this category, causing market volatility and investor flight to quality. A **black swan risk** is an event that is rare and difficult to predict but has an important impact. Investors with the appropriate time horizon and risk tolerance may make tactical changes to their investment choices as a result of these events. Long-term changes are unlikely to be necessary.

Geopolitical Risk and the Investment Process

Risks with a medium-term impact may begin to impair companies' processes, costs, and investment opportunities, resulting in lower valuations. These risks tend to be distributed toward specific sectors, meaning they will affect some companies much more than others.

Long-term risks may have important environmental, social, governance, and other impacts. This can affect an investor's asset allocation—including choice of asset classes and investment styles—for a long-term horizon; however, the immediate impact on portfolios is likely to be more limited.

Exhibit 14: Risk Velocity

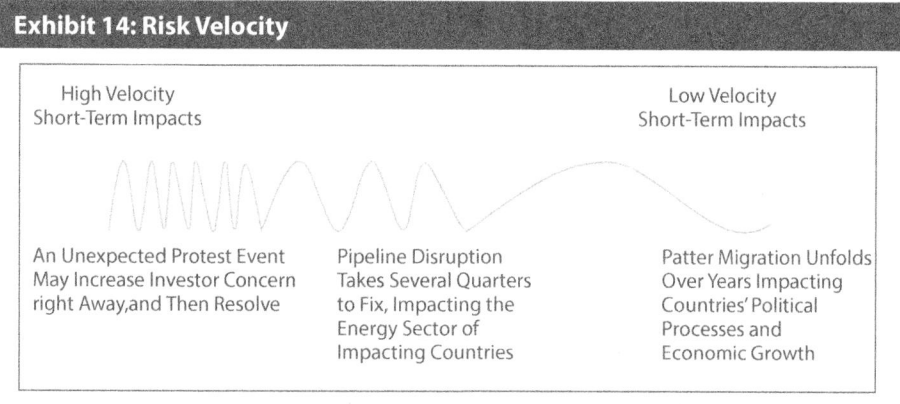

Note that some risks have more than one speed of impact on investments. The United Kingdom's referendum outcome to exit the EU had some immediate impacts, notably a decline in the value of the British pound sterling and other forms of market volatility. Over time, low-velocity impacts have become more apparent and more lasting for investors. Higher transaction costs and the unwind of previous forms of political cooperation—including the freedom of movement between the United Kingdom and the EU—are generating important impacts on investment outcomes and overall economic growth.

EXAMPLE 11

Geopolitical Risk Velocity and Investor Reaction

1. Match the potential velocity of a geopolitical risk with the *most likely* investor reaction among those listed in the following table:

Geopolitical Risk Velocity	Investor Reaction
1. Low	A. Adjust investments in specific sectors
2. Medium	B. Flight to quality
3. High	C. Adjust asset allocation

Solution:

Option 1 (Low) matches with C (Adjust asset allocation).

Option 2 (Medium) matches with A (Adjust investments in specific sectors).

Option 3 (High) matches with B (Flight to quality).

> **EXAMPLE 12**
>
> ## Geopolitical Risk and the Investor
>
> 1. Describe the three areas that an investor should consider when assessing geopolitical risk.
>
>   **Solution:**
>
>   An investor should consider the following three areas when assessing geopolitical risk: the likelihood it will occur, the velocity of its impact, and the size and nature of that impact. The likelihood that it will occur considers the probability that geopolitical risk will occur. The velocity of its impact is the pace at which it affects an investor portfolio. The impact can manifest in many ways and can be discrete in size or broad in nature.

Impact of Geopolitical Risk

A risk's impact on investor portfolios can manifest in many different ways. For the sake of this framework for assessing risk, suffice it to say that investors should consider the size of any risk's impact when gauging its importance to the investment process. A high-impact risk may merit extensive study of its drivers and motivations, whereas a low-impact risk may not. In addition, the size of a risk's impact may be compounded by external factors. For example, risk tends to have a greater impact on markets experiencing a general contraction or economic downturn.

Impact may also be discrete or broad in nature. Discrete impacts are those that affect only one company or sector at a time, whereas broad impacts are felt more holistically by a sector, a country, or the global economy. Cyber risks may be considered in this light. In the event of a cyberattack, only the companies and investment strategies exposed to that company will be affected. However, cyber risks may also have a broader impact by increasing monitoring, due diligence, and security costs for all companies and investors seeking to avoid them.

When assessing geopolitical risk for portfolio management, investors should consider all three geopolitical risk factors—likelihood, velocity, and size and nature of impact—together. For example, a highly likely risk with very little impact to the portfolio may not merit extensive analysis and investor attention. However, a highly impactful risk with a low likelihood of occurring may merit building a scenario for response but not regular monitoring and assessment. Between these extremes, investors must consider their goals and risk tolerance to identify high-priority risks.

Scenario Analysis

Geopolitical risks seldom develop in linear fashion, making it difficult to monitor and forecast their likelihood, velocity, and impact on a portfolio as well as difficult to address those changes through portfolio action. As a result, many investors deploy an approach that includes scenario analysis and signposting rather than a single point forecast.

Scenario analysis is the process of evaluating portfolio outcomes across potential circumstances or states of the world. Scenarios help investment teams understand where they stand with respect to a risk that might cause them to change their behavior. Scenario analysis can strengthen a team's conviction about its prioritization and calls to action, thereby helping it make good investment choices at opportune moments.

Scenarios can take the form of qualitative analysis, quantitative measurement, or both. A simple framework for qualitative scenario building begins with developing a base case for the event. What is the most impactful outcome of the risk? How likely is that risk/outcome to occur in the first place? From there, investors can consider upside and downside scenarios. Is it a persistent tail risk or a short-term shock? How are markets likely to recover once the event has taken place? Considering alternate futures for key risks will drive more precise perspective around what constitutes key developments in the most important risks.

Quantitative scenarios can vary widely by sophistication. One form of a simple quantitative scenario is a stylized scenario in which portfolio sensitivity is measured against one key factor relevant to the portfolio, such as interest rates, asset prices, or exchange rates. Another involves using circumstances from extreme events to help build quantitative tests for portfolio resilience. It is important to have reasonable ambitions, however. Quantitative scenarios can be complicated because of the secondary and linked impacts of geopolitical risks to securities in the portfolio.

Good scenario building can prompt investors to alter their risk prioritization, making it a useful tool not only for tracking risks but also for deciding which portfolio actions may be valuable to take. Good scenario analysis also requires a consistent commitment of investors' time and resources. Teams that read similar research or speak with similar client groups may be affected by **groupthink**, the practice of thinking or making decisions as a group in a way that discourages creativity or individual responsibility. For scenario analysis to be useful in portfolio management, teams must work hard to build creative processes, identify and track scenarios, and assess the need for action on a regular basis.

Tracking Risks According to Signposts

To build a portfolio's resilience to unexpected change, asset managers develop processes in advance that allow for rapid course correction. In other words, by creating plans for addressing priority risks as they occur, investors can help reduce the events' impact on investment outcomes.

One important process is identifying signposts for priority risk. A **signpost** is an indicator, market level, data piece, or event that signals a risk is becoming more or less likely. An analyst can think of signposts like a traffic light. If quantitative and qualitative evidence suggest that a risk is low in likelihood, velocity, or impact, then the signposts are flashing green, or no action needed. If signposts are flashing amber, indicating that a risk is medium in likelihood, velocity, or impact, then higher caution and preparedness against that risk may be warranted. As a risk rises in likelihood, velocity, or impact, an action plan may be necessary.

Identifying signposts should equip a team to differentiate signal from noise and react when signposts flash red. For instance, when the market environment moves to either risk-on or risk-off, it is important to identify what actions should be taken next or communications made. Good signposts are anchored in the key assumptions made up-front around a scenario and mark whether a scenario is materializing.

Let's return to our example of the United Kingdom's Brexit referendum for context. Before 2014, signposts for geopolitical risk in the United Kingdom may have flashed "green." Attitudes toward European Union membership were divided, and while there is always a possibility of disruptive geopolitical change, a reduction in political cooperation with the European Union was not clearly defined. Then, when the referendum was announced in 2015, signposts for disruptive change became more likely and faster in potential velocity, resulting in a higher required level of portfolio manager attention. In May 2016, when phone polls suggested that the "leave" vote was moving to the majority, signposts flashed "red" and attentive portfolio managers prepared action plans for election day.

Identifying the right signposts can require some trial and error. A basic rule of thumb for distinguishing signal from noise is the distinction between politics and policy. For example, there can be a big difference in "politics" between two leaders, but the "policies" they enact are what create larger or more durable portfolio impacts. Political developments can serve as meaningful signposts, as they can indicate a change in the risk's likelihood or pace. However, analysts are frequently knocked off course by following developments that do not necessarily indicate a change in real economic or market outcomes. Instead, analysts should look for policy changes to guide their portfolio management decisions.

Some combinations of economic and financial market circumstances serve as strong warnings of potential trouble. For example, high inflation and deteriorating employment can signal political unrest. A pegged currency and rapidly declining export value (particularly for commodities exporters) can prompt a change in exchange rate policy. Often, particularly for emerging markets, these signposts will change before official data are released. If a portfolio relies on country-level economic conditions, data screens should be used to help identify any red flags early.

Manifestations of Geopolitical Risk

If geopolitical risk takes many forms, its impact on investor portfolios is just as multifaceted. High-velocity risks are most likely to manifest in market volatility through prompt changes in asset prices. Commonly affected asset prices include commodities, foreign exchange, equities, and bond prices (via changes in interest rates).

One example is the market response to economic shutdowns related to the COVID-19 pandemic (Exhibit 15). Using the United States as an example, the S&P 500 Index fell from a level of 3,386 on 19 February 2020 to 2,237.4 on 23 March, a decline of nearly 34%. Bonds also experienced volatility. Global investors' "flight to safety" pushed up US bond prices. The US 10-year Treasury yield fell from 1.5661 to a low of 0.5407 during that period, a decline of nearly 68 percent. This volatility was not permanent but created ample risk—and opportunity—for investors during that time.

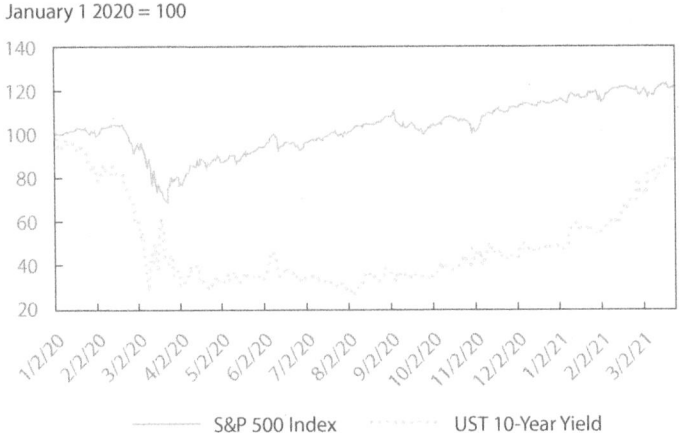

Exhibit 15: US Market Reaction to the COVID-19 Pandemic, 1 January 2020 to 23 March 2021

Source: Bloomberg Finance LP.

Low-velocity geopolitical risks can have a more prolonged impact on investor inputs. Sustained disruption may result in smaller revenues, higher costs, or both, which can negatively affect a company's valuation. Here, too, the COVID-19 pandemic is an instructive example. While risk asset valuations improved over the course of the pandemic, disruptions to mobility and consumption had long-lasting impacts on company revenues and supply chains.

For countries, regions, or sectors perceived to be at more consistent risk of geopolitical disruption, investors may require higher compensation, effectively increasing the discount rate investors use when valuing those securities. Portfolio investment flows face greater volatility because of geopolitical factors, and investors will factor in a higher risk premium. This dynamic is a key reason why asset prices in emerging and frontier markets are typically maintained at a discount to those in developed countries that are perceived to have a lower threat of risk.

GEOPOLITICAL RISK INDEX

In a 2019 paper, two analysts at the US Federal Reserve Board of Governors built the Geopolitical Risk Index (GPR) based on a tally of news articles covering geopolitical tensions and their impact on economic events. The purpose of the index is to measure real-time geopolitical risk as perceived by the press, the public, global investors, and policymakers in a way that is consistent over time.

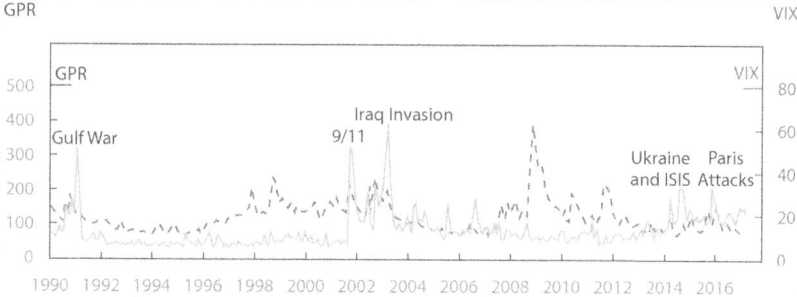

Through their construction of the GPR, the authors made three important observations. First, they found that high levels of geopolitical risk reduce US investment, employment, and price level of the stock market. Second, and taking this observation deeper, the authors found that individual firm's investment falls more in industries positively exposed to geopolitical risk and that firms reduce investment in the wake of idiosyncratic geopolitical risk events. Finally, they studied the adverse effect of geopolitical events themselves as well as the threat of adverse events, finding that the threat of events had a larger impact over time.

EXAMPLE 13

Geopolitical Risk

1. True or False: Higher-velocity geopolitical risks are *most* likely to have a prolonged impact on investor inputs.

   Explain your selection.

   A. True

   B. False

   Solution:

   B is correct. Higher-velocity risks are most likely to manifest in market volatility via prompt changes in asset prices. Lower-velocity geopolitical risks are likely to have a prolonged impact on investor inputs. The terrorist attacks of 11 September 2001 in the United States are an example of a higher-velocity geopolitical risk as the market had a sharp downturn and rebounded in a relatively short amount of time.

EXAMPLE 14

Geopolitical Risk

1. True or false: The probability and impact of geopolitical risks influence relative asset price discount rates across emerging and developed markets.

    Explain your selection.

    A. True

    B. False

    Solution:

    A is correct. For countries, regions, or sectors perceived to be at more consistent risk of geopolitical disruption, investors may require higher compensation, effectively increasing the discount rate used in valuation. When portfolio investment flows face greater volatility because of geopolitical factors, investors will factor in a higher risk premium. This explains why asset prices in emerging markets typically are maintained at a discount to those in developed countries perceived to have a lower threat of geopolitical risk, with the latter more likely to experience lower probability risks with lesser impacts.

Acting on Geopolitical Risk

Determining the likelihood, velocity, and impact of a risk may help an investor to assign priority to which risks might be most important. But if the risk does occur, what, if anything, can be done about it? Even if an investor could anticipate every risk and its impact on their portfolios, they must still consider whether and how to act in the face of such threats. A final step in incorporating geopolitical risk into the portfolio management process thus requires that geopolitical risk analysis be translated into investment action as appropriate for investor goals, risk tolerance, and time horizon.

Taking a top-down approach, asset allocators may consider geopolitical risk in their asset allocation strategy. The likelihood, velocity, and impact of risks may affect key capital markets assumptions as well as an asset allocator's positioning in certain countries or regions. For example, countries with a long history of using a multilateral approach may be considered more reliable investments and see increased investor flows. In contrast, those countries experiencing consistent military threat may have lower economic and investment growth potential because of consistent disruptions. The asset allocator would thus allocate more capital to the countries with lower expected risk profiles.

At the portfolio management level, investors can consider geopolitical risk as a factor in multifactor models. Imagine an analyst assessing global car manufacturers. A company with highly diversified production may be exposed to more risk (i.e., higher likelihood), but production would be less likely to come to a halt given the multiple production alternatives (i.e., lower impact). When making a buy or sell recommendation, the analyst may consider relative geopolitical risk exposure as a factor in their analysis. Disruptive threats may be used as a binary yes-or-no factor or they can affect the confidence intervals around factors related to momentum, valuation, market sentiment, or the economic cycle.

Ultimately, the importance of geopolitical risk to the investment process depends on investor objectives, risk tolerance, and time horizon. For an investor with low risk tolerance, reducing exposure to geopolitical risk may be appropriate, whether through low-volatility investment choices or through hedging.

For an investor with a long time horizon, a geopolitical event like an exogenous shock could be a buying opportunity. For an investor nearing retirement, however, that same exogenous shock can have a major negative impact on their terminal portfolio value.

The extensive political, economic, and financial cooperation in which countries, companies, and organizations participate may raise the stakes of geopolitical risk analysis for global investors. Changes in the style and momentum of international cooperation can have an important impact on capital markets. Global investors ignore those risks at their peril.

PRACTICE PROBLEMS

1. Which of the following statements regarding a country's political cooperation is *most* accurate?
    A. If a country is engaged in military conflict, there is a higher cost to cooperation.
    B. A country with few internal resources is not likely to rely on political cooperation.
    C. Interest prioritization does not determine the depth and nature of political cooperation.

2. A consequence of one of the disadvantages of globalization is that:
    A. pay differences between countries have narrowed.
    B. emerging market trade flows have grown more important.
    C. greater economic and financial cooperation has increased interdependence.

3. Which of the following outcomes is *most* likely a result of globalization?
    A. Unequal gains
    B. Increased independence
    C. Decreased access to talent

4. A US company expanding critical spare part inventories for local customers made at its existing Canadian facility after a supply chain disruption is *most likely* using the coping tactic of:
    A. reshoring the essentials.
    B. reglobalizing production.
    C. doubling down on key markets.

5. An example of a geopolitical multifaceted tool for furthering national interests is:
    A. cabotage.
    B. armed conflict.
    C. nationalization of key export industries.

6. Which of these is most likely to be described as an event risk?
    A. An earthquake
    B. An election
    C. An ongoing civil war

7. Exogenous risks are *best* described as those that:
    A. are known and evolve and expand over a period of time.

Practice Problems

    B. revolve around set dates, such as elections, new legislation, or other date-driven milestones, such as holidays or political anniversaries.

    C. are sudden or unanticipated and impact either a country's cooperative stance, the ability of non-state actors to globalize, or both.

8. Which of the following statements about geopolitical threats in the investment environment is *most* accurate?
    - **A.** Geopolitical risk is not always present in the investment environment.
    - **B.** Highly collaborative, interconnected countries are vulnerable to geopolitical risk.
    - **C.** Geopolitical risk tends to have less of an impact on markets already experiencing a general contraction or economic downturn.

9. An applicable conclusion drawn from the Geopolitical Risk Index (GPR) is that:
    - **A.** high geopolitical risk results in tangible macroeconomic effects.
    - **B.** recurring geopolitical risk events lead to reduced corporate investment.
    - **C.** the adverse impact of actual events is greater over time than that of the threat of such events.

10. The basic geopolitical risk type *most likely* in comparison to have the smallest degree of uncertainty is:
    - **A.** exogenous risk.
    - **B.** event risk.
    - **C.** thematic risk.

SOLUTIONS

1. A is correct. If a country is engaged in military conflict, there is a higher cost to cooperation. B is incorrect because a country with few internal resources is likely to rely on political cooperation. C is incorrect because interest prioritization does determine the depth and nature of political cooperation.

2. C is correct. Through the process of greater economic and financial cooperation, companies may become dependent on other countries' resources for their supply chains. On aggregate, this can result in the nation itself becoming dependent on other nations for certain resources (such as rare earth metals, cobalt, or copper). If there is a disruption to the supply chain, including via a moment of political non-cooperation, then firms may not be able to produce the good themselves.

   A is incorrect because the narrowing of pay differences between countries results from a motivation to pursue globalization, which is related to one of its advantages. It is an important way for companies to increase profitability by reducing their costs. Although wage differentials remain, they are decreasing. B is incorrect because the proportion of flows between developed economies as a share of overall trade continuing to decline as emerging market trade flows rise is a function of increased international investment. This increased investment has provided beneficial aggregate economic benefits, such as increased choice, higher quality goods, increased competition among firms, higher efficiency, and increased labor mobility.

3. A is correct. Unequal accrual of economic and financial gains is a cost of globalization because improvement on the aggregate does not mean improvement for everyone. B is incorrect because globalization leads to *interdependency* as companies may become dependent on other countries' resources for their supply chains. C is incorrect because rather than decreased access to talent, a country might actually globalize to improve access to talent as cooperation and globalization can lead to increased access to resources.

4. A is correct. The COVID-19 pandemic has highlighted the need for certain essential supply chains to be rebuilt domestically for emergency situations, with availability of critical spare parts being an analogy. The close integration of the US and Canadian economies through the revised USMCA agreement effectively makes expanded production at an existing Canadian factory an example of reducing manufacturing risk by relocating to home countries via reshoring. B is incorrect because instead of reducing manufacturing risk by duplicating or fortifying its supply chain, the company is simply continuing to use its existing capacity more intensively. C is incorrect because although the production is intended to better supply its home market, there is no evidence that the company is expanding its presence in the US market or shifting its focus to the exclusion of available opportunities elsewhere.

5. A is correct. Cabotage is the right to transport passengers or goods within a country by a foreign firm. Many countries—including those with multilateral trade agreements—impose restrictions on cabotage across transportation subsectors, meaning that shippers, airlines, and truck drivers are not allowed to transport goods and services within another country's borders. Allowing cabotage requires coordination on areas like physical security and economic coordination, a highly multilateral (multifaceted tool) process. B is incorrect because armed conflict is the most extreme example of a national security tool. It can be either internal or external to a country in taking a direct and active approach to wield-

ing influence. C is incorrect because nationalization of key export industries is an economic tool. This process of transferring an activity or industry from private to state control is a non-cooperative approach to asserting economic control.

6. B is correct. Event risk evolves around set dates, such as elections and new legislation, or other date-driven milestones, such as holidays or political anniversaries known in advance. The other choices could not be known in advance. An earthquake (A) is an example of an exogenous risk. An ongoing civil war (C) is an example of a thematic risk.

7. C is correct. Exogenous risks are best described as those that are sudden or unanticipated and that affect either a country's cooperative stance, the ability of non-state actors to globalize, or both. A is incorrect because thematic (not exogenous) risks are known risks that evolve and expand over a period of time. B is incorrect because event (not exogenous) risks are those that evolve around set dates, including elections, new legislation, or other date-driven milestones.

8. B is correct. Although highly collaborative and globalized countries are, on balance, less likely to experience geopolitical risk because the political, economic, and financial costs of partners inflicting those risks are higher than less collaborative countries, the same interconnectedness may make them more vulnerable to geopolitical risk. A is incorrect because geopolitical risk is always present in the investment environment. C is incorrect because geopolitical risk tends to have a greater impact on markets already experiencing a general contraction or economic downturn.

9. A is correct. The GPR creators found that high levels of geopolitical risk reduce US investment, employment, and price level of the stock market. B is incorrect because firms reduce investment in the wake of idiosyncratic events, which would be unlikely to repeat. C is incorrect because the threat of an event was shown to have a larger impact over time than that of the actual events themselves.

10. B is correct. *Event risk* evolves around set dates, such as elections or new legislation, or other date-driven milestones, such as holidays or political anniversaries. Analysts can thus look to political calendars as a predictable starting point for determining the occurrence of event risk, with time to devise a suitable response.

    A is incorrect because exogenous risk is sudden and unanticipated. Examples include sudden uprisings, invasions, or the aftermath of natural disasters. The timing and range of its effects thus have the greatest unknowns. C is incorrect because thematic risks are known risks that evolve and expand over a period of time. Climate change, pattern migration, the rise of populist forces, and the ongoing threat of terrorism fall into this category. These are more foreseeable than exogenous risks, but with their extended interval of exposure, planned responses likely require continual adjustments.

LEARNING MODULE 6

International Trade

by Usha Nair-Reichert, PhD, and Daniel Robert Witschi, PhD, CFA.

Usha Nair-Reichert, PhD, is at Georgia Institute of Technology (USA). Daniel Robert Witschi, PhD, CFA (Switzerland).

LEARNING OUTCOMES	
Mastery	*The candidate should be able to:*
☐	describe the benefits and costs of international trade
☐	compare types of trade restrictions, such as tariffs, quotas, and export subsidies, and their economic implications
☐	explain motivations for and advantages of trading blocs, common markets, and economic unions

INTRODUCTION

From an investment perspective, it is important for global investors to understand existing trade policies. Such policies can affect the volume and value of trade and thus can affect the return on investment. Investors need to be aware of potential changes in the government's trade policy. Such changes have important implications for firm profitability and growth by affecting the demand for its products and its pricing. There has been much debate among economists on the role of trade and trade policy and its impact on the overall economy. This learning module examines the benefits and cost of international trade. It then describes trade restrictions and their implications and discusses the motivation for, and advantages of, the different types of trading blocs or trade agreements.

> **LEARNING MODULE OVERVIEW**
>
> - The most compelling arguments supporting international trade are:
>   - countries gain from exchange and specialization,
>   - industries experience greater economies of scale,
>   - households and firms have greater product variety,
>   - competition is increased, and

- resources are allocated more efficiently.
- Newer models of trade focus on the gains from trade that result from economies of scale, greater product variety, and increased competition.
- Opponents of free trade point to the potential for greater income inequality and the loss of jobs in developed market countries as a result of import competition.
- The fact that trade increases overall welfare does not mean that every individual consumer and producer is better off. What it does mean is that the winners could, in theory, compensate the losers and still be better off.
- Trade restrictions (or trade protection) are government policies that limit the ability of domestic households and firms to trade freely with other countries.
- Tariffs are taxes that a government levies on imported goods. The primary objective of tariffs is to protect domestic industries that produce the same or similar goods. They also may aim to reduce a trade deficit.
- The net welfare effect of tariffs is the sum of consumer surplus, producer surplus and government tax revenue. The loss in consumer surplus is greater than the sum of the gain in producer surplus and government revenue and results in a deadweight loss to the country's welfare.
- A quota restricts the quantity of a good that can be imported into a country, generally for a specified period of time. A voluntary export restraint (VER) is a trade barrier under which the exporting country agrees to limit its exports of the good to its trading partners to a specific number of units.
- An export subsidy is a payment by the government to a firm for each unit of a good that is exported. Its goal is to stimulate exports.
- A regional trading bloc is a group of countries that have signed an agreement to reduce and progressively eliminate barriers to trade and the movement of factors of production among the members of the bloc.
- There are many different types of regional trading blocs, depending on the level of integration that takes place. These include free trade areas, customs union, common market, and economic union.
- Trade creation occurs when regional integration results in the replacement of higher-cost domestic production by lower-cost imports from other members. Trade diversion occurs when lower-cost imports from non-member countries are replaced with higher-cost imports from members.

2 BENEFITS AND COSTS OF TRADE

☐ describe the benefits and costs of international trade

Over the past few decades, the global economy has experienced rapid growth in trade and a growing interdependence among countries. This has led to a debate among policy makers over whether the expansion of trade has been helpful for individual national economies. This lesson examines the possible benefits and costs of international trade.

Benefits and Costs of International Trade

The benefits and costs of international trade are widely debated. The most compelling arguments supporting international trade are as follows: countries gain from exchange and specialization, industries experience greater economies of scale, households and firms have greater product variety, competition is increased, and resources are allocated more efficiently.

Gains from exchange occur when trade enables each country to receive a higher price for its exports (and greater profit) or pay a lower price for imported goods instead of producing these goods domestically at a higher cost (i.e., less efficiently). This exchange, in turn, leads to a more efficient allocation of resources by increasing production of the export good and reducing production of the import good in each country (trading partner). This efficiency allows for consumption of a larger bundle of goods, thus increasing overall welfare. The fact that trade increases overall welfare does not mean, of course, that every individual consumer and producer is better off. What it does mean is that the winners could, in theory, compensate the losers and still be better off.

Trade also leads to greater efficiency by fostering specialization based on comparative advantage. Traditional trade models, such as the Ricardian model and the Heckscher–Ohlin model, focus on specialization and trade according to comparative advantage arising from differences in technology and factor endowments, respectively.

Newer models of trade focus on the gains from trade that result from economies of scale, greater product variety, and increased competition. In an open economy, increased competition from foreign firms reduces the monopoly power of domestic firms and forces them to become more efficient, in contrast to a closed economy. Industries that exhibit increasing returns to scale (e.g., the automobile and steel industries) benefit from increased market size as a country starts trading because the average cost of production declines as output increases in these industries. Monopolistically competitive models of trade have been used to explain why there is significant two-way trade (known as *intra-industry trade*) between countries within the same industry. Intra-industry trade occurs when a country exports and imports goods in the same product category or classification.

A monopolistically competitive industry has many firms; each firm produces a unique or differentiated product: it does not have any exit or entry barriers, and long-run economic profits are zero. In such a model, even though countries may be similar, they gain from trade because each country focuses on the production and export of one or more varieties of the good and imports other varieties of the good. For example, the European Union exports and imports different types of cars. Consumers gain from having access to a greater variety of final goods. Firms benefit from greater economies of scale because firms both within and outside the EU are able to sell their goods in both markets. Hence, scale economies allow firms to benefit from the larger market size and experience lower average cost of production as a result of trade.

Research suggests that trade liberalization can lead to increased real (i.e., inflation-adjusted) GDP although the strength of this relationship is still debated. The positive influence of trade on GDP can arise from more efficient allocation of resources, learning by doing, higher productivity, knowledge spillovers, and trade-induced changes in policies and institutions that affect the incentives for innovation. In industries that embrace "learning by doing," such as the semiconductor industry, the cost of production per unit declines as output increases because of expertise and experience acquired in the process of production. Trade can lead to increased exchange of ideas, freer flow of technical expertise, and greater awareness of changing consumer tastes and preferences in global markets. It also can contribute to the development of higher quality and more effective institutions and policies that encourage domestic innovation. For example, studies have shown that foreign research and development (R&D) has beneficial effects on domestic productivity, which become stronger the more open an economy is to foreign trade. For example, some estimate that about a quarter of the benefits of R&D investment in a G–7 country accrues to their trading partners. Consider Logitech, a Swiss company that manufactures computer mice. To win original equipment manufacturer (OEM) contracts from IBM and Apple, Logitech needed to develop innovative designs and provide high-volume production at a low cost. So in the late 1980s, the company moved to Taiwan Region, which had a highly qualified labor force, competent parts suppliers, a rapidly expanding local computer industry, and offered Logitech space in a science park at a competitive rate. Soon thereafter, Logitech was able to secure the Apple contract.

Opponents of free trade point to the potential for greater income inequality and the loss of jobs in developed countries as a result of import competition. As a country moves toward free trade, adjustments will be made in domestic industries that are exporters as well as in those that face import competition. Resources (investments) may need to be reallocated into or out of an industry depending on whether that industry is expanding (exporters) or contracting (i.e., facing import competition). As a result of this adjustment process, less-efficient firms may be forced to exit the industry, which, in turn, may lead to higher unemployment and the need for displaced workers to be retrained for jobs in expanding industries. The counter argument is that although there may be short-term and even some medium-term costs, these resources are likely to be more effectively (re-)employed in other industries in the long run. Nonetheless, the adjustment process is virtually certain to impose costs on some groups of stakeholders.

> **QUESTION SET**
>
> Consider two countries that each produce two goods. Suppose the cost of producing cotton relative to lumber is lower in Cottonland than in Lumberland.
>
> 1. How would trade between the two countries affect the lumber industry in Lumberland?
>
>   **Solution:**
>
>   The lumber industry in Lumberland would benefit from trade. Because the cost of producing lumber relative to producing cotton is lower in Lumberland than in Cottonland (i.e., lumber is relatively cheap in Lumberland), Lumberland will export lumber and the industry will expand.
>
> 2. How would trade between the two countries affect the lumber industry in Cottonland?
>
>   **Solution:**
>
>   The lumber industry in Cottonland would not benefit from trade, at least in the short run. Because lumber is relatively expensive to produce in Cottonland, the domestic lumber industry will shrink as lumber is imported from Lumberland.

3. What would happen to the lumber industry workers in Cottonland in the long run?

   Solution:

   The overall welfare effect in both countries is positive. However, in the short run, many lumber producers in Cottonland (and cotton producers in Lumberland) are likely to find themselves without jobs as the lumber industry in Cottonland and the cotton industry in Lumberland contract. Those with skills that also are needed in the other industry may find jobs fairly quickly. Others are likely to do so after some re-training. In the long run, displaced workers should be able to find jobs in the expanding export industry. Those who remain in the import-competing industry, however, may be permanently worse off because their industry-specific skills are now less valuable. Thus, even in the long run, trade does not necessarily make every stakeholder better off. But the winners could compensate the losers and still be better off, so the overall welfare effect of opening trade is positive.

4. What is the meaning of the expression "gains from trade"?

   Solution:

   Gains from trade imply that the overall benefits of trade outweigh the losses from trade. It does not mean that all stakeholders (producers, consumers, government) benefit (or benefit equally) from trade.

5. What are some of the benefits from trade?

   Solution:

   Some of the benefits from trade include the following: gains from exchange and specialization based on relative cost advantage; gains from economies of scale as the companies add new markets for their products; greater variety of products available to households and firms; greater efficiency from increased competition; and more efficient allocation of resources.

TRADE RESTRICTIONS AND AGREEMENTS—TARIFFS, QUOTAS, AND EXPORT SUBSIDIES

3

☐ compare types of trade restrictions, such as tariffs, quotas, and export subsidies, and their economic implications

Trade restrictions (or trade protection) are government policies that limit the ability of domestic households and firms to trade freely with other countries. Examples of trade restrictions include tariffs, import quotas, voluntary export restraints (VER), subsidies, embargoes, and domestic content requirements. **Tariffs** are taxes that a government levies on imported goods. **Quotas** restrict the quantity of a good that can be imported into a country, generally for a specified period of time. A voluntary export restraint is similar to a quota but is imposed by the exporting country. An **export subsidy** is paid by the government to the firm when it exports a unit of a good that is being subsidized. The goal is to promote exports, but it reduces welfare by encouraging production and trade that is inconsistent with comparative advantage. **Domestic content provisions** stipulate that some percentage of the value added or components used in production should be of domestic origin. Trade restrictions are imposed by countries for several reasons, including protecting established domestic industries from foreign competition, protecting new industries from foreign competition until they mature (infant industry argument), protecting and increasing domestic employment, protecting strategic industries for national security reasons, generating revenue from tariffs (especially for developing countries), and retaliation against trade restrictions imposed by other countries.

Capital restrictions are defined as controls placed on foreigners' ability to own domestic assets or domestic residents' ability to own foreign assets. Thus, in contrast with trade restrictions, which limit the openness of goods markets, capital restrictions limit the openness of financial markets and will be addressed later.

Tariffs

Tariffs are taxes that a government levies on imported goods. The primary objective of tariffs is to protect domestic industries that produce the same or similar goods. They also may aim to reduce a trade deficit. Tariffs reduce the demand for imported goods by increasing their price above the free trade price. The economic impact of a tariff on imports in a small country is illustrated in Exhibit 1. In this context, a small country is not necessarily small in size, population, or GDP. Instead, a **small country** is one that is a price taker in the world market for a product and cannot influence the world market price. For example, by many measures, Brazil is a large country, but it is a price taker in the world market for cars. A large country, however, is a large importer of the product and can exercise some influence on price in the world market. When a large country imposes a tariff, the exporter reduces the price of the good to retain some of the market share it could lose if it did not lower its price.

This reduction in price alters the terms of trade and represents a redistribution of income from the exporting country to the importing country. So, in theory, it is possible for a large country to increase its welfare by imposing a tariff if (1) its trading partner does not retaliate and (2) the deadweight loss as a result of the tariff (see below) is smaller than the benefit of improving its terms of trade. Global welfare, however, would still experience a net reduction—the large country cannot gain by imposing a tariff unless it imposes an even larger loss on its trading partner.

In Exhibit 1, the world price (free trade price) is P^*. Under free trade, domestic supply is Q^1, domestic consumption is Q^4, and imports are Q^1Q^4. After the imposition of a per-unit tariff t, the domestic price increases to P_t, which is the sum of the world price and the per-unit tariff t. At the new domestic price, domestic production increases to Q^2 and domestic consumption declines to Q^3, resulting in a reduction in imports to Q^2Q^3.

Exhibit 1: Welfare Effects of Tariff and Import Quota

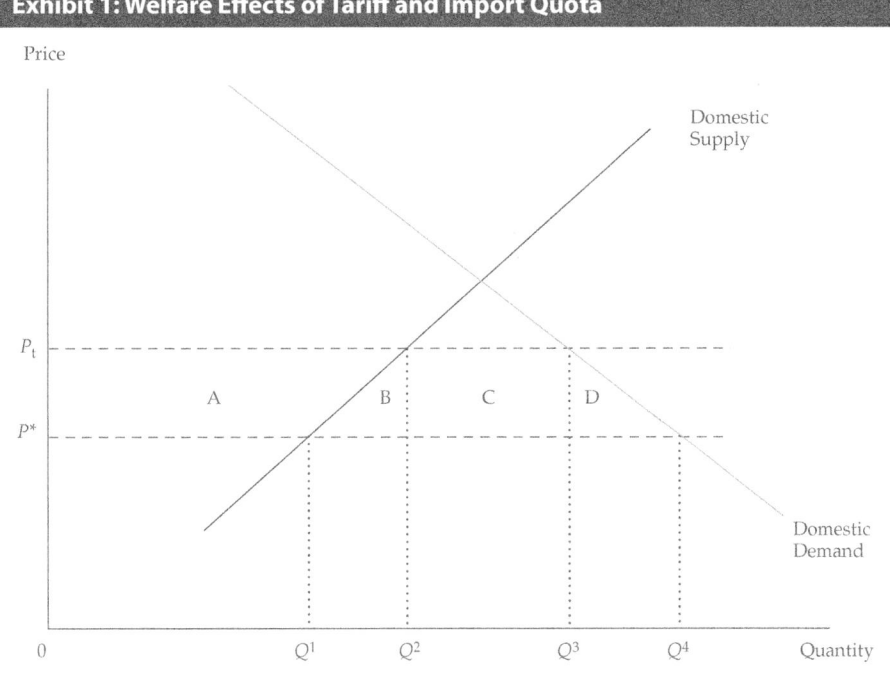

The welfare effects of the tariff can be summarized as follows:

- Consumers suffer a loss of consumer surplus because of the increase in price. In Exhibit 1, this effect is represented by areas A + B + C + D.
- Local producers gain producer surplus from a higher price for their output. This effect is represented by area A.
- The government gains tariff revenue on imports Q^2Q^3. This effect is represented by area C.

The net welfare effect is the sum of these three effects and is summarized in Exhibit 2. The loss in consumer surplus is greater than the sum of the gain in producer surplus and government revenue and results in a deadweight loss to the country's welfare of B + D.

Exhibit 2: Welfare Effects of an Import Tariff or Quota

	Importing Country
Consumer surplus	− (A + B + C + D)
Producer surplus	+A
Tariff revenue *or* Quota rents	+C
National welfare	− B − D

Tariffs create deadweight loss because they give rise to inefficiencies on both the consumption and production side. B represents inefficiencies in production. Instead of being able to import goods at the world price P^*, tariffs encourage inefficient producers whose cost of production is greater than P^* to enter (or remain in) the market, leading to an inefficient allocation of resources. On the consumption side, tariffs prevent mutually beneficial exchanges from occurring because consumers who were willing to pay more than P^* but less than P_t are now unable to consume the good.

EXAMPLE 1

Analysis of a Tariff

South Africa manufactures 110,000 tons of paper. However, domestic demand for paper is 200,000 tons. The world price for paper is USD5.00 per ton. South Africa will import 90,000 tons of paper from the world market at free trade prices. If the South African government (a small country) decides to impose a tariff of 20 percent on paper imports, the price of imported paper will increase to USD6.00. Domestic production after the imposition of the tariff increases to 130,000 tons, while the quantity demanded declines to 170,000 tons.

1. Calculate the loss in consumer surplus arising from the imposition of the tariff on imported paper.

   Solution:

   The loss in consumer surplus = USD1 × 170,000 + 1/2 × USD1 × 30,000 = USD185,000. This calculation is represented by areas A + B + C + D in Exhibit 1.

2. Calculate the gain in producer surplus arising from the imposition of the tariff.

   Solution:

   Gain in producer surplus = USD1 × 110,000 + 1/2 × (USD1 × 20,000) = USD120,000; Area A in Exhibit 1.

3. Calculate the gain in government revenue arising from the imposition of the tariff.

   Solution:

   Change in government revenue = USD1 × 40,000 = USD40,000; Area C in Exhibit 1.

4. Calculate the deadweight loss arising from the imposition of the tariff.

   Solution:

   Deadweight loss because of the tariff = 1/2 × USD1 × 20,000 + 1/2 × USD1 × 30,000 = USD 25,000; Areas B + D in Exhibit 1.

Quotas

A quota restricts the quantity of a good that can be imported into a country, generally for a specified period of time. An **import license** specifies the quantity that can be imported. For example, the European Union operates a system of annual import quotas for steel producers who are not members of the World Trade Organization. A key difference between tariffs and quotas is that the government is able to collect the revenue generated from a tariff. This effect is uncertain under a quota. With quotas, foreign producers can often raise the price of their goods and earn greater profits than they would without the quota. These profits are called **quota rents**. In Exhibit 1, if the quota is Q^2Q^3, the equivalent tariff that will restrict imports to Q^2Q^3 is t and the domestic price after the quota is P_t. This is the same as the domestic price after the tariff t was imposed. Area C, however, is now the quota rent or profits that are likely to be captured by the foreign producer rather than tariff revenue that is captured by the domestic government. If the foreign producer or foreign government captures the quota rent, C, then the welfare loss to the importing country, represented by areas B + D + C in Exhibit 1, under a quota is greater than under the equivalent tariff. If the government of the country that imposes the quota can capture the quota rents by auctioning the import licenses for a fee, then the welfare loss under the quota is similar to that of a tariff, represented by areas B + D.

A VER is a trade barrier under which the exporting country agrees to limit its exports of the good to its trading partners to a specific number of units. The main difference between an import quota and a VER is that the former is imposed by the importer, whereas the latter is imposed by the exporter. The VER allows the quota rent resulting from the decrease in trade to be captured by the exporter (or exporting country), whereas in the case of an import quota, there is ambiguity regarding who captures the quota rents. Hence, a VER results in welfare loss in the importing country. For example, in 1981, the Japanese government imposed VERs on automobile exports to the United States.

Export Subsidies

An export subsidy is a payment by the government to a firm for each unit of a good that is exported. Its goal is to stimulate exports. But it interferes with the functioning of the free market and may distort trade away from comparative advantage. Hence, it reduces welfare. *Countervailing duties* are duties that are levied by the importing country against subsidized exports entering the country. As an example, agricultural subsidies in developed countries, notably the EU, have been a contentious issue in trade negotiations with emerging market countries and developed market countries that are agricultural exporters, such as New Zealand and Australia.

In the case of an export subsidy, the exporter has the incentive to shift sales from the domestic to the export market because it receives the international price plus the per-unit subsidy for each unit of the good exported. This scenario raises the price in the domestic market by the amount of the subsidy in the small country case (price before subsidy plus subsidy). In the large country case, the world price declines as the large country increases exports. The net welfare effect is negative in both the large and small country cases, with a larger decline in the large country case. In the large country case, the decline in world prices implies that a part of the subsidy is transferred to the foreign country, unlike in the small country case.

Exhibit 3 summarizes some of these effects.

Exhibit 3: Summary of Some of the Effects of Trade Restrictions

Panel A. Effects of Alternative Trade Policies

	Tariff	Import Quota	Export Subsidy	VER
Impact on	Importing country	Importing country	Exporting country	Importing country
Producer surplus	Increases	Increases	Increases	Increases
Consumer surplus	Decreases	Decreases	Decreases	Decreases

Panel A. Effects of Alternative Trade Policies

	Tariff	Import Quota	Export Subsidy	VER
Government revenue	Increases	Mixed (depends on whether the quota rents are captured by the importing country through sale of licenses or by the exporters)	Falls (government spending rises)	No change (rent to foreigners)
National welfare	Decreases in small country Could increase in large country	Decreases in small country Could increase in large country	Decreases	Decreases

Panel B. Effects of Alternative Trade Policies on Price, Production, Consumption, and Trade

	Tariff	Import Quota	Export Subsidy	VER
Impact on	Importing country	Importing country	Exporting country	Importing country
Price	Increases	Increases	Increases	Increases
Domestic consumption	Decreases	Decreases	Decreases	Decreases
Domestic production	Increases	Increases	Increases	Increases
Trade	Imports decrease	Imports decrease	Exports increase	Imports decrease

> **EXAMPLE 2**
>
> ## Analysis of Trade Restrictions
>
> Thailand, a small country, has to decide whether to impose a tariff or a quota on the import of computers. You are considering investing in a local firm that is a major importer of computers.
>
> 1. What will be the impact of a tariff on prices, quantity produced, and quantity imported in Thailand (the importing country)?
>
>   **Solution:**
>
>   A tariff imposed by a small country, such as Thailand, raises the price of computers in the importing country, reduces the quantity imported, and increases domestic production.
>
> 2. If Thailand imposes a tariff, what will the impact be on prices in the exporting country?
>
>   **Solution:**
>
>   A tariff imposed by a small country would not change the price of computers in the exporting country.
>
> 3. How would a tariff affect consumer surplus, producer surplus, and government revenue in Thailand?
>
>   **Solution:**
>
>   When a small country imposes a tariff, it reduces consumer surplus, increases producer surplus, and increases government revenue in that country.

4. Explain whether the net welfare effect of a tariff is the same as that of a quota.

   Solution:

   The quota can lead to a greater welfare loss than a tariff if the quota rents are captured by the foreign government or foreign firms.

5. Which policy, a tariff or a quota, would be most beneficial to the local importer in which you may invest and why?

   Solution:

   A tariff will hurt importers because it will reduce their share of the computer market in Thailand. The impact of a quota depends on whether or not the importers can capture a share of the quota rents. Assuming importers can capture at least part of the rents, they will be better off with a quota.

6. If Thailand were to negotiate a VER with the countries from which it imports computers, would this be better or worse than an import quota for the local importing firm in which you may invest? Why?

   Solution:

   The VER would not be better for the local importer than the import quota and would most likely be worse. Under the VER, all of the quota rents will be captured by the exporting countries whereas with an import quota at least part of the quota rents may be captured by local importers.

It is important to understand existing trade policies and the potential for policy changes that may affect return on investment. Changes in the government's trade policy can affect the pattern and value of trade and may result in changes in industry structure. These changes may have important implications for firm profitability and growth because they can affect the goods a firm can import or export; change demand for its products; affect its pricing policies; and create delays through increased paperwork, procurement of licenses, approvals, and so on. For example, changes in import policies that affect the ability of a firm to import vital inputs for production may increase the cost of production and reduce firm profitability.

TRADING BLOCS AND REGIONAL INTEGRATION   4

☐ explain motivations for and advantages of trading blocs, common markets, and economic unions

There has been a proliferation of trading blocs or regional trading agreements (RTA) in recent years. Important examples of regional integration include the United States-Mexico-Canada Agreement (USMCA) and the European Union (EU). A regional trading bloc is a group of countries that have signed an agreement to reduce and progressively eliminate barriers to trade and movement of factors of production among the members of the bloc. It may or may not have common trade barriers against countries that are not members of the bloc.

Types Of Trading Blocs

There are many different types of regional trading blocs, depending on the level of integration that takes place. **Free trade areas** (FTA) are one of the most prevalent forms of regional integration in which all barriers to the flow of goods and services among members have been eliminated. However, each country maintains its own polices against non-members. The USMCA among the United States, Canada, and Mexico is an example of an FTA. A **customs union** extends the FTA by not only allowing free movement of goods and services among members but also by creating a common trade policy against non-members. In 1947, Belgium, the Netherlands, and Luxemburg (Benelux) formed a customs union that became part of the European Community in 1958.

The **common market** is the next level of economic integration that incorporates all aspects of the customs union and extends it by allowing free movement of factors of production among members. The Southern Cone Common Market (MERCOSUR) of Argentina, Brazil, Paraguay, and Uruguay is an example of a common market. An **economic union** requires an even greater degree of integration. It incorporates all aspects of a common market and in addition requires common economic institutions and coordination of economic policies among members. The European Community became the European Union in 1993. If the members of the economic union decide to adopt a common currency, then it is also a **monetary union**. For example, with the adoption of the euro, 19 EU member countries also formed a monetary union.

EXAMPLE 3

Trading Blocs

1. Chile and Australia have a free trade with each other but have separate trade barriers on imports from other countries. Chile and Australia are a part of a(n):

    A. FTA.

    B. economic union.

    C. customs union.

    D. common market.

    Solution:

    A is correct. Chile and Australia do not a have customs union because they do not have a common trade policy with respect to other trade partners (C is incorrect). A common market or an economic union entail even more integration (B and D are incorrect).

2. An RTA that removes all tariffs on imports from member countries, and has common external tariffs against all non-members, but does not advance further in deepening economic integration is called a(n):

    A. FTA.

    B. economic union.

    C. customs union.

D. common market.

Solution:

C is correct. A basic FTA does not entail common external tariffs (A is incorrect), whereas a common market and an economic union entail integration beyond common external tariffs (B and D are incorrect).

Regional Integration

Regional integration is popular because eliminating trade and investment barriers among a small group of countries is easier, politically less contentious, and quicker than multilateral trade negotiations under the World Trade Organization (WTO). The WTO is a negotiating forum that deals with the rules of global trade between nations and where member countries can sort out trade disputes. Trade negotiations launched by the WTO have included contentious issues of specific concern to developing countries, such as the cost of implementing trade policy reform in developing countries, market access in developed countries for developing countries' agricultural products, and access to affordable pharmaceuticals in developing countries. Despite decades of negotiations, limited progress has been made on these and other major issues. Hence, it is not surprising to see a renewed interest in bilateral and multilateral trade liberalization on a smaller scale. Policy coordination and harmonization are also easier among a smaller group of countries. Regional integration can be viewed as a movement toward freer trade.

Regional integration results in preferential treatment for members compared with non-members and can lead to changes in the patterns of trade. Member countries move toward freer trade by eliminating or reducing trade barriers against each other, leading to a more efficient allocation of resources. Regional integration also may result in trade and production being shifted from a lower-cost non-member who still faces trade barriers to a higher-cost member who faces no trade barriers. This shift leads to a less-efficient allocation of resources and could reduce welfare. Hence, two static effects are direct results of the formation of the customs union: trade creation and trade diversion.

Trade Creation and Diversion

Trade creation occurs when regional integration results in the replacement of higher-cost domestic production by lower-cost imports from other members. For example, consider two hypothetical countries, Qualor and Vulcan. Qualor produces 10 million shirts annually and imports 2 million shirts from Vulcan, which has a lower cost of production. Qualor has 10 percent tariffs on imports from Vulcan. Qualor and Vulcan then agree to form a customs union. Qualor reduces its production of shirts to 7 million and now imports 11 million shirts from Vulcan. The decline in Qualor's domestic production (from 10 million to 7 million shirts) is replaced by importing 3 million additional shirts from the low-cost producer, Vulcan. This scenario represents trade creation. The rest of the additional imports (6 million shirts) represents increased consumption by Qualor's consumers because the price of shirts declines after formation of the custom union.

Trade diversion occurs when lower-cost imports from non-member countries are replaced with higher-cost imports from members. In the previous example, suppose Qualor initially imposes a 10 percent tariff on imports from both Vulcan and Aurelia. Aurelia is the lowest-cost producer of shirts, so Qualor initially imports 2 million shirts from Aurelia instead of from Vulcan. Qualor and Vulcan then form a customs union, which eliminates tariffs on imports from Vulcan but maintains a 10 percent tariff on imports from Aurelia. Now trade diversion could occur if the free trade price on imports from Vulcan is lower than the price on imports from Aurelia.

Even though Aurelia is the lowest-cost producer, it may be a higher-priced source of imports because of the tariff. If this is the case, then Qualor will stop importing from Aurelia, a non-member, and divert its imports to Vulcan, a member of the RTA. Both trade creation and trade diversion are possible in an RTA. If trade creation is larger than trade diversion, then the net welfare effect is positive. There are concerns, however, that this may not always be the case.

Costs and Benefits of Regional Trading Blocs

The benefits ascribed to free trade—greater specialization according to comparative advantage, reduction in monopoly power because of foreign competition, economies of scale from larger market size, learning by doing, technology transfer, knowledge spillovers, greater foreign investment, and better quality intermediate inputs at world prices—also apply to regional trading blocs. In addition, fostering greater interdependence among members of the regional trading bloc reduces the potential for conflict. Members of the bloc also have greater bargaining power and political clout in the global economy by acting together instead of as individual countries.

Considerable spillover of growth across borders is evident among member countries of the Organisation for Economic Co-operation and Development (OECD), which are highly integrated both as a group and within their own geographic regions. The long-run growth of integrated countries is interconnected because members have greater access to each other's markets. Strong growth in any RTA country could have a positive impact on growth in other RTA member countries. RTAs also enhance the benefits of good policy and lead to convergence in living standards. For example, growth spillovers are likely to be much smaller among Sub-Saharan African countries because of a lack of integration arising from deficiencies in RTAs and inadequate levels of transportation and telecommunications infrastructure. One study estimated what the cumulative loss in real GDP between 1970 and 2000 would have been if Switzerland, which is landlocked and fully integrated with both its immediate neighbors and the world economy, had been subject to the same level of spillovers as the Central African Republic. Under such a scenario, Switzerland's GDP per capita in 2000 would have been 9.3 percent lower. The cumulative GDP loss would have been USD334 billion (constant US dollars, 2000), which was the equivalent of 162 percent of Switzerland's real GDP in 2000.

Although regional integration has many advantages, it may impose costs on some groups. For example, there was significant concern in the United States that fewer trade restrictions and especially low-skilled labor-intensive imports from Mexico could hurt low-skilled workers. Adjustment costs arose as import competition caused inefficient firms to exit the market, and the workers in those firms were at least temporarily unemployed as they sought new jobs. However, the surviving firms experienced an increase in productivity, and US consumers benefited from the increase in product varieties imported from Mexico. One study estimated that the product varieties exported from Mexico to the United States had grown by an average of 2.2 percent a year across all industries. While USMCA imposed estimated private costs of nearly USD5.4 billion a year in the United States during 1994–2002, these costs were offset by an average welfare gain of USD5.5 billion a year accruing from increased varieties imported from Mexico. Consumer gains from more varieties of products continued over time as long as the imports continued, whereas adjustment costs arising from job losses declined over time. In 2003, the gain from increased product varieties from Mexico was USD11 billion, far exceeding the adjustment costs of USD5.4 billion.

It is important to recognize, however, that workers displaced by regional integration may have to bear long-term losses if they are unable to find jobs with wages comparable with the jobs they lost or they remain unemployed for a long period of time. For example, although import competition was certainly not the only factor that led to a dramatic contraction of the US automobile industry, the impact on employment in that industry is likely to be permanent and many former autoworkers, especially older workers, may never find comparable jobs.

Concerns regarding national sovereignty, especially where big and small nations may be part of the same bloc, also have been an impediment to the formation of FTAs. The proposal for a South Asian regional bloc has faced challenges regarding India's role because it is one of the biggest economies in the region.

Challenges to Deeper Integration

The formation of an RTA and its potential progression from an FTA to deeper integration in the form of a customs union, common market, or economic union face at least two challenges. First, cultural differences and historical considerations—for example, wars and conflicts—may complicate the social and political process of integration. Second, maintaining a high degree of economic integration limits the extent to which member countries can pursue independent economic and social policies. Free trade and mobility of labor and capital tend to thwart policies aimed at controlling relative prices or quantities within a country, while balance-of-payments and fiscal credibility considerations limit the viability of divergent macroeconomic policies. This situation is especially true in the case of a monetary union because monetary policy is not under the control of individual countries and currency devaluation or revaluation is not available as a tool to correct persistent imbalances. When persistent imbalances do arise, they may lead to a crisis that spills over to other countries facing similar problems. The Greek fiscal crisis in 2010 is a case in point. In May 2010, Standard & Poor's reduced the credit ratings on Greece's government from investment grade to junk status. It also downgraded the government debt of Spain and Portugal. These countries were suffering from a combination of high government deficits and slow GDP growth. The credit downgrades increased fears that Greece, in particular, would default on its debt and cause economic turmoil not only among the healthier countries in the EU but also in the United States and Asia. The EU and the International Monetary Fund (IMF) agreed on a USD145 billion (EUR110 billion) bailout for Greece in May 2010 and provided Ireland with a financing package of about USD113 billion (EUR85 billion) in November 2010.

Investment Implications

Regional integration is important from an investment perspective because it offers new opportunities for trade and investment. The cost of doing business in a large, single, regional market is lower and firms can benefit from economies of scale. Note, however, that differences in tastes, culture, and competitive conditions still exist among members of a trading bloc. These differences may limit the potential benefits from investments within the bloc. In addition, depending on the level of integration and the safeguards in place, problems faced by individual member countries in an RTA may quickly spread to other countries in the bloc.

> **QUESTION SET**
>
> Bagopia, Cropland, and Technopia decide to enter into an RTA. In the first stage, they decide to sign an FTA. After several successful years, they decide that it is time to form a common market.

1. Does an FTA make exporting firms in member countries more attractive as investment options?

   Solution:

   The first stage, where there is free movement of goods and services among RTA members, is called an FTA. It makes exporting firms a more attractive investment proposition because they are able to serve markets in member countries without the additional costs imposed by trade barriers.

2. How does the common market affect firms doing business in these countries compared with an FTA?

   Solution:

   Unlike an FTA, a common market allows for free movement of factors of production, such as labor and capital, among the member economies. Like an FTA, it provides access to a much larger market and free movement of goods and services. But the common market can create more profitable opportunities for firms than an FTA by allowing them to locate production in and purchase components from anywhere in the common market according to comparative advantage.

PRACTICE PROBLEMS

1. Which of the following statements *best* describes the benefits of international trade?

    A. Countries gain from exchange and specialization.

    B. Countries receive lower prices for their exports and pay higher prices for imports.

    C. Countries gain from trade because all individuals and companies benefit in the long term.

2. Which of the following statements *best* describes the costs of international trade?

    A. Countries without an absolute advantage in producing a good cannot benefit significantly from international trade.

    B. Resources may need to be allocated into or out of an industry and less-efficient companies may be forced to exit an industry, which in turn may lead to higher unemployment.

    C. Loss of manufacturing jobs in developed countries as a result of import competition means that developed countries benefit far less than developing countries from trade.

3. Suppose the cost of producing tea relative to copper is lower in Tealand than in Copperland. With trade, the copper industry in Copperland would *most likely*:

    A. expand.

    B. contract.

    C. remain stable.

4. Which type of trade restriction would most likely increase domestic government revenue?

    A. Tariff

    B. Import quota

    C. Export subsidy

5. Which of the following trade restrictions is likely to result in the greatest welfare loss for the importing country?

    A. A tariff

    B. An import quota

    C. A voluntary export restraint

6. A large country can:

    A. benefit by imposing a tariff.

    B. benefit with an export subsidy.

C. not benefit from any trade restriction.

7. If Brazil and South Africa have free trade with each other, a common trade policy against all other countries, but no free movement of factors of production between them, then Brazil and South Africa are part of a(n):

    A. customs union.

    B. common market.

    C. FTA.

8. Which of the following factors *best* explains why regional trading agreements are more popular than larger multilateral trade agreements?

    A. Minimal displacement costs

    B. Trade diversions benefit members

    C. Quicker and easier policy coordination

SOLUTIONS

1. A is correct. Countries gain from exchange when trade enables each country to receive a higher price for exported goods or pay a lower price for imported goods. This leads to more efficient resource allocation and allows consumption of a larger variety of goods.

2. B is correct. Resources may need to be reallocated into or out of an industry, depending on whether that industry is an exporting sector or an import-competing sector of that economy. As a result of this adjustment process, less-efficient companies may be forced to exit the industry, which in turn may lead to higher unemployment and the need for retraining so that displaced workers may find jobs in expanding industries.

3. A is correct. The copper industry in Copperland would benefit from trade. Because the cost of producing copper relative to producing tea is lower in Copperland than in Tealand, Copperland will export copper and the industry will expand.

4. A is correct. The imposition of a tariff will most likely increase domestic government revenue. A tariff is a tax on imports collected by the importing country's government.

5. C is correct. With a voluntary export restraint, the price increase induced by restricting the quantity of imports (= quota rent for equivalent quota = tariff revenue for equivalent tariff) accrues to foreign exporters or the foreign government.

6. A is correct. By definition, a large country is big enough to affect the world price of its imports and exports. A large country can benefit by imposing a tariff if its terms of trade improve by enough to outweigh the welfare loss arising from inefficient allocation of resources.

7. A is correct. A customs union extends an FTA by not only allowing free movement of goods and services among members, but also by creating common trade policy against non-members. Unlike a more integrated common market, a customs union does not allow free movement of factors of production among members.

8. C is correct. Regional trading agreements are politically less contentious and quicker to establish than multilateral trade negotiations (e.g., under the World Trade Organization). Policy coordination and harmonization is easier among a smaller group of countries.

LEARNING MODULE 7

Capital Flows and the FX Market

by William A. Barker, PhD, CFA, Paul D. McNelis, and Jerry Nickelsburg, PhD.

William A. Barker, PhD, CFA (Canada). Paul D. McNelis is at Gabelli School of Business, Fordham University (USA). Jerry Nickelsburg, PhD, is at the Anderson School of Management, University of California, Los Angeles (USA).

LEARNING OUTCOMES	
Mastery	The candidate should be able to:
☐	describe the foreign exchange market, including its functions and participants, distinguish between nominal and real exchange rates, and calculate and interpret the percentage change in a currency relative to another currency
☐	describe exchange rate regimes and explain the effects of exchange rates on countries' international trade and capital flows
☐	describe common objectives of capital restrictions imposed by governments

INTRODUCTION

The foreign exchange market, which is the largest trading market in the world, facilitates international trade and capital flows. Numerous participants use this market for a wide variety of financial, business, trade, and hedging purposes. As with any trading market, the foreign exchange market uses various terms and conventions that allow participants to understand quoting mechanisms and the factors affecting pricing and then to conduct trades. International capital flows are the primary determinant of short- to medium-term exchange rate movements, and exchange rate movements affect the trade balance between countries. Given the relative economic stability and objectives of different national governments, countries use a range of exchange rate regimes, which are described in this module. These lessons introduce and expand upon these topics to lay the groundwork for a more detailed understanding of the foreign exchange market.

LEARNING MODULE OVERVIEW

- The foreign exchange market is the largest market in the world.

- Nominal spot exchange rates are quoted in the market and are inputs for analysts to determine real exchange rates, which reflect the relationship between domestic and foreign price levels and indicate the relative purchasing power between countries. To track exchange rate movements, calculating the percentage change in a currency relative to another currency enables market participants to understand price changes and use these percentages in market trades.
- Exchange rate regimes can be floating or fully fixed, and various political and economic forces drive countries to use one of a number of intermediate regimes.
- The impact of exchange rates and other factors on a country's trade balance is mirrored by their impact on that country's capital flows.
- Although the free flow of capital between countries is most beneficial economically, governments may restrict capital inflows or outflows to address domestic policy and strategic or defense-related objectives. These restrictions allow governments to avoid capital flight in times of macroeconomic crisis and limit capital inflows, which may hurt the competitiveness of domestic firms.

2. THE FOREIGN EXCHANGE MARKET AND EXCHANGE RATES

describe the foreign exchange market, including its functions and participants, distinguish between nominal and real exchange rates, and calculate and interpret the percentage change in a currency relative to another currency

Introduction and the Foreign Exchange Market

The foreign exchange (FX) market—the market in which currencies are traded against each other—is by far the world's largest market. Current estimates put daily turnover at approximately USD6.6 trillion for 2019. This is about 10 to 15 times larger than daily turnover in global fixed-income markets and about 50 times larger than global turnover in equities.

The FX market is a truly global market that operates 24 hours a day, each business day. It involves market participants from every time zone connected through electronic communications networks that link players as large as multibillion-dollar investment funds and as small as individuals trading for their own account—all brought together in real time. International trade would be impossible without the trade in currencies that facilitates it and so too would cross-border capital flows that connect all financial markets globally through the FX market.

These factors make FX a key market for investors and market participants to understand. The world economy is increasingly transnational in nature, with both production processes and trade flows often determined more by global factors than by domestic considerations. Likewise, investment portfolio performance increasingly reflects global determinants because pricing in financial markets responds to the array of investment opportunities available worldwide, not just locally. All of these factors

The Foreign Exchange Market and Exchange Rates

funnel through, and are reflected in, the FX market. As investors shed their "home bias" and invest in FX, the exchange rate—the price at which foreign-currency-denominated investments are valued in terms of the domestic currency—becomes an increasingly important determinant of portfolio performance.

Even investors adhering to a purely "domestic" portfolio mandate are increasingly affected by what happens in the FX market. Given the globalization of the world economy, most large companies depend heavily on their foreign operations (e.g., by some estimates about 30 percent of S&P 500 Index earnings are from outside the United States). Almost all companies are exposed to some degree of foreign competition, and the pricing for domestic assets—equities, bonds, real estate, and others—also depend on demand from foreign investors. All of these various influences on investment performance reflect developments in the FX market.

The FX Market

To understand the FX market, it is necessary to become familiar with some of its basic conventions. Individual currencies often are referred to by standardized three-letter codes that the market has agreed upon through the International Organization for Standardization (ISO). Exhibit 1 lists some of the major global currencies and their identification codes.

Exhibit 1: Standard Currency Codes

Three-Letter Currency Code	Currency
AUD	Australian dollar
BRL	Brazilian real
CAD	Canadian dollar
CHF	Swiss franc
CNY	Chinese yuan
EUR	Euro
GBP	British pound sterling
HKD	Hong Kong dollar
INR	Indian rupee
JPY	Japanese yen
KRW	South Korean won
MXN	Mexican peso
NOK	Norwegian krone
NZD	New Zealand dollar
RUB	Russian ruble
SEK	Swedish krona
SGD	Singapore dollar
USD	US dollar
ZAR	South African rand

It is important to understand the difference between referring to an *individual currency* and an *exchange rate*. One can hold an individual currency (e.g., in a EUR100 million deposit); an exchange rate, however, is the price of one currency in terms of another (e.g., the exchange rate between the euro and the US dollar). An individual currency can be singular, but two currencies always are involved in an exchange rate: the price of one currency relative to another. The exchange rate is the number of units of one currency (called the *price currency*) that one unit of another currency (called the *base currency*) will buy. An equivalent way of describing the exchange rate is as the cost of one unit of the base currency in terms of the price currency.

This distinction between individual currencies and exchange rates is important because, as we will see in a later lesson, these three-letter currency codes can be used both ways. For example, when used as an exchange rate in the professional FX market, EUR is understood to be the exchange rate between the euro and US dollar. Be aware of the context (either as a currency or as an exchange rate) in which these three-letter currency codes are being used. To avoid confusion, this lesson will identify exchange rates using the convention of "A/B," referring to the number of units of currency A that one unit of currency B will buy. For example, a USD/EUR exchange rate of 1.1700 means that 1 euro will buy 1.1700 US dollars (i.e., 1 euro costs 1.1700 US dollars). In this case, the euro is the base currency and the US dollar is the price currency. A decrease in this exchange rate would mean that the euro costs less or that fewer US dollars are needed to buy one euro. In other words, a decline in this exchange rate indicates that the US dollar is *appreciating* against the euro or, equivalently, the euro is *depreciating* against the US dollar.

These exchange rates are referred to as *nominal* exchange rates. In contrast, *real* exchange rates are indexes that often are constructed by economists and other market analysts to assess changes in the relative purchasing power of one currency compared with another. Creating these indexes requires adjusting the nominal exchange rate by using the price levels in each country of the currency pair (hence the name "real exchange rates") to compare the relative purchasing power between countries.

In a world of homogenous goods and services, and with no market frictions or trade barriers, the relative purchasing power across countries would tend to equalize: Why would you pay more, in real terms, domestically for a "widget" if you could import an identical "widget" from overseas at a cheaper price? This basic concept is the intuition behind a theory known as purchasing power parity (PPP), which describes the long-term equilibrium of nominal exchange rates. PPP asserts that nominal exchange rates adjust so that identical goods (or baskets of goods) will have the same price in different markets. Or, put differently, the purchasing power of different currencies is equalized for a standardized basket of goods.

In practice, the conditions required to enforce PPP are not satisfied: Goods and services are not identical across countries; countries typically have different baskets of goods and services produced and consumed; many goods and services are not traded internationally; there are trade barriers and transaction costs (e.g., shipping costs and import taxes); and capital flows are at least as important as trade flows in determining nominal exchange rates. As a result, nominal exchange rates exhibit persistent deviations from PPP. Moreover, relative purchasing power among countries displays a weak, if any, tendency toward long-term equalization. A simple example of a cross-country comparison of the purchasing power of a standardized good is the Big Mac index produced by the *Economist*, which shows the relative price of this standardized hamburger in different countries. The Big Mac index shows that fast-food hamburger prices can vary widely internationally and that this difference in purchasing power is typical of most goods and services. Hence, movements in real exchange rates provide meaningful information about changes in relative purchasing power among countries.

Consider the case of an individual who wants to purchase goods from a foreign country. The individual would be able to buy fewer of these goods if the nominal spot exchange rate for the foreign currency appreciated or if the foreign price level increased. Conversely, the individual could buy more foreign goods if the individual's domestic income increased. (For this example, we will assume that changes in the individual's income are proportional to changes in the domestic price level.) Hence, in *real* purchasing power terms, the real exchange rate that an individual faces is an increasing function of the nominal exchange rate (quoted in terms of the number of units of domestic currency per one unit of foreign currency) and the foreign price level and a decreasing function of the domestic price level. The *higher* the real exchange rate is, the *fewer* foreign goods, in real terms, the individual can purchase and the *lower* that individual's relative purchasing power will be compared with the other country.

An equivalent way of viewing the real exchange rate is that it represents the relative price levels in the domestic and foreign countries. Mathematically, we can represent the foreign price level in terms of the domestic currency as follows:

Foreign price level in domestic currency = $S_{d/f} \times P_f$,

where $S_{d/f}$ is the spot exchange rate (quoted in terms of the number of units of domestic currency per one unit of foreign currency) and P_f is foreign price level quoted in terms of the foreign currency. We can define the domestic price level, in terms of the domestic currency, as P_d. Hence, the ratio between the foreign and domestic price levels is as follows:

Real exchange rate$_{(d/f)}$ = $(S_{d/f} P_f)/P_d = S_{d/f} \times (P_f/P_d)$.

For example, for a British consumer wanting to buy goods made in the Eurozone, the real exchange rate (defined in GBP/EUR terms; note that the domestic currency for the United Kingdom is the price currency, not the base currency) will be an increasing function of the nominal spot exchange rate (GBP/EUR) and the Eurozone price level and a decreasing function of the UK price level. This is written as follows:

Real exchange rate$_{\frac{GBP}{EUR}}$ = $S_{\frac{GBP}{EUR}} \times \left(\frac{CPI_{eur}}{CPI_{UK}}\right)$.

We can examine the effect of movements in the domestic and foreign price levels, and the nominal spot exchange rate, on the real purchasing power of an individual in the United Kingdom wanting to purchase Eurozone goods. Assume that the nominal spot exchange rate (GBP/EUR) increases by 10 percent, the Eurozone price level increases by 5 percent, and the UK price level increases by 2 percent. The change in the real exchange rate is then as follows:

$$\left(1 + \frac{\Delta S_{\frac{d}{f}}}{S_{\frac{d}{f}}}\right) \times \frac{\left(1 + \frac{\Delta P_f}{P_f}\right)}{\left(1 + \frac{\Delta P_d}{P_d}\right)} - 1$$

$$= (1 + 10\%) \times \frac{1 + 5\%}{1 + 2\%} - 1 \approx 10\% + 5\% - 2\% \approx 13\%.$$

In this case, the real exchange rate for the UK-based individual has *increased* about 13 percent, meaning that it now costs *more*, in real terms, to buy Eurozone goods. Or put differently, the UK individual's real purchasing power relative to Eurozone goods has *declined* by about 13 percent. An easy way to remember this relationship is to consider the real exchange rate (stated with the domestic currency as the price currency) as representing the real price you face to purchase foreign goods and services: The *higher* the price is (real exchange rate), the *lower* your relative purchasing power will be.

The real exchange rate for a currency can be constructed for the domestic currency relative to a single foreign currency or relative to a basket of foreign currencies. In either case, these real exchange rate indexes depend on the assumptions made by the analyst creating them. Several investment banks and central banks create proprietary measures of real exchange rates. Note that real exchange rates are *not* quoted or traded in global FX markets: They are only indexes created by analysts to understand the international competitiveness of an economy and the real purchasing power of a currency.

In this context, real exchange rates can be useful for understanding trends in international trade and capital flows and hence can be seen as one of the influences on nominal spot exchange rates. As an example, consider the exchange rate between the Indian rupee and the US dollar. During 2018, the nominal rupee exchange rate against the US dollar (INR/USD) rose by approximately 6.7 percent—meaning that the US dollar appreciated against the rupee. However, the annual inflation rates in the United States and India were different during 2018—approximately 2.5 percent for the United States and 4.7 percent for India. This means that the real exchange rate (in INR/USD terms) was depreciating less rapidly than the nominal INR/USD exchange rate:

$$\left(1 + \%\Delta S_{\frac{INR}{USD}}\right) \times \frac{(1 + \%\Delta P_{US})}{(1 + \%\Delta P_{India})} - 1 \approx +6.7\% + 2.5\% - 4.7\% \approx 4.5\%.$$

This combination of a much weaker rupee and a higher Indian inflation rate meant that the real exchange rate faced by India was increasing, thus decreasing Indian purchasing power in US dollar terms.

Movements in real exchange rates can have a similar effect as movements in nominal exchange rates in terms of affecting relative prices and hence trade flows. Even if the nominal spot exchange rate does not move, differences in inflation rates between countries affect their relative competitiveness.

Although real exchange rates can exert some influence on nominal exchange rate movements, they are only one of many factors; it can be difficult to disentangle all of these inter-relationships in a complex and dynamic FX market. As discussed earlier, PPP is a poor guide to predicting future movements in nominal exchange rates because these rates can deviate from PPP equilibrium—and even continue to trend away from their PPP level—for years at a time. Hence, it should not be surprising that real exchange rates, which reflect changes in relative purchasing power, have a poor track record as a predictor of future nominal exchange rate movements.

EXAMPLE 1

Nominal and Real Exchange Rates

An investment adviser located in Sydney, Australia, is meeting with a local client who is looking to diversify her domestic bond portfolio by adding investments in fixed-rate, long-term bonds denominated in the Hong Kong dollar. The client frequently visits Hong Kong SAR, and many of her annual expenses are denominated in the Hong Kong dollar. The client, however, is concerned about the foreign currency risks of offshore investments and whether the investment return on her Hong Kong-dollar-denominated investments will maintain her purchasing power—both domestically (i.e., for her Australian-dollar-denominated expenses) and for her foreign trips (i.e., Hong Kong-dollar-denominated expenses for her visits to Hong Kong SAR). The investment adviser explains the effect of changes in nominal and real exchange rates to the client and illustrates this explanation by making the following statements:

Statement 1 All else equal, an increase in the nominal AUD/HKD exchange rate will lead to an increase in the Australia-dollar-denominated value of your foreign investment.

Statement 2 All else equal, an increase in the nominal AUD/HKD exchange rate means that your relative purchasing power for your Hong Kong SAR trips will increase (based on paying for your trip with the income from your Hong Kong-dollar-denominated bonds).

Statement 3 All else equal, an increase in the Australian inflation rate will lead to an increase in the real exchange rate (AUD/HKD). A higher real exchange rate means that the relative purchasing power of your Australian-dollar-denominated income is higher.

Statement 4   All else equal, a decrease in the nominal exchange rate (AUD/HKD) will decrease the real exchange rate (AUD/HKD) and increase the relative purchasing power of your Australian-dollar-denominated income.

To demonstrate the effects of the changes in inflation and nominal exchange rates on relative purchasing power, the adviser uses the following scenario:

"Suppose that the AUD/HKD exchange rate increases by 5 percent, the price of goods and services in Hong Kong SAR goes up by 5 percent, and the price of Australian goods and services goes up by 2 percent."

1. Statement 1 is:

   A. correct.

   B. incorrect, because based on the quote convention the investment's value would be decreasing in Australian dollar terms.

   C. incorrect, because the nominal Australian dollar value of the foreign investments will depend on movements in the Australian inflation rate.

   Solution:

   A is correct. Given the quoting convention, an increase in the AUD/HKD rate means that the base currency (Hong Kong dollar) is appreciating (one Hong Kong dollar will buy more Australian dollars). This increases the nominal value of the Hong Kong-dollar-denominated investments when measured in Australian dollar terms.

2. Statement 2 is:

   A. correct.

   B. incorrect, because purchasing power is not affected in this case.

   C. incorrect, because based on the quote convention, the client's relative purchasing power would be decreasing.

   Solution:

   B is correct. When paying for Hong Kong-dollar-denominated expenses with Hong Kong-dollar-denominated income, the value of the AUD/HKD spot exchange rate (or any other spot exchange rate) would not be relevant. In fact, this is a basic principle of currency risk management: reducing FX risk exposures by denominating assets and liabilities (or income and expenses) in the same currency.

3. Statement 3 is:

   A. correct.

   B. incorrect with respect to the real exchange rate only.

   C. incorrect with respect to both the real exchange rate and the purchasing power of Australian dollar -denominated income.

   Solution:

   C is correct. An increase in the Australian (i.e., domestic) inflation rate means that the real exchange rate (measured in domestic/foreign, or AUD/HKD, terms) would be decreasing, not increasing. Moreover, an increase in the real exchange rate ($R_{AUD/HKD}$) would be equivalent to a reduction of the purchasing power of the Australian client: Goods and services denominated in Hong Kong dollar would cost more.

4. Statement 4 is:

    A. correct.

    B. incorrect with respect to the real exchange rate.

    C. incorrect with respect to the purchasing power of Australian dollar-denominated income.

    Solution:

    A is correct. As the spot AUD/HKD exchange rate decreases, the Hong Kong dollar is depreciating against the Australian dollar; or equivalently, the Australian dollar is appreciating against the Hong Kong dollar. This is reducing the real exchange rate ($R_{AUD/HKD}$) and increasing the Australian client's purchasing power.

5. Based on the adviser's scenario and assuming that the Hong Kong dollar value of the Hong Kong dollar bonds remained unchanged, the nominal Australian dollar value of the client's Hong Kong dollar investments would:

    A. decrease by about 5 percent.

    B. increase by about 5 percent.

    C. remain about the same.

    Solution:

    B is correct. As the AUD/HKD spot exchange rate increases by 5 percent, the Hong Kong dollar is appreciating against the Australian dollar by 5 percent and, all else equal, the value of the Hong Kong-dollar-denominated investment is increasing by 5 percent in Australian dollar terms.

6. Based on the adviser's scenario, the change in the relative purchasing power of the client's Australian-dollar-denominated income is *closest* to:

    A. −8 percent.

    B. +8 percent.

    C. +12 percent.

    Solution:

    A is correct. The real exchange rate ($R_{AUD/HKD}$) is expressed as follows:

    $$R_{\frac{AUD}{HKD}} = S_{\frac{AUD}{HKD}} \times \frac{P_{HKD}}{P_{AUD}}.$$

    The information in the adviser's scenario can be expressed as follows:

    $$\%\Delta R_{\frac{AUD}{HKD}} \approx \%\Delta S_{\frac{AUD}{HKD}} + \%\Delta P_{HKD} - \%\Delta P_{AUD} \approx +5\% + 5\% - 2\% \approx +8\%.$$

    Because the real exchange rate (expressed in AUD/HKD terms) has gone up by about 8 percent, the real purchasing power of the investor based in Australia has declined by about 8 percent. This can be seen from the fact that Hong Kong dollar has appreciated against the Australian dollar in nominal terms, and the Hong Kong SAR price level has also increased. This increase in the cost of Hong Kong SAR goods and services (measured in Australian dollars) is only partially offset by the small (2 percent) increase in the investor's income (assumed equal to the change in the Australian price level).

> **QUESTION SET**
>
> 1. A decrease in the real exchange rate (quoted in terms of domestic currency per unit of foreign currency) is *most likely* to be associated with an increase in which of the following?
>
>   **A.** Foreign price level.
>
>   **B.** Domestic price level.
>
>   **C.** Nominal exchange rate.
>
>   **Solution:**
>
>   B is correct. The real exchange rate (quoted in terms of domestic currency per unit of foreign currency) is given as follows:
>
>   Real exchange rate$_{(d/f)}$ = $S_{d/f} \times (P_f/P_d)$.
>
>   An increase in the domestic price level (P_d) *decreases* the real exchange rate because it implies an *increase* in the relative purchasing power of the domestic currency.

Market Participants

We now turn to the counterparties that participate in FX markets. As mentioned previously, an extremely diverse universe of market participants ranges in size from multi-billion-dollar investment funds to individuals trading for their own account (including foreign tourists exchanging currencies at airport kiosks).

To understand the various market participants, it is useful to separate them into broad categories. One broad distinction is between what the market refers to as the *buy side* and the *sell side*. The sell side generally consists of large FX trading banks (such as Citigroup, UBS, and Deutsche Bank); the buy side consists of clients who use these banks to undertake FX transactions (i.e., buy FX products) from the sell-side banks.

The buy side can be further broken down into several categories:

- *Corporate accounts*: Corporations of all sizes undertake FX transactions during cross-border purchases and sales of goods and services. Many of their FX flows also are related to cross-border investment flows—such as international mergers and acquisitions (M&A) transactions, investment of corporate funds in foreign assets, and foreign currency borrowing.

- *Real money accounts*: These are investment funds managed by insurance companies, mutual funds, pension funds, endowments, exchange-traded funds (ETFs), and other institutional investors. These accounts are referred to as real money because they usually are restricted in their use of leverage or financial derivatives. This feature distinguishes them from leveraged accounts (discussed next), although many institutional investors often engage in some form of leverage, either directly through some use of borrowed funds or indirectly using financial derivatives.

- *Leveraged accounts*: This category, often referred to as the professional trading community, consists of hedge funds, proprietary trading shops, commodity trading advisers (CTAs), high-frequency algorithmic traders, and the proprietary trading desks at banks—and, indeed, almost any active trading account that accepts and manages FX risk for profit. The professional trading community accounts for a large and growing proportion of daily FX market turnover. These active trading accounts also have a wide diversity of trading styles. Some are macro-hedge funds that take long-term FX positions based on their views of the underlying economic fundamentals of a currency. Others are high-frequency algorithmic traders that use technical trading strategies (such as those based on moving averages or Fibonacci levels) and whose trading cycles and investment horizons are sometimes measured in milliseconds.

- *Retail accounts*: The simplest example of a retail account is the archetypical foreign tourist exchanging currency at an airport kiosk. However, as electronic trading technology has reduced the barriers to entry into FX markets and the costs of FX trading, there has been a huge surge in speculative trading activity by retail accounts—consisting of individuals trading for their own accounts as well as smaller hedge funds and other active traders. This category also includes households using electronic trading technology to move their savings into foreign currencies (e.g., this is relatively widespread among households in Japan). It is estimated that retail trading accounts for as much as 10 percent of all spot transactions in some currency pairs and that this proportion is growing.

- *Governments*: Public entities of all types often have FX needs, ranging from relatively small (e.g., maintaining consulates in foreign countries) to large (e.g., military equipment purchases or maintaining overseas military bases). Sometimes these flows are purely transactional—the business simply needs to be done—and sometimes government FX flows reflect, at least in part, the public policy goals of the government. Some government FX business resembles that of investment funds, although sometimes with a public policy mandate as well. In some countries, public sector pension plans and public insurance schemes are run by a branch of the government. One example is the Caisse de dépôt et placement du Québec, which was created by the Québec provincial government in Canada to manage that province's public sector pension plans. The Caisse, as it is called, is a relatively large player in financial markets, with nearly CAD420 billion of assets under management at the end of 2021. Although it has a mandate to invest these assets for optimal return, it is also called upon to help promote the economic development of Québec. Many governments—both at the federal and provincial/state levels—issue debt in foreign currencies; this, too, creates FX flows. Such supranational agencies as the World Bank and the African Development Bank issue debt in a variety of currencies as well.

- *Central banks*: These entities sometimes intervene in FX markets to influence either the level or trend in the domestic exchange rate. This often occurs when the central banks judge their domestic currency to be too weak and when the exchange rate has overshot any concept of equilibrium level (e.g., because of a speculative attack) to the degree that the exchange rate no longer reflects underlying economic fundamentals. Alternatively, central banks also intervene when the FX market has become so erratic and dysfunctional that end-users such as corporations can no longer transact necessary FX business. Conversely, central banks sometimes intervene when they believe that their domestic currency has become too strong, to the point that it undercuts that country's export competitiveness. The Bank of Japan intervened against yen strength versus the US dollar in 2004 and again in March 2011 after the massive earthquake and nuclear disaster. Similarly, in 2010, 2013, and again in 2015, the Swiss National Bank intervened against strength in the Swiss franc versus the euro by selling the Swiss franc on the euro–Swiss (CHF/EUR) cross-rate. Central bank reserve managers are frequent participants in FX markets to manage their country's FX reserves.

In this context, they act much like real money investment funds—although generally with a cautious, conservative mandate to safeguard the value of their country's FX reserves. The FX reserves of some countries are enormous, and central bank participation in FX markets can sometimes have a material impact on exchange rates even when these reserve managers are not intervening for public policy purposes. Total FX reserves reached nearly USD13 trillion at the end of 2021.

This largely reflects the rapid growth in foreign reserves held by Asian central banks, because these countries typically run large current account surpluses with the United States and other developed market economies. Reserve accumulation by energy-exporting countries in the Middle East and elsewhere is also a factor. As of the end of 2021, nearly 60 percent of global allocated currency reserves were held in US dollars, while just over 20 percent was held in euros, the second most widely held currency in central bank FX reserves.

- *Sovereign wealth funds (SWFs)*: Many countries with large current account surpluses have diverted some of the resultant international capital flows into SWFs rather than into FX reserves managed by central banks. Although SWFs are government entities, their mandate is usually more oriented toward purely investment purposes rather than public policy purposes. As such, SWFs can be thought of as akin to real money accounts, although some SWFs can employ derivatives or engage in aggressive trading strategies. It generally is understood that SWFs use their resources to help fulfill the public policy mandate of their government owners. The SWFs of many current account surplus countries (such as exporting countries in East Asia (e.g., Singapore) or oil-exporting countries (e.g., Kuwait) are enormous, and their FX flows can be an important determinant of exchange rate movements in almost all of the major currency pairs.

The sell side generally consists of the FX dealing banks that sell FX products to the buy side. The following sell-side distinctions can be made.

- A large and growing proportion of the daily FX turnover is accounted for by the very largest money center dealing banks, such as Deutsche Bank, Citigroup, UBS, HSBC, and a few other multinational banking behemoths. Maintaining a competitive advantage in FX requires huge fixed-cost investments in the electronic technology that connects the FX market, and it also requires a broad, global client base. As a result, only the largest first-tier banks are able to compete successfully in providing competitive price quotes to clients across the broad range of FX products. In fact, among the largest FX dealing banks, a large proportion of their business is crossed internally, meaning that these banks are able to connect buyers and sellers within their own extremely diverse client base and have no need to show these FX flows outside of the bank.

- All other banks fall into the second and third tier of the FX market sell side. Many of these financial institutions are regional or local banks with well-developed business relationships, but they lack the economies of scale, broad global client base, or information technology (IT) expertise required to offer competitive pricing across a wide range of currencies and FX products. In many cases, these are banks in emerging markets that do not have the business connections or credit lines required to access the FX market on a cost-effective basis on their own. As a result, these banks often outsource

FX services by forming business relationships with the larger tier-one banks; otherwise, they depend on the deep, competitive liquidity provided by the largest FX market participants.

The categories presented are based on functions that are closely associated with the named groups. However, in some cases, functions typifying a group also may be assumed by or shared with another group. For example, sell-side banks provide FX price quotes. Hedge funds and other large players, however, may access the professional FX market on equal terms with the dealing banks and effectively act as market makers.

One of the most important ideas to draw from this categorization of market participants is that there is an extremely wide variety of FX market participants, reflecting a complex mix of trading motives and strategies that can vary with time. Most market participants reflect a combination of hedging and speculative motives in tailoring their FX risk exposures. Among public sector market participants, public policy motives also may be a factor. The dynamic, complex interaction of FX market participants and their trading objectives make it difficult to analyze or predict movements in FX rates with any precision or to describe the FX market adequately with simple characterizations.

BEST PRACTICES IN FOREIGN EXCHANGE MARKETS

As an important element of trade and cross-border capital flows and a key determinant of portfolio performance, the transparency and proper functioning of foreign exchange markets is of critical importance to market participants in meeting their financial goals and objectives. However, as a truly global market, the FX market lacks the regulatory oversight of domestic exchanges, although the Bank for International Settlements (BIS) mentioned earlier, oversees and periodically surveys FX market activity worldwide.

In an effort initiated by the BIS Markets Committee, the Global Foreign Exchange Committee (GFXC) was established in 2017 by FX market participants, including central banks, large global banks, and buy-side firms, to ensure a "robust, fair, liquid, open, and appropriately transparent" FX market in which users can transact at competitive prices using best practices established in a voluntary FX Global Code. These practices address such principles as ethics, governance, execution, information sharing, confirmation and settlement, and risk management and compliance.

Market Composition

In this section, we first describe components of the FX market, then present a descriptive overview of the global FX market drawn from the 2016 Triennial Survey undertaken by the Bank for International Settlements (BIS).

In addition to spot transactions, the FX market includes forward transactions and **FX swaps**. Forwards are transactions made using forward exchange rates with settlement at agreed-upon future dates, and forward rates can be used to manage FX risk. The combination of spot and forward transactions can be used to create FX swaps. These instruments are used for hedging purposes and to raise foreign currency at more favorable rates, and their trading constitutes the largest daily volume of the FX market.

The BIS is an umbrella organization for the world's central banks. Every three years, participating central banks undertake a survey of the FX market in their jurisdictions, the results of which are aggregated and compiled at the BIS. The survey, taken in April 2016, gives a broad indication of the current size and distribution of global FX market flows.

As of April 2016, the BIS estimates that average daily turnover in the traditional FX market (composed of spot, outright forward, and FX swap transactions) totaled approximately USD5.1 trillion. Exhibit 2 shows the approximate percentage allocation among FX product types, including both traditional FX products and exchange-traded FX derivatives. Note that this table of percentage allocations adds exchange-traded derivatives to the BIS estimate of average daily turnover of USD5.1 trillion; the "Spot" and "Outright forwards" categories include only transactions that are not executed as part of a swap transaction.

Exhibit 2: FX Turnover by Instrument

Instrument	FX Turnover (%)
Spot	33
Outright forwards	14
Swaps[a]	49
FX options	5
Total	100

Note: Swaps includes FX and currency swaps. An "FX swap" is not the same as a "currency swap"; a currency swap is generally used for multiple periods and payments. May not add to 100% due to rounding.
[a] *Includes both FX and currency swaps.*

The survey also provides a percentage breakdown of the average daily flows between sell-side banks (called the interbank market), between banks and financial customers (all non-bank financial entities, such as real money and leveraged accounts, SWFs, and central banks), and between banks and non-financial customers (such as corporations, retail accounts, and governments). The breakdown is provided in Exhibit 3. It bears noting that the proportion of average daily FX flow accounted for by financial clients is much larger than that for non-financial clients. The BIS also reports that the proportion of financial client flows has been growing rapidly, and in 2010, it exceeded interbank trading volume for the first time. This underscores the fact that only a minority of the daily FX flow is accounted for by corporations and individuals buying and selling foreign goods and services. Huge investment pools and professional traders account for a large and growing proportion of the FX business.

Exhibit 3: FX Flows by Counterparty

Counterparty	FX Flows (%)
Interbank	42
Financial clients	51
Non-financial clients	8

Note: May not add to 100% due to rounding.

The 2016 BIS survey also identified the top five currency pairs in terms of their percentage share of average daily global FX turnover. These are shown in Exhibit 4. Note that each of these most active pairs includes the US dollar (USD).

Exhibit 4: FX Turnover by Currency Pair

Currency Pair	Percent of Market (%)
USD/EUR	23.1
JPY/USD	17.8
USD/GBP	9.3
USD/AUD	5.2
CAD/USD	4.3

The largest proportion of global FX trading occurs in London, followed by New York. This means that FX markets are most active between approximately 8:00 a.m. and 11:30 a.m. New York time, when banks in both cities are open. (The official London close is at 11:00 a.m. New York time, but London markets remain relatively active for a period after that.) Tokyo is the third-largest FX trading hub.

EXAMPLE 2

Market Participants and Composition of Trades

The investment adviser based in Sydney, Australia, makes the following statements to her client when describing some of the basic characteristics of the FX market:

Statement 1   "FX transactions for spot settlement see the most trade volume in terms of average daily turnover because the FX market is primarily focused on settling international trade flows."

Statement 2   "The most important FX market participants on the buy side are corporations engaged in international trade; on the sell side they are the local banks that service their FX needs."

1. Statement 1 is:

    A. correct.

    B. incorrect with respect to the importance of spot settlements.

    C. incorrect both with respect to the importance of spot settlements and international trade flows.

Solution:

C is correct. Although the media generally focus on the spot market when discussing FX, the majority of average daily trade volume involves the FX swap market as market participants either roll over or modify their existing hedging and speculative positions (or engage in FX swap financing). Although it is true that all international trade transactions eventually result in some form of spot settlement, this typically generates a great deal of hedging (and speculative) activity in advance of spot settlement. Moreover, an important group of FX market participants engages in purely speculative positioning with no intention of ever delivering/receiving the principal amount of the trades. Most FX trading volume is not related to international trade: Portfolio flows (cross-border capital movements) and speculative activities dominate.

2. Statement 2 is:

    A. correct.

B. incorrect with respect to corporations engaged in international trade.

C. incorrect with respect to both corporations and the local banks that service their trade needs.

Solution:

C is correct. The most important FX market participants in terms of average daily turnover are found not among corporations engaged in international trade but among huge investment managers, both private (e.g., pension funds) and public (e.g., central bank reserve managers or sovereign wealth funds). A large and growing amount of daily turnover is also being generated by high-frequency traders who use computer algorithms to automatically execute extremely high numbers of speculative trades (although their individual ticket sizes are generally small, they add up to large aggregate flows). On the sell side, the largest money center banks (e.g., Deutsche Bank, Citigroup, HSBC, UBS) are increasingly dominating the amount of trading activity routed through dealers. Regional and local banks are increasingly being marginalized in terms of their share of average daily turnover in FX markets.

QUESTION SET

1. Which of the following counterparties is *most likely* to be considered a sell-side FX market participant?

   A. A large corporation that borrows in foreign currencies

   B. A sovereign wealth fund that influences cross-border capital flows

   C. A multinational bank that trades FX with its diverse client base

   Solution:

   C is correct. The sell-side parties generally consist of large banks that sell FX and related instruments to buy-side clients. These banks act as market makers, quoting exchange rates at which they will buy (the bid price) or sell (the offer price) the base currency.

Exchange Rate Quotations

Exchange rates represent the relative price of one currency in terms of another. This price can be represented in two ways: (1) currency A buys how many units of currency B; or (2) currency B buys how many units of currency A. Of course, these two prices are simply the inverse of each other.

To distinguish between these two prices, market participants sometimes distinguish between *direct* and *indirect* exchange rates. In the quoting convention A/B (where there are a certain number of units of currency A per one unit of currency B), we refer to currency A as the *price currency* (or quote currency); currency B is referred to as the *base currency*. (The reason for this choice of names will become clear.) The base currency is always set at a quantity of one. A *direct* currency quote takes the domestic country as the price currency and the foreign country as the base currency. For example, for a Paris-based trader, the domestic currency would be the euro (EUR) and a foreign currency would be the UK pound (GBP). For this Paris-based trader, a *direct* quote would be EUR/GBP. An exchange rate quote of EUR/GBP = 1.1211 means that GBP1 costs EUR1.1211. For this Paris-based trader, an *indirect* quote has the domestic currency—the euro—as the base currency. An indirect quote of GBP/EUR = 0.8920 means that EUR1 costs GBP0.8920. *Direct and indirect quotes are just the inverse (reciprocal) of each other.*

The professional FX market does not use the convention of describing exchange rates as either being direct or indirect because determining the domestic currency and the foreign currency depends on where one is located. For a London-based market participant, the UK pound (GBP) is the domestic currency and the euro (EUR) is a foreign currency. For a Paris-based market participant, it would be the other way around.

To avoid confusion, the FX market has developed a set of market conventions that all market participants typically adhere to when making and asking for FX quotes. Exhibit 5 displays some of these for the major currencies: the currency code used for obtaining exchange rate quotes, how the market lingo refers to this currency pair, and the actual ratio—price currency per unit of base currency—represented by the quote.

Exhibit 5: Exchange Rate Quote Conventions

FX Rate Quote Convention	Name Convention	Actual Ratio (Price currency/Base currency)
EUR	Euro	USD/EUR
JPY	Dollar–yen	JPY/USD
GBP	Sterling	USD/GBP
CAD	Dollar–Canada	CAD/USD
AUD	Aussie	USD/AUD
NZD	Kiwi	USD/NZD
CHF	Swiss franc	CHF/USD
EURJPY	Euro–yen	JPY/EUR
EURGBP	Euro–sterling	GBP/EUR
EURCHF	Euro–Swiss	CHF/EUR
GBPJPY	Sterling–yen	JPY/GBP
EURCAD	Euro–Canada	CAD/EUR
CADJPY	Canada–yen	JPY/CAD

Several things should be noted in this exhibit. First, the three-letter currency codes in the first column (for FX rate quotes) refer to what are considered to be the major exchange rates. Remember that an exchange rate is the price of one currency in terms of another: Two currencies are always involved in the price. This is different from referring to a single currency in its own right. For example, one can refer to the euro (EUR) as a *currency*; but if we refer to a euro *exchange rate* (EUR), it is always the price of the euro in terms of another currency, in this case the US dollar. This is because in the professional FX market, the three-letter code EUR is always taken to refer to the euro–US dollar exchange rate, which is quoted in terms of the number of US dollars per euro (USD/EUR). Second, the six-letter currency codes in the first column refer to some of the major *cross-rates*. This topic will be covered in the next section, but generally these are secondary exchange rates and are not as common as the main exchange rates. (Note that three-letter codes are always in terms of an exchange rate involving the US dollar, but the six-letter codes are not.) Third, when both currencies are mentioned in the code or the name convention, *the base currency is always mentioned first, the opposite order of the actual ratio* (*price currency/base currency*). Thus, the code for "Sterling–yen" is "GBPJPY," but the actual number quoted is the number of yen per sterling (JPY/GBP). Note also that *the codes may appear in a variety of formats that all mean the same thing.* For example, GBPJPY might instead appear as GBP:JPY or GBP–JPY. Fourth, regardless of where a market participant is located, there is always a mix of direct and indirect quotes in common market usage. For example, a trader based in Toronto, Canada, will typically refer to the euro–Canada and Canada–yen exchange rates—a mixture of direct (CAD/EUR) and indirect (JPY/CAD) quotes for that Canada-based trader. No overall consistency is observed in this mixture of direct and indirect quoting conventions in the professional FX market; a market participant must get familiar with how the conventions are used. In general, however, there is a hierarchy for quoting conventions. For quotes involving the euro, it serves as the base currency (e.g., GBP/EUR). Next in the priority sequence, for quotes involving the British pound (but not the euro), it serves as the base currency (e.g., USD/GBP). Finally, for quotes involving the US dollar (but not the GBP or EUR), it serves as the base currency (e.g., CAD/USD). Exceptions among the major currencies are the Australian and New Zealand dollars: they serve as the base currency when quoted against the US dollars (i.e., USD/AUD, USD/NZD).

Another concept involving exchange rate quotes in professional FX markets is that of a *two-sided price.* When a client asks a bank for an exchange rate quote, the bank will provide a "*bid*" (the price at which the bank is willing to buy the currency) and an "*offer*" (the price at which the bank is willing to sell the currency). But *two* currencies are referenced in an exchange rate quote, which is always the price of one currency relative to the other. So, which currency is being bought and which is being sold in this two-sided price quote? In this situation, the lingo involving the price currency (or quote currency) and the base currency, explained earlier, becomes useful. *The two-sided price quoted by the dealer is in terms of buying/selling the base currency.* It shows the number of units of the *price* currency that the client will receive from the dealer for one unit of the base currency (the bid) and the number of units of the price currency that the client must sell to the dealer to obtain one unit of the base currency (the offer). Consider the case of a client that is interested in a transaction involving the Swiss franc (CHF) and the euro (EUR). As we have read, the market convention is to quote this as euro–Swiss (CHF/EUR). The euro is the base currency, and the two-sided quote (price) shows the number of units of the price currency (CHF) that must be paid or will be received for EUR1. For example, a two-sided price in euro–Swiss (CHF/EUR) might look like: 1.1583–1.1585. The client will receive CHF1.1583 for selling EUR1 to the dealer and must pay CHF1.1585 to the dealer to buy EUR1. Note that *the price is shown in terms of the price currency* and that *the bid is always less than the offer*: The bank buys the base currency (euro, in this case) at the low price and sells the base currency at the high price. Buying low and selling high is profitable for banks, and spreading clients—trying to widen the bid/offer spread—is how dealers try to increase their profit margins. Note, however, that the electronic dealing systems currently used in professional FX markets are extremely efficient in connecting buyers and sellers globally. Moreover, this worldwide competition for business has compressed most bid/offer spreads to very tight levels. For simplicity, in the remainder of this reading, we will focus on exchange rates as a single number (with no bid/offer spread).

One last point in exchange rate quoting conventions is that most major spot exchange rates are typically quoted to four decimal places. One exception among the major currencies involves the yen, for which spot exchange rates are usually quoted to two decimal places. (For example, a USD/EUR quote would be expressed as 1.1701, whereas a JPY/EUR quote would be expressed as 130.98.) This difference involving the yen comes from the fact that the units of yen per unit of other currencies typically is relatively large, and hence extending the exchange rate quote to four decimal places is viewed as unnecessary.

Regardless of which quoting convention is used, changes in an exchange rate can be expressed as a percentage appreciation of one currency against the other: One simply has to be careful in identifying which currency is the price currency and which is the base currency. For example, suppose the exchange rate for the euro (USD/EUR) increases from 1.1500 to 1.2000. This represents an (unannualized) percentage change of the following:

$$\frac{1.2000}{1.1500} - 1 = 4.35\%.$$

This represents a 4.35 percent appreciation in the euro against the US dollar (and not an appreciation of the US dollar against the euro) because the USD/EUR exchange rate is expressed with the US dollar as the price currency.

Note that this appreciation of the euro against the US dollar also can be expressed as a depreciation of the US dollar against the euro; but in this case, the depreciation is not equal to 4.35 percent. Inverting the exchange rate quote from USD/EUR to EUR/USD, so that the euro is now the price currency, leads to the following:

$$\frac{\left(\frac{1}{1.2000}\right)}{\left(\frac{1}{1.1500}\right)} - 1 = \frac{1.1500}{1.2000} - 1 = -4.17\%.$$

Note that the US dollar depreciation is not the same, in percentage terms, as the euro appreciation. Mathematically, these percentages will always be different.

EXAMPLE 3

Exchange Rate Conventions

A dealer based in New York City provides a spot exchange rate quote of 18.8590 MXN/USD to a client in Mexico City. The inverse of 18.8590 is 0.0530.

1. From the perspective of the Mexican client, the *most* accurate statement is that the:

    A. direct exchange rate quotation is equal to 0.0530.

    B. direct exchange rate quotation is equal to 18.8590.

    C. indirect exchange rate quotation is equal to 18.8590.

    Solution:

    B is correct. A direct exchange rate uses the domestic currency as the price currency and the foreign currency as the base currency. For an MXN/USD quote, the Mexican peso is the price currency; therefore, the direct quote for the Mexican client is 18.8590 (it costs MXN18.8590 to purchase USD1). Another way of understanding a *direct* exchange rate quote is that it is the price of one unit of foreign currency in terms of your own currency. This purchase of a unit of foreign currency can be thought of as a purchase much like any other you might make; think of the unit of foreign currency as just another item that you might be purchasing with your domestic currency. For example, for someone based in Canada, a liter of milk might cost about CAD1.25 at a time when USD1 costs about CAD1.30. This *direct* currency quote uses the *domestic* currency (the Canadian dollar, in this case) as the *price* currency and simply gives the price of a unit of foreign currency that is being purchased.

2. If the bid/offer quote from the dealer was 18.8580–18.8600 MXN/USD, then the bid/offer quote in USD/MXN terms would be *closest* to:

    A. 0.05302–0.05303.

B. 0.05303–0.05302.

C. 0.053025–0.053025.

Solution:

A is correct. An MXN/USD quote is the amount of Mexican pesos the dealer is bidding (offering) to buy (sell) USD1. The dealer's bid to buy USD1 at MXN18.8580 is equivalent to the dealer paying MXN18.8580 to buy USD1. Dividing both terms by 18.8580 means the dealer is paying (i.e., selling) MXN1 to buy USD0.05303. This is the offer in USD/MXN terms: The dealer offers to sell MXN1 at a price of USD0.05303. In USD/MXN terms, the dealer's bid for MXN1 is 0.05302, calculated by inverting the offer of 18.8600 in MXN/USD terms (1/18.8600 = 0.05302). Note that in any bid/offer quote, no matter which base or price currencies are used, the bid is always lower than the offer.

EXCHANGE RATE REGIMES: IDEALS AND HISTORICAL PERSPECTIVE

☐ describe exchange rate regimes and explain the effects of exchange rates on countries' international trade and capital flows

FX rates affect international capital flows and trading relationships. These rate movements are based on the relative economic stability and efficiency of the trading countries involved. As a result, countries having higher or lower economic or trading volatility use different exchange regimes to address their economic objectives. This lesson describes these factors and concludes with an example from Malaysia.

Highly volatile exchange rates create uncertainty that undermines the efficiency of real economic activity and the financial transactions required to facilitate that activity. Exchange rate volatility also has a direct impact on investment decisions because it is a key component of the risk inherent in foreign (i.e., foreign-currency-denominated) assets. Exchange rate volatility is also a critical factor in selecting hedging strategies for foreign currency exposures.

The amount of FX rate volatility will depend, at least in part, on the institutional and policy arrangements associated with trade in any given currency. Virtually every exchange rate is managed to some degree by central banks. The policy framework that each central bank adopts is called an *exchange rate regime*. Although there are many potential variations, these regimes fall into a few general categories. Before describing each of these types, we consider the possibility of an ideal regime and provide some historical perspective on the evolution of currency arrangements.

The Ideal Currency Regime

The ideal currency regime would have three properties. First, the exchange rate between any two currencies would be credibly fixed. This would eliminate currency-related uncertainty with respect to the prices of goods and services as well as real and financial assets. Second, all currencies would be fully convertible (i.e., currencies could be freely exchanged for any purpose and in any amount). This condition ensures the unrestricted flow of capital. Third, each country would be able to undertake fully independent monetary policy in pursuit of domestic objectives, such as growth and inflation targets.

Unfortunately, these three conditions are not consistent. If the first two conditions were satisfied—credibly fixed exchange rates and full convertibility—then there would really be only one currency in the world. Converting from one national currency to another would have no more significance (indeed less) than deciding whether to carry coins or paper currency in your wallet. Any attempt to influence interest rates, asset prices, or inflation by adjusting the supply of one currency versus another would be futile. Thus, independent monetary policy is not possible if exchange rates are credibly fixed and currencies are fully convertible. *There can be no ideal currency regime.*

The impact of the currency regime on a country's ability to exercise independent monetary policy is a recurring theme in open-economy macroeconomics. It will be covered in more detail in other readings; however, it is worth emphasizing the basic point by considering what would happen in an idealized world of perfect capital mobility. If the exchange rate were credibly fixed, then any attempt to decrease default-free interest rates in one country below those in another—that is, to undertake independent, expansionary monetary policy—would result in a potentially unlimited outflow of capital because funds would seek the higher return. The central bank would be forced to sell foreign currency and buy domestic currency to maintain the fixed exchange rate. The loss of reserves and reduction in the domestic money supply would put upward pressure on domestic interest rates until rates were forced back to equality, negating the initial expansionary policy. Similarly, a contractionary monetary policy (higher interest rates) would be thwarted by an inflow of capital.

The situation is quite different, however, with a floating exchange rate. A decrease in the domestic interest rate would make the domestic currency less attractive. The resulting depreciation of the domestic currency would shift demand toward domestically produced goods (i.e., exports rise and imports fall), reinforcing the expansionary impact of the initial decline in the interest rate. Similarly, a contractionary increase in the interest rate would be reinforced by appreciation of the domestic currency.

In practice, of course, capital is not perfectly mobile, and the impact on monetary policy is not so stark. The fact remains, however, that fixed exchange rates limit the scope for independent monetary policy and that national monetary policy regains potency and independence, at least to some degree, if the exchange rate is allowed to fluctuate or restrictions are placed on convertibility. In general, the more freely the exchange rate is allowed to float and the more tightly convertibility is controlled, the more effective the central bank can be in addressing domestic macroeconomic objectives. The downside, of course, is the potential distortion of economic activity caused by exchange rate risk and inefficient allocation of financial capital.

Historical Perspective on Currency Regimes

How currencies exchange for one another has evolved over the centuries. At any point in time, different exchange rate systems may coexist; still, the world economy tends to have one dominant system. Throughout most of the 19th century and the early 20th century until the start of World War I, the US dollar and the British pound sterling operated on the "classical gold standard." The price of each currency was fixed in terms of gold. Gold was the numeraire (the unit in terms of which other goods, services, and assets were priced) for each currency; therefore, it was indirectly the numeraire for all other prices in the economy. Many countries (e.g., the colonies of the United Kingdom) fixed their currencies relative to sterling and were therefore implicitly also operating on the classical gold standard.

The classical gold standard operated by what is called the *price-specie-flow mechanism*. This mechanism operated through the impact of trade imbalances on capital flows, namely gold. As countries experienced a trade surplus, they accumulated gold as payment, their domestic money supply expanded by the amount dictated by the fixed parity, prices rose, and exports fell. Similarly, when a country ran a trade deficit, there was an automatic outflow of gold, a contraction of the domestic money supply, and a fall in prices leading to increased exports.

In this system, national currencies were backed by gold. A country could print only as much money as its gold reserve allowed. The system was limited by the amount of gold, but it was self-adjusting and inspired confidence. With a fixed stock of gold, the price-specie-flow mechanism would work well. Still, new gold discoveries as well as more efficient methods of refining gold would enable a country to increase its gold reserves and increase its money supply apart from the effect of trade flows. In general, however, trade flows drove changes in national money supplies.

Economic historians disagree about the effect of the classical gold standard on overall macroeconomic stability. Was it destabilizing? On the one hand, monetary policy was tied to trade flows, so a country could not engage in expansionary policies when there was a downturn in the non-traded sector. On the other hand, tying monetary policy to trade flows kept inflation in check.

During the 1930s, the use of gold as a clearing device for settlement of trade imbalances, combined with increasing protectionism on the part of economies struggling with depression as well as episodes of deflation and hyperinflation, created a chaotic environment for world trade. As a consequence of these factors, world trade dropped by more than 50 percent and the gold standard was abandoned.

In the latter stages of World War II, a new system of fixed exchange rates with periodic realignments was devised by John Maynard Keynes and Harry Dexter White, representing the UK and US Treasuries, respectively. The Bretton Woods system, named after the town where it was negotiated, was adopted by 44 countries in 1944. From the end of the war until the collapse of the system in the early 1970s, the United States, Japan, and most of the industrial countries of Europe maintained a system of fixed parities for exchange rates between currencies. When the parities were significantly and persistently out of line with the balancing of supply and demand, there would be a realignment of currencies with some appreciating in value and others depreciating in value. These periodic realignments were viewed as a part of standard monetary policy.

By 1973, with chronic inflation taking hold throughout the world, most nations abandoned the Bretton Woods system in favor of a flexible exchange rate system under what are known as the Smithsonian Agreements. Milton Friedman had called for such a system as far back as the 1950s. His argument was that the fixed parity system with periodic realignments would become unsustainable. When the inevitable realignments were imminent, large speculative profit opportunities would appear. Speculators would force the hand of monetary policy authorities, and their actions would distort the data needed to ascertain appropriate trade-related parities. It is better, he argued, to let the market, rather than central bank governors and treasury ministers, determine the exchange rate.

After 1973, most of the industrial world changed to a system of flexible exchange rates. The original thinking was that the forces that caused exchange rate chaos in the 1930s—poor domestic monetary policy and trade barriers—would not be present in a flexible exchange rate regime, and therefore exchange rates would move in response to the exchange of goods and services among countries. However, exchange rates moved around much more than anyone expected. Academic economists and financial analysts alike soon realized that the high degree of exchange rate volatility was the manifestation of a highly liquid, forward-looking asset market. Investment-driven FX transactions—for both long-term investment and short-term speculation—mattered much more in setting the spot exchange rate than anyone had previously imagined.

There are costs, of course, to a high degree of exchange rate volatility. These include difficulty planning without hedging exchange rate risks—a form of insurance cost, domestic price fluctuations, uncertain costs of raw materials, and short-term interruptions in financing transactions. For these reasons, in 1979 the European Economic Community opted for a system of limited flexibility, the European Exchange Rate Mechanism (ERM).

Initially, the system called for European currency values to fluctuate within a narrow band called "the snake," but this system did not last long. The end of the Cold War and the reunification of Germany created conditions ripe for speculative attack. In the early 1990s, the United Kingdom was in a recession and the government's monetary policy leaned toward low interest rates to stimulate economic recovery. Germany was issuing large amounts of debt to pay for reunification, and the German central bank (the Deutsche Bundesbank) opted for high interest rates to ensure price stability. Capital began to flow from sterling to Deutsche marks to obtain the higher interest rate. The Bank of England tried to lean against these flows and maintain the exchange rate within the ERM, but eventually it began to run out of marks to sell. Because it was almost certain that devaluation would be required, holders of sterling rushed to purchase marks at the old rate, and the speculative attack forced the United Kingdom out of the ERM in September 1992, only two years after it finally had joined the system.

Despite these difficulties, 1999 saw the creation of a common currency for most Western European countries, without Switzerland or the United Kingdom, called the euro. The hope was that the common currency would increase transparency of prices across borders in Europe, enhance market competition, and facilitate more efficient allocation of resources. The drawback, of course, is that each member country lost the ability to manage its exchange rate and therefore to engage in independent monetary policy.

QUESTION SET

1. An exchange rate:

    A. is most commonly quoted in real terms.

    B. is the price of one currency in terms of another.

    C. between two currencies ensures that they are fully convertible.

    Solution:

    B is correct. The exchange rate is the number of units of the price currency that one unit of the base currency will buy. Equivalently, it is the number of units of the price currency required to buy one unit of the base currency.

2. Which of the following is *not* a condition of an ideal currency regime?

    A. Fully convertible currencies

    B. Fully independent monetary policy

    C. Independently floating exchange rates

    Solution:

    C is correct. An ideal currency regime would have credibly fixed exchange rates among all currencies. This would eliminate currency-related uncertainty with respect to the prices of goods and services as well as real and financial assets.

A Taxonomy of Currency Regimes

Although the pros and cons of fixed and flexible exchange rate regimes continue to be debated, regimes have been adopted that lie somewhere between these polar cases. In some cases, the driving force is the lack of credibility with respect to sound monetary policy. An economy with a history of hyperinflation may be forced to adopt a form of fixed-rate regime because its promise to maintain a sound currency with a floating rate regime would not be credible. This has been a persistent issue in Latin America. In other cases, the driving force is as much political as it is economic. The decision to create the euro was strongly influenced by the desire to enhance political union within the European Community, whose members had been at war with each other twice in the 20th century.

As of April 2008, the International Monetary Fund (IMF) classified exchange rate regimes into the eight categories shown in Exhibit 6.

Exhibit 6: Exchange Rate Regimes for Selected Economies as of 30 April 2008

Type of Regime	Currency Anchor		
	US Dollar	Euro	Basket/None
No separate legal tender			
Dollarized	Ecuador, El Salvador, Marshall Islands, Micronesia, Palau, Panama, Timor-Leste, Zimbabwe	Kosovo, Montenegro, San Marino	Kiribati, Tuvalu
Monetary union		EMU: Austria, Belgium, Cyprus, Estonia, Finland, France, Germany, Greece, Ireland, Italy, Latvia, Luxembourg, Lithuania, Malta, Netherlands, Portugal, Slovak Rep., Slovenia, Spain	
Currency board	Djibouti, Hong Kong SAR, Antigua and Barbuda	Bosnia and Herzegovina, Bulgaria	Brunei Darussalam
Fixed parity	Aruba, The Bahamas, Bahrain, Barbados, Belize, Curaçao and Saint Maarten, Eritrea, Jordan, Oman, Qatar, Saudi Arabia, South Sudan, Turkmenistan, UAE, Venezuela	Cabo Verde, Comoros, Denmark, São Tomé and Príncipe WAEMU: Benin, Burkina Faso, Côte d'Ivoire, Guinea-Bissau, Mali, Niger, Senegal, Togo CEMAC: Cameroon, Central African Rep., Chad, Rep. of Congo, Equatorial Guinea, Gabon	Fiji, Kuwait, Libya, Morocco, Samoa, Bhutan, Lesotho, Namibia, Nepal, Swaziland
Target zone		Slovak Republic	Syria
Crawling peg	Nicaragua		Botswana
Crawling band	Honduras, Jamaica	Croatia	China, Ethiopia, Uzbekistan, Armenia, Dominican Republic, Guatemala, Argentina, Belarus, Haiti, Switzerland, Tunisia

Type of Regime	Currency Anchor		
	US Dollar	Euro	Basket/None
Managed float	Cambodia, Liberia		Algeria, Iran, Syria, The Gambia, Myanmar, Nigeria, Rwanda, Czech Rep., Costa Rica, Malaysia, Mauritania Pakistan, Russia, Sudan, Vanuatu
Independent float	Australia, Canada, Chile, Japan, Mexico, Norway, Poland, Sweden, United Kingdom, Somalia, United States	Albania, Brazil, Colombia, Georgia, Ghana, Hungary, Iceland, Indonesia, Israel, Korea, Moldova, New Zealand, Paraguay, Peru	Philippines, Romania, Serbia, South Africa, Thailand, Turkey, Uganda

Global financial markets are too complex and diverse to be fully captured by this (or any other) classification system. A government's control over the domestic currency's exchange rate will depend on many factors; for example, the degree of capital controls used to prevent the free flow of funds in and out of the economy. Also, even under an "independent float" regime, monetary authorities will occasionally intervene in FX markets to influence the value of their domestic currency. Additionally, the specifics of exchange rate policy implementation are subject to change.

This means that the classifications in Exhibit 6 are somewhat arbitrary and subject to interpretation, and they change over time. The important point is that the prices and flows in FX markets will, to varying degrees, reflect the legal and regulatory framework imposed by governments, not just "pure" market forces. Governments have a variety of motives and tools to attempt to manage exchange rates. The taxonomy in Exhibit 6 can be used to help understand the main distinctions among currency regimes and the rationales for adopting them, but the specific definitions should not be interpreted too rigidly. Instead, the focus should be on the diversity of FX markets globally as well as the implications of these various currency regimes for market pricing.

Arrangements with No Separate Legal Tender

The IMF identifies two types of arrangements for countries that do not have their own legal tender. In the first, known as *dollarization*, the country uses the currency of another nation as its medium of exchange and unit of account. In the second, the country participates in a monetary union whose members share the same legal tender. In either case, the country gives up the ability to conduct its own monetary policy.

In principle, a country could adopt any currency as its medium of exchange and unit of account, but the main reserve currency, the US dollar, is an obvious choice—hence the name dollarization. Many countries are dollarized: East Timor, El Salvador, Ecuador, and Panama, for example. By adopting another country's currency as legal tender, a dollarized country inherits that country's currency credibility, but not its creditworthiness. For example, although local banks may borrow, lend, and accept deposits in US dollars, they are not members of the US Federal Reserve System, nor are they backed by deposit insurance from the Federal Deposit Insurance Corporation. Thus, interest rates on US dollars in a dollarized economy need not be, and generally are not, the same as on dollar deposits in the United States.

Dollarization imposes fiscal discipline by eliminating the possibility that the central bank will be induced to monetize government debt (i.e., to persistently purchase government debt with newly created local currency). For countries with a history of fiscal excess or a lack of monetary discipline, dollarizing the economy can facilitate growth of international trade and capital flows if it creates an expectation of economic and financial stability. In the process, however, it removes another potential source of stabilization—domestic monetary policy.

The European Economic and Monetary Union (EMU) is the most prominent example of the second type of arrangement lacking separate legal tender. Each EMU member country uses the euro as its currency. Although member countries cannot have their own monetary policies, they jointly determine monetary policy through their representation at the European Central Bank (ECB). As with dollarization, a monetary union confers currency credibility on members with a history of fiscal excess or a lack of monetary discipline. As shown by the 2010 EMU sovereign debt crisis, however, a monetary union alone cannot confer creditworthiness.

Currency Board System

The IMF defines a *currency board system* (CBS) as follows:

> A monetary regime based on an explicit legislative commitment to exchange domestic currency for a specified foreign currency at a fixed exchange rate, combined with restrictions on the issuing authority to ensure fulfillment of its legal obligation. This implies that domestic currency will be issued only against foreign exchange and it remains fully backed by foreign assets.

Hong Kong SAR has the leading example of a long-standing (since 1983) currency board. US dollar reserves are held to cover, at the fixed parity, the entire *monetary base*—essentially bank reserves plus all Hong Kong dollar notes and coins in circulation. Note that Hong Kong-dollar-denominated bank deposits are not fully collateralized by US dollar reserves; to do so would mean that banks could not lend against their deposits. The Hong Kong Monetary Authority (HKMA) does not function as a traditional central bank under this system because the obligation to maintain 100 percent foreign currency reserves against the monetary base prevents it from acting as a lender-of-last-resort for troubled financial institutions. It can, however, provide short-term liquidity by lending against foreign currency collateral.

A CBS works much like the classical gold standard in that expansion and contraction of the monetary base are directly linked to trade and capital flows. As with the gold standard, a CBS works best if domestic prices and wages are very flexible, non-traded sectors of the domestic economy are relatively small, and the global supply of the reserve asset grows at a slow, steady rate consistent with long-run real growth with stable prices. The first two of these conditions are satisfied in Hong Kong SAR. Until and unless Hong Kong SAR selects a new reserve asset, however, the third condition depends on US monetary policy.

In practice, the HKD exhibits modest fluctuations around the official parity of HKD/USD = 7.80 because the HKMA buys (sells) US dollars at a pre-announced level slightly below (above) the parity. Persistent flows on one side of this convertibility zone or the other result in interest rate adjustments rather than exchange rate adjustments. Inside the zone, however, the exchange rate is determined by the market and the HKMA is free to conduct limited monetary operations aimed at dampening transitory interest rate movements.

One of the advantages of a CBS as opposed to dollarization is that the monetary authority can earn a profit by paying little or no interest on its liability—the monetary base—and can earn a market rate on its asset—the foreign currency reserves. This profit is called *seigniorage*. Under dollarization, the seigniorage goes to the monetary authority whose currency is used.

Fixed Parity

A simple fixed-rate system differs from a CBS in two important respects. First, there is no legislative commitment to maintaining the specified parity. Thus, market participants know that the country may choose to adjust or abandon the parity rather than endure other, potentially more painful, adjustments. Second, the target level of FX reserves is discretionary; it bears no particular relationship to domestic monetary aggregates. Thus, although monetary independence is ultimately limited as long as the exchange peg is maintained, the central bank can carry out traditional functions, such as serving as lender of last resort.

In the conventional fixed-rate system, the exchange rate may be pegged to a single currency—for example, the US dollar—or to a basket index of the currencies of major trading partners. There is a band of up to ±1 percent around the parity level within which private flows are allowed to determine the exchange rate. The monetary authority stands ready to spend its foreign currency reserves, or buy foreign currency, to maintain the rate within these bands.

The credibility of the fixed parity depends on the country's willingness and ability to offset imbalances in private sector demand for its currency. Both excess and deficient private demand for the currency can exert pressure to adjust or abandon the parity. Excess private demand for the domestic currency implies a rapidly growing stock of FX reserves, expansion of the domestic money supply, and potentially accelerating inflation. Deficient demand for the currency depletes FX reserves and exerts deflationary pressure on the economy. If market participants believe the FX reserves are insufficient to sustain the parity, then that belief may be self-fulfilling because the resulting speculative attack will drain reserves and may force an immediate devaluation. Thus, the level of reserves required to maintain credibility is a key issue for a simple fixed exchange rate regime.

Target Zone

A target zone regime has a fixed parity with fixed horizontal intervention bands that are somewhat wider—up to ±2 percent around the parity—than in the simple fixed parity regime. The wider bands provide the monetary authority with greater scope for discretionary policy.

Active and Passive Crawling Pegs

Crawling pegs for the exchange rate—usually against a single currency, such as the US dollar—were common in the 1980s in Latin America, particularly Brazil, during the high inflation periods. To prevent a run on the US dollar reserves, the exchange rate was adjusted frequently (weekly or daily) to keep pace with the inflation rate. Such a system was called a passive crawl. An adaptation used in Argentina, Chile, and Uruguay was the active crawl: The exchange rate was pre-announced for the coming weeks with changes taking place in small steps. The aim of the active crawl was to manipulate expectations of inflation. Because the domestic prices of many goods were directly tied to import prices, announced changes in the exchange rate would effectively signal future changes in the inflation rate of these goods.

Fixed Parity with Crawling Bands

A country can also have a fixed central parity with crawling bands. Initially, a country may fix its rates to a foreign currency to anchor expectations about future inflation, but then the country may gradually permit increasing flexibility in the form of a pre-announced widening band around the central parity. Such a system has the desirable property of allowing a gradual exit strategy from the fixed parity. A country might want to introduce greater flexibility and greater scope for monetary policy, but it may not yet have the credibility or financial infrastructure for full flexibility. In this case, it can maintain a fixed parity with slowly widening bands.

Managed Float

A country may simply follow an exchange rate policy based on either internal or external policy targets—intervening or not to achieve trade balance, price stability, or employment objectives. Such a policy, often called *dirty floating*, invites trading partners to respond likewise with their exchange rate policy and potentially decreases stability in FX markets as a whole. The exchange rate target, in terms of either a level or a rate of change, typically is not explicit.

Independently Floating Rates

In this case, the exchange rate is left to market determination and the monetary authority is able to exercise independent monetary policy aimed at achieving such objectives as price stability and full employment. The central bank also has latitude to act as a lender of last resort to troubled financial institutions, if necessary.

It should be clear from recent experience that the concepts of float, managed float, crawl, and target zone are not hard and fast rules. Central banks do occasionally engage, implicitly or explicitly, in regime switches—even in countries nominally following an independently floating exchange rate regime. For example, when the US dollar appreciated in the mid-1980s with record US trade deficits, then-US Treasury Secretary James Baker engineered the Plaza Accord, in which Japan and Germany implemented an appreciation of their currencies against the US dollar. (The Plaza Accord is so named because it was negotiated at the Plaza Hotel in New York City.) This 1985 policy agreement involved a combination of fiscal and monetary policy measures by the countries involved as well as direct intervention in FX markets. The Plaza Accord was a clear departure from a pure independently floating exchange rate system.

There are more recent examples of government intervention in FX markets. In September 2000, the ECB, the Federal Reserve Board, the Bank of Japan, the Bank of England, and the Bank of Canada engaged in "concerted" intervention to support the value of the euro, a "freely floating" currency that was then under pressure within FX markets. (This intervention was described as "concerted" because it was pre-arranged and coordinated among the central banks involved.) During 2010, many countries engaged in unilateral intervention to prevent the rapid appreciation of their currencies against the US dollar. Several of these countries also employed various fiscal and regulatory measures (e.g., taxes on capital inflows) to further affect exchange rate movements.

The important point to draw from this discussion is that exchange rates not only reflect private sector market forces but also will be influenced, to varying degrees, by the legal and regulatory framework (currency regimes) within which FX markets operate. Moreover, they will occasionally be influenced by government policies (fiscal, monetary, and intervention) intended to manage exchange rates. All of these can vary widely among countries and are subject to change with time.

Nonetheless, the most widely traded currencies in FX markets (the US dollar, yen, euro, UK pound, Swiss franc, and the Canadian and Australian dollars) are typically considered to be free floating, although subject to relatively infrequent intervention.

EXAMPLE 4

Exchange Rate Regimes

An investment adviser in Los Angeles, United States, is meeting with a client who wishes to diversify her portfolio by including more international investments. To evaluate the suitability of international diversification for the client, the adviser attempts to explain some of the characteristics of FX markets. The adviser points out that exchange rate regimes affect the performance of domestic economies as well as the amount of FX risk posed by international investments.

The client and her adviser discuss potential investments in Hong Kong SAR, Panama, and Canada. The adviser notes that the currency regimes of Hong Kong SAR, Panama, and Canada are a currency board, dollarization, and a free float, respectively. The adviser tells his client that these regimes imply different degrees of FX risk for her portfolio.

The discussion between the investment adviser and his client then turns to potential investments in other markets with different currency regimes. The adviser notes that some markets are subject to fixed parity regimes against the US dollar. The client asks whether a fixed parity regime would imply less foreign currency risk for her portfolio than would a currency board. The adviser replies: "Yes, a fixed parity regime means a constant exchange rate and is more credible than a currency board."

The adviser goes on to explain that in some markets, exchange rates are allowed to vary, although with different degrees of FX market intervention to limit exchange rate volatility. Citing examples, he notes that mainland China has a crawling peg regime with reference to the US dollar, but the average daily percentage changes in the mainland China/US exchange rate are very small compared with the average daily volatility for a freely floating currency. The adviser also indicates that Denmark has a target zone regime with reference to the euro, and South Korea usually follows a freely floating currency regime but sometimes switches to a managed float regime. The currencies of mainland China, Denmark, and South Korea are the yuan renminbi (CNY), krone (DKK), and won (KRW), respectively.

1. Based solely on the exchange rate risk the client would face, what is the correct ranking (from most to least risky) of the following investment locations?

   A. Panama, Canada, Hong Kong SAR
   B. Canada, Hong Kong SAR, Panama
   C. Hong Kong SAR, Panama, Canada

   Solution:

   B is correct. The CAD/USD exchange rate is a floating exchange rate, and Canadian investments would therefore carry exchange rate risk for a US-based investor. Although Hong Kong SAR follows a currency board system, the HKD/USD exchange rate nonetheless does display some variation, albeit much less than in a floating exchange rate regime. In contrast, Panama has a dollarized economy (i.e., it uses the US dollar as the domestic currency); therefore, there is no FX risk for a US investor.

2. Based solely on their FX regimes, which investment location is least likely to import inflation or deflation from the United States?

   A. Canada
   B. Panama
   C. Hong Kong SAR

   Solution:

   A is correct. The Canadian dollar floats independently against the US dollar leaving the Bank of Canada able to adjust monetary policy to maintain price stability. Neither Hong Kong SAR (currency board) nor Panama (dollarized) can exercise independent monetary policy to buffer its economy from the inflationary or deflationary consequences of US monetary policy.

3. The adviser's reply about fixed parity regimes is incorrect with regard to:

   A. credibility.
   B. a constant exchange rate.
   C. both a constant exchange rate and credibility.

   Solution:

   C is correct. A fixed exchange rate regime does not mean that the exchange rate is rigidly fixed at a constant level. In practice, both a fixed-rate regime and a currency board allow the exchange rate to vary within a band around the stated parity level. Thus, both regimes involve at least a modest amount of exchange rate risk. The fixed parity regime exposes the investor to the additional risk that the parity may not be maintained. In a fixed parity regime, the level of foreign currency reserves is discretionary and typically only a small fraction of the domestic money supply. With no legal obligation to maintain the parity, the monetary authority may adjust the parity (devalue or revalue its currency) or allow its currency to float if doing so is deemed to be less painful than other adjustment mechanisms (e.g., fiscal restraint). In contrast, a currency board entails a legal commitment to maintain the parity and to fully back the domestic currency with reserve currency assets. Hence, there is little risk that the parity will be abandoned.

4. Based on the adviser's categorization of mainland China's currency regime, if the US dollar is depreciating against the South Korean won, then it is *most* likely correct that the Chinese yuan is:

   A. fixed against the South Korean won.
   B. appreciating against the South Korean won.
   C. depreciating against the South Korean won.

   Solution:

   C is correct. If the Chinese yuan is subject to a crawling peg with very small daily adjustments versus the US dollar, and the US dollar is depreciating against the South Korean won, then the Chinese yuan *mostlikely* would be depreciating against the South Korean won as well. In fact, this was an important issue in FX markets through the latter part of 2010: As the US dollar depreciated against most Asian currencies (and less so against the Chinese yuan), many Asian countries felt that they were losing their competitive export advantage because the Chinese yuan was so closely tied to the US dollar. This led many Asian countries to intervene in FX markets against the strength of their domestic currencies to avoid losing an export pricing advantage against the Chinese mainland.

5. Based on the adviser's categorization of Denmark's currency regime, it would be *most* correct to infer that the:

   A. krone is allowed to float against the euro within fixed bands.
   B. Danish central bank will intervene if the exchange rate strays from its target level.
   C. target zone will be adjusted periodically to manage inflation expectations.

   Solution:

   A is correct. A target zone means that the exchange rate between the euro and Danish krone (DKK) will be allowed to vary within a fixed band (as of 2010, the target zone for the DKK/EUR is a ±2.5 percent band). This does not mean that the DKK/EUR rate is fixed at a certain level (B is incorrect) or that the target zone will vary to manage inflation expectations (this is a description of a crawling peg, which makes C incorrect).

6. Based on the adviser's categorization of South Korea's currency policy, it would be *most* correct to infer that the Korean:

   A. central bank is engineering a gradual exit from a fixed-rate regime.

   B. government is attempting to peg the exchange rate within a predefined zone.

   C. won is allowed to float, but with occasional intervention by the Korean central bank.

   Solution:

   C is correct. Similar to the monetary authorities responsible for many of the world's major currencies, the South Korean policy typically involves letting market forces determine the exchange rate (an independent floating rate regime). But this approach does not mean that market forces are the sole determinant of the won exchange rate. As with most governments, the South Korean policy is to intervene in FX markets when movements in the exchange rate are viewed as undesirable (a managed float). For example, during the latter part of 2010, South Korea and many other countries intervened in FX markets to moderate the appreciation of their currencies against the US dollar. Answer A describes a fixed parity with a crawling bands regime, and B describes a target zone regime: Both answers are incorrect.

QUESTION SET

1. In practice, both a fixed parity regime and a target zone regime allow the exchange rate to float within a band around the parity level. The *most likely* rationale for the band is that the band allows the monetary authority to:

   A. be less active in the currency market.

   B. earn a spread on its currency transactions.

   C. exercise more discretion in monetary policy.

   Solution:

   C is correct. Fixed exchange rates impose severe limitations on the exercise of independent monetary policy. With a rigidly fixed exchange rate, domestic interest rates, monetary aggregates (e.g., money supply), and credit conditions are dictated by the requirement to buy/sell the currency at the rigid parity. Even a narrow band around the parity level allows the monetary authority to exercise some discretionary control over these conditions. In general, the wider the band, the more independent control the monetary authority can exercise.

2. A fixed exchange rate regime in which the monetary authority is legally required to hold FX reserves backing 100 percent of its domestic currency issuance is best described as:

   A. dollarization.

   B. a currency board.

> **C.** a monetary union.
>
> **Solution:**
>
> B is correct. With a currency board, the monetary authority is legally required to exchange domestic currency for a specified foreign currency at a fixed exchange rate. It cannot issue domestic currency without receiving foreign currency in exchange, and it must hold that foreign currency as a 100 percent reserve against the domestic currency issued. Thus, the country's monetary base (bank reserves plus notes and coins in circulation) is fully backed by FX reserves.

Exchange Rates and the Trade Balance: Introduction

Just as a family that spends more than it earns must borrow or sell assets to finance the excess, a country that imports more goods and services than it exports must either borrow from or sell assets to foreign entities to finance the trade deficit. Conversely, a country that exports more goods and services than it imports must invest the excess either by lending to foreigners or by buying assets from foreigners. Thus, a trade deficit (surplus) must be exactly matched by an offsetting *capital account* surplus (deficit). This implies that any factor that affects the trade balance must have an equal and opposite impact on the capital account, and vice versa. To put this differently, the *impact of exchange rates and other factors on the trade balance must be mirrored by their impact on capital flows*: They cannot affect one without affecting the other.

Using a fundamental identity from macroeconomics, the relationship between the trade balance and expenditure/saving decisions can be expressed as follows:

$$X - M = (S - I) + (T - G),$$

where X represents exports, M is imports, S is private savings, I is investment in plant and equipment, T is taxes net of transfers, and G is government expenditure. From this relationship, we can see that a trade surplus ($X > M$) must be reflected in a fiscal surplus ($T > G$), an excess of private saving over investment ($S > I$), or both. Because a fiscal surplus can be viewed as government saving, we can summarize this relationship more simply by saying that a trade surplus means the country saves more than enough to fund its investment (I) in plant and equipment. The excess saving is used to accumulate financial claims on the rest of the world. Conversely, a trade deficit means the country does not save enough to fund its investment spending (I) and must reduce its net financial claims on the rest of the world.

Although this identity provides a key link between real expenditure and saving decisions and the aggregate flow of financial assets into or out of a country, it does not tell us what type of financial assets will be exchanged or in what currency they will be denominated. All that can be said is that asset prices and exchange rates at home and abroad must adjust so that all financial assets are willingly held by investors.

If investors anticipate a significant change in an exchange rate, they will try to sell the currency that is expected to depreciate and buy the currency that is expected to appreciate. This implies an incipient (i.e., potential) flow of capital from one country to the other, which must either be accompanied by a simultaneous shift in the trade balance or be discouraged by changes in asset prices and exchange rates. Because expenditure/saving decisions and prices of goods change much more slowly than financial investment decisions and asset prices, most of the adjustment usually occurs within the financial markets. That is, *asset prices and exchange rates adjust so that the potential flow of financial capital is mitigated and actual capital flows remain consistent with trade flows*. In a fixed exchange rate regime, the central bank offsets the private capital flows in the process of maintaining the exchange rate peg and the adjustment occurs in other asset prices, typically interest rates, until and unless the central bank is forced to allow the exchange rate to adjust. In a floating exchange rate regime, the main adjustment is often a rapid change in the exchange rate that dampens an investor's conviction that further movement will be forthcoming. Thus, *capital flows—potential and actual—are the primary determinant of exchange rate movements in the short to intermediate term.* Trade flows become increasingly important in the long term as expenditure and saving decisions as well as the prices of goods and services adjust.

> **QUESTION SET**
>
> 1. A country with a trade deficit will *most likely*:
>   - **A.** have an offsetting capital account surplus.
>   - **B.** save enough to fund its investment spending.
>   - **C.** buy assets from foreigners to fund the imbalance.
>
>   **Solution:**
>
>   A is correct. A trade deficit must be exactly matched by an offsetting capital account surplus to fund the deficit. A capital account surplus reflects borrowing from foreigners (an increase in domestic liabilities) and/or selling assets to foreigners (a decrease in domestic assets). A capital account surplus is often referred to as a "capital inflow" because the net effect is foreign investment in the domestic economy.

4 CAPITAL RESTRICTIONS

☐ describe common objectives of capital restrictions imposed by governments

Governments restrict inward and outward flow of capital for many reasons. For example, the government may want to meet some objective regarding employment or regional development, or it may have a strategic or defense-related objective. Many countries require approval for foreigners to invest in their country and for citizens to invest abroad. Control over inward investment by foreigners results in restrictions on how much can be invested, and on the type of industries in which capital can be invested. For example, such strategic industries as defense and telecommunications are often subject to ownership restrictions. Outflow restrictions can include restrictions on repatriation of capital, interest, profits, royalty payments, and license fees. Citizens are often limited in their ability to invest abroad, especially in FX-scarce economies, and there can be deadlines for repatriation of income earned from any investments abroad.

Economists consider free movement of financial capital to be beneficial because it allows capital to be invested where it will earn the highest return. Inflows of capital also allow countries to invest in productive capacity at a rate that is higher than could be achieved with domestic savings alone, and it can enable countries to achieve a higher rate of growth. Long-term investments by foreign firms that establish a presence in the local economy can bring in not only much needed capital but also new technology, skills, and advanced production and management practices as well as create spillover benefits for local firms. Investment by foreign firms can create a network of local suppliers if they source some of their components locally. Such suppliers may receive advanced training and spillover benefits from a close working relationship with the foreign firms. On the one hand, increased competition from foreign firms in the market may force domestic firms to become more efficient. On the other hand, it is possible that the domestic industry may be hurt because domestic firms that are unable to compete are forced to exit the market.

In times of macroeconomic crisis, capital mobility can result in capital flight out of the country, especially if most of the inflow reflects short-term portfolio flows into stocks, bonds, and other liquid assets rather than foreign direct investment in productive assets. In such circumstances, capital restrictions are often used in conjunction with other policy instruments, such as fixed exchange rate targets. Capital restrictions and fixed exchange rate targets are complementary instruments because in a regime of perfect capital mobility, governments cannot achieve domestic and external policy objectives simultaneously using only standard monetary and fiscal policy tools. By limiting the free flow of capital, capital controls provide a way to exercise control over a country's external balance, whereas more traditional macro-policy tools are used to address other objectives.

Modern capital controls were developed by the belligerents in World War I as a method to finance the war effort. At the start of the war, all major powers restricted capital outflows (i.e., the purchase of foreign assets or loans abroad). These restrictions raised revenues by keeping capital in the domestic economies, facilitating the taxation of wealth, and producing interest income. Moreover, capital controls helped to maintain a low level of interest rates, reducing the governments' borrowing costs on their liabilities. Since World War I, controls on capital outflows have been used similarly in other countries, mostly developing nations, to generate revenue for governments or to permit them to allocate credit in their domestic economies without risking capital flight. In broad terms, a capital restriction is any policy designed to limit or redirect capital flows. Such restrictions may take the form of taxes, price or quantity controls, or outright prohibitions on international trade in assets. Price controls may take the form of special taxes on returns to international investment, taxes on certain types of transactions, or mandatory reserve requirements—that is, a requirement forcing foreign parties wishing to deposit money in a domestic bank account to deposit some percentage of the inflow with the central bank for a minimum period at zero interest. Quantity restrictions on capital flows may include rules imposing ceilings or requiring special authorization for new or existing borrowing from foreign creditors. Or administrative controls may have an impact on cross-border capital movements in which a government agency must approve transactions for certain types of assets.

Effective implementation of capital restrictions may entail non-trivial administration costs, particularly if the measures have to be broadened to close potential loopholes. Protecting the domestic financial markets by capital restrictions also may postpone necessary policy adjustments or impede private-sector adaptation to changing international circumstances. Most important, controls may give rise to negative market perceptions, which may, in turn, make it more costly and difficult for the country to access foreign funds.

In a study on the effectiveness of capital controls, the International Monetary Fund considered restrictions on capital outflows and inflows separately. The authors concluded that for restrictions on capital inflows to be effective (i.e., not circumvented), the coverage needs to be comprehensive and the controls need to be implemented forcefully. Considerable administrative costs are incurred in continuously extending, amending, and monitoring compliance with the regulations. Although controls on inflows appeared to be effective in some countries, it was difficult to distinguish the impact of the controls from the impact of other policies, such as strengthening of prudential regulations, increased exchange rate flexibility, and adjustment of monetary policy. In the case of capital outflows, the imposition of controls during episodes of financial crisis seems to have produced mixed results, providing only temporary relief of varying duration to some countries, while successfully shielding others (e.g., Malaysia) and providing them with sufficient time to restructure their economies.

> **EXAMPLE 5**
>
> ### Historical Example—Capital Restrictions: Malaysia's Capital Controls in 1998–2001
>
> After the devaluation of the Thai baht in July 1997, Southeast Asia suffered from significant capital outflows that led to falling local equity and real estate prices and declining exchange rates. To counter the outflows of capital, the IMF urged many of the countries in the region to increase interest rates, thus making their assets more attractive to foreign investors. Higher interest rates, however, weighed heavily on the domestic economies. In response to this dilemma, Malaysia imposed capital controls on 1 September 1998. These controls prohibited transfers between domestic and foreign accounts, eliminated credit facilities to offshore parties, prevented repatriation of investment until 1 September 1999, and fixed the exchange rate of the Malaysian ringgit at 3.8 per US dollar. In February 1999, a system of taxes on capital flows replaced the prohibition on repatriation of capital. Although the details were complex, the net effect was to discourage short-term capital flows while permitting long-term transactions. By imposing capital controls, Malaysia hoped to regain monetary independence and to be able to cut interest rates without provoking a fall in the value of its currency as investors avoided Malaysian assets. The imposition of outflow controls indeed curtailed speculative capital outflows and allowed interest rates to be reduced substantially. At the same time, under the umbrella of the capital controls, the authorities pursued bank and corporate restructuring and achieved a strong economic recovery in 1999 and 2000. With the restoration of economic and financial stability, administrative controls on portfolio outflows were replaced by a two-tier, price-based exit system in February 1999, which was finally eliminated in May 2001. Although Malaysia's capital controls did contribute to a stabilization of its economy, they came with long-term costs associated with the country's removal from the MSCI developed equity market index, an important benchmark in the institutional asset management industry, and its relegation to the emerging market universe. The Malaysian market was no longer seen as on par with developed equity markets whose institutional and regulatory frameworks provide a higher standard of safety for investors. As a result, a number of market analysts suggested that it became more difficult for Malaysia to attract net long-term capital inflows.
>
> 1. Under what economic circumstances were Malaysia's capital restrictions imposed?
>
>   **Solution:**
>
>   As a result of the Southeast Asian crisis, Malaysia suffered substantial net capital outflows pushing up the domestic interest rate level.
>
> 2. What was the ultimate objective of Malaysia's capital restrictions?
>
>   **Solution:**
>
>   The restrictions were designed to limit and redirect capital flows to allow the government to reduce interest rates and pursue bank and corporate restructurings.

3. How successful were the country's capital restrictions?

   Solution:

   Although the capital controls helped stabilize Malaysia's economy, they contributed to a change in investors' perception of Malaysian financial markets and the removal of the Malaysian equity market from the MSCI benchmark universe of developed equity markets. This situation undermined international demand for Malaysian equities and made it more difficult to attract net long-term capital inflows.

PRACTICE PROBLEMS

1. What will be the effect on a direct exchange rate quote if the domestic currency appreciates?

   A. Increase

   B. Decrease

   C. No change

2. An executive from Switzerland checks into a hotel room in Spain and is told by the manager that EUR1 will buy CHF1.2983. From the executive's perspective, an indirect exchange rate quote would be:

   A. EUR0.7702 per CHF1.

   B. CHF0.7702 per EUR1.

   C. EUR1.2983 per CHF1.

3. Over the past month, the Swiss franc (CHF) has depreciated 12 percent against the British pound (GBP). How much has the pound sterling appreciated against the Swiss franc?

   A. 12 percent

   B. Less than 12 percent

   C. More than 12 percent

4. An exchange rate between two currencies has increased to 1.4500. If the base currency has appreciated by 8 percent against the price currency, the initial exchange rate between the two currencies was *closest* to:

   A. 1.3340.

   B. 1.3426.

   C. 1.5660.

SOLUTIONS

1. B is correct. In the case of a direct exchange rate, the domestic currency is the price currency (the numerator) and the foreign currency is the base currency (the denominator). If the domestic currency appreciates, then fewer units of the domestic currency are required to buy one unit of the foreign currency, and the exchange rate (domestic per foreign) declines. For example, if British pound sterling (GBP) appreciates against the euro (EUR), then euro–sterling (GBP/EUR) might decline.

2. A is correct. An indirect quote takes the foreign country as the price currency and the domestic country as the base currency. To get Swiss francs—which is the executive's domestic currency—as the base currency, the quote must be stated as EUR/CHF. Using the manager's information, the indirect exchange rate is (1/1.2983) = 0.7702.

3. C is correct. The appreciation of the British pound against the Swiss franc is the inverse of the 12 percent depreciation of the Swiss franc against the pound sterling: [1/(1 − 0.12)] − 1 = (1/0.88) − 1 = 0.1364, or 13.64%.

4. B is correct. The percentage appreciation of the base currency can be calculated by dividing the appreciated exchange rate by the initial exchange rate. In this case, the unknown is the initial exchange rate. The initial exchange is the value of X that satisfies the formula:

   $1.4500/X = 1.08$

   Solving for X leads to $1.45/1.08 = 1.3426$.

LEARNING MODULE 8

Exchange Rate Calculations

LEARNING OUTCOMES

Mastery	The candidate should be able to:
☐	calculate and interpret currency cross-rates
☐	explain the arbitrage relationship between spot and forward exchange rates and interest rates, calculate a forward rate using points or in percentage terms, and interpret a forward discount or premium

INTRODUCTION

The foreign exchange market facilitates international currency and trade flows, and it is important to understand how currency exchange rates are calculated. Market participants can also derive cross-rates to expand trading opportunities by determining quotes for currencies not directly traded. Understanding the concept of arbitrage relationships in the foreign exchange market provides a basis for understanding the interrelationships between four key market inputs. Global entities trade currencies for a wide variety of purposes and understanding the relationships between the market factors affecting spot and forward rates is crucial. These interactions are reinforced by the calculations in the second lesson.

LEARNING MODULE OVERVIEW

- An exchange rate between two currencies that are not expressly quoted on the market is known as a cross-rate and can be calculated using conventional currency quotes.
- Three conventional currency market quotes can be used with one inversion to calculate a cross-rate.
- Discrepancies in exchange rates can create arbitrage opportunities but they are rare due to market efficiencies.
- The premium of a forward exchange rate over a spot rate is quoted in terms of forward points, which are also called swap points.
- Forward rates are directly proportional to currency spot rates, the interest rate differential, and the maturity of the forward contract.

- As a result of the interrelationship among these four variables, any variable can be calculated by using the other three as inputs.

2. CROSS-RATE CALCULATIONS

calculate and interpret currency cross-rates

Global currencies are bought, sold, and exchanged in the foreign exchange (FX) market. In this decentralized market, participants trade currencies utilizing exchange rates, which typically reflect an efficient market. This section will cover the use of cross exchange rate relationships (cross-rates) to calculate exchange rates between two currencies using a third currency. It also will introduce calculations used in the FX market to trade currencies.

Given two exchange rates involving three currencies, it is possible to back out the cross-rate. For example, as we have seen in a prior lesson, the FX market convention is to quote the exchange rate between the US dollar and the euro as euro–dollar (USD/EUR). The FX market also quotes the exchange rate between the Canadian dollar and US dollar as dollar–Canada (CAD/USD). Given these two exchange rates, it is possible to back out the cross-rate between the euro and the Canadian dollar, which according to market convention is quoted as euro–Canada (CAD/EUR). This calculation is shown as follows:

$$\frac{CAD}{USD} \times \frac{USD}{EUR} = \frac{CAD}{\cancel{USD}} \times \frac{\cancel{USD}}{EUR} = \frac{CAD}{EUR}.$$

Hence, to get a euro–Canada (CAD/EUR) quote, we must multiply the dollar–Canada (CAD/USD) quote by the euro–dollar (USD/EUR) quote. For example, assume the exchange rate for dollar–Canada is 1.3020 and the exchange rate for euro–dollar is 1.1701. Using these spot exchange rates, the euro–Canada cross-rate equals:

1.3020 × 1.1701 = 1.5235 CAD per EUR.

The professional FX market does not use the convention of direct or indirect quotes because these conventions depend on one's location to determine the domestic versus foreign currencies. Instead, the market uses rate quotes on defined conventional currency pairs. Sometimes, to get a cross-rate using several currency quotes, it is necessary to invert a quote to get an intermediary currency that can be canceled out in the equation to obtain the cross-rate. For example, to get a Canada–yen (JPY/CAD) quote, one typically uses the dollar–Canada (CAD/USD) rate and dollar–yen (JPY/USD) rate, which are the market conventions. This Canada–yen calculation requires that the dollar–Canada rate (CAD/USD) be inverted to a Canada–dollar (USD/CAD) quote for the calculations to work, as follows:

$$\left(\frac{CAD}{USD}\right)^{-1} \times \frac{JPY}{USD} = \frac{USD}{CAD} \times \frac{JPY}{USD} = \frac{\cancel{USD}}{CAD} \times \frac{JPY}{\cancel{USD}} = \frac{JPY}{CAD}.$$

Hence, to get a Canada–yen (JPY/CAD) quote, we must first invert the dollar–Canada (CAD/USD) quote before multiplying by the dollar–yen (JPY/USD) quote. Market quotes for most currencies are quoted to four decimal places; however, the Japanese yen exchange rate is quoted to two decimal places. For example, assume that we have spot exchange rates of 1.3020 for dollar–Canada (CAD/USD) and 111.94 for dollar–yen (JPY/USD). The dollar–Canada rate of 1.3020 inverts to 0.7680; multiplying this value by the dollar–yen quote of 111.94 gives the following Canada–yen quote:

Cross-Rate Calculations

0.7680 × 111.94 = 85.97 JPY per CAD.

Market participants asking for a quote in a cross-rate currency pair typically will not need to do this calculation themselves: Either the dealer or the electronic trading platform will provide a quote in the specified currency pair. (For example, a client asking for a quote in Canada–yen will receive that quote from the dealer; he will not be given separate dollar–Canada and dollar–yen quotes to do the calculation.) Dealers providing the quotes often have to do this calculation themselves if only because the dollar–Canada and dollar–yen currency pairs often trade on different trading desks and involve different traders. Electronic dealing machines used in both the interbank market and bank-to-client markets often provide this mathematical operation to calculate cross-rates automatically.

Because market participants can receive both a cross-rate quote (e.g., Canada–yen) as well as the component underlying exchange rate quotes (e.g., dollar–Canada and dollar–yen), these cross-rate quotes must be consistent with the previous equation; otherwise, the market will arbitrage the mispricing. Extending our example, we calculate a Canada–yen (JPY/CAD) rate of 85.97 based on underlying dollar–Canada (CAD/USD) and dollar–yen (JPY/USD) rates of 1.3020 and 111.94, respectively. Now suppose that at the same time a misguided dealer quotes a Canada–yen rate of 86.20. This is a different price in Canada–yen for an identical service—that is, converting yen into Canadian dollars. Hence, any trader could buy CAD1 at the lower price of JPY85.97 and then turn around and sell CAD1 at JPY86.20 (recall our earlier discussion of how price and base currencies are defined). The riskless arbitrage profit is JPY0.23 per CAD1. The arbitrage—called *triangular arbitrage* (we use "tri-" because it involves three currencies—would continue until the price discrepancy was removed.

In reality, however, these discrepancies in cross-rates rarely occur because both human traders and automatic trading algorithms are constantly on alert for any pricing inefficiencies. In practice, and for the purposes of this lesson, we can consider cross-rates as being consistent with their underlying exchange rate quotes and can assume that given any two exchange rates involving three currencies, we can back out the third cross-rate.

EXAMPLE 1

Cross-Rates and Percentage Changes

A research report produced by a dealer includes the following spot rate quotes:

Currency	Spot Rate	Expected Spot Rate in One Year
USD/EUR	1.1701	1.1619
CHF/USD	0.9900	0.9866
USD/GBP	1.3118	1.3066

1. The spot CHF/EUR cross-rate is *closest* to:

    A. 0.8461.

    B. 0.8546.

    C. 1.1584.

    Solution:

    C is correct:

    $$\frac{CHF}{EUR} = \frac{USD}{EUR} \times \frac{CHF}{USD} = 1.1701 \times 0.9900 = 1.1584$$

2. The spot GBP/EUR cross-rate is *closest* to:

   A. 0.8920.
   B. 1.1211.
   C. 1.4653.

   Solution:

   A is correct:

   $$\frac{GBP}{EUR} = \frac{USD}{EUR} \times \left(\frac{USD}{GBP}\right)^{-1} = \frac{USD}{EUR} \times \frac{GBP}{USD} = \frac{1.1701}{1.3118} = 0.8920$$

3. Based on the research report, the euro is expected to appreciate by how much against the US dollar over the next year?

   A. −0.7 percent
   B. +0.7 percent
   C. +1.0 percent

   Solution:

   A is correct. The euro is the base currency in the USD/EUR quote, and the expected decrease in the USD/EUR rate indicates that the euro is depreciating. In one year, it will cost less, in US dollars, to buy one euro. Mathematically:

   $$\frac{1.1619}{1.1701} - 1 = -0.7\%$$

4. Based on the research report, how much is the US dollar expected to appreciate against the British pound sterling over the next year?

   A. +0.6 percent
   B. −0.4 percent
   C. +0.4 percent

   Solution:

   C is correct. The British pound is the base currency in the USD/GBP quote, and the expected decrease in the USD/GBP rate means that the British pound is expected to depreciate against the US dollar. Or equivalently, the US dollar is expected to appreciate against the British pound. Mathematically:

   $$\left(\frac{1.3066}{1.3118}\right)^{-1} - 1 = \frac{1.3118}{1.3066} - 1 = +0.4\%$$

5. Over the next year, the Swiss franc is expected to:

   A. depreciate against the British pound.
   B. depreciate against the euro.
   C. appreciate against the British pound, euro, and US dollar.

   Solution:

   C is correct: Because the question does not require calculating the magnitude of the appreciation or depreciation, we can use the Swiss franc as either the price currency or the base currency. In this case, it is easier to use the Swiss franc as the price currency. CHF/USD is expected to decline from 0.9900 to 0.9866, so the Swiss franc is expected to be stronger (i.e., it should appreciate against the US dollar). CHF/EUR is currently 1.1584 (see the solution to problem 1) and is expected to be 1.1463 (= 0.9866 × 1.1619), so the Swiss franc is expected to appreciate against the euro. CHF/GBP is currently 1.2987 (= 0.9900 × 1.3118) and is expected to be 1.2891 (= 0.9866 × 1.3066), so the Swiss franc is also expected to appreciate against the British pound.

Alternatively, we can derive this answer intuitively. According to the research report, the CHF/USD rate is expected to decline: That is, the US dollar is expected to depreciate against the Swiss franc, or alternatively, the Swiss franc is expected to appreciate against the US dollar. The USD/EUR and USD/GBP rates are also decreasing, meaning that the euro and British pound are expected to depreciate against the US dollar, or alternatively, the US dollar is expected to appreciate against the euro and British pound. If the Swiss franc is expected to appreciate against the US dollar and the US dollar is expected to appreciate against both the euro and British pound, it follows that the Swiss franc is expected to appreciate against both the euro and British pound.

6. Based on the research report, which of the following lists the three currencies from strongest to weakest over the next year?

   A. US dollar, British pound, euro
   B. US dollar, euro, British pound
   C. Euro, US dollar, British pound

   Solution:

   A is correct. USD/EUR is expected to decline from 1.1701 to 1.1619, while USD/GBP is expected to decline from 1.3118 to 1.3066. So, the US dollar is expected to be stronger than both the euro and British pound. GBP/EUR is currently 0.8920 [= $(1.3118)^{-1}$ × 1.1701] and is expected to be 0.8893 [= $(1.3066)^{-1}$ × 1.1619], so the British pound is expected to be stronger than the euro.

7. Based on the research report, which of the following lists the three currencies in order of appreciating the most to appreciating the least (in percentage terms) against the US dollar over the next year?

   A. British pound, Swiss franc, euro
   B. Swiss franc, British pound, euro
   C. Euro, Swiss franc, British pound

   Solution:

   B is correct. The USD/EUR rate depreciates by −0.7 percent (= [1.1619/1.1701] − 1), which is the depreciation of the base currency euro against the US dollar. The USD/GBP rate declines −0.4 percent (= [1.3066/1.3118] − 1), which is the depreciation of the British pound against the US dollar. Inverting the CHF/USD rate to a USD/CHF convention shows that the base currency Swiss franc appreciates by +0.35 percent against the US dollar (= [1.0136/1.0101] − 1).

3

FORWARD RATE CALCULATIONS

☐ explain the arbitrage relationship between spot and forward exchange rates and interest rates, calculate a forward rate using points or in percentage terms, and interpret a forward discount or premium

This lesson continues the previous discussion of the FX market by considering the interactions between spot and forward rates, interest rates, and maturities, which exist because of arbitrage relationships. The relationships among these four factors are maintained because of market efficiencies, and any one factor can be determined using the other three as inputs. In addition, this lesson covers the methods of calculating forward rates in point and percentage terms as well as forward discounts and premiums for these rate relationships.

In professional FX markets, forward exchange rates typically are quoted in terms of points (also sometimes referred to as "pips"). The points on a forward rate quote are simply the difference between the forward exchange rate quote and the spot exchange rate quote, with the points scaled so that they can be related to the last decimal in the spot quote. When the forward rate is higher than the spot rate, the points are positive and the base currency is said to be trading at a *forward premium*. Conversely, if the forward rate is less than the spot rate, the points (forward rate minus spot rate) are negative and the base currency is said to be trading at a *forward discount*. Of course, if the base currency is trading at a forward premium, then the price currency is trading at a forward discount, and vice versa.

This can best be explained by means of an example. Assume the spot euro–dollar exchange rate (USD/EUR) is 1.15885 and the one-year forward rate is 1.19532. Hence, the forward rate is trading at a premium to the spot rate (the forward rate is larger than the spot rate) and the one-year forward points are quoted as +364.7. This +364.7 comes from the following calculation:

1.19532 − 1.15885 = +0.03647.

Recall that most non-yen exchange rates are quoted to four decimal places. In this case, we would scale up by four decimal places (multiply by 10,000) so that this +0.03647 would be represented as +364.7 points. Notice that the points are scaled to the size of the last digit in the spot exchange rate quote—usually the fourth decimal place. Notice as well that points typically are quoted to one (or more) decimal places, meaning that the forward rate will typically be quoted to five or more decimal places. The exception among the major currencies is the yen, which is typically quoted to two decimal places for spot rates. Here, forward points are scaled up by two decimal places—the last digit in the spot rate quote—by multiplying the difference between forward and spot rates by 100.

Typically, quotes for forward rates are shown as the number of forward points at each maturity, the time between spot settlement and the settlement of the forward contract. These forward points are also called *swap points* because an FX swap consists of simultaneous spot and forward transactions. In our example, a trader would have faced a spot rate and forward points in the euro–dollar (USD/EUR) currency pair similar to those in Exhibit 1,

Forward Rate Calculations

Exhibit 1: Sample Spot and Forward Quotes

Maturity	Spot Rate or Forward Points
Spot	1.15885
One week	+5.6
One month	+27.1
Three months	+80.9
Six months	+175.6
Twelve months	+364.7

Notice that the absolute number of points generally increases with maturity. This is because the number of points is proportional to the yield differential between the two countries (the Eurozone and the United States, in this case) scaled by the term to maturity. Given the interest rate differential, the longer the term to maturity, the greater the absolute number of forward points. Similarly, given the term to maturity, a wider interest rate differential implies a greater absolute number of forward points. (This relationship will be explained and demonstrated in more detail later in this lesson.)

To convert any of these quoted forward points into a forward rate, one would divide the number of points by 10,000 (to scale down to the fourth decimal place, the last decimal place in the spot quote) and then add the result to the spot exchange rate quote. (As mentioned previously, exchange rates for the Japanese yen, such as the JPY/USD exchange rate, are quoted to two decimal places only, so forward points for the dollar–yen currency pair are divided by 100.) For example, using the data in Exhibit 1 for USD/EUR, the three-month forward rate in this case would be as follows:

$$1.15885 + \left(\frac{+80.9}{10,000}\right) = 1.15885 + 0.00809 = 1.16694.$$

Occasionally, one will see the forward rate or forward points represented as a percentage of the spot rate rather than as an absolute number of points. Continuing the previous example, the three-month forward rate for USD/EUR can be represented as follows:

$$\frac{1.15885 + 0.00809}{1.15885} - 1 = \left(\frac{1.16694}{1.15885}\right) - 1 = +0.698\%.$$

This shows that either the forward rate or the forward points can be used to calculate the percentage discount (or premium) in the forward market—in this case, +0.698 percent rounding to three decimal places. To convert a spot quote into a forward quote when the points are shown as a percentage, one simply multiplies the spot rate by one plus the percentage premium or discount:

$$1.15885 \times (1 + 0.698\%) = 1.15885 \times (1.0000 + 0.00698) \approx 1.16694.$$

Note that, rounded to the fifth decimal place, this is equal to our previous calculation. However, it is typically the case in professional FX markets that forward rates will be quoted in terms of pips rather than percentages.

Arbitrage Relationships

We now turn to the interaction between spot rates, forward rates, and interest rates and how their relationship is derived. Forward exchange rates are based on an arbitrage relationship that equates the investment return on two alternative but equivalent investments. Consider the case of an investor with funds to invest. For simplicity, we will assume that one unit of the investor's domestic currency will be invested for one period. One alternative is to invest for one period at the domestic risk-free rate (r_d); at the end of the period, the amount of funds held is equal to $(1 + r_d)$. An alternative investment is to convert this one unit of domestic currency to foreign currency using the spot rate of $S_{f/d}$ (number of units of foreign currency per one unit of domestic currency). This can be invested for one period at the foreign risk-free rate; at the end of the period, the investor would have $S_{f/d}(1 + r_f)$ units of foreign currency. These funds must then be converted back to the investor's domestic currency. If the exchange rate to be used for this end-of-period conversion was pre-contracted at the start of the period (i.e., a forward rate was used), it would eliminate any FX risk from converting at a future, unknown spot rate. Given the assumed exchange rate convention (foreign/domestic), the investor would obtain $(1/F_{f/d})$ units of the domestic currency for each unit of foreign currency sold forward. Note that this process of converting domestic funds in the spot FX market, investing at the foreign risk-free rate, and then converting back to the domestic currency with a forward rate is termed "swap financing."

Hence, we have two alternative investments—both are risk free because both are invested at risk-free interest rates and because any FX risk was eliminated (hedged) by using a forward rate. Because these two investments are equal in risk characteristics, they must have the same return. Bearing in mind that the currency quoting convention is the number of foreign currency units per single domestic unit (f/d), this relationship can be stated as follows:

$$(1 + r_d) = S_{f/d}(1 + r_f)\left(\frac{1}{F_{f/d}}\right).$$

This is an arbitrage relationship because it describes two alternative investments (one on either side of the equal sign) that should have equal returns. If they do not, a riskless arbitrage opportunity exists because an investor can sell short the investment with the lower return and invest the funds in the investment with the higher return; the difference between the two returns is pure profit. It is because of this arbitrage relationship that the all-in financing rate using swap financing is close to the domestic interest rate.

This formula is perhaps the easiest and most intuitive way to remember the formula for the forward rate because this formula is based directly on the underlying intuition (the arbitrage relationship of two alternative but equivalent investments, one on either side of the equal sign). Also, the right-hand side of the equation, for the hedged foreign investment alternative, is arranged in proper time sequence: (1) convert domestic to foreign currency; then (2) invest the foreign currency at the foreign interest rate; and finally (3) convert the foreign currency back to the domestic currency. Recall that this equation is based on an f/d exchange rate quoting convention. If the exchange rate data were presented in d/f form, one could either invert these quotes back to f/d form and use the previous equation or use the following equivalent equation:

$$(1 + r_d) = (1/S_{d/f})(1 + r_f)F_{d/f}.$$

If this latter equation were used, remember that forward and spot exchange rates are now being quoted on a d/f convention.

This arbitrage equation can be rearranged as needs require. For example, to get the formula for the forward rate, the previous equation can be restated as follows:

$$F_{f/d} = S_{f/d}\left(\frac{1 + r_f}{1 + r_d}\right).$$

Given the spot exchange rate and the domestic and foreign risk-free interest rates, the forward rate is the value that completes this equation and eliminates any arbitrage opportunity. For example, let's assume that the spot exchange rate ($S_{f/d}$) is 1.6535, the domestic 12-month risk-free rate is 3.50 percent, and the foreign 12-month risk-free rate is 5.00 percent. The 12-month forward rate ($F_{f/d}$) must then be equal to:

$$1.6535\left(\frac{1.0500}{1.0350}\right) = 1.6775.$$

Forward Rate Calculations

Suppose instead that, with the spot exchange rate and interest rates unchanged, you were given a quote on the 12-month forward rate ($F_{f/d}$) of 1.6900. Because this misquoted forward rate does not agree with the arbitrage equation, it would present a riskless arbitrage opportunity. This can be calculated by using the arbitrage equation to compute the return on the two alternative investment strategies. The return on the domestic-only investment approach is the domestic risk-free rate (3.50 percent). In contrast, the return on the hedged foreign investment when this misquoted forward rate is put into the arbitrage equation equals:

$$S_{f/d}(1 + r_f)\left(\frac{1}{F_{f/d}}\right) = 1.6535(1.05)\left(\frac{1}{1.6900}\right) = 1.0273.$$

This results in a return of 2.73 percent. Hence, the investor could make riskless arbitrage profits by borrowing at the higher foreign risk-free rate, selling the foreign currency at the spot exchange rate, hedging the currency exposure (buying the foreign currency back) at the misquoted forward rate, investing the funds at the lower domestic risk-free rate, and thereby getting a profit of 77 basis points (3.50% − 2.73%) for each unit of domestic currency involved—all with no upfront commitment of the investor's own capital. Any such opportunity in real-world financial markets would be quickly "arbed" away. In this example, the investor actually borrows at the higher of the two interest rates but makes a profit because the foreign currency is underpriced in the forward market.

The underlying arbitrage equation can also be rearranged to show the forward rate as a percentage of the spot rate:

$$\frac{F_{f/d}}{S_{f/d}} = \left(\frac{1 + r_f}{1 + r_d}\right).$$

This shows that, given an *f/d* quoting convention, the forward rate will be higher than (be at a premium to) the spot rate if foreign interest rates are higher than domestic interest rates. More generally, and regardless of the quoting convention, *the currency with the higher (lower) interest rate will always trade at a discount (premium) in the forward market.*

One context in which forward rates are quoted as a percentage of spot rates occurs when forward rates are interpreted as expected future spot rates, as follows:

$$F_t = S_{t+1}.$$

Substituting this expression into the previous equation and doing some rearranging leads to the following:

$$\frac{S_{t+1}}{S_t} - 1 = \%\Delta S_{t+1} = \left(\frac{r_f - r_d}{1 + r_d}\right).$$

This shows that if forward rates are interpreted as expected future spot rates, the expected percentage change in the spot rate is proportional to the interest rate differential ($r_f - r_d$).

It is intuitively appealing to see forward rates as expected future spot rates. However, this interpretation of forward rates should be used cautiously. The direction of the expected change in spot rates is somewhat counterintuitive. All else being equal, an increase in domestic interest rates (e.g., the central bank tightens monetary policy) would typically be expected to lead to an increase in the value of the domestic currency. In contrast, the previous equation indicates that, all else equal, a higher domestic interest rate implies slower expected appreciation (or greater expected depreciation) of the domestic currency (recall that this equation is based on an *f/d* quoting convention).

More important, historical data show that forward rates are poor predictors of future spot rates. Although various econometric studies suggest that forward rates may be unbiased predictors of future spot rates (i.e., they do not systematically over- or under-estimate future spot rates), this is not particularly useful information because the margin of error for these forecasts is so large. As mentioned in the Introduction, the FX market is far too complex and dynamic to be captured by a single variable, such as the level of the yield differential between countries. Moreover, according to the formula for the forward rate, forward rates are based on domestic and foreign interest rates. This means that anything that affects the level and shape of the yield curve in either the domestic or foreign market will also affect the relationship between spot and forward exchange rates. In other words, FX markets do not operate in isolation but rather reflect almost all factors affecting other markets globally; anything that affects expectations or risk premia in these other markets will reverberate in forward exchange rates as well. Although the level of the yield differential is one factor that the market may look at in forming spot exchange rate expectations, it is only one of many factors. (Many traders look to the trend in the yield differential rather than the level of the differential.) Moreover, a lot of noise in FX markets makes almost any model—no matter how complex—a relatively poor predictor of spot rates at any given point in the future. In practice, FX traders and market strategists do *not* base either their currency expectations or trading strategies solely on forward rates.

For the purposes of this lesson, *it is best to understand forward exchange rates simply as a product of the arbitrage equation outlined earlier and forward points as being related to the (time-scaled) interest rate differential between the two countries.* Reading any more than that into forward rates or interpreting them as the "market forecast" can be potentially misleading.

Forward Discounts and Premiums

We now continue our discussion of forward discounts and premiums based on spot and interest rates and add the impact of maturity. To understand the relationship between maturity and forward points, we need to generalize our arbitrage formula slightly. Suppose the investment horizon is a fraction, τ, of the period for which the interest rates are quoted. Then the interest earned in the domestic and foreign markets would be (r_d τ) and (r_f τ), respectively. Substituting this into our arbitrage relationship and solving for the difference between the forward and spot exchange rates gives the following:

$$F_{f/d} - S_{f/d} = S_{f/d}\left(\frac{r_f - r_d}{1 + r_d \tau}\right)\tau.$$

This equation shows that forward points (appropriately scaled) are proportional to the spot exchange rate and to the interest rate differential and approximately (but not exactly) proportional to the horizon of the forward contract.

For example, suppose that we wanted to determine the 30-day forward exchange rate given a 30-day domestic risk-free interest rate of 2.00 percent per year, a 30-day foreign risk-free interest rate of 3.00 percent per year, and a spot exchange rate ($S_{f/d}$) of 1.6555. The risk-free assets used in this arbitrage relationship are typically bank deposits quoted using the London Interbank Offered Rate (Libor) for the currencies involved. The day count convention for Libor deposits is actual/360. Incorporating the fractional period (τ) and inserting the data into the forward rate equation leads to the following 30-day forward rate:

$$F_{f/d} = S_{f/d}\left(\frac{1 + r_f \tau}{1 + r_d \tau}\right) = 1.6555\left(\frac{1 + 0.0300\left[\frac{30}{360}\right]}{1 + 0.0200\left[\frac{30}{360}\right]}\right) = 1.6569.$$

This means that, for a 30-day term, forward rates are trading at a premium of 14 pips (1.6569 − 1.6555). This can also be calculated using the previous formula for swap points:

$$F_{f/d} - S_{f/d} = S_{f/d}\left(\frac{r_f - r_d}{1 + r_d \tau}\right)\tau = 1.6555\left(\frac{0.0300 - 0.0200}{1 + 0.0200\left[\frac{30}{360}\right]}\right)\left[\frac{30}{360}\right] = 0.0014.$$

Forward Rate Calculations

As should be clear from this expression, the absolute number of swap points will be closely related to the term of the forward contract (i.e., approximately proportional to τ = actual/360). For example, leaving the spot exchange rate and interest rates unchanged, and setting the term of the forward contract to 180 days, we obtain the following:

$$F_{f/d} - S_{f/d} = 1.6555 \left(\frac{0.0300 - 0.0200}{1 + 0.0200 \left[\frac{180}{360} \right]} \right) \left[\frac{180}{360} \right] = 0.0082.$$

This leads to the forward rate trading at a premium of 82 pips. The increase in the number of forward points is approximately proportional to the increase in the term of the contract (from 30 days to 180 days). Note that although the term of the 180-day forward contract is six times longer than that of a 30-day contract, the number of forward points is not exactly six times larger: 6 × 14 = 84.

Similarly, the number of forward points is proportional to the spread between foreign and domestic interest rates ($r_f - r_d$). For example, with reference to the original 30-day forward contract, let's set the foreign interest rate to 4.00 percent leaving the domestic interest rate and spot exchange rate unchanged. This doubles the interest rate differential ($r_f - r_d$) from 1.00 percent to 2.00 percent; it also doubles the forward points (rounding to four decimal places), as follows:

$$F_{f/d} - S_{f/d} = 1.6555 \left(\frac{0.0400 - 0.0200}{1 + 0.0200 \left[\frac{30}{360} \right]} \right) \left[\frac{30}{360} \right] = 0.0028.$$

EXAMPLE 2

Forward Rate Calculations

A French company recently finalized a sale of goods to a UK-based client and expects to receive a payment of GBP50 million in 32 days. The corporate treasurer at the French company wants to hedge the FX risk of this transaction and receives the following exchange rate information from a dealer:

GBP/EUR spot rate	0.8752
One-month forward points	−1.4

1. According to the exchange rate information, the treasurer could hedge the FX risk by:

    A. buying euro (selling British pounds) at a forward rate of 0.87380.

    B. buying euro (selling British pounds) at a forward rate of 0.87506.

    C. selling euro (buying British pounds) at a forward rate of 0.87506.

    Solution:

    B is correct. The French company would want to convert the British pound to its domestic currency, the euro (it wants to sell British pounds and buy euros). The forward rate would be equal to: 0.8752 + (−1.4/10,000) = 0.87506.

2. According to the exchange rate information, the *best* interpretation of the forward discount shown is that:

    A. the euro is expected to depreciate over the next 30 days.

    B. one-month UK interest rates are higher than those in the Eurozone.

C. one-month Eurozone interest rates are higher than those in the United Kingdom.

Solution:

C is correct. A forward discount indicates that interest rates in the base currency country (France, in this case, which uses the euro) are higher than those in the price currency country (the United Kingdom).

3. According to the exchange rate information, if the 12-month forward rate is 0.87295 GBP/EUR, then the 12-month forward points are *closest* to:

   A. −22.5.
   B. −2.25.
   C. −0.00225.

   Solution:

   A is correct. The number of forward points is equal to the scaled difference between the forward rate and the spot rate. In this case: 0.87295 − 0.87520 = −0.00225. This is then multiplied by 10,000 to convert to the number of forward points.

4. If a second dealer quotes GBP/EUR at a 12-month forward discount of 0.30 percent on the same spot rate, the French company could:

   A. trade with either dealer because the 12-month forward quotes are equivalent.
   B. lock in a profit in 12 months by buying euros from the second dealer and selling it to the original dealer.
   C. lock in a profit in 12 months by buying euros from the original dealer and selling it to the second dealer.

   Solution:

   B is correct. A 0.30 percent discount means that the second dealer will sell euros 12 months forward at 0.8752 × (1 − 0.0030) = 0.87257, a lower price per euro than the original dealer's quote of 0.87295. Buying euros at the cheaper 12-month forward rate (0.87257) and selling the same amount of euros 12 months forward at the higher 12-month forward rate (0.87295) means a profit of (0.87295 − 0.87257 = GBP0.00038) per euro transacted, receivable when both forward contracts settle in 12 months.

5. If the 270-day Libor rates (annualized) for the euro and British pound are 1.370 percent and 1.325 percent, respectively, and the spot GBP/EUR exchange rate is 0.8489, then the number of forward points for a 270-day forward rate ($F_{GBP/EUR}$) is *closest* to:

   A. −22.8.
   B. −3.8.
   C. −2.8.

   Solution:

   C is correct, because the forward rate is calculated as:

Forward Rate Calculations

$$F_{\frac{GBP}{EUR}} = S_{\frac{GBP}{EUR}}\left(\frac{1 + r_{GBP}\left[\frac{Actual}{360}\right]}{1 + r_{EUR}\left[\frac{Actual}{360}\right]}\right) = 0.8489\left(\frac{1 + 0.01325\left[\frac{270}{360}\right]}{1 + 0.01370\left[\frac{270}{360}\right]}\right) = 0.84862.$$

This shows that the forward points are at a discount of: 0.84862 − 0.84890 = −0.00028, or −2.8 points. This can also be seen using the swap points formula:

$$F_{\frac{GBP}{EUR}} - S_{\frac{GBP}{EUR}} = 0.8489\left(\frac{0.01325 - 0.01370}{1 + 0.01370\left[\frac{270}{360}\right]}\right)\left[\frac{270}{360}\right] = -0.00028.$$

The calculation of −3.8 points omits the day count (270/360), and −22.8 points gets the scaling wrong.

PRACTICE PROBLEMS

The following information relates to questions 1-2

A dealer provides spot rate quotes for the following currencies:

Currency	Spot rate
CNY/HKD	0.8422
CNY/ZAR	0.9149
CNY/SEK	1.0218

1. The spot ZAR/HKD cross-rate is *closest* to:

   A. 0.9205.

   B. 1.0864.

   C. 1.2978.

2. Another dealer is quoting the ZAR/SEK cross-rate at 1.1210. The arbitrage profit that can be earned is *closest* to:

   A. ZAR3671 per million Swedish krona traded.

   B. SEK4200 per million South African rand traded.

   C. ZAR4200 per million Swedish krona traded.

3. A BRL/MXN spot rate is listed by a dealer at 0.1378. The six-month forward rate is 0.14193. The six-month forward points are *closest* to:

   A. −41.3.

   B. +41.3.

   C. +299.7.

4. A three-month forward exchange rate in CAD/USD is listed by a dealer at 1.0123. The dealer also quotes three-month forward points as a percentage at 6.8 percent. The CAD/USD spot rate is *closest* to:

   A. 0.9478.

   B. 1.0550.

   C. 1.0862.

5. If the base currency in a forward exchange rate quote is trading at a forward discount, which of the following statements is *most* accurate?

   A. The forward points will be positive.

Practice Problems

    B. The forward percentage will be negative.

    C. The base currency is expected to appreciate versus the price currency.

6. A forward premium indicates:

    A. an expected increase in demand for the base currency.

    B. the interest rate is higher in the base currency than in the price currency.

    C. the interest rate is higher in the price currency than in the base currency.

7. The JPY/AUD spot exchange rate is 82.42, the Japanese yen interest rate is 0.15 percent, and the Australian dollar interest rate is 4.95 percent. If the interest rates are quoted on the basis of a 360-day year, the 90-day forward points in JPY/AUD would be *closest* to:

    A. −377.0.

    B. −97.7.

    C. 98.9.

SOLUTIONS

1. A is correct. To get to the ZAR/HKD cross-rate, it is necessary to take the inverse of the CNY/ZAR spot rate and then multiply by the CNY/HKD exchange rate:

   ZAR/HKD = (CNY/ZAR)$^{-1}$ × (CNY/HKD)
   = (1/0.9149) × 0.8422 = 0.9205

2. C is correct. The ZAR/SEK cross-rate from the original dealer is (1.0218/0.9149) = 1.1168, which is lower than the quote from the second dealer. To earn an arbitrage profit, a currency trader would buy Swedish krona (sell South African rand) from the original dealer and sell Swedish krona (buy South African rand) to the second dealer. On SEK1 million, the profit would be:

   SEK1,000,000 × (1.1210 − 1.1168) = ZAR4,200

3. B is correct. The number of forward points equals the forward rate minus the spot rate, or 0.14193 − 0.1378 = 0.00413, multiplied by 10,000: 10,000 × 0.00413 = 41.3 points. By convention, forward points are scaled so that ±1 forward point corresponds to a change of ±1 in the last decimal place of the spot exchange rate.

4. A is correct. Given the forward rate and forward points as a percentage, the unknown in the calculation is the spot rate. The calculation is as follows:

   Spot rate × (1 + Forward points as a percentage) = Forward rate

   Spot rate × (1 + 0.068) = 1.0123

   Spot = 1.0123/1.068 = 0.9478

5. B is correct. The base currency trading at a forward discount means that 1 unit of the base currency costs less for forward delivery than for spot delivery (i.e., the forward exchange rate is less than the spot exchange rate). The forward points, expressed either as an absolute number of points or as a percentage, are negative.

6. C is correct. To eliminate arbitrage opportunities, the spot exchange rate (S), the forward exchange rate (F), the interest rate in the base currency (r_d, and the interest rate in the price currency (r_f) must satisfy:

   $F_{f/d} / S_{f/d} = (1+r_f \tau \,/\, 1+r_d \tau)$.

   According to this formula, the base currency will trade at forward premium ($F > S$) if, and only if, the interest rate in the price currency is higher than the interest rate in the base currency ($r_f > r_d$).

7. B is correct. The forward exchange rate is given by:

   $$F_{\frac{JPY}{AUD}} = S_{\frac{JPY}{AUD}}\left(\frac{1+r_{JPY}\tau}{1+r_{AUD}\tau}\right) = 82.42\left(\frac{1+0.0015\left[\frac{90}{360}\right]}{1+0.0495\left[\frac{90}{360}\right]}\right)$$

   = 82.42 × 0.98815 = 81.443.

   The forward points are as follows:

   100 × (F × S) = 100 × (81.443 − 82.42) = 100 × (−0.977) = −97.7.

   Because the spot exchange rate is quoted with two decimal places, the forward points are scaled by 100.

Glossary

Abandonment option The option to terminate an investment at some future time if the financial results are disappointing.

Abnormal return The return on an asset in excess of the asset's required rate of return; the risk-adjusted return.

Absolute dispersion The amount of variability present without comparison to any reference point or benchmark.

Accelerated book build An offering of securities by an investment bank acting as principal that is accomplished in only one or two days.

Accounting profit Income as reported on the income statement, in accordance with prevailing accounting standards, before the provisions for income tax expense. Also called *income before taxes* or *pretax income*.

Accredited investors Investors that meet certain minimum regulatory net worth or other requirements in order to invest in certain types of alternative assets.

Accrued interest The amount of interest in currency or par value terms of a fixed-income instrument that accumulates from the last coupon payment until the trade settlement date. The amount is paid by the buyer to the seller.

Action lag Delay from policy decisions to implementation.

Active investment An approach to investing in which the investor seeks to outperform a given benchmark.

Active return The return on a portfolio minus the return on the portfolio's benchmark.

Activist Short for "activist shareholder." Managers secure sufficient equity holdings to allow them to seek a position in a company's board and influence corporate policies or direction.

Activity ratios Ratios that measure how well a company is managing key current assets and working capital over time.

Ad hoc committee A small group of lenders or bondholders who negotiate with an issuer on debt restructuring and refinancing before the issuer submits a final proposal to the wider group of all lenders and bondholders.

Add-on pricing A pricing approach based on high-margin optional features, customizations, and additional content.

Add-on rate A yield or pricing convention for money market instrument quotations. It is the interest earned on an instrument, derived from the difference between the price and face value, expressed as a percentage of the price and multiplied by the periodicity of the annual rate.

Agency costs Direct and indirect costs borne by the principal in a principal-agent relationship owing primarily to information asymmetries. Agency costs include the costs of monitoring and assessing the agent as well as missed opportunities.

Agency RMBS Securities created by the pooling of residential mortgage-backed securities in the United States by either the Federal National Mortgage Association (Fannie Mae) or the Federal Home Loan Mortgage Corporation (Freddie Mac). These RMBS carry the full faith and credit of the government, essentially a guarantee with respect to timely payment of interest and repayment of principal.

All-or-nothing (AON) orders An order that includes the instruction to trade only if the trade fills the entire quantity (size) specified.

Allocationally efficient A characteristic of a market, a financial system, or an economy that promotes the allocation of resources to their highest value uses.

Altcoin A cryptocurrency other than Bitcoin.

Alternative data Data that are generated from non-traditional sources, such as social media and sensor networks.

Alternative hypothesis The hypothesis that is accepted if the null hypothesis is rejected.

Alternative investment markets Market for investments other than traditional securities investments (i.e., traditional common and preferred shares and traditional fixed income instruments). The term usually encompasses direct and indirect investment in real estate (including timberland and farmland) and commodities (including precious metals); hedge funds, private equity, and other investments requiring specialized due diligence.

Alternative trading systems Trading venues that function like exchanges but that do not exercise regulatory authority over their subscribers except with respect to the conduct of the subscribers' trading in their trading systems. Also called *electronic communications networks* or *multilateral trading facilities*.

American depository receipt A US dollar-denominated security that trades like a common share on US exchanges.

American depository share The underlying shares on which American depository receipts are based. They trade in the issuing company's domestic market.

American options Options that may be exercised at any time from contract inception until maturity.

American-style Type of option contract that can be exercised at any time up to the option's expiration date.

Amortization The process of allocating the cost of intangible long-term assets having a finite useful life to accounting periods; the allocation of the amount of a bond premium or discount to the periods remaining until bond maturity.

Amortizing debt A loan or bond with a payment schedule that calls for periodic payments of interest and repayments of principal.

Analysis of variance (ANOVA) A table that presents the sums of squares, degrees of freedom, mean squares, and F-statistic for a regression model.

Analytical duration Estimates of duration using mathematical formulas. Estimates of the impact of yield changes on bond prices using analytical duration implicitly assume that benchmark yields and spreads are independent variables and are uncorrelated.

Anchoring and adjustment bias An information-processing bias in which the use of a psychological heuristic influences the way people estimate probabilities.

Annual general meeting (AGM) A yearly meeting of the corporate board of directors and shareholders, typically held in person and digitally, during which votes on directors, compensation plans, shareholder resolutions, and any other matters properly brought forward at the meeting are held. Issuer management may also make presentations and hold events.

Anomalies Apparent deviations from market efficiency.

Antidilutive With reference to a transaction or a security, one that would increase earnings per share (EPS) or result in EPS higher than the company's basic EPS—antidilutive securities are not included in the calculation of diluted EPS.

Arbitrage 1) The simultaneous purchase of an undervalued asset or portfolio and sale of an overvalued but equivalent asset or portfolio, in order to obtain a riskless profit on the price differential. Taking advantage of a market inefficiency in a risk-free manner. 2) The condition in a financial market in which equivalent assets or combinations of assets sell for two different prices, creating an opportunity to profit at no risk with no commitment of money. In a well-functioning financial market, few arbitrage opportunities are possible. 3) A risk-free operation that earns an expected positive net profit but requires no net investment of money.

Arbitrageurs Traders who engage in arbitrage. See *arbitrage*.

Arithmetic mean The sum of the observations divided by the number of observations.

Artificial intelligence (AI) Computer systems that are capable of performing tasks that previously required human intelligence. AI methods are sometimes better suited to identify complex, non-linear relationships than are traditional quantitative and statistical methods.

Ask The price at which a dealer or trader is willing to sell an asset, typically qualified by a maximum quantity (ask size). See *offer*.

Ask size The maximum quantity of an asset that pertains to a specific ask price from a trader. For example, if the ask for a share issue is $30 for a size of 1,000 shares, the trader is offering to sell at $30 up to 1,000 shares.

Asset allocation The process of determining how investment funds should be distributed among asset classes.

Asset class A group of assets that have similar characteristics, attributes, and risk–return relationships.

Asset utilization ratios Ratios that measure how efficiently a company performs day-to-day tasks, such as the collection of receivables and management of inventory.

Asset-backed commercial paper Secured form of commercial paper issuance. Loans or receivables are sold to a special purpose entity that issues the ABCP and makes interest and principal payments to investors from asset cash flows.

Asset-backed securities (ABS) A type of bond issued by a legal entity called a special purpose entity created solely to own assets such as loans, receivables, and mortgages and to distribute cash flows to ABS investors. Generally, ABS backed by mortgages are known as mortgage-backed securities (MBS) while ABS refer to non-mortgage ABS.

Asset-backed token A token that represents the ownership of a physical asset that does not exist on the blockchain and whose value is based on the underlying asset.

Asset-based valuation models Valuation based on estimates of the market value of a company's assets.

Asymmetric information Also known as *information asymmetry*; the differential of information between corporate insiders and outsiders regarding the company's performance and prospects. Managers typically have more information about the company's performance and prospects than owners and creditors.

At-the-money Describes a unique situation in which the price of the underlying is equal to an option's exercise price. Like an out-of-the-money option, the intrinsic value is zero.

Auction/reverse auction models Pricing models that establish prices through bidding (by sellers in the case of reverse auctions).

Autarky Countries seeking political self-sufficiency with little or no external trade or finance. State-owned enterprises control strategic domestic industries.

Automatic stabilizer A countercyclical factor that automatically comes into play as an economy slows and unemployment rises.

Availability bias An information-processing bias in which people take a heuristic approach to estimating the probability of an outcome based on how easily the outcome comes to mind.

Available-for-sale Under US GAAP, debt securities not classified as either held-to-maturity or held-for-trading securities. The investor is willing to sell but not actively planning to sell. In general, available-for-sale debt securities are reported at fair value on the balance sheet, with unrealized gains included as a component of other comprehensive income.

Average revenue (AR) Total revenue divided by quantity sold.

Backfill Bias A problem whereby certain surviving hedge funds may be added to databases and various hedge fund indexes only after they are initially successful and start to report their returns. Also see *survivorship bias*.

Backup line of credit A type of credit enhancement provided by a bank to an issuer of commercial paper to ensure that the issuer will have access to sufficient liquidity to repay maturing commercial paper if issuing new paper is not a viable option.

Backwardation A downward-sloping, or inverted, forward curve in a futures market.

Balance sheet ratios Financial ratios involving balance sheet items only.

Balanced With respect to a government budget, one in which spending and revenues (taxes) are equal.

Balloon payment A large payment required at maturity to retire a bond's outstanding principal amount.

Base rates The reference rate on which a bank bases lending rates to all other customers.

Base-rate neglect A type of representativeness bias in which the base rate or probability of the categorization is not adequately considered.

Basic EPS Net earnings available to common shareholders (i.e., net income minus preferred dividends) divided by the weighted average number of common shares outstanding.

Basis risk The possibility that the expected value of a derivative differs unexpectedly from that of the underlying.

Basket of listed depository receipts (BLDR) An exchange-traded fund (ETF) that represents a portfolio of depository receipts.

Bayes' formula The rule for updating the probability of an event of interest—given a set of prior probabilities for the event, information, and information given the event—if you receive new information.

Bearer bonds Bonds for which ownership is not recorded; only the clearing system knows who the bond owner is.

Behavioral finance A field of finance that examines the psychological variables that affect and often distort the investment decision making of investors, analysts, and portfolio managers.

Behind the market Said of prices specified in orders that are worse than the best current price; e.g., for a limit buy order, a limit price below the best bid.

Benchmark A bond used to compare against another bond to discern attributes, often a government bond with the same or similar time-to-maturity as the bond under analysis.

Benchmark spread The difference in yield-to-maturity between a bond and that of a benchmark bond.

Best bid The highest bid in the market.

Best effort offering An offering of a security using an investment bank in which the investment bank, as agent for the issuer, promises to use its best efforts to sell the offering but does not guarantee that a specific amount will be sold.

Best offer The lowest offer (ask price) in the market.

Best-in-class An ESG implementation approach that seeks to identify the most favorable companies in an industry based on ESG considerations.

Beta A measure of systematic risk that is based on the covariance of an asset's or portfolio's return with the return of the overall market; a measure of the sensitivity of a given investment or portfolio to movements in the overall market.

Bid The price at which a dealer or trader is willing to buy an asset, typically qualified by a maximum quantity.

Bid size The maximum quantity of an asset that pertains to a specific bid price from a trader.

Big data The vast amount of information being generated by both traditional sources—for example, stock exchanges, companies, governments—and non-traditional sources—for example, electronic devices, social media, sensor networks, and company exhaust.

Bilateralism The conduct of political, economic, financial, or cultural cooperation between two countries. Countries engaging in bilateralism may have relations with many different countries but in one-at-a-time agreements without multiple partners. Typically, countries exist on a spectrum between bilateralism and multilateralism.

Bimodal A distribution that has two most frequently occurring values.

Bitcoin A cryptocurrency using blockchain technology that was created in 2009.

Bivariate correlation Also known as Pearson correlation. A parametric measure of the relationship between two variables.

Black swan risk An event that is rare and difficult to predict but has an important impact.

Block brokers A broker (agent) that provides brokerage services for large-size trades.

Blockchain A type of digital ledger in which information is recorded sequentially and then linked together and secured using cryptographic methods.

Blue chip Widely held large market capitalization companies that are considered financially sound and are leaders in their respective industry or local stock market.

Board of directors A body or individual selected by a limited company's member(s) or shareholder(s), in a manner determined by the company's charter, that manages the company. Typically, for larger companies, boards of directors appoint and oversee executive management.

Bond equivalent yield A money market interest rate quoted on a 365-day add-on rate basis.

Bond indenture A legal document between a bond issuer and investors that governs each party's rights and responsibilities.

Bond market vigilantes Bond market participants who might reduce their demand for long-term bonds, thus pushing up their yields.

Bondholders Investors in an entity's securitized debt claims, such as commercial paper, notes, and bonds. Common types of bondholders include investment funds and institutional investors.

Bonds Contractual agreements between an issuer and bondholders.

Bonus issue of shares A type of dividend in which a company distributes additional shares of its common stock to shareholders instead of cash.

Book building Investment bankers' process of compiling a "book" or list of indications of interest to buy part of an offering.

Book value The net amount shown for an asset or liability on the balance sheet; book value may also refer to the company's excess of total assets over total liabilities. Also called *carrying value*.

Boom An expansionary phase characterized by economic growth "testing the limits" of the economy.

Bootstrap A resampling method that repeatedly draws samples with replacement of the selected elements from the original observed sample. Bootstrap is usually conducted by using computer simulation and is often used to find standard error or construct confidence intervals of population parameters.

Bottom-up analysis An investment selection approach that focuses on company-specific circumstances rather than emphasizing economic cycles or industry analysis.

Box and whisker plot A graphic for visualizing the dispersion of data across quartiles. It consists of a box with "whiskers" connected to the box.

Breakeven point Represents the price of the underlying in a derivative contract in which the profit to both counterparties would be zero.

Bridge financing Interim financing that provides funds until permanent financing can be arranged.

Broker An agent who executes orders to buy or sell securities on behalf of a client in exchange for a commission.

Brokered market A market in which brokers arrange trades among their clients.

Broker–dealer A financial intermediary (often a company) that may function as a principal (dealer) or as an agent (broker) depending on the type of trade.

Brownfield investments The third stage of development of an infrastructure asset. Brownfield investments involve expanding existing facilities and may involve privatization of public assets or a sale leaseback of completed greenfield projects. They are characterized by a shorter investment period with immediate cash flows and an operating history.

Budget surplus/deficit The difference between government revenue and expenditure for a stated fixed period of time.

Bullet bond A bond whose principal repayment is made entirely at maturity.

Bundling A pricing approach that refers to combining multiple products or services so that customers are incentivized or required to buy them together.

Business cycles Are recurrent expansions and contractions in economic activity affecting broad segments of the economy.

Business model A concise description of how a business works and makes revenues and profits, including its customers, products or services, channels for reaching customers, and pricing.

Businesses Organization entities formed and managed for the purpose of providing a return or economic benefits to its investors and owners.

Buy-side firm An investment management company or other investor that uses the services of brokers or dealers (i.e., the client of the sell side firms).

Buyback A transaction in which a company buys back its own shares. Unlike stock dividends and stock splits, share repurchases use corporate cash.

Cabotage The right to transport passengers or goods within a country by a foreign firm. Many countries—including those with multilateral trade agreements—impose restrictions on cabotage across transportation subsectors, meaning that shippers, airlines, and truck drivers are not allowed to transport goods and services within another country's borders.

Call market A market in which trades occur only at a particular time and place (i.e., when the market is called).

Call money rate The interest rate that buyers pay for their margin loan.

Call option The right to buy an underlying.

Call period The time during which the issuer of a callable bond can exercise the call option.

Call price The price at which the issuer of a callable bond has the right to purchase the bond from investors.

Call protection period The time during which the issuer of a callable bond is not allowed to exercise the call option.

Call risk The uncertain maturity and limited price appreciation associated with callable bonds.

Callable bond A bond containing an embedded call option that gives the issuer the right to buy the bond back from the investor at specified prices on predetermined dates.

Cannibalization A transfer of sales or market share from one product to another product owned by the same company. It tends to occur when the two products are actual or perceived substitutes.

Capacity The ability of the borrower to make its debt payments on time.

Capital Other company resources available that reduce reliance on debt.

Capital allocation The process that companies use for decision making on capital investments—those projects with a life of one year or longer.

Capital allocation line (CAL) A graph line that describes the combinations of expected return and standard deviation of return available to an investor from combining the optimal portfolio of risky assets with the risk-free asset.

Capital asset pricing model (CAPM) An equation describing the expected return on any asset (or portfolio) as a linear function of its beta relative to the market portfolio.

Capital expenditure Expenditure on physical capital (fixed assets).

Capital investments An expenditure for an asset or resource with a useful life of more than one year.

Capital market expectations (CME) Expectations concerning the risk and return prospects of asset classes.

Capital market line (CML) The line with an intercept point equal to the risk-free rate that is tangent to the efficient frontier of risky assets; represents the efficient frontier when a risk-free asset is available for investment.

Capital market securities Fixed-income securities with original maturities greater than one year.

Capital markets Financial markets that trade securities of longer duration, such as bonds and equities.

Capital restrictions Controls placed on foreigners' ability to own domestic assets and/or domestic residents' ability to own foreign assets.

Capital structure The mix of debt and equity that a company uses to finance its business; a company's specific mix of long-term financing.

Capital-indexed bond A type of index-linked bond for which changes in the index are captured with adjustments to the principal. A common example is Treasury Inflation Protected Securities (TIPS) issued by the United States government.

Capital-intensive businesses Companies or business activities that are characterized by a relatively low fixed asset turnover, a high percentage of capital expenditures to sales, or a high net-working-capital-to-sales ratio.

Capital-light businesses Also known as *asset light businesses*, companies or business activities characterized by relatively high fixed asset turnover, a low percentage of capital expenditures to sales, or a low net-working-capital-to-sales ratio.

Carried interest A performance fee (also referred to as an incentive fee, or carry) that is applied based on excess returns above a hurdle rate.

Carrying Investing and holding an asset for a period of time.

Carrying amount The amount at which an asset or liability is valued according to accounting principles.

Carrying value Of a fixed-income instrument is the purchase price plus (minus) the amortized amount of the discount (premium) if the bond is purchased at a price below (above) par value.

Cartel Participants in collusive agreements that are made openly and formally.

Cash conversion cycle The amount of time between an issuer paying its suppliers in cash and receiving cash from its customers.

Cash flow additivity principle The principle that dollar amounts indexed at the same point in time are additive.

Cash flow from operations A cash profit measure over a period for an issuer's primary business activities. It includes cash from customers as well as interest and dividends received from financial investments, less cash paid to employees and suppliers as well as taxes paid to governments and interest paid to lenders.

Cash flow hedge Refers to a specific **hedge accounting** classification in which a derivative is designated as absorbing the variable cash flow of a floating-rate asset or liability, such as foreign exchange, interest rates, or commodities.

Cash markets Markets in which specific assets are exchanged at current prices. Cash markets are often referred to as **spot markets**.

Cash prices The current prices prevailing in **cash markets**.

Cash ratio A measure of liquidity that is the ratio of cash and marketable securities to current liabilities.

Catch-up clause A clause in an agreement that favors the GP. For a GP who earns a 20% performance fee, a catch-up clause allows the GP to receive 100% of the distributions above the hurdle rate *until* she receives 20% of the profits generated, and then every excess dollar is split 80/20 between the LPs and GP.

CDS credit spread Reflects the credit spread of a credit default swap (CDS) derivative contract. As with cash bonds, CDS credit spreads depend on the probability of default (POD) and the loss given default (LGD).

Central bank digital currencies (CBDCs) A tokenized version of the currency issued by the central bank, such as a digital bank note or coin, and a digital liability of the central bank.

Central bank funds market The market in which deposit-taking banks that have an excess reserve with their national central bank can lend money to banks that need funds for maturities ranging from overnight to one year. Called the federal or fed funds market in the United States.

Central bank funds rate The interest rate at which central bank funds are bought (borrowed) and sold (lent) for maturities ranging from overnight to one year. Called federal or fed funds rate in the United States.

Central clearing mandate A requirement instituted by global regulatory authorities following the 2008 global financial crisis that most **over-the-counter (OTC)** derivatives be **cleared** by a **central counterparty (CCP)**.

Central counterparty (CCP) An economic entity that assumes the **counterparty credit risk** between derivative **counterparties**, one of which is typically a financial intermediary. CCPs provide **clearing** and **settlement** for most **derivative contracts**.

Central limit theorem The theorem that states the sum (and the mean) of a set of independent, identically distributed random variables with finite variances is normally distributed, whatever distribution the random variables follow.

Certificate of deposit (CD) An instrument that represents a specified amount of funds on deposit with a bank for a specified maturity and interest rate. CDs are issued in various denominations and can be negotiable or non-negotiable.

Channels Venues where a company markets and/or delivers its products and services.

Character The quality of a debt issuer's management.

Checking accounts Bank deposits with no stated maturity available for transactional purposes that pay little or no interest. Also known as a *demand deposit*.

Circuit breaker A pause in intraday trading for a brief period if a price limit is reached.

Classical cycle Refers to fluctuations in the level of economic activity when measured by GDP in volume terms.

Clawback A requirement that the general partner return any funds distributed as incentive fees until the limited partners have received their initial investment and a percentage of the total profit.

Clearing An exchange's process of verifying the execution of a transaction, exchange of payments, and recording of participants.

Clearing instructions Instructions that indicate how to arrange the final settlement ("clearing") of a trade.

Clearinghouse An entity associated with a futures market that acts as middleman between the contracting parties and guarantees to each party the performance of the other.

Closed-end fund A mutual fund in which no new investment money is accepted. New investors invest by buying existing shares, and investors in the fund liquidate by selling their shares to other investors.

Cluster sampling A procedure that divides a population into subpopulation groups (clusters) representative of the population and then randomly draws certain clusters to form a sample.

Co-investing In co-investing, the investor invests in assets *indirectly* through the fund but also possesses rights (known as co-investment rights) to invest *directly* in the same assets. Through co-investing, an investor is able to make an investment *alongside* a fund when the fund identifies deals.

Code of ethics An established guide that communicates an organization's values and overall expectations regarding member behavior. A code of ethics serves as a general guide for how community members should act.

Coefficient of determination (R^2) The percentage of the variation of the dependent variable that is explained by the independent variable. It is a measure of goodness of fit of a regression model.

Coefficient of variation The ratio of a set of observations' standard deviation to the observations' mean value.

Cognitive cost The effort involved in processing new information and updating beliefs.

Cognitive dissonance The mental discomfort that occurs when new information conflicts with previously held beliefs or cognitions.

Cognitive errors Behavioral biases resulting from faulty reasoning; cognitive errors stem from basic statistical, information-processing, or memory errors.

Coincident economic indicators Turning points that are usually close to those of the overall economy; they are believed to have value for identifying the economy's present state.

Collateral Assets or financial guarantees underlying a debt obligation that are above and beyond the issuer's promise to pay.

Collateral manager Buys and sells debt obligations for and from the CDO's collateral pool to generate sufficient cash flows to meet the obligations to the CDO bondholders.

Collateralized bond obligations (CBOs) CDOs backed by high-yield corporate and emerging market bonds.

Collateralized debt obligations (CDOs) Securities backed by a diversified pool of one or more debt obligations. CDOs can be backed by a broad range of debt.

Collateralized loan obligations (CLOs) CDOs backed by leveraged bank loans.

Collateralized mortgage obligations Securitize mortgage pass-through securities or multiple pools of loans. CMOs are structured to redistribute the cash flows to different bond classes or tranches and create securities that have different exposures to prepayment risk.

Commercial paper (CP) Short-term, negotiable, unsecured promissory note that represents a debt obligation of the issuer.

Committed (regular) lines of credit Bank commitments to extend credit; the commitment is considered a short-term liability and is usually in effect for 364 days (one day short of a full year).

Committed capital The amount that the limited partners have agreed to provide to the private equity fund.

Commodities A product or service from a firm that is indistinguishable from products or services of competing firms, usually conforming to a common standard or grade imposed by convention or regulation.

Commoditization A process by which competing products become less differentiated over time and become interchangeable "commodities" in the eyes of customers. This process is typically associated with declining profitability for the selling firms.

Commodity producers A firm that makes and/or sells commodities.

Commodity swap A type of swap involving the exchange of payments over multiple dates as determined by specified reference prices or indexes relating to commodities.

Common market Level of economic integration that incorporates all aspects of the customs union and extends it by allowing free movement of factors of production among members.

Common shares A type of security that represents an ownership interest in a company. Also called *common stock*.

Common stock A type of security that represents an ownership interest in a company. Also called *common shares*.

Common-size analysis The restatement of financial statement items using a common denominator or reference item that allows one to identify trends and major differences; an example is an income statement in which all items are expressed as a percent of revenue.

Companies Organization entities formed and managed for the purpose of providing a return or economic benefits to its investors and owners.

Company research report A document that presents an analyst's investment recommendation on an issuer and its securities, supported by financial modeling, industry overviews and competitive analyses, valuation scenarios, ESG considerations, and investment risks.

Complete markets Informally, markets in which the variety of distinct securities traded is so broad that any desired payoff in a future state-of-the-world is achievable.

Concession agreement A contractual arrangement under which an entity (also known as a grantor) establishes terms and conditions with a developer or operator (referred to as a concessionaire) to plan, build, operate, finance, and maintain an infrastructure asset for a specific period.

Conditional expected value The expected value of a stated event given that another event has occurred.

Conditional pass-through covered bonds Convert to pass-through securities after the original maturity date if all bond payments have not yet been made.

Conditional variances The variance of one variable, given the outcome of another.

Conditions The general economic, competitive, and business environment faced by all borrowers that may affect their ability to service or refinance debt.

Confidence level The complement of the level of significance.

Confirmation bias A belief perseverance bias in which people tend to look for and notice what confirms their beliefs, to ignore or undervalue what contradicts their beliefs, and to misinterpret information as support for their beliefs.

Consensus protocol A set of rules governing how blocks can join the blockchain that is designed to resist attempts at malicious manipulation up to a certain level of security; it can be either a proof of work or a proof of stake.

Conservatism bias A belief perseverance bias in which people maintain their prior views or forecasts by inadequately incorporating new information.

Constant yield-price trajectory A graphical depiction of the relationship between time to maturity and a bond price, assuming no default, that shows that a bond price approaches par as time passes.

Constituent securities With respect to an index, the individual securities within an index.

Contango Refers to spot price below forward price in a futures market.

Contingency provision Clause in a legal document that allows for some action if a specific event or circumstance occurs.

Contingency table A table of the frequency distribution of observations classified on the basis of two discrete variables.

Contingent claim A type of derivative in which one of the *counterparties* determines whether and when the trade will settle. An *option* is a common type of contingent claim.

Contingent convertible bonds Bonds that automatically convert to equity if a specific event or circumstance occurs, such as the issuer's equity capital falling below the minimum requirement set by regulators.

Continuous trading market A market in which trades can be arranged and executed any time the market is open.

Continuously compounded return The natural logarithm of 1 plus the holding period return, or equivalently, the natural logarithm of the ending price over the beginning price.

Contract manufacturers Companies that make products for other companies that meet specific terms and specifications.

Contract size Amount(s) used for calculation to price and value the derivative. The contract size is often referred to as "notional amount or notional principal."

Contraction The period of a business cycle after the peak and before the trough; often called a *recession* or, if exceptionally severe, called a *depression*.

Contraction risk The risk of earlier repayment of a mortgage-backed security than expected.

Contractionary Tending to cause the real economy to contract.

Contractionary fiscal policy A fiscal policy that has the objective to make the real economy contract.

Contribution margin A profitability measure using variable costs: unit price less unit variable cost. It can also be expressed as a percentage of price or sales.

Controlling shareholder An individual or entity that owns a majority of the voting rights in a corporation.

Convenience sampling A procedure of selecting an element from a population on the basis of whether or not it is accessible to a researcher or how easy it is for a researcher to access the element.

Convenience yield A non-cash benefit of holding a physical commodity versus a derivative.

Conversion price For a convertible bond, the price per share at which the bond can be converted into shares.

Conversion ratio Number of common shares received in exchange for each preferred share after a predetermined period.

Conversion value For a convertible bond, the value of the bond if it is converted at the market price of the shares. Also called *parity value*.

Convertible bond A bond that gives the bondholder the right to exchange the bond for a specified number of common shares in the issuing company.

Convertible debt A debt instrument that gives the holder the right to exchange the instrument for a specified number of common shares in the issuing company.

Convertible preference shares A type of equity security that entitles shareholders to convert their shares into a specified number of common shares.

Convexity An interest rate risk measure used in conjunction with duration; captures the degree of nonlinearity (curvature) in the relation between price change and yield change.

Convexity adjustment A measure that is used to complement modified duration to capture the second-order effect of yield changes on a bond's price. It is equal to the annual convexity statistic times one-half times the given change in the yield-to-maturity squared.

Convexity bias Refers to the difference in price changes for a given change in yield between interest rate futures and interest rate forward contracts. That is, interest rate forwards exhibit a non-linear or convex relationship between price and yield, while the price–yield relationship is linear for interest rate futures.

Cooperation The process by which countries work together toward some shared goal or purpose. These goals may, and often do, vary widely—from strategic or military concerns, to economic influence, to cultural preferences.

Cooperative country A country that engages and reciprocates in rules standardization; harmonization of tariffs; international agreements on trade, immigration, or regulation; and allowing the free flow of information, including technology transfer.

Core real estate strategies Strategies with exposure to well-leased, high-quality commercial and residential real estate in the best markets, generally offered by open-end funds. Investors expect core real estate to deliver stable returns, primarily from income from the property.

Core-plus real estate strategies Value-add investments that require modest redevelopment or upgrades to lease any vacant space together with possible alternative use of the underlying properties. Compared to core real estate strategies, these may be appealing for investors seeking higher returns and willing to accept additional risks from development, redevelopment, repositioning, and leasing.

Corporate issuers Limited companies or corporations that seek financing in financial markets by, for example, issuing debt or equity securities.

Corporations Another term for limited companies, though often used to refer to public limited companies. See *limited company*, *private limited company*, and *public limited company*.

Correlation A measure of the linear relationship between two random variables.

Correlation coefficient A number between −1 and +1 that measures the consistency or tendency for two investments to act in a similar way. It is used to determine the effect on portfolio risk when two assets are combined.

Cost averaging The periodic investment of a fixed amount of money.

Cost of capital The cost of financing for a company; the rate of return that suppliers of capital require as compensation for their contribution of capital (also called *opportunity cost of funds*).

Cost of carry The net of the costs and benefits related to owning an underlying asset for a specific period.

Cost of debt The required return on debt financing for a company, such as when it issues a bond, takes out a bank loan, or leases an asset through a finance lease.

Cost of equity The return required by equity investors to compensate for both the time value of money and the risk. Also referred to as the required rate of return on common stock or the required return on equity.

Counterparty Legal entities entering a **derivative contract**.

Counterparty credit risk The likelihood that a **counterparty** is unable to meet its financial obligations under the contract.

Counterparty risk The risk that the other party to a contract will fail to honor the terms of the contract.

Country The geopolitical environment as well as the legal and political system faced by all issuers in a jurisdiction that may affect debt payment.

Coupon Periodic interest payments paid by a bond issuer to investors, typically expressed as a percentage of par on an annual basis.

Cournot assumption Assumption in which each firm determines its profit-maximizing production level assuming that the other firms' output will not change.

Covariance A measure of the co-movement (linear association) between two random variables.

Covenants The terms and conditions of lending agreements that the issuer must comply with; they specify the actions that an issuer is obligated to perform (affirmative covenant) or prohibited from performing (negative covenant).

Credit default swap (CDS) A type of credit derivative in which one party, the credit protection buyer who is seeking credit protection against a third party, makes a series of regularly scheduled payments to the other party, the credit protection seller. The seller makes no payments until a credit event occurs.

Credit enhancements Provisions or methods that allow a borrower improve their creditworthiness in a structured transaction.

Credit event An event that defines a payout in a credit derivative. Events are usually defined as bankruptcy, failure to pay an obligation, or an involuntary debt restructuring.

Credit facilities Loan agreements with pre-specified terms and limits but with fluctuating balances based on borrower-specific needs at different points in time, analogous to a credit card.

Credit migration risk The risk that a bond issuer's creditworthiness deteriorates, or migrates lower, leading investors to believe the risk of default is higher. Also called **downgrade risk**.

Credit rating Letter-grade, qualitative measures of an issuer's ability to meet its debt obligations based on both the probability of default and the expected loss under a default scenario.

Credit rating agencies Institutions that issue and maintain credit ratings. The three largest are Standard & Poor's, Moody's, and Fitch Ratings.

Credit risk The expected economic loss under a potential borrower default over the life of the contract

Credit spread A premium over and above the current government bond yield.

Credit spread risk The risk of greater expected loss due to changes in credit conditions as a result of macroeconomic, market, and/or issuer-related factors.

Credit tranching Internal credit enhancement where cash flows into a senior/subordinate structure.

Credit-linked notes Bonds whose coupon changes when the bonds' credit rating changes.

Critical values Values of the test statistic at which the decision changes from fail to reject the null hypothesis to reject the null hypothesis.

Cross-default clause Covenant or contract clause that specifies borrowers are considered in default if they default on another debt obligation.

Cross-sectional analysis Also called relative analysis. Analysis that involves comparisons across individuals in a group over a given time period or at a given point in time.

Crossing networks Trading systems that match buyers and sellers who are willing to trade at prices obtained from other markets.

Crowdsourcing A business model that enables users to contribute directly to a product, service, or online content.

Cryptocurrency An electronic medium of exchange that lacks physical form.

Cryptocurrency wallet A storage unit for public and/or private keys for cryptocurrency transactions. These wallets may be a physical device, program, or service.

Cryptography An algorithmic process to encrypt data, making the data unusable if received by unauthorized parties.

Cumulative preference shares Preference shares for which any dividends that are not paid accrue and must be paid in full before dividends on common shares can be paid.

Cumulative voting A voting process whereby shareholders can accumulate and vote all their shares for a single candidate in an election, as opposed to having to allocate their voting rights evenly among all candidates.

Currencies Monies issued by national monetary authorities.

Currency Money issued by national monetary authorities.

Currency swap A swap in which each party makes interest payments to the other in different currencies.

Current government spending With respect to government expenditures, spending on goods and services that are provided on a regular, recurring basis including health, education, and defense.

Current ratio A measure of liquidity that is the ratio of current assets to current liabilities.

Current yield The sum of the coupon payments received over the year divided by the flat price. Also called the income, interest yield, or running yield.

Customs union Extends the free trade area (FTA) by not only allowing free movement of goods and services among members, but also creating a common trade policy against nonmembers.

CVaR Conditional VaR, a tail loss measure. The weighted average of all loss outcomes in the statistical distribution that exceed the VaR loss.

Daily settlement A specific process of *mark-to-market* by a central clearing party in which the profits and losses of all counterparties to derivatives contracts are determined using settlement prices for each contract.

Dark pools Alternative trading systems that do not display the orders that their clients send to them.

Data mining The practice of determining a model by extensive searching through a dataset for statistically significant patterns.

Data science An interdisciplinary field that harnesses advances in computer science, statistics, and other disciplines for the purpose of extracting information from big data (or data in general).

Data snooping The practice of determining a model by extensive searching through a dataset for statistically significant patterns.

Day order An order that is good for the day on which it is submitted. If it has not been filled by the close of business, the order expires unfilled.

Days of inventory on hand (DOH) The average number of days it would take to sell the amount of inventory on hand. It is calculated as either the ending or average balance of inventories divided by (cost of goods sold/days in the period).

Days payable outstanding (DPO) The average number of days it takes a company to pay its suppliers. It is calculated as either the ending or average balance of accounts payable divided by (cost of goods sold/days in the period).

Days sales outstanding (DSO) The average number of days it takes for a company to receive payment from customers who purchase goods or services on credit. It is calculated as either the ending or average balance of accounts receivable divided by (revenues/days in the period).

Dealers Financial intermediaries, such as commercial banks or investment banks, who transact as **counterparties** with derivative end users.

Debt A claim against an entity to receive cash, stock, or other assets at a future date. From the perspective of the debtor or borrower, an obligation to pay cash, stock, or other assets at a future date. Generally, debt claims are unconditional and are senior to equity claims.

Debt service coverage ratio A ratio in which the net operating income of a real estate investment for a specific period is divided by the amount of debt service to be paid during the same time period.

Debt tax shield The tax benefit from interest paid on debt being tax deductible from income, equal to the marginal tax rate multiplied by the value of the debt.

Debt-to-assets ratio A solvency ratio calculated as total debt divided by total assets.

Debt-to-capital ratio A solvency ratio calculated as total debt divided by total debt plus total shareholders' equity.

Debt-to-equity ratio A solvency ratio calculated as total debt divided by total shareholders' equity.

Debt-to-income ratio (DTI) Residential lending metric that compares an individual's monthly debt payments to their monthly pre-tax, gross income.

Debut issuer An issuer approaching the bond market for the first time.

Deciles Quantiles that divide a distribution into 10 equal parts.

Declaration date The day that the corporation issues a statement declaring a specific dividend.

Decreasing returns to scale When a production process leads to increases in output that are proportionately smaller than the increase in inputs.

Deductible temporary differences Temporary differences that result in a reduction of or deduction from taxable income in a future period when the balance sheet item is recovered or settled.

Deep learning An area of artificial intelligence in which a system uses neural networks to perform multistage, non-linear data processing to identify patterns. Also called *deep learning nets*.

Deep learning nets See *Deep learning*.

Deep-in-the-money option An option that is highly likely to be exercised.

Deep-out-of-the-money option An option that is highly unlikely to be exercised.

Default When a borrower on a mortgage loan fails to meet the obligations of the loan.

Default risk premium An extra return that compensates investors for the possibility that the borrower will fail to make a promised payment at the contracted time and in the contracted amount.

Defeasance Mechanism that allows prepayment on mortgage, but the borrower must purchase a portfolio of government securities that fully replicates the cash flows of the remaining scheduled principal and interest payments, including the balloon loan balance, on the loan.

Defensive interval ratio A liquidity ratio that estimates the number of days that an entity could meet cash needs from liquid assets; calculated as (cash + short-term marketable investments + receivables) divided by daily cash expenditures.

Deferred coupon bonds Bonds that pay no coupons for their first few years but then pay a higher coupon than they otherwise normally would for the remainder of their life. Also called *split coupon bonds*.

Deferred tax assets A balance sheet asset that arises when an excess amount is paid for income taxes relative to accounting profit. The taxable income is higher than accounting profit and income tax payable exceeds tax expense. The company expects to recover the difference during the course of future operations when tax expense exceeds income tax payable.

Deferred tax liabilities A balance sheet liability that arises when a deficit amount is paid for income taxes relative to accounting profit. The taxable income is less than the accounting profit and income tax payable is less than tax expense. The company expects to eliminate the liability over the course of future operations when income tax payable exceeds tax expense.

Defined benefit pension plans (DB plans) Plans in which the company promises to pay a certain annual amount (defined benefit) to the employee after retirement. The company bears the investment risk of the plan assets.

Defined contribution pension plans Individual accounts to which an employee and typically the employer makes contributions during their working years and expect to draw on the accumulated funds at retirement. The employee bears the investment and inflation risk of the plan assets.

Deflation Negative inflation.

Degree of financial leverage The ratio of percentage change in net income to percentage change in operating income over a period. It is a measure of how sensitive net income is to changes in operating income, driven by the firm's use of debt in its capital structure.

Degree of operating leverage (DOL) The ratio of percentage change in operating income to percentage change in sales over a period. It is a measure of how sensitive operating income is to changes in sales, driven by the fixed and variable cost composition of operating expenses.

Delta The relationship between the option price and the underlying price, which reflects the sensitivity of the price of the option to changes in the price of the underlying. Delta is a good approximation of how an option price will change for a small change in the stock.

Demand shock A typically unexpected disturbance to demand, such as an unexpected interruption in trade or transportation.

Dependent variable The variable that is explained by a regression model.

Depository bank A bank that raises funds from depositors and other investors and lends it to borrowers.

Depository institutions Commercial banks, savings and loan banks, credit unions, and similar institutions that raise funds from depositors and other investors and lend it to borrowers.

Depository receipt A security that trades like an ordinary share on a local exchange and represents an economic interest in a foreign company.

Depreciation The process of systematically allocating the cost of long-lived (tangible) assets to the periods during which the assets are expected to provide economic benefits.

Derivative A financial instrument that derives its value from the performance of an underlying asset.

Derivative contract A legal agreement between counterparties with a specific **maturity**, or length of time, until the closing of the transaction, or **settlement**.

Derivative pricing rule A pricing rule used by crossing networks in which a price is taken (derived) from the price that is current in the asset's primary market.

Derivatives A financial instrument whose value depends on the value of some underlying asset or factor (e.g., a stock price, an interest rate, or exchange rate).

Differentiated products A product or service from a firm that is distinguishable or distinct from those of competing firms. It is customers who determine and value whether a product is differentiated.

Diffuse prior The assumption of equal prior probabilities.

Diffusion index Reflects the proportion of the index's components that are moving in a pattern consistent with the overall index.

Digital assets The umbrella term covering assets that can be created, stored, and transmitted electronically and have associated ownership or use rights. Digital assets include a variety of assets, such as cryptocurrencies, tokens (security and utility), and digital collectables.

Diluted EPS The EPS that would result if all dilutive securities were converted into common shares.

Dilution An increase in the number of shares outstanding from share issuance that decreases the percentage of shares owned by existing shareholders.

Direct investing Occurs when an investor makes a direct investment in an asset without the use of an intermediary.

Direct lending Providing capital directly from private debt investors.

Direct listing Where the equity of a security is floated on the public markets directly, without underwriters, reducing the complexity and cost of the transaction.

Direct sales Marketing and/or delivering products and services to customers without an intermediary or third party between the customer and seller.

Direct taxes Taxes levied directly on income, wealth, and corporate profits.

Discount factor The price equivalent of a zero rate. Also may be stated as the present value of a currency unit on a future date.

Discount rate A yield or pricing convention for money market instrument quotations. It is the interest earned on an instrument, derived from the difference between the price and face value, expressed as a percentage of the face value and multiplied by the periodicity of the annual rate.

Discounted cash flow models Valuation models that estimate the intrinsic value of a security as the present value of the future benefits expected to be received from the security.

Discriminatory pricing rule A pricing rule used in continuous markets in which the limit price of the order or quote that first arrived determines the trade price.

Diseconomies of scale Increase in cost per unit resulting from increased production.

Dispersion The variability of a population or sample of observations around the central tendency.

Display size The size of an order displayed to public view.

Disposition effect As a result of loss aversion, an emotional bias whereby investors are reluctant to dispose of losers. This results in an inefficient and gradual adjustment to deterioration in fundamental value.

Distressed debt Debt of mature companies in financial difficulty, in bankruptcy, or likely to default on debt.

Distressed/restructuring These strategies focus on securities of companies either in or perceived to be near bankruptcy. In one approach, hedge funds simply purchase fixed-income securities trading at a significant discount to par but that are still senior enough to be backed by sufficient corporate assets.

Distributed ledger A type of database that can be shared among entities in a network.

Distributed ledger technology (DLT) Technology based on a distributed ledger.

Diversification ratio The ratio of the standard deviation of an equally weighted portfolio to the standard deviation of a randomly selected security.

Dividend A distribution paid to shareholders based on the number of shares owned.

Dividend discount model (DDM) A present value model of stock value that views the intrinsic value of a stock as present value of the stock's expected future dividends.

Dividend payout ratio The ratio of cash dividends paid to earnings for a period.

Dividends Distributions of profits and/or net assets from a corporation to its shareholders. While often in cash, dividends can be also be paid in stock or assets, such as property.

Divisor A number (denominator) used to determine the value of a price return index. It is initially chosen at the inception of an index and subsequently adjusted by the index provider, as necessary, to avoid changes in the index value that are unrelated to changes in the prices of its constituent securities.

Domestic bonds A type of bond for which the issuer's domicile and jurisdiction of issuance are the same.

Domestic content provisions Stipulate that some percentage of the value added or components used in production should be of domestic origin.

Double taxation The taxation of business income at both the entity and personal or owner levels. In most jurisdictions, this taxation scheme applies to public limited companies.

Downside risk The potential for loss.

Drag on liquidity An action or event that reduces available funds or delays cash inflows.

Drivers Causative factors that explain the level of and changes in an output variable.

DSC ratio A property's annual net operating income (NOI) divided by the debt service.

Dual-class structure A capital structure that includes at least two classes of equity shares with unequal voting rights.

Dupont analysis An approach to decomposing return on investment, e.g., return on equity, as the product of other financial ratios.

Duration The percentage change in bond price given an unanticipated small change in interest rates.

Duration gap The difference between a bond's Macaulay duration and its investor's investment horizon.

Dynamic pricing A pricing approach that charges different prices at different times. Specific examples include off-peak pricing, "surge" pricing, and "congestion" pricing.

Early repayment option May entitle the borrower to prepay all or part of the outstanding mortgage principal prior to maturity. This creates a risk from the lender's or investor's viewpoint because the cash flow amounts and timing cannot be known with certainty.

Earnings surprise The portion of a company's earnings that is unanticipated by investors and, according to the efficient market hypothesis, merits a price adjustment.

Economic indicators Economic statistics provided by government and established private organizations that contain information on an economy's recent past activity or its current or future position in the business cycle.

Economic infrastructure investments A category of infrastructure investments that support economic activity through transportation assets, information and communication technology assets, and utility and energy assets.

Economic stabilization Reduction of the magnitude of economic fluctuations.

Economic union Incorporates all aspects of a common market and in addition requires common economic institutions and coordination of economic policies among members.

Economies of scale A decline in costs per unit as output grows, generally resulting from having fixed costs in the cost structure that are spread over more units of output.

Economies of scope A decline in costs per unit as the number of product or business lines increases, generally resulting from having shared costs between the product lines.

Effective annual rate An interest rate with a periodicity of one.

Effective convexity An interest rate risk statistic that measures the non-linear/second-order effect of changes in the benchmark yield curve on a bond's price.

Effective duration The sensitivity of the bond's price to an instantaneous parallel shift in a benchmark yield curve—for example, the government par curve.

Efficient market A market in which asset prices reflect new information quickly and rationally. See also, *informationally efficient market*.

Either/or fee A custom fee arrangement whereby major investors are offered a structure where managers agree to charge *either* a lower management fee *or* a higher incentive fee, whichever is greater.

Electronic communications networks (ECNs) See *alternative trading systems* and *multilateral trading facilities*.

Embedded derivative A derivative within an underlying, such as a callable, putable, or convertible bond.

Embedded options Contingency provisions found in a bond's indenture representing rights that enable their holders to take advantage of interest rate movements. They can be exercised by the issuer, by the bondholder, or automatically depending on the course of interest rates.

Emotional biases Behavioral biases resulting from reasoning influenced by feelings; emotional biases stem from impulse or intuition.

Empirical duration Estimates of duration calculated over time and in different interest rate environments. Unlike analytical duration, empirical duration estimates do not assume that benchmark yields and spreads are independent variables and are uncorrelated.

Employee stock ownership plan (ESOP) A type of employee benefit plan in which a company sets up a trust fund to receive contributions of newly issued shares or cash to buy existing shares. Contributions are tax deductible up to certain limits. Shares in the trust fund are allocated to individual employees based on relative pay or a formula.

Endowment bias An emotional bias in which people value an asset more when they hold rights to it than when they do not.

Enterprise risk management An overall assessment of a company's risk position. A centralized approach to risk management sometimes called firmwide risk management.

Enterprise value (EV) Total company value (the market value of debt, common equity, and preferred equity) minus the value of cash and investments.

Equal weighting An index weighting method in which an equal weight is assigned to each constituent security at inception.

Equity Ownership interest in an entity. A residual claim on the assets of an entity after more senior claims, such as debt, have been satisfied. Also known as *net assets*.

Equity swap A swap transaction in which at least one cash flow is tied to the return on an equity portfolio position, often an equity index.

Error term Represents the difference between the observed value of the independent variable and that expected from the true underlying population relation between the dependent and independent variable.

Estimated parameters In a simple linear regression, the estimated parameters are the intercept and slope of the fitted line.

Ether A programmable cryptocurrency created on the Ethereum blockchain in 2015 that allows for the execution of smart contracts.

Ethical principles Beliefs regarding what is good, acceptable, or obligatory behavior and what is bad, unacceptable, or forbidden behavior.

Ethics The study of moral principles or of making good choices. Ethics encompasses a set of moral principles and rules of conduct that provide guidance for our behavior.

Eurobonds A type of bond issued internationally, outside the jurisdiction of the country in whose currency the bond is denominated.

European options Options that may be exercised only at contract maturity.

European-style Said of an option contract that can only be exercised on the option's expiration date.

Event risk Risk that evolves around set dates, such as elections, new legislation, or other date-driven milestones, such as holidays or political anniversaries, known in advance. Example: Brexit referendum.

Ex-dividend date The first date that a share trades without (i.e., "ex") the right to receive the declared dividend for the period.

Excess kurtosis Degree of kurtosis (fatness of tails) relative to the kurtosis of the normal distribution.

Excess spread Surplus difference of yield remaining after payments to bondholders are made after expenses are made and losses are covered.

Exchange A rules-based, open access market venue where financial instruments are traded, with price and volume transparency accessible by issuers, investors, and their intermediaries.

Exchange-traded derivative (ETD) Futures, options, and other financial contracts available on exchanges.

Exchanges Places where traders can meet to arrange their trades.

Execution instructions Instructions that indicate how to fill an order.

Exercise The decision to transact the underlying by an option holder.

Exercise date The day that an option is exercised by its holder. For a call option, the day the strike price is paid and underlying is purchased. For a put option, when the strike price is received and the underlying is sold.

Exercise price The pre-agreed execution price specified in an option contract. Sometimes, this price is referred to as the strike price.

Exogenous risk A sudden or unanticipated risk that impacts either a country's cooperative stance, the ability of non-state actors to globalize, or both. Examples include sudden uprisings, invasions, or the aftermath of natural disasters.

Expansion The period of a business cycle after its lowest point and before its highest point.

Expansionary Tending to cause the real economy to grow.

Expansionary fiscal policy Fiscal policy aimed at achieving real economic growth.

Expected exposure (EE) The size of the investor's claim at the time of default.

Expected loss (EL) Default probability times loss severity given default.

Expected return on the portfolio Denoted as $(E(R_p))$. The weighted average of the expected returns (R_1 to R_n) on the component securities using their respective weights (w_1 to w_n).

Expected value of a random variable The probability-weighted average of the possible outcomes of a random variable.

Expert system A type of computer programming, often based on "if–then" rules, that attempts to simulate the knowledge base and analytical abilities of human experts in specific problem-solving contexts.

Export subsidy Paid by the government to the firm when it exports a unit of a good that is being subsidized.

Exposure at default (EAD) The size of the investor's claim at the time of default.

Extension risk The risk of later repayment of a mortgage-backed security than expected.

External credit enhancements Provisions or methods from a third party that allow a borrower improve their creditworthiness in a structured transaction.

External debt Sovereign debt owed to foreign creditors.

Extra dividend A dividend paid by a company that does not pay dividends on a regular schedule, or a dividend that supplements regular cash dividends with an extra payment.

Extraordinary general meetings (EGMs) Meetings besides an AGM of the corporate board and shareholders, typically held to deliberate and vote on urgent matters. Corporate charters and bylaws specify who can call an EGM and under what conditions.

Extreme value theory A branch of statistics that focuses primarily on extreme outcomes.

Face value The amount of principal on a bond, also known as par value.

Factoring arrangement When a company sells its accounts receivable to a lender (known as a factor) that assumes responsibility for the credit-granting and collection process.

Fair value A market-based measure of an investment based on observable or derived assumptions to determine a price that market participants would use to exchange an asset or liability in an orderly transaction at a specific time.

Fair value hedge Refers to a specific **hedge accounting** designation that applies when a derivative is deemed to offset the fluctuation in fair value of an asset or liability.

Fallen angels Formerly investment-grade issuers whose credit quality has deteriorated since the time of issuance.

Fat-Tailed Describes a distribution that has fatter tails than a normal distribution (also called leptokurtic).

Fed funds rate The US interbank lending rate on overnight borrowings of reserves.

Federal funds rate The US interbank lending rate on overnight borrowings of reserves. Also known as *Fed Funds rate*.

Fiat money Money that is not convertible into any other commodity.

Fiduciary call A combination of a purchased call option and investment in a risk-free bond with face value of the option's exercise price.

Fill or kill See *immediate or cancel order*.

Finance lease A type of lease which is more akin to the purchase or sale of the underlying asset.

Financial leverage The use of debt in the capital structure. Measured using ratios such as operating income to operating income less interest expense, total assets to total equity, or debt to equity.

Financial leverage ratio A measure of financial leverage calculated as average total assets divided by average total equity.

Financial risk The risk arising from a company's capital structure and, specifically, from the level of debt and debt-like obligations.

Fintech Technological innovation in the financial services industry, specifically with the design and delivery of financial services and products. It may also refer more broadly to companies involved in developing the new technologies and their applications, as well as the business sector that includes such companies.

Firm commitment A pre-determined amount (price and quantity) is agreed to be exchanged at settlement. Examples of firm commitments include forward contracts, futures contracts, and swaps.

First lien Security interest in a property that gives the lender the right to seize the collateral if the borrower does not pay as agreed.

First lien debt Debt secured by a pledge of certain assets that could include buildings, but it may also include property and equipment, licenses, patents, brands, etc.

First mortgage debt Debt secured by a pledge of a specific property.

Fiscal multiplier The ratio of a change in national income to a change in government spending.

Fiscal policy The use of taxes and government spending to affect the level of aggregate expenditures.

Fixed charge coverage A solvency ratio measuring the number of times interest and lease payments are covered by operating income, calculated as (EBIT + lease payments) divided by (interest payments + lease payments).

Fixed charge coverage ratio A measure of how well a company's earnings covers its fixed expenses, which may include debt payments, interest expense, and lease costs.

Fixed-income instruments Debt instruments such as loans or bonds.

Fixed-income securities Fixed-income instruments designed to be more easily tradeable than a loan, such as a bond.

Fixed-price call A contingency provision that grants an issuer the right to buy back a bond at a predetermined price in the future.

Fixed-rate payer The counterparty paying fixed cash flows in a swap contract. May also be referred to as the floating-rate receiver.

Flat price The full price of a bond minus accrued interest. Flat prices are usually quoted by bond dealers.

Float-adjusted market-capitalization weighting An index weighting method in which the weight assigned to each constituent security is determined by adjusting its market capitalization for its market float.

Floating-rate notes Notes on which interest payments are not fixed but instead vary from period to period depending on the current level of a reference interest rate. Also known as *floaters*.

Floating-rate payer The counterparty paying the variable cash flows in a swap contract. May also be referred to as the fixed-rate receiver.

Forecast object A variable on or related to an issuer's financial statements that an analyst makes a projection for. Examples include drivers of financial statements, financial statement lines, and summary measures like EBITDA.

Foreclosure Allows a lender to take possession of the property and ultimately sell the property to recover funds toward satisfying the outstanding debt obligation.

Foreign bonds A type of bond for which the issuer's domicile and jurisdiction of issuance are different.

Foreign currency reserves Holding by the central bank of non-domestic currency deposits and non-domestic bonds.

Foreign direct investments (FDI) Long-term investments in the productive capacity of a foreign country.

Foreign exchange gains (or losses) Gains (or losses) that occur when the exchange rate changes between the investor's currency and the currency that foreign securities are denominated in.

Forward contract A **derivative contract** for the future exchange of an **underlying** at a fixed price set at contract signing.

Forward price Represents the price agreed upon in a forward contract to be exchanged at the contract's maturity date, T. This price is shown in equations as $F_0(T)$.

Forward price-to-earnings ratio A P/E calculated on the basis of a forecast of EPS; a stock's current price divided by next year's expected earnings.

Forward rate agreement (FRA) An OTC derivatives contract in which counterparties agree to apply a specific interest rate to a future time period.

Founders class shares A way to entice early participation in startup funds whereby managers offer incentives that entitle investors to a lower fee structure and/or other favorable terms.

Framing bias An information-processing bias in which a person answers a question differently based on the way in which it is asked (framed).

Franchising A situation where an owner of an asset and associated intellectual property divests the asset and licenses intellectual property to a third-party operator (franchisee) in exchange for royalties. Franchisees operate under the constraints of a franchise agreement.

Free cash flow The actual cash that would be available to the company's investors after making all investments necessary to maintain the company as an ongoing enterprise (also referred to as free cash flow to the firm); the internally generated funds that can be distributed to the company's investors (e.g., shareholders and bondholders) without impairing the value of the company.

Free cash flow hypothesis The hypothesis that higher debt levels discipline managers by forcing them to make fixed debt service payments and by reducing the company's free cash flow.

Free float The portion of a listed company's equity securities that are not held by insiders, strategic investors, sponsors, founders, and so on, that are more freely available for trading.

Free trade areas One of the most prevalent forms of regional integration, in which all barriers to the flow of goods and services among members have been eliminated.

Free-cash-flow-to-equity models Valuation models based on discounting expected future free cash flow to equity.

Freemium business model A pricing approach that allows customers a certain level of usage or functionality at no charge. Those who wish to use more must pay.

Frequency table A representation of the frequency of occurrence of two discrete variables.

Full price The price of a bond including any accrued interest owed to the seller. It is the flat price plus accrued interest.

Fully amortizing loan A loan or bond with a payment schedule that calls for the complete repayment of principal over the instrument's time to maturity.

Fund investing In fund investing, the investor invests in assets indirectly by contributing capital to a fund as part of a group of investors. Fund investing is available for all major alternative investment types.

Fund of funds Funds that hold a portfolio of hedge funds; also called *funds of hedge funds*.

Fundamental analysis The examination of publicly available information and the formulation of forecasts to estimate the intrinsic value of assets.

Fundamental growth These strategies use fundamental analysis to identify companies expected to exhibit high growth and capital appreciation.

Fundamental long/short In this strategy, the hedge fund takes a long position in companies that are trading at inexpensive levels compared to their potential intrinsic value and shorts those that trade in the other direction, with the intention of reversing this trade to obtain alpha.

Fundamental value These strategies use fundamental analysis to identify undervalued and unloved companies for which there is a possibility that a corporate turnaround, with future revenue and cash flow growth, will result in higher valuations.

Fundamental weighting An index weighting method in which the weight assigned to each constituent security is based on its underlying company's size. It attempts to address the disadvantages of market-capitalization weighting by using measures that are independent of the constituent security's price.

Fungible Freely exchangeable, interchangeable, or substitutable with other things of the same type. Money and commodities are the most common examples.

Futures contract A variation of a forward contract that has essentially the same basic definition but with some additional features, such as a clearinghouse guarantee against credit losses, a daily settlement of gains and losses, and an organized electronic or floor trading facility.

Futures contract basis point value (BPV) The change in price of a futures contract given a 1 basis point (0.01%) change in yield.

Futures contracts Forward contracts with standardized sizes, dates, and underlyings that trade on futures exchanges.

Futures margin account An account held by an exchange clearinghouse for each derivatives counterparty. The funds in such an account are used to ensure that counterparties do not default on their contract obligation.

Futures price The pre-agreed price at which a futures contract buyer (seller) agrees to pay (receive) for the underlying at the maturity date of the futures contract.

FX swap The combination of a spot and a forward FX transaction.

G-spread Yield spread in basis points between a bond's yield-to-maturity and that of an actual or interpolated government bond. It represents the return for bearing risks relative to the government bond.

Game theory The set of tools decision makers use to incorporate responses by rival decision makers into their strategies.

Gamma A numerical measure of how sensitive an option's delta (the sensitivity of the derivative's price) is to a change in the value of the underlying.

Gate A provision that when implemented limits or restricts redemptions for a period of time.

General collateral repo Rather than involving a specific security, a repo that instead references a specific group of securities as eligible collateral (such as government bonds of a specific maturity).

General collateral repo rate The interest rate on a general collateral repo.

General obligation (GO) bonds Unsecured bonds issued by a non-sovereign government which are backed by the taxing authority of the issuer.

General obligation bonds Also known as GO bonds. Bonds issued by non-sovereign governments for general purposes and repaid from tax cash flows.

General partners (GPs) Owners of a general partnership or limited partnership with unlimited liability and other attributes as specified in the partnership agreement.

General partnership A business organizational form owned entirely by general partners.

Geophysical resource endowment Includes such factors as livable geography and climate as well as access to food and water, which are necessary for sustainable growth. Geophysical resource endowment is highly unequal among countries.

Geopolitics The study of how geography affects politics and international relations. These relations matter for investments because they contribute to important drivers of investment performance, including economic growth, business performance, market volatility, and transaction costs.

Gilts Bonds issued by the UK government.

Global depository receipt (GDR) A depository receipt that is issued outside of the company's home country and outside of the United States.

Global minimum-variance portfolio The portfolio on the minimum-variance frontier with the smallest variance of return.

Global registered share (GRS) A common share that is traded on different stock exchanges around the world in different currencies.

Globalization The process of interaction and integration among people, companies, and governments worldwide. It is marked by the spread of products, information, jobs, and culture across borders.

Gold standard With respect to a currency, if a currency is on the gold standard a given amount can be converted into a prespecified amount of gold.

Good-on-close An execution instruction specifying that an order can only be filled at the close of trading. Also called *market-on-close*.

Good-on-open An execution instruction specifying that an order can only be filled at the opening of trading.

Good-till-cancelled order An order specifying that it is valid until the entity placing the order has cancelled it (or, commonly, until some specified amount of time such as 60 days has elapsed, whichever comes sooner).

Goodwill An intangible asset that represents the excess of the purchase price of an acquired company over the value of the net identifiable assets acquired.

Governance tokens In permissionless networks, governance tokens serve as votes to determine how the particular network is run.

Government debt management Government policies that relate to the issuance of debt securities, typically handled by a treasurer or finance ministry.

Government equivalent yield Measures quoted using actual/actual day counts.

Grant date The day that terms of compensation are communicated by an issuer and accepted by an employee recipient.

Green bonds Bonds used in green finance whereby the proceeds are earmarked toward environmental-related products.

Greenfield investments The first stage of development of an infrastructure asset. Greenfield investments involve developing new assets and new infrastructure with the intention either to lease or sell the assets to the government after construction or to hold and operate the assets. Greenfield investors typically invest alongside strategic investors or developers that specialize in developing the underlying assets.

Gross profit margin The ratio of gross profit to revenues.

Groupthink The practice of thinking or making decisions as a group in a way that discourages creativity or individual responsibility. For scenario analysis to be useful in portfolio management, teams must work hard to build creative processes, identify scenarios, track these scenarios, and assess the need for action on a regular cadence.

Growth cycle Refers to fluctuations in economic activity around the long-term potential trend growth level, focusing on how much actual economic activity is below or above trend growth in economic activity.

Growth option The option to make additional investments in a project at some future time if the financial results are strong. Also called *expansion option*.

Growth rate cycle Refers to fluctuations in the growth rate of economic activity.

Haircut The difference between the market value of the security used as collateral and the value of the loan. Also called *repo margin*.

Halo effect An emotional bias that extends a favorable evaluation of some characteristics to other characteristics.

Hard commodities Traded natural resources, such as crude oil and metals, with markets often involving the physical delivery of the underlying upon settlement.

Hard hurdle rate Hurdle rate where the manager earns fees on annual returns in excess of the hurdle rate.

Hard-bullet covered bonds Type of security where if payments do not occur according to the original schedule of a covered bond, a bond default is triggered and bond payments are accelerated.

Harmonic mean A type of weighted mean computed as the reciprocal of the arithmetic average of the reciprocals.

Hedge The **derivative contract** used in **hedging** an exposure.

Hedge accounting Accounting standard(s) that allow an issuer to offset a hedging instrument (usually a derivative) against a hedged transaction or balance sheet item to reduce financial statement volatility.

Hedge funds Private investment vehicles that may invest in public equities or publicly traded fixed-income assets, private capital, and/or real assets, but they are distinguished by their investment *approach* rather than by the investments themselves.

Hedge ratio The proportion of an underlying that will offset the risk associated with a derivative position.

Hedging The use of a derivative contract to offset or neutralize existing or anticipated exposure to an **underlying**.

Hegemony Countries that are regional or even global leaders and use their political or economic influence of others to control resources.

Held-to-maturity Debt (fixed-income) securities that a company intends to hold to maturity; these are presented at their original cost, updated for any amortisation of discounts or premiums.

Herding Clustered trading that may or may not be based on information.

Herfindahl-Hirschman Index (HHI) A measure of market concentration, calculated as the sum of the squares of competitor market shares. Antitrust regulators in some countries consider markets with an HHI between 1,500 and 2,500 moderately concentrated and consider markets with an HHI over 2,500 highly concentrated.

Heteroskedasticity Non-constant variance across all observations.

Hidden order An order that is exposed not to the public but only to the brokers or exchanges that receive it.

Hidden revenue business model Business models that provide services to users at no charge and generate revenues elsewhere.

High yield Bond issuers and issues rated BB+ (Ba1 on Moody's scale) or lower. Also known as speculative grade and junk.

High-water mark The highest value, net of fees, that a fund has reached in history. It reflects the highest cumulative return used to calculate an incentive fee.

Hindsight bias A bias with selective perception and retention aspects in which people may see past events as having been predictable and reasonable to expect.

Holder-of-record date The date that a shareholder listed on the corporation's books will be deemed to have ownership of the shares for purposes of receiving an upcoming dividend.

Holding period return The single-period internal rate of return for a real estate property that includes property income and the change in property value over the period.

Home bias A preference for securities listed on the exchanges of one's home country.

Homogeneity of expectations The assumption that all investors have the same economic expectations and thus have the same expectations of prices, cash flows, and other investment characteristics.

Homoskedasticity Constant variance across all observations.

Horizon yield An investor's total rate of return on a fixed income instrument over their holding period, including reinvested coupon payments. It is an internal rate of return expressed as an annualized rate.

Hostile takeover When a potential acquirer seeks to acquire a company (the target) against the wishes of the target's board of directors. Typically, a tender offer is used to carry out the hostile takeover, against which a board might use a poison pill in its defense.

Household A person or a group of people living in the same residence, taken as a basic unit in economic analysis.

Human capital The present value of an individual's future expected labor income.

Hurdle rate The rate of return that a project's IRR must exceed for the project to be accepted by the company.

Hypothesis A proposed explanation or theory that can be tested.

Hypothesis testing The process of testing of hypotheses about one or more populations using statistical inference.

I-spread Also known as interpolated spread, it is the yield spread for a bond over the standard swap rate in that currency of the same tenor.

Iceberg order An order in which the display size is less than the order's full size.

If-converted method A method for accounting for the effect of convertible securities on earnings per share (EPS) that specifies what EPS would have been if the convertible securities had been converted at the beginning of the period, taking account of the effects of conversion on net income and the weighted average number of shares outstanding.

Illusion of control bias A bias in which people tend to believe that they can control or influence outcomes when, in fact, they cannot.

Immediate or cancel order An order that is valid only upon receipt by the broker or exchange. If such an order cannot be filled in part or in whole upon receipt, it cancels immediately. Also called *fill or kill*.

Impact lag The lag associated with the result of actions affecting the economy with delay.

Implied forward rate An interest rate or yield over a future period implied by the current term structure of interest rates.

Import license Specifies the quantity of a good that can be imported into a country.

In-the-money Describes an option with a positive intrinsic value.

Income tax paid The actual amount paid for income taxes in the period; not a provision, but the actual cash outflow.

Income tax payable The income tax owed by the company on the basis of taxable income.

Increasing returns to scale When a production process leads to increases in output that are proportionately larger than the increase in inputs.

Incurrence test A financial ratio or other measurement taken prior to an action such as debt issuance, usually on a pro forma basis taking the action into account. Satisfaction of the test (e.g., leverage ratio below a certain value) is linked to covenants between the issuer and investors.

Indenture A written contract between a lender and borrower that specifies the terms of the loan, such as interest rate, interest payment schedule, or maturity.

Independent With reference to events, the property that the occurrence of one event does not affect the probability of another event occurring. With reference to two random variables X and Y, they are independent if and only if $P(X,Y) = P(X)P(Y)$.

Independent directors Members of a corporation's board of directors who do not have an employment or familial relationship with the company, nor do they have a relationship that would impair their independence such as an economic interest in a vendor or competitor of the company.

Independent variable An explanatory variable in a regression model.

Independently and identically distributed With respect to random variables, the property of random variables that are independent of each other but follow the identical probability distribution.

Index-linked bonds A bond whose coupon payments or principal repayment is linked to a specified index.

Indexing An investment strategy in which an investor constructs a portfolio to mirror the performance of a specified index.

Indicator variable A variable that takes on only one of two values, 0 or 1, based on a condition. In simple linear regression, the slope is the difference in the dependent variable for the two conditions. Also referred to as a *dummy variable*.

Indifference curve A curve representing all the combinations of two goods or attributes such that the consumer is entirely indifferent among them.

Indirect taxes Taxes such as taxes on spending, as opposed to direct taxes.

Inflation premium An extra return that compensates investors for expected inflation.

Inflation reports A type of economic publication put out by many central banks.

Inflation-linked bonds Debt instruments that link the principal and interest to inflation.

Information cascade The transmission of information from those participants who act first and whose decisions influence the decisions of others.

Information-motivated traders Traders that trade to profit from information that they believe allows them to predict future prices.

Informationally efficient market A market in which asset prices reflect new information quickly and rationally.

Infrastructure A type of real asset that is intended for public use and provides essential services. These assets are typically long-lived fixed assets, such as bridges and toll roads.

Initial coin offering (ICO) An unregulated process whereby companies raise capital by selling crypto-tokens to investors in exchange for fiat money or another agreed-upon cryptocurrency.

Initial margin The ratio of the price of collateral to the value of cash exchanged in a repo; a value over 1.0 or 100% indicates overcollateralization.

Initial margin requirement The margin requirement on the first day of a transaction as well as on any day in which additional margin funds must be deposited.

Initial public offering (IPO) The first issuance of common shares to the public by a formerly private corporation.

Inside directors Members of a corporation's board of directors who are not independent. Typically, inside directors are employees or founders (and their family) of the company.

Insolvency Refers to the condition in which firm value is below the face value of debt used to finance the firm's assets.

Institution An established organization or practice in a society or culture. An institution can be a formal structure, such as a university, organization, or process backed by law; or it can be informal, such as a custom or behavioral pattern important to society. Institutions can, but need not be, formed by national governments. Examples of institutions include non-governmental organizations, charities, religious customs, family units, the media, political parties, and educational practice.

Intangible assets Assets without a physical form, such as patents and trademarks.

Interbank market The market of loans and deposits between banks for maturities ranging from overnight to one year.

Intercept The estimated value of the dependent variable when the independent variable is zero.

Interest coverage A solvency ratio calculated as EBIT divided by interest payments.

Interest coverage ratio A measure of an issuer's ability to service its debt, typically the ratio of operating income or EBIT to interest expense.

Interest rate A rate of return that reflects the relationship between differently dated cash flows; a discount rate.

Interest rate swap A swap in which the underlying is an interest rate. Can be viewed as a currency swap in which both currencies are the same and can be created as a combination of currency swaps.

Interest-indexed bond A type of index-linked bond for which changes in the index are captured with adjustments to interest payments.

Internal credit enhancements Provisions or methods a borrower initiates to improve their creditworthiness in a structured transaction, such as overcollateralization or excess spread.

Internal rate of return The discount rate that makes net present value equal 0; the discount rate that makes the present value of an investment's costs (outflows) equal to the present value of the investment's benefits (inflows).

Internal rate of return (IRR) The discount rate that makes net present value equal 0; the discount rate that makes the present value of an investment's costs (outflows) equal to the present value of the investment's benefits (inflows).

Internet of things The vast array of physical devices, home appliances, smart buildings, vehicles, and other items that are embedded with electronics, sensors, software, and network connections that enable the objects in the system to interact and share information.

Interquartile range The difference between the third and first quartiles of a dataset.

Intrinsic value The amount gained (per unit) by an option buyer if an option is exercised at any given point in time. May be referred to as the exercise value of the option.

Investment banks Financial intermediaries that provide advice to their mostly corporate clients and help them arrange transactions such as initial and seasoned securities offerings.

Investment grade Bond issuers and issues rated BBB- (Baa3 on Moody's scale).

Investment policy statement A written planning document that describes a client's investment objectives and risk tolerance over a relevant time horizon, along with the constraints that apply to the client's portfolio.

Issue rating A rating which seeks to capture the probability of default or expected loss of the issuer's senior unsecured bonds.

Issuer rating A rating which seeks to capture the credit risk of a specific financial obligation of an issuer which takes such factors as seniority into account.

J-curve effect Represents the initial negative return in the capital commitment phase followed by an acceleration of returns through the capital deployment phase.

Jackknife A resampling method that repeatedly draws samples by taking the original observed data sample and leaving out one observation at a time (without replacement) from the set.

January effect Calendar anomaly that stock market returns in January are significantly higher compared to the rest of the months of the year, with most of the abnormal returns reported during the first five trading days in January. Also called *turn-of-the-year effect*.

Joint probability function A function giving the probability of joint occurrences of values of stated random variables.

Judgmental sampling A procedure of selectively handpicking elements from the population based on a researcher's knowledge and professional judgment.

Junior debt Debt obligation with lower priority of payment than senior debt obligations.

Key rate duration Also known as partial duration, is a measure of a bond's sensitivity to a change in the benchmark yield at a specific maturity.

Keynesians Economists who believe that fiscal policy can have powerful effects on aggregate demand, output, and employment when there is substantial spare capacity in an economy.

Kurtosis The statistical measure that indicates the combined weight of the tails of a distribution relative to the rest of the distribution.

Lagging economic indicators Turning points that take place later than those of the overall economy; they are believed to have value in identifying the economy's past condition.

Law of one price A principle that states that if two investments have the same or equivalent future cash flows regardless of what will happen in the future, then these two investments should have the same current price.

Lead underwriter The lead investment bank in a syndicate of investment banks and broker–dealers involved in a securities underwriting.

Leading economic indicators Turning points that usually precede those of the overall economy; they are believed to have value for predicting the economy's future state, usually near-term.

Legal tender Something that must be accepted when offered in exchange for goods and services.

Lender of last resort An entity willing to lend money when no other entity is ready to do so.

Leptokurtic Describes a distribution that has fatter tails than a normal distribution (also called fat-tailed).

Lessee Tenant or property user that enters a lease with a property owner or lessor.

Lessor Property owner or manager that leases a property to a tenant or property user.

Level of significance The probability of a Type I error in testing a hypothesis.

Leverage A measure for identifying a potentially influential high-leverage point.

Leveraged buyout A transaction whereby the target company management team converts the target to a privately held company by using heavy borrowing to finance the purchase of the target company's outstanding shares.

Leveraged buyout (LBO) An acquirer (typically an investment fund specializing in LBOs) uses a significant amount of debt to finance the acquisition of a target and then pursues restructuring actions, with the goal of exiting the target with a sale or public listing.

Leveraged buyouts Buyout equity transactions that utilize a high proportion of debt financing to make a company acquisition.

Leveraged loan Where private debt investor firms borrow money to make a direct loan to a borrower.

Leveraged loans Loans made to a borrower or issuer with relatively lower credit quality and/or higher leverage.

Liability-driven investing An investment industry term that generally encompasses asset allocation that is focused on funding an investor's liabilities in institutional contexts.

Licensing arrangements Rights to produce a product or have access to intangible assets using someone else's brand name in return for a royalty (often a percentage of revenues).

Lien A legal right or claim to property by a creditor.

Likelihood The probability of an observation, given a particular set of conditions.

Limit order Instructions to a broker or exchange to obtain the best price immediately available when filling an order, but in no event accept a price higher than a specified (limit) price when buying or accept a price lower than a specified (limit) price when selling.

Limit order book The book or list of limit orders to buy and sell that pertains to a security.

Limited company A business organizational form owned by shareholders or members with limited liability who elect a board of directors to appoint management. Generally, limited companies have indefinite life and easier transfer of ownership interests than limited partnerships.

Limited liability partnership (LLP) A business organizational form available in some jurisdictions owned entirely by limited partners with limited liability.

Limited partners (LPs) Owners of a limited partnership with limited liability and other attributes as specified in the partnership agreement.

Limited partnership A business organizational form owned by a general partner and limited partners.

Limited partnership agreement (LPA) A legal document that outlines the rules of the partnership and establishes the framework that ultimately guides the fund's operations throughout its life.

Lin-log model A functional form for transforming regression model data in which the dependent variable is linear but the independent variable is logarithmic.

Linear derivatives Firm commitment derivative contracts in which the contract's payoff/profit function is linear with respect to the price of the underlying.

Liquid market Said of a market in which traders can buy or sell with low total transaction costs when they want to trade.

Liquidity The extent to which a company is able to meet its short-term obligations using cash flows and those assets that can be readily transformed into cash.

Liquidity premium An extra return that compensates investors for the risk of loss relative to an investment's fair value if the investment needs to be converted to cash quickly.

Liquidity ratios Financial ratios measuring the company's ability to meet its short-term obligations to creditors as they come due.

Liquidity risk A divergence in the cash flow timing of a derivative versus that of an underlying transaction.

Liquidity trap A condition in which the demand for money becomes infinitely elastic (horizontal demand curve) so that injections of money into the economy will not lower interest rates or affect real activity.

Load fund A mutual fund in which, in addition to the annual fee, a percentage fee is charged to invest in the fund and/or for redemptions from the fund.

Loan-to-value ratio (LTV) Ratio of the amount of the mortgage to the property's value. The lower the LTV, the higher the borrower's equity. From the lender's perspective, the higher the borrower's equity, the less likely the borrower is to default.

Loans Debt instruments agreed to between a borrower and lender, typically a bank.

Lockout or revolving period For an ABS with a non-amortizing collateral pool, such as credit card debt, is the period in which the cash proceeds from principal repayments are reinvested in additional loans with a principal equal to the principal repaid. During this period, there is no prepayment risk and potential default risk is generally limited. When the lockout period is over, principal repayments are used to pay off the outstanding principal on the ABS. Lockout period and revolving period are interchangeable.

Lockup period The minimum holding period before investors are allowed to make withdrawals or redeem shares from a fund. Its purpose is to allow the hedge fund manager the required time to implement and potentially realize a strategy's expected results.

Log-lin model A functional form for transforming regression model data in which the dependent variable is logarithmic but the independent variable is linear.

Log-log model A functional form for transforming regression model data in which both the dependent and independent variables are in logarithmic form.

Long A trading position in a **derivative contract** that gains value as the price of the **underlying** moves higher.

Long position A position in an asset or contract in which one owns the asset or has an exercisable right under the contract.

Long-run average total cost The curve describing average total cost when no costs are considered fixed.

Loss aversion The tendency of people to dislike losses more than they like comparable gains.

Loss given default (LGD) The investor's loss conditional on an issuer event of default.

Loss severity Portion of a bond's value (including unpaid interest) an investor loses in the event of default.

Loss-aversion bias A bias in which people tend to strongly prefer avoiding losses as opposed to achieving gains.

Low-cost producer A firm with lower production costs than its industry competitors.

M^2 An appraisal measure that indicates what a portfolio would have returned, assuming the same total risk as the market index.

M^2 alpha Difference between the risk-adjusted performance of the portfolio and the performance of the benchmark.

Macaulay duration The present-value weighted average time to receipt of cash flows for fixed-income instrument, also the holding period needed to balance coupon reinvestment risk and price risk for a one-time instantaneous "parallel" shift in the yield curve once the bond purchase is settled. It is named after Frederick Macaulay, the Canadian economist who introduced the concept in 1938.

Machine learning (ML) Involves computer-based techniques that seek to extract knowledge from large amounts of data without making any assumptions about the data's underlying probability distribution. The goal of ML algorithms is to automate decision-making processes by generalizing, or "learning," from known examples to determine an underlying structure in the data.

Maintenance capital expenditures Investments in assets to keep them in operation or increase their efficiency without extending their useful lives.

Maintenance margin Minimum balance set below the initial margin that each contract buyer and seller must hold in the futures margin account from trade initiation until final settlement at maturity.

Maintenance margin requirement The margin requirement on any day other than the first day of a transaction.

Management buy-in A type of leveraged buyout where the current management team is replaced with the acquiring team involved in managing the company.

Management buyout A type of leveraged buyout where the current management team participates in the acquisition.

Management guidance Management of public companies may publicly provide targets for earnings, revenues, and other measures (e.g., capital expenditures) for the next quarter, year, or longer term. Guidance can be detailed or rather directional and is often updated throughout the year. Initial guidance for next fiscal year might be provided during the fourth-quarter earnings call and updated for completed quarters, and new information provided at the first-, second-, and third-quarter earnings calls. Also known simply as *guidance*.

Margin call Request to a derivatives contract counterparty to immediately deposit funds to return the futures margin account balance to the initial margin.

Margin financing A financing arrangement whereby the prime broker lends shares, bonds, or derivatives and the hedge fund (or investment manager) deposits cash or other collateral into a margin account at the prime broker based on certain fractions of the investment positions.

Margin loan Money borrowed from a broker to purchase securities.

Marginal propensity to consume The proportion of an additional unit of disposable income that is consumed or spent; the change in consumption for a small change in income.

Marginal propensity to save The proportion of an additional unit of disposable income that is saved (not spent).

Mark to market (MTM) The practice in which a central clearing party assigns profits and losses to counterparties to derivative contracts. In exchange-traded markets, this practice takes place daily and is often referred to as daily settlement.

Market anomaly Change in the price or return of a security that cannot directly be linked to current relevant information known in the market or to the release of new information into the market.

Market bid–ask spread The difference between the best bid and the best offer.

Market discount rate The rate of return required by investors given the risk of the bond investment, also known as the required yield or required rate of return.

Market float The number of shares that are available to the investing public.

Market makers Over-the-counter (OTC) dealers who typically enter into offsetting bilateral transactions with one another to transfer risk to other parties.

Market model A regression equation that specifies a linear relationship between the return on a security (or portfolio) and the return on a broad market index.

Market multiple models Valuation models based on share price multiples or enterprise value multiples.

Market neutral These strategies use quantitative, fundamental, and technical analysis to identify under- and overvalued equity securities. The hedge fund takes long positions in undervalued securities and short positions in overvalued securities, while seeking to maintain a market-neutral net position.

Market order Instructions to a broker or exchange to obtain the best price immediately available when filling an order.

Market reference rate A market-determined interest rate used as the underlying in financial instruments and contracts such as variable-rate debt and interest rate swaps. An example is the Secured Overnight Financing Rate (SOFR), which is an overnight cash borrowing rate collateralized by US Treasuries. Other MRRs include the euro short-term rate (€STR) and the Sterling Overnight Index Average (SONIA).

Market reference rate (MRR) The interest rate underlying used in interest rate swaps. These rates typically match those of loans or other short-term obligations. Survey-based Libor rates used as reference rates in the past have been replaced by rates based on a daily average of observed market transaction rates. For example, the Secured Overnight Financing Rate (SOFR) is an overnight cash borrowing rate collateralized by US Treasuries. Other MRRs include the euro short-term rate (€STR) and the Sterling Overnight Index Average (SONIA).

Market risk Risk related to market movements, e.g., unexpected changes in share prices, interest rates, currency exchange rates, and commodity prices.

Market share A company's or product's revenue expressed as a percentage of its market size.

Market size Total sales for a good or service, which can be calculated on a global or more regional basis.

Market value The price at which an asset or security can currently be bought or sold in an open market.

Market-capitalization weighting An index weighting method in which the weight assigned to each constituent security is determined by dividing its market capitalization by the total market capitalization (sum of the market capitalization) of all securities in the index. Also called *value weighting*.

Market-on-close An execution instruction specifying that an order can only be filled at the close of trading.

Marketable limit order A buy limit order in which the limit price is placed above the best offer, or a sell limit order in which the limit price is placed below the best bid. Such orders generally will partially or completely fill right away.

Markowitz efficient frontier The graph of the set of portfolios offering the maximum expected return for their level of risk (standard deviation of return).

Master limited partnership (MLP) Has similar features to limited partnerships but is usually a more liquid investment that is often publicly traded.

Master repurchase agreement A legal document governing all repo trades between two parties.

Match funding Financing an asset with a source, such as a loan or bond, that is aligned with certain attributes of the asset, such as duration and the respective streams of income and financing costs.

Material (materiality) Refers to information that is decision-useful for a reasonable investor.

Glossary

Matrix pricing An estimation process for financial instruments based on the prices of comparable instruments.

Maturity The date of a fixed-income instrument's final payment to investors.

Maturity premium An extra return that compensates investors for the increased sensitivity of the market value of debt to a change in market interest rates as maturity is extended.

Maturity structure of interest rates Also known as the term structure of interest rates, refers to the difference in interest rates or benchmark yields by time-to-maturity.

Mean absolute deviation With reference to a sample, the mean of the absolute values of deviations from the sample mean.

Mean square error (MSE) Calculated as the sum of squares error (SSE) divided by the degrees of freedom, which are the number of observations minus the number of independent variables minus one. Since simple linear regression has just one independent variable, the degrees of freedom calculation is the number of observations minus 2.

Mean square regression (MSR) Calculated as the sum of squares regression (SSR) divided by the number of independent variables in the regression model. In simple linear regression, there is only one independent variable, so MSR equals SSR.

Mean–variance analysis An approach to portfolio analysis using expected means, variances, and covariances of asset returns.

Measure of central tendency A quantitative measure that specifies where data are centered.

Measures of location Quantitative measures that describe the location or distribution of data. They include not only measures of central tendency but also other measures, such as percentiles.

Median The value of the middle item of a set of items that has been sorted into ascending or descending order (i.e., the 50th percentile).

Meme coin A type of altcoin that is often inspired by a joke.

Mental accounting bias An information-processing bias in which people treat one sum of money differently from another equal-sized sum based on which mental account the money is assigned to.

Merger arbitrage Generally, these strategies involve going long (buying) the stock of the company being acquired at a discount to its announced takeover price and going short (selling) the stock of the acquiring company when the merger or acquisition is announced.

Mesokurtic Describes a distribution with kurtosis equal to that of the normal distribution, namely, kurtosis equal to three.

Mezzanine debt Refers to private credit subordinated to senior secured debt but senior to equity in the borrower's capital structure.

Mezzanine-stage financing Mezzanine venture capital that prepares a company to go public as it continues to expand capacity and enhance its growth trajectory. It represents the bridge financing needed to fund a private firm until it can execute an IPO or be sold.

Miner A validator of transactions on the blockchain that locks blocks of transactions into the blockchain and receives compensation for this process in the form of a digital asset.

Minimum efficient scale The smallest output that a firm can produce such that its long-run average total cost is minimized.

Minimum-variance portfolio The portfolio with the minimum variance for each given level of expected return.

Minority shareholder An individual or entity that owns less than a majority of the voting rights in a corporation.

Mode The most frequently occurring value in a distribution.

Modern portfolio theory (MPT) The analysis of rational portfolio choices based on the efficient use of risk.

Modified duration The first derivative of a bond's price with respect to its yield, this statistic is a measure of interest rate risk used to estimate the percentage price change for a given change in yield-to-maturity.

Monetarists Economists who believe that the rate of growth of the money supply is the primary determinant of the rate of inflation.

Monetary policy Actions taken by a nation's central bank to affect aggregate output and prices through changes in bank reserves, reserve requirements, or its target interest rate.

Monetary transmission mechanism The process whereby a central bank's interest rate gets transmitted through the economy and ultimately affects the rate of increase of prices.

Monetary union An economic union in which the members adopt a common currency.

Money convexity A measure that is used to complement modified duration to capture the second-order effect of yield changes on a bond's price, expressed in currency terms.

Money duration A measure of the price change of a fixed-income instrument in currency units from a change in yield-to-maturity. The money duration can be stated per 100 of par value or in terms of the actual position size. In the United States, money duration is commonly called "dollar duration."

Money market The market for short-term debt instruments (one-year maturity or less).

Money market securities Fixed-income securities with original maturities of one year or less.

Money-weighted return The internal rate of return on a portfolio, taking account of all cash flows.

Moneyness Expresses the relationship between an option's value and its exercise price across the full range of possible underlying prices.

Monopolistic competition Highly competitive form of imperfect competition; the competitive characteristic is a notably large number of firms, while the monopoly aspect is the result of product differentiation.

Monopoly In pure monopoly markets, there are no substitutes for the given product or service. There is a single seller, which exercises considerable power over pricing and output decisions.

Monte Carlo simulation A technique that uses the inverse transformation method for converting a randomly generated uniformly distributed number into a simulated value of a random variable of a desired distribution. Each key decision variable in a Monte Carlo simulation requires an assumed statistical distribution; this assumption facilitates incorporating non-normality, fat tails, and tail dependence as well as solving high-dimensionality problems.

Moral principles Beliefs regarding what is good, acceptable, or obligatory behavior and what is bad, unacceptable, or forbidden behavior.

Mortgage loan Agreement to finance real estate by the collateral of a specified property that obliges the borrower to make a predetermined series of payments to the lender.

Mortgage pass-through security Security created when mortgage lenders pool mortgages together and sell securities to investors. The cash flow from the mortgage pool—monthly payments of principal, interest, and prepayments—are "passed through" to the security holders.

Mortgage-backed securities Debt obligations that represent claims to the cash flows from pools of mortgage loans, most commonly on residential property.

Mortgage-backed securities (MBS) Bonds created from the securitization of mortgages.

Multi-factor model A model that explains a variable in terms of the values of a set of factors.

Multi-market indexes Comprised of indexes from different countries, designed to represent multiple security markets.

Multilateral trading facilities See *alternative trading systems*.

Multilateralism The conduct of countries who participate in mutually beneficial trade relationships and extensive rules harmonization. Private firms are fully integrated into global supply chains with multiple trade partners. Examples of multilateral countries include Germany and Singapore.

Multiple of invested capital (MOIC) A simplified calculation that measures the total value of all distributions and residual asset values relative to an initial total investment; also known as a *money multiple*.

Multiple-price auction A debt securities auction in which bidders receive distinct prices based on their bids.

Multiplier models Valuation models based on share price multiples or enterprise value multiples.

Mutual fund A comingled investment pool in which investors in the fund each have a pro-rata claim on the income and value of the fund.

Nash equilibrium When two or more participants in a non-coop-erative game have no incentive to deviate from their respective equilibrium strategies given their opponent's strategies.

Nationalism The promotion of a country's own economic interests to the exclusion or detriment of the interests of other nations. Nationalism is marked by limited economic and financial cooperation. These actors may focus on national production and sales, limited cross-border investment and capital flows, and restricted currency exchange.

Natural language processing (NLP) A field of research within the field of text analytics and at the intersection of computer science, AI, and linguistics that focuses on developing computer programs to analyze and interpret human language.

Natural resources These include commodities (hard and soft), agricultural land (farmland), and timberland.

Negative externalities A cost to a third party because of the production or consumption of a good or service.

Negative pledge clause Limitations on investments, the disposal of assets, or issuance of debt senior to existing obligations. Negative covenants seek to ensure that an issuer maintains the ability to make interest and principal payments.

Net cash An issuer's total debt less cash and marketable securities. When the balance is negative it is referred to as net cash.

Net debt An issuer's total debt less cash and marketable securities. When the balance is positive it is referred to as net debt.

Net investment hedge Refers to a specific **hedge accounting** designation that applies when either a foreign currency bond or a derivative, such as an FX swap or forward, is used to offset the exchange rate risk of the equity of a foreign operation.

Net present value (NPV) The present value of an investment's cash inflows (benefits) minus the present value of its cash outflows (costs).

Net profit margin An indicator of profitability, calculated as net income divided by revenue; indicates how much of each dollar of revenues is left after all costs and expenses. Also called *profit margin* or *return on sales*.

Net tax rate The tax rate net of transfer payments.

Net working capital Working capital excluding short-term items unrelated to business operations, such as cash, marketable securities, and short-term debt.

Network effects A business model that enables users to contribute directly to a product, service, or online content.

Neural networks A type of computer program design based on how the human brain learns and processes information.

Neutral rate of interest The rate of interest that neither spurs on nor slows down the underlying economy.

No-load fund A mutual fund in which there is no fee for investing in the fund or for redeeming fund shares, although there is an annual fee based on a percentage of the fund's net asset value.

Node Each value on a binomial tree from which successive moves or outcomes branch.

Non-agency RMBS MBS backed by residential mortgages that are issued by private entities and not guaranteed by a federal agency or a GSE.

Non-amortizing loans Type of debt where there are no scheduled principal repayments.

Non-cooperative country A country with inconsistent and even arbitrary rules; restricted movement of goods, services, people, and capital across borders; retaliation; and limited technology exchange.

Non-cumulative preference shares Preference shares for which dividends that are not paid in the current or subsequent periods are forfeited permanently (instead of being accrued and paid at a later date).

Non-financial risks Risks that arise from sources other than changes in the external financial markets, such as changes in accounting rules, legal environment, or tax rates.

Non-fungible token (NFT) A unique cryptographic token on the blockchain that cannot be replicated and is used to represent ownership of physical assets, such as artwork, real estate, or other assets.

Non-linear derivatives Derivatives, such as options or other contingent claims, with payoff/profit profiles that are non-linear (asymmetric) with respect to the price of the underlying.

Non-participating preference shares Preference shares that do not entitle shareholders to share in the profits of the company. Instead, shareholders are only entitled to receive a fixed dividend payment and the par value of the shares in the event of liquidation.

Non-probability sampling A sampling plan dependent on factors other than probability considerations, such as a sampler's judgment or the convenience to access data.

Non-recourse loan Loan in which the lender does not have a claim against the borrower and thus can look only to the property to recover the outstanding mortgage balance.

Non-state actors Those that participate in global political, economic, or financial affairs but do not directly control national security or country resources. Examples of non-state actors are non-governmental organizations (NGOs), multinational companies, charities, and even influential individuals, such as business leaders or cultural icons.

Nonparametric test A test that is not concerned with a parameter or that makes minimal assumptions about the population from which a sample comes.

Nonsystematic risk Unique risk that is local or limited to a particular asset or industry that need not affect assets outside of that asset class.

Normal distribution A continuous, symmetric probability distribution that is completely described by its mean and its variance.

Normalized earnings The expected level of mid-cycle earnings for a company in the absence of any unusual or temporary factors that affect profitability (either positively or negatively).

Notching Ratings adjustment methodology where specific issues from the same borrower may be assigned different credit ratings.

Notice period The length of time (typically 30–90 days) in advance that investors may be required to notify a fund of their intent to redeem some or all of their investment. This allows a fund manager to liquidate a position in an orderly fashion without magnifying losses.

Novation process A process that substitutes the initial **swap execution facility (SEF)** contract with identical trades facing the **central counterparty (CCP)**. The CCP serves as **counterparty** for both financial intermediaries, eliminating bilateral **counterparty credit risk** and providing **clearing** and **settlement** services.

Null hypothesis The hypothesis that is tested.

Off-the-run Seasoned government bonds that are often less liquid.

Off-the-run securities Sovereign debt securities outstanding other than on-the-sun securities. Off-the-run securities are less liquid than on-the-run securities.

Offer The price at which a dealer or trader is willing to sell an asset, typically qualified by a maximum quantity (ask size).

Official interest rate An interest rate that a central bank sets and announces publicly; normally the rate at which it is willing to lend money to the commercial banks. Also called *official policy rate* or *policy rate*.

Official policy rate An interest rate that a central bank sets and announces publicly; normally the rate at which it is willing to lend money to the commercial banks.

Oligopoly Market structure with a relatively small number of firms supplying the market.

Omnichannel Refers to a company selling its products or services in multiple channels, such as in store and online.

On-the-run Most recently issued, and liquid, government bonds.

On-the-run securities The most recently issued and liquid sovereign debt securities.

Open interest The number of outstanding contracts.

Open market operations The purchase or sale of bonds by the national central bank to implement monetary policy. The bonds traded are usually sovereign bonds issued by the national government.

Open-end fund A mutual fund that accepts new investment money and issues additional shares at a value equal to the net asset value of the fund at the time of investment.

Operating cycle The length of time between a company's acquisition of goods or raw materials and the collection of cash from sales to customers.

Operating efficiency ratios Ratios that measure how efficiently a company performs day-to-day tasks, such as the collection of receivables and management of inventory.

Operating leases A type of lease which is more akin to the rental of the underlying asset.

Operating leverage The sensitivity of a firm's operating profit to a change in revenues, determined by the composition of fixed and variable operating costs.

Operating profit margin A profitability ratio calculated as operating income (i.e., income before interest and taxes) divided by revenue. Also called *operating margin*.

Operational deposits Bank deposits generated by clearing, custody, and cash management activities.

Operational independence A bank's ability to execute monetary policy and set interest rates in the way it thought would best meet the inflation target.

Operational risk The risk that arises from inadequate or failed people, systems, and internal policies, procedures, and processes, as well as from external events that are beyond the control of the organization but that affect its operations.

Operationally efficient Said of a market, a financial system, or an economy that has relatively low transaction costs.

Opportunistic real estate strategies Include major redevelopment, repurposing of assets, taking on large vacancies, or speculating on significant improvement in market conditions. These may be appealing for investors seeking higher returns and willing to accept additional risks from development, redevelopment, repositioning, and leasing.

Opportunity cost The value that investors forgo by choosing a particular course of action; the value of something in its best alternative use.

Optimal capital structure The capital structure at which the value of the company is maximized.

Option A primary example of a **contingent claim**. A **derivative contract** that provides the buyer the right, but not the obligation, to buy or sell an **underlying**.

Option contract See *option*.

Option premium An amount that is paid upfront from the option buyer to the option seller. Reflects the value of the option buyer's right to exercise in the future.

Option-adjusted price The sum of a bond's flat price and value of an embedded option.

Option-adjusted spread Or OAS for a bond is its Z-spread adjusted for the value of an embedded option.

Option-adjusted yield A yield measure for a bond adjusted for embedded options.

Order A specification of what instrument to trade, how much to trade, and whether to buy or sell.

Order precedence hierarchy With respect to the execution of orders to trade, a set of rules that determines which orders execute before other orders.

Order-driven markets A market (generally an auction market) that uses rules to arrange trades based on the orders that traders submit; in their pure form, such markets do not make use of dealers.

Ordinary shares Equity shares that are subordinate to all other types of equity (e.g., preferred equity). Also called *common stock* or *common shares*.

Organizational form A legal and tax classification of a business, specific to a jurisdiction, that determines the organization's legal identity, owner–manager relationship, owner liability, taxation, and access to financing.

Out-of-the-money Describes an option with zero intrinsic value because the option buyer would not rationally exercise the option. An example of such would be the case in which the price of the underlying is less than the option's exercise price for a call option.

Over-the-counter (OTC) Refers to derivative markets in which **derivative contracts** are created and traded between derivatives end users and **dealers**, or financial intermediaries, such as commercial banks or investment banks.

Overcollateralization Credit enhancement technique where collateral underlying the transaction exceeds the face value of the issued bonds.

Overconfidence bias A bias in which people demonstrate unwarranted faith in their own intuitive reasoning, judgments, and/or cognitive abilities.

Overfitting When a machine learning model learns the input and target dataset too precisely, making the system more likely to discover false relationships or unsubstantiated patterns that will lead to prediction errors.

P-value The smallest level of significance at which the null hypothesis can be rejected.

Par rate A yield-to-maturity that makes the present value of a bond's cash flows equal to par.

Par swap rate The fixed swap rate that equates the present value of all future expected floating cash flows to the present value of fixed cash flows.

Par value The amount of principal on a bond, also known as face value.

Parallel shift When all maturities along a yield curve increase or decrease in yield in the same direction by the same magnitude. A parallel shift in the yield curve is implicitly assumed in analytical duration and convexity.

Parameter A descriptive measure computed from or used to describe a population of data, conventionally represented by Greek letters.

Parametric test Any test (or procedure) concerned with parameters or whose validity depends on assumptions concerning the population generating the sample.

Pari passu clause A covenant or contract clause that ensures a debt obligation is treated the same as the borrower's other senior debt instruments and is not subordinated to similar obligations.

Partially amortizing bond A loan or bond with a payment schedule that calls for the complete repayment of principal over the instrument's time to maturity.

Participating preference shares Preference shares that entitle shareholders to receive the standard preferred dividend plus the opportunity to receive an additional dividend if the company's profits exceed a pre-specified level.

Pass-through businesses Businesses that, by virtue of their organizational form and/or other legal and regulatory attributes, do not pay entity-level taxes on income or loss; income or loss is passed through to owners, who pay personal taxes.

Pass-through rate The coupon rate of a mortgage pass-through security that is received by the investor after administrative charges. It is lower than the weighted average mortgage rate earned on the underlying pool of mortgages because of administrative charges. The pass-through rate that the investor receives is said to be "net interest" or "net coupon."

Passive investment In the fixed-income context, it is investment that seeks to mimic the prevailing characteristics of the overall investments available in terms of credit quality, type of borrower, maturity, and duration rather than express a specific market view.

Payable date The day that the company actually mails out (or electronically transfers) a dividend payment.

Payment date The day that the company actually mails out (or electronically transfers) a dividend payment.

Payment-in-kind A bond feature whereby coupon payments can be fully or partially paid in the form of additional issuance or added to the principal amount.

Payments system The system for the transfer of money.

Pearson correlation A parametric measure of the relationship between two variables.

Pecking order theory The theory that managers consider how their actions might be interpreted by outsiders and thereby order their preferences for various forms of corporate financing. Forms of financing that are least visible to outsiders (e.g., internally generated funds) are most preferable to managers, and those that are most visible (e.g., equity issuance) are least preferable.

Penetration pricing A discount pricing approach used when a firm willingly sacrifices margins in order to build scale and market share.

Percentiles Quantiles that divide a distribution into 100 equal parts that sum to 100.

Perfect competition A market structure in which the individual firm has virtually no impact on market price, because it is assumed to be a very small seller among a very large number of firms selling essentially identical products.

Performance evaluation The measurement and assessment of the outcomes of investment management decisions.

Performance fee Fee paid to the general partner from the limited partner(s) based on realized net profits.

Period costs Costs (e.g., executives' salaries) that cannot be directly matched with the timing of revenues and which are thus expensed immediately.

Periodicity Number of periods in a year, used for compound interest. The periodicity of a fixed-income instrument usually matches the frequency of its coupon payments.

Permanent differences Differences between tax and financial reporting of revenue (expenses) that will not be reversed at some future date. These result in a difference between the company's effective tax rate and statutory tax rate and do not result in a deferred tax item.

Permissioned networks Networks that are fully open only to select participants on a DLT network.

Permissionless networks Networks that are fully open to any user on a DLT network.

Perpetual bonds Bonds with no stated maturity date.

Perpetuity A perpetual annuity, or a set of never-ending level sequential cash flows, with the first cash flow occurring one period from now.

PESTLE analysis A framework for analyzing factors that influence an industry's economic outcomes.

Pet projects A capital investment that is pursued by management but is not economically justifiable by a disinterested party. Motivations for pet projects include self-dealing and vanity.

Physical risks Economic and financial losses from the increase in the severity and frequency of extreme weather due to climate change—for example, the loss of coastal real estate from a storm.

PIPE (private investment in public equity) A private offering to select investors with fewer disclosures and lower transaction costs that allows the issuer to raise capital more quickly and cost effectively.

Platykurtic Describes a distribution that has relatively less weight in the tails than the normal distribution (also called thin-tailed).

Pledge A legal right or claim to property by a creditor. Also called a lien.

Poison pill Officially known as a shareholder rights plan, a poison pill is a hostile-takeover defense adopted by boards of directors according to rules specified in the corporate charter. There are several types of poison pills. Generally, they allow shareholders, *excluding* the shareholder making the hostile bid and their affiliates, to buy newly issued shares at a discounted price. The share issuance would dilute the bidder's ownership percentage, rendering it impossible for the bidder to attain control.

Policy rate An interest rate that a central bank sets and announces publicly; normally the rate at which it is willing to lend money to the commercial banks.

Portfolio companies The individual companies owned by a private equity firm.

Portfolio investment flows Short-term investments in foreign assets, such as stocks or bonds.

Portfolio planning The process of creating a plan for building a portfolio that is expected to satisfy a client's investment objectives.

Position The quantity of an asset that an entity owns or owes.

Posterior probability An updated probability that reflects or comes after new information.

Power of a test The probability of correctly rejecting the null—that is, rejecting the null hypothesis when it is false.

Pre-funding period Allows the trust to acquire during a certain period of time after the close of the transaction.

Preference shares A type of equity interest which ranks above common shares with respect to the payment of dividends and the distribution of the company's net assets upon liquidation. They have characteristics of both debt and equity securities. Also called *preferred stock*.

Preferred stock See *preference shares*.

Premium In the case of bonds, premium refers to the amount by which a bond is priced above its face (par) value. In the case of an option, the amount paid for the option contract.

Prepayment option May entitle the borrower to prepay all or part of the outstanding mortgage principal prior to maturity. This creates a risk from the lender's or investor's viewpoint because the cash flow amounts and timing cannot be known with certainty.

Prepayment risk The risk that the some or all of a mortgage-backed security's principal is repaid at a different speed than expected, either in the form of contraction risk (or earlier repayment than expected) or extension risk (later repayment).

Present value models Valuation models that estimate the intrinsic value of a security as the present value of the future benefits expected to be received from the security. Also called *discounted cash flow models*.

Pretax margin A profitability ratio calculated as earnings before taxes divided by revenue.

Price discrimination A pricing approach that charges different prices to different customers based on their willingness to pay.

Price index Represents the average prices of a basket of goods and services.

Price limits Establish a band relative to the previous day's settlement price within which all trades must occur.

Price multiple A ratio that compares the share price with some sort of monetary flow or value to allow evaluation of the relative worth of a company's stock.

Price priority The principle that the highest priced buy orders and the lowest priced sell orders execute first.

Price return Measures *only* the price appreciation or percentage change in price of the securities in an index or portfolio.

Price return index An index that reflects *only* the price appreciation or percentage change in price of the constituent securities. Also called *price index*.

Price stability In economics, refers to an inflation rate that is low on average and not subject to wide fluctuation.

Price takers Producers that must accept whatever price the market dictates.

Price value of a basis point (PVBP) An estimate of the change in the full price of a bond given a 1 bp change in its yield-to-maturity. The PVBP is also called the "PV01," standing for the "price value of an 01" or "present value of an 01," where "01" means 1 bp. In the United States, it is commonly called the "DV01" for the "dollar value" of 1 bp.

Price weighting An index weighting method in which the weight assigned to each constituent security is determined by dividing its price by the sum of all the prices of the constituent securities.

Price-setting option The option to adjust prices when demand or supply varies from what is forecast.

Price-to-earnings ratio (P/E) The ratio of share price to earnings per share.

Pricing power A company's ability to set prices and other economic terms with customers without affecting its sales volumes.

Primary bond markets Fixed-income markets comprised of issuers issuing bonds to investors to raise capital, often intermediated by a third-party such as an investment bank.

Primary capital markets (primary markets) The market where securities are first sold and the issuers receive the proceeds.

Primary dealer Financial institution that is authorized to deal in new issues of sovereign bonds and that serves primarily as a trading counterparty of the office responsible for issuing sovereign bonds.

Primary market The market where securities are first sold and the issuers receive the proceeds.

Prime broker A broker that provides services that commonly include custody, administration, lending, short borrowing, and trading.

Prime loans Lending made to borrowers of high credit quality with strong employment and credit histories, a low DTI, substantial equity in the underlying property, and a first lien on the mortgaged property serving as the collateral for the loan.

Principal The amount that an issuer agrees to repay the debtholders on the maturity date.

Principal-agent relationship An arrangement in which one party (the agent) has authority to act for or on behalf of another party (the principal). Such an arrangement imposes a duty on the agent to act in the principal's best interest.

Prior probabilities Probabilities reflecting beliefs prior to the arrival of new information.

Priority of claims Priority of payment, with the most senior or highest ranking debt having the first claim on the cash flows and assets of the issuer.

Private capital Funding provided to companies that is not sourced from the public markets.

Private company A company, typically a limited company, that does not list its equity securities on an exchange.

Private debt Capital extended to companies through a loan or other form of debt.

Private debtholders Investors in an entity's non-securitized debt claims, such as a loan or lease. The most common type of private debtholder is a bank.

Private equity Equity investment capital raised from sources other than public markets and traditional institutions.

Private equity fund A hedge fund that seeks to buy, optimize, and ultimately sell portfolio companies to generate profits. See *venture capital fund*.

Private equity securities Securities that are not listed on public exchanges and have no active secondary market. They are issued primarily to institutional investors via non-public offerings, such as private placements.

Private investment in public equity (PIPE) An investment in the equity of a publicly traded firm that is made at a discount to the market value of the firm's shares.

Private limited company A type of limited company in many jurisdictions with pass-through taxation but restrictions on the number of shareholders or members and on the transfer of ownership interest.

Private placement A sale of debt or equity securities to a small group of investors on an unregulated basis. The terms of the offering are negotiated by the issuer and investors.

Probability of default (POD) The likelihood that an issuer fails to make full and timely payments of principal and interest; typically an annualized measure.

Probability sampling A sampling plan that allows every member of the population to have an equal chance of being selected.

Probability tree diagram A diagram with branches emanating from nodes representing either mutually exclusive chance events or mutually exclusive decisions.

Production flexibility option The option to alter production when demand varies from what is forecast.

Profession An occupational group that has specific education, expert knowledge, and a framework of practice and behavior that underpins community trust, respect, and recognition.

Profit margin An indicator of profitability, calculated as net income divided by revenue; indicates how much of each dollar of revenues is left after all costs and expenses.

Profitability ratios Ratios that measure a company's ability to generate profitable sales from its resources (assets).

Prospectus Legal document in securitization that describes the structure of the transaction, including the priority and amount of payments to be made to the servicer, administrators, and the ABS holders, as well as the credit enhancements used in the securitization.

Protective put A strategy of purchasing an underlying asset and purchasing a put on the same asset.

Proxy contest When a shareholder or group of shareholders campaigns for certain matters they have submitted to a shareholder vote, often a slate of directors who oppose the incumbent board and management. The incumbent board and management simultaneously campaign for their side.

Proxy voting A form of casting a ballot in an election in which a voter authorizes a representative to vote on their behalf according to instructions. In corporate elections, proxy ballots are cast by shareholders that direct a representative, typically the corporate secretary, to enter their votes as instructed.

Public (listed) company A company with its equity securities traded on an exchange.

Public limited companies A type of limited company in many jurisdictions with entity-level taxation but no restrictions on the number of shareholders or transferability of ownership interest; the most suitable organizational form for a company that seeks to go public.

Public–private partnership A long-term contractual relationship between the public and private sectors for the purpose of having the private sector deliver a project or service traditionally provided by the public sector. Infrastructure is increasingly being financed privately through public–private partnerships by local, regional, and national governments.

Public–private partnership (PPP) An agreement between the public sector and the private sector to finance, build, and operate public infrastructure, such as hospitals and toll roads.

Pull on liquidity An action or event that accelerates cash outflows.

Purchase agreement Legal document in a securitization transaction that outlines the representations and warranties that the seller makes about the assets sold.

Pure discount bonds Bonds that do not pay interest during their life. They are issued at a discount to par value and redeemed at par. Also called zero-coupon bonds.

Put An option that gives the holder the right to sell an underlying asset to another party at a fixed price over a specific period of time.

Put option The right to sell an underlying.

Putable bonds Bonds that give the bondholder the right to sell the bond back to the issuer at a predetermined price on specified dates.

Put–call forward parity Describes the no-arbitrage condition in which at $t = 0$ the present value of the price of a long forward commitment plus the price of the long put must equal the price of the long call plus the price of the risk-free asset (with face value of the exercise price of both the call and the put).

Put–call parity Describes the no-arbitrage condition in which at $t = 0$ the price of the long underlying asset plus the price of the long put must equal the price of the long call plus the price of the risk-free asset (with face value of the exercise price of both the call and the put).

Quantile A value at or below which a stated fraction of the data lies. Also referred to as a fractile.

Quantitative easing An expansionary monetary policy based on aggressive open market purchase operations.

Quartiles Quantiles that divide a distribution into four equal parts.

Quick ratio A measure of liquidity that is the ratio of cash, marketable securities, and receivables to current liabilities.

Quintiles Quantiles that divide a distribution into five equal parts.

Quota rents Profits that foreign producers can earn by raising the price of their goods higher than they would without a quota.

Quotas Government policies that restrict the quantity of a good that can be imported into a country, generally for a specified period of time.

Quote-driven market A market in which dealers acting as principals facilitate trading.

Quoted margin Specified spread of a floating rate instrument over a market reference rate or benchmark.

Range The difference between the maximum and minimum values in a dataset.

Rapid amortization provisions Provisions in receivable ABS that may require early principal amortization if specific events occur. Such provisions are referred to as early amortization and are included to safeguard the credit quality of the issue, particularly during the revolving period.

Razor, razorblade pricing A pricing approach that combines a low price on a piece of equipment and high-margin pricing on repeat-purchase consumables.

Real assets Generally, these are tangible physical assets, such as real estate, infrastructure, and natural resources, but they also include such intangibles as patents, intellectual property, and goodwill. Real assets generate current or expected future cash flows and/or are considered a store of value.

Real estate Includes borrowed or ownership capital in buildings or land. Developed land includes commercial and industrial real estate, residential real estate, and infrastructure.

Real option A right, but not an obligation, for management to make a decision with respect to a capital investment that alters future cash flows from the original forecasted scenario.

Real risk-free interest rate The single-period interest rate for a completely risk-free security if no inflation were expected.

Rebalancing In the context of asset allocation, a discipline for adjusting the portfolio to align with the strategic asset allocation.

Rebalancing policy The set of rules that guide the process of restoring a portfolio's asset class weights to those specified in the strategic asset allocation.

Recapitalization Recapitalization via private equity describes the steps a firm takes to increase or introduce leverage to its portfolio company and pay itself a dividend out of the new capital structure.

Recognition lag The lag in government response to an economic problem resulting from the delay in confirming a change in the state of the economy.

Recourse loan Loan in which the lender has a claim against the borrower for the shortfall (deficiency) between the amount of the outstanding mortgage balance and the proceeds received from the sale of the property.

Recovery rate (RR) The percentage of an outstanding debt claim recovered when an issuer defaults

Redemption fee A fee charged to discourage redemptions and to offset the transaction costs for remaining investors in the fund.

Refinancing rate A type of central bank policy rate.

Regionalism In between the two extremes of bilateralism and multilateralism. In regionalism, a group of countries cooperate with one another. Both bilateralism and regionalism can be conducted at the exclusion of other groups. For example, regional blocs may agree to provide trade benefits to one another and increase barriers for those outside of that group.

Registered bonds Bonds for which ownership is recorded by either name or serial number.

Regression analysis Allows us to test hypotheses about the relationship between two variables, by quantifying the strength of the relationship between the two variables, and to use one variable to make predictions about the other variable.

Regression coefficients The collective term for the intercept and slope coefficients in the regression model.

Regret The feeling that an opportunity has been missed; typically, an expression of *hindsight bias*.

Regret-aversion bias An emotional bias in which people tend to avoid making decisions that will result in action out of fear that the decision will turn out poorly.

Relative dispersion The amount of dispersion relative to a reference value or benchmark.

Reopening Issuing bonds by increasing the size of an existing bond issue with a price significantly different from par.

Replication A strategy in which a derivative's cash flow stream may be recreated using a combination of long or short positions in an underlying asset and borrowing or lending cash.

Repo rate The interest rate on a repurchase agreement.

Representativeness bias A belief perseverance bias in which people tend to classify new information based on past experiences and classifications.

Repurchase agreement (Repo) A form of collateralized loan involving the sale of a security with a simultaneous agreement by the seller to buy back the same security from the purchaser at an agreed-on price and future date. The party who sells the security at the inception of the repurchase agreement and buys it back at maturity is borrowing money from the other party, and the security sold and subsequently repurchased represents the collateral.

Repurchase date The date when the party who sold the security at the inception of a repurchase agreement buys back the security from the cash lending counterparty.

Repurchase price The price at which the party who sold the security at the inception of the repurchase agreement buys back the security from the cash lending counterparty.

Required margin Yield spread of a floating rate instrument such that the instrument is priced at par value on a rate reset date.

Required rate of return The rate of return required by investors given the risk of the bond investment, also known as the market discount rate or required yield.

Required yield The rate of return required by investors given the risk of the bond investment, also known as the market discount rate of required rate of return.

Required yield spread The difference in yield-to-maturity between a bond and that of a government benchmark bond with the same or similar time-to-maturity.

Resampling A statistical method that repeatedly draws samples from the original observed data sample for the statistical inference of population parameters.

Reserve currency A currency held by global central banks in significant quantities and widely used to conduct international trade and financial transactions.

Reserve requirement The requirement for banks to hold reserves in proportion to the size of deposits.

Residual The amount of deviation of an observed value of the dependent variable from its estimated value based on the fitted regression line.

Restricted domestic currency A currency with limited convertibility into other currencies due to illiquidity.

Return on assets (ROA) A profitability ratio calculated as net income divided by average total assets; indicates a company's net profit generated per dollar invested in total assets.

Return on equity (ROE) A profitability ratio calculated as net income divided by average shareholders' equity.

Return on invested capital (ROIC) A measure of the profitability of a company relative to the amount of capital invested by the equityholders and debtholders.

Return on sales An indicator of profitability, calculated as net income divided by revenue; indicates how much of each dollar of revenues is left after all costs and expenses. Also referred to as *net profit margin*.

Return-generating model A model that can provide an estimate of the expected return of a security given certain parameters and estimates of the values of the independent variables in the model.

Revenue bonds Bonds issued by non-sovereign governments related to a government sponsored project expected to generate future cash flow as a primary source of repayment.

Reverse repurchase agreement A repurchase agreement viewed from the perspective of the cash lending counterparty.

Reverse stock split A reduction in the number of shares outstanding with a corresponding increase in share price, but no change to the company's underlying fundamentals.

Revolving credit agreements The most reliable form of short-term bank borrowing facilities; they are in effect for multiple years (e.g., three to five years) and can have optional medium-term loan features. Also known as *revolvers*.

Rho The change in a given derivative instrument for a given small change in the risk-free interest rate, holding everything else constant. Rho measures the sensitivity of the option to the risk-free interest rate.

Ricardian equivalence An economic theory that implies that it makes no difference whether a government finances a deficit by increasing taxes or issuing debt.

Risk Exposure to uncertainty. The chance of a loss or adverse outcome as a result of an action, inaction, or external event.

Risk averse The assumption that an investor will choose the least risky alternative.

Risk aversion The degree of an investor's inability and unwillingness to take risk.

Risk budgeting The establishment of objectives for individuals, groups, or divisions of an organization that takes into account the allocation of an acceptable level of risk.

Risk exposure The state of being exposed or vulnerable to a risk. The extent to which an organization is sensitive to underlying risks.

Risk governance The top-down process and guidance that directs risk management activities to align with and support the overall enterprise.

Risk management The process of identifying the level of risk an organization wants, measuring the level of risk the organization currently has, taking actions that bring the actual level of risk to the desired level of risk, and monitoring the new actual level of risk so that it continues to be aligned with the desired level of risk.

Risk management framework The infrastructure, process, and analytics needed to support effective risk management in an organization.

Risk premium An extra return expected by investors for bearing some specified risk.

Risk shifting Actions to change the distribution of risk outcomes.

Risk tolerance the level of risk an investor is willing and able to bear.

Risk transfer Actions to pass on a risk to another party, often, but not always, in the form of an insurance policy.

Risk-neutral pricing A no-arbitrage derivative value established separately from investor views on risk that uses underlying asset volatility and the risk-free rate to calculate the present value of future cash flows.

Risk-neutral probability The computed probability used in binomial option pricing by which the discounted weighted sum of expected values of the underlying equal the current option price. Specifically, this probability is computed using the risk-free rate and assumed up gross return and down gross return of the underlying.

Rollover risk The likelihood that a property owner will lose an existing tenant and forgo income until a new one is found.

Safety-first rules Rules for portfolio selection that focus on the risk that portfolio value or portfolio return will fall below some minimum acceptable level over some time horizon.

Sample correlation coefficient A standardized measure of how two variables in a sample move together. It is the ratio of the sample covariance to the product of the two variables' standard deviations.

Sample covariance A measure of how two variables in a sample move together.

Sample excess kurtosis A sample measure of the degree of a distribution's kurtosis in excess of the normal distribution's kurtosis.

Sample mean The sum of the sample observations divided by the sample size.

Sample skewness A sample measure of the degree of asymmetry of a distribution.

Sample standard deviation The positive square root of the sample variance.

Sample variance The sum of squared deviations around the mean divided by the degrees of freedom.

Sample-size neglect A type of representativeness bias in which financial market participants incorrectly assume that small sample sizes are representative of populations (or "real" data).

Sampling distribution The distribution of all distinct possible values that a statistic can assume when computed from samples of the same size randomly drawn from the same population.

Sampling error The difference between the observed value of a statistic and the estimate resulting from using subsets of the population.

Sampling plan The set of rules used to select a sample.

Saving deposits Bank deposits typically held for non-transactional purposes that often have a stated term.

Scatter plot A two-dimensional graphical plot of paired observations of values for the independent and dependent variables in a simple linear regression.

Scenario analysis A variation of the valuation process combining a base case with alternative outcomes, allowing the incorporation of more favorable or adverse scenarios in the valuation process.

Scraping An automated, large-scale, algorithm-driven approach that retrieves otherwise unstructured data available on websites and creates data in a more structured format.

Seasoned offering An offering in which an issuer sells additional units of a previously issued security.

Glossary

Secondary bond markets Fixed-income markets comprised of investors trading existing bonds amongst themselves.

Secondary market The market where securities are traded among investors.

Secondary precedence rules Rules that determine how to rank orders placed at the same time.

Secondary sale Sale of a private company stake to another private equity firm or group of financial buyers.

Secondary-stage investments The second stage of development of an infrastructure asset. Secondary-stage investments involve existing infrastructure facilities or fully operational assets that do not require further investment or development over the investment horizon. These assets generate immediate cash flow and returns expected over the investment period.

Sector indexes Indexes that represent and track different economic sectors—such as consumer goods, energy, finance, health care, and technology—on either a national, regional, or global basis.

Secured With collateral; secured debt is backed by the cash flows of the issuer and the collateral as a secondary source of repayment.

Secured loans Loans collateralized by an asset of the borrower.

Security Evidence of equity or debt interest or in an entity or a related right, such as a derivative. Often standardized to conform to security exchange requirements.

Security characteristic line A plot of the excess return of a security on the excess return of the market.

Security market index A portfolio of securities representing a given security market, market segment, or asset class.

Security market line The graphical representation of the CAPM formula, showing the relationship between expected return and beta.

Security selection The process of selecting individual securities; typically, security selection has the objective of generating superior risk-adjusted returns relative to a portfolio's benchmark.

Security tokens Digitizes the ownership rights associated with publicly traded securities.

Segmenting A process of identifying and grouping customers by decision-useful attributes.

Self-attribution bias A bias in which people take too much credit for successes (*self-enhancing*) and assign responsibility to others for failures (*self-protecting*).

Self-control bias A bias in which people fail to act in pursuit of their long-term, overarching goals because of a lack of self-discipline.

Self-investment limits With respect to investment limitations applying to pension plans, restrictions on the percentage of assets that can be invested in securities issued by the pension plan sponsor.

Sell-side firm A broker/dealer that sells securities and provides independent investment research and recommendations to their clients (i.e., buy-side firms).

Semi-strong-form efficient market A market in which security prices reflect all publicly known and available information.

Semiannual bond basis yield Also known as a semiannual bond equivalent yield, it is an annualized interest rate with a periodicity of two.

Semiannual bond equivalent yield Also known as a semiannual bond basis yield, it is an annualized interest rate with a periodicity of two.

Senior debt A debt obligation with higher priority of payment than junior debt obligations.

Senior unsecured debt The highest-ranked debt in an issuer's capital structure which is a general obligation of the borrower.

Seniority Priority of payment of various debt obligations.

Sensitivity analysis A form of analysis used to determine the impact of a change in one or more key variables affecting investment returns or valuation.

Separately managed account (SMA) An investment portfolio managed exclusively for the benefit of an individual or institution.

Separately managed accounts Accounts that are managed in accordance with an investor's specific investment preferences and risk tolerance.

Service period The time between the grant and vesting dates for an employee share-based award, usually measured in years.

Settlement The closing date at which the counterparties of a derivative contract exchange payment for the underlying as required by the contract.

Settlement price The price determined by an exchange's clearinghouse in the daily settlement of the mark-to-market process. The price reflects an average of the final futures trades of the day.

Share class Types of equity securities that have different voting rights—for example, an issuer may issue Class A shares that carry one vote per share and Class B shares that carry ten votes per share.

Share repurchase A transaction in which a company buys back its own shares. Unlike stock dividends and stock splits, share repurchases use corporate cash.

Shareholder activism A range of actions by a corporation's shareholders that are intended to result in some change in the corporation, typically a change in the board of directors, management, or business strategy.

Shareholder derivative lawsuit A legal action by a shareholder on behalf of a company, not the shareholder personally, against a third party. Often, the third party is a director or manager who the shareholder believes has harmed the company.

Shareholder engagement Shareholder engagement reflects active ownership by investors in which the investor seeks to influence a corporation's decisions on ESG matters, either through dialogue with corporate officers or votes at a shareholder assembly (in the case of equity).

Shareholder theory of corporate governance Espoused by Milton Friedman in his famous 1970 essay, the shareholder theory holds that the objective of a business is to increase profits and shareholder value.

Shareholders Hold a direct equity position in a firm, and both individual persons and financial institutions can be shareholders. The term comes from the individual or investment firm literally having a share of the company. It is most commonly used when talking about the rights and responsibilities that come with being an "owner" of a company, such as stewardship, voting, and engagement. This differentiates it from a situation where an individual or an investment firm lends money or invests in a bond (in other words, they are not an equityholder of a company). Because bond investors do not have a share and are not owners of a company, they cannot vote. Nonetheless, expectations around engagement are increasing for those who invest in loans and bonds as well, making the difference between the two terms more subtle.

Shares Units of ownership interest in a limited company.

Sharpe ratio The average return in excess of the risk-free rate divided by the standard deviation of return; a measure of the average excess return earned per unit of standard deviation of return. Also known as the *reward-to-variability ratio*.

Shelf registration A type of public offering that allows the issuer to file a single, all-encompassing offering circular that covers a series of bond issues.

Short A trading position in a **derivative contract** that gains value as the price of the **underlying** moves lower.

Short biased These strategies use quantitative, technical, and fundamental analysis to short overvalued equity securities with limited or no long-side exposures.

Short position A position in an asset or contract in which one has sold an asset one does not own, or in which a right under a contract can be exercised against oneself.

Short selling A transaction in which borrowed securities are sold with the intention to repurchase them at a lower price at a later date and return them to the lender.

Short-run average total cost The curve describing average total cost when some costs are considered fixed.

Shortfall risk The risk that portfolio value or portfolio return will fall below some minimum acceptable level over some time horizon.

Shutdown point The point at which average revenue is equal to the firm's average variable cost.

Side letter A side agreement created between the GP and specific LPs. These agreements exist *outside* the LPA. These agreements provide additional terms and conditions related to the investment agreement.

Signpost An indicator, market level, data piece, or event that signals a risk is becoming more or less likely. An analyst can think of signposts like a traffic light.

Simple linear regression (SLR) An approach for estimating the linear relationship between a dependent variable and a single independent variable by minimizing the sum of the squared deviations between the fitted line and the observed values.

Simple random sample A subset of a larger population created in such a way that each element of the population has an equal probability of being selected to the subset.

Simple random sampling The procedure of drawing a sample to satisfy the definition of a simple random sample.

Simple yield The sum of the coupon payments plus the straight-line amortized share of the gain or loss divided by the bond's flat price. Simple yields are used mostly to quote JGBs.

Simulation A technique for exploring how a target variable (e.g. portfolio returns) would perform in a hypothetical environment specified by the user, rather than a historical setting.

Simulation trial A complete pass through the steps of a simulation.

Single-price auction A debt securities auction in which all bidders pay the same price.

Sinking fund Provisions that reduce the credit risk of a bond issue by requiring the issuer to retire a portion of the bond's principal outstanding each year.

Situational influences External factors, such as environmental or cultural elements, that shape our behavior.

Skewed Not symmetrical.

Skewness A quantitative measure of skew (lack of symmetry); a synonym of skew. It is computed as the average cubed deviation from the mean standardized by dividing by the standard deviation cubed.

Slope coefficient The change in the estimated value of the dependent variable for a one-unit change in the value of the independent variable.

Small country A country that is a price taker in the world market for a product and cannot influence the world market price.

Smart beta Involves the use of transparent, rules-based strategies as a basis for investment decisions.

Smart contracts Computer programs that are designed to self-execute on the basis of pre-specified terms and conditions agreed to by parties to a contract.

Social infrastructure investments A category of infrastructure investments that are directed toward human activities and include such assets as educational, health care, social housing, and correctional facilities, with the focus on providing, operating, and maintaining the asset infrastructure.

Soft commodities Standardized agricultural products, such as cattle and corn, with markets often involving the physical delivery of the underlying upon settlement.

Soft hurdle rate Hurdle rate where the fee is calculated on the entire return when the hurdle is exceeded. With a soft hurdle, GPs are able to catch up performance fees once the hurdle threshold is exceeded.

Soft power A means of influencing another country's decisions without force or coercion. Soft power can be built over time through actions, such as cultural programs, advertisement, travel grants, and university exchange.

Soft-bullet covered bonds Delay the bond default and payment acceleration of bond cash flows until a new final maturity date, which is usually up to a year after the original maturity date.

Solvency Refers to the condition in which firm value exceeds the face value of debt used to finance the firm's assets.

Solvency ratios Ratios that measure a company's ability to meet its long-term obligations.

Solvency risk The risk that an organization does not survive or succeed because it runs out of cash, even though it might otherwise be solvent.

Sophisticated investors Individuals or entities that are permitted in a jurisdiction to trade unregistered or, generally, less regulated securities, including shares of privately held companies; also called *accredited investors*.

Sovereign immunity A principle limiting the legal recourse of bondholders holding national government debt from forcing the issuer to declare bankruptcy or liquidate assets to settle debt claims.

Spearman rank correlation coefficient A measure of correlation applied to ranked data.

Special dividend A dividend paid by a company that does not pay dividends on a regular schedule, or a dividend that supplements regular cash dividends with an extra payment.

Special purpose acquisition company A "blank check" company that exists solely for the purpose of acquiring an unspecified private company within a predetermined period or return capital to investors.

Special purpose entity (SPE) Also referred to as a special purpose vehicle or SPV, this legal entity is created for a specific economic purpose. In the case of a project SPV, the entity's sole purpose is to facilitate the construction, operation, and financing of an infrastructure asset over its contractual life.

Special purpose vehicle See *special purpose entity*.

Special situations An area of private capital investment which targets return by investing in stressed, distressed, or event-driven opportunities.

Split ratings Complex risks viewed very differently by rating agencies

Sponsored A type of depository receipt in which the foreign company whose shares are held by the depository has a direct involvement in the issuance of the receipts.

Spot curve Yields-to-maturity on a series of default-risk-free zero-coupon bonds.

Spot markets Markets in which specific assets are exchanged at current prices. Spot markets are often referred to as **cash markets**.

Spot prices The current prices prevailing in **spot markets**.

Spot rates Yields-to-maturity on default-risk-free zero-coupon bonds.

Spread The difference in yield-to-maturity between a bond and that of a another bond.

Spread risk Bond price risk arising from changes in the yield spread on credit-risky bonds; reflects changes in the market's assessment and/or pricing of credit migration (or downgrade) risk and market liquidity risk.

Spurious correlation Refers to: 1) correlation between two variables that reflects chance relationships in a particular dataset; 2) correlation induced by a calculation that mixes each of two variables with a third variable; and 3) correlation between two variables arising not from a direct relation between them but from their relation to a third variable.

Stablecoin A cryptocurrency that aims to maintain a stable value relative to a specified asset or to a pool or basket of assets.

Stackelberg model A prominent model of strategic decision making in which firms are assumed to make their decisions sequentially.

Staggered board A structure of board elections in which only part of the board is elected simultaneously—for example, only one-third of the board may be up for election each year, so the board can be replaced over three years, not in one year if all seats were elected annually. This structure fosters greater continuity of board members but is an obstacle for shareholders seeking to effect change.

Stakeholder theory of corporate governance An expansion of the shareholder theory of corporate governance under which the objective of a business is to maximize value for, and balance the interests of, a broad group of stakeholders, including shareholders, employees, society, and the non-human environment.

Stakeholders Any party with an interest, financial or non-financial, in an entity or its actions.

Standard deviation The positive square root of the variance; a measure of dispersion in the same units as the original data.

Standard error of the estimate A measure of the distance between the observed values of the dependent variable and those predicted from the estimated regression. The smaller this value, the better the fit of the model. Also known as the standard error of the regression and the root mean square error.

Standard error of the forecast Used to provide an interval estimate around the estimated regression line. It is necessary because the regression line does not describe the relationship between the dependent and independent variables perfectly.

Standard error of the slope coefficient Calculated for simple linear regression by dividing the standard error of the estimate by the square root of the variation of the independent variable.

Standardization The process of creating protocols for the production, sale, transport, or use of a product or service. Standardization occurs when relevant parties agree to follow these protocols together. It helps support expanded economic and financial activities, such as trade and capital flows that support higher economic growth and standards of living, across borders.

Standards of conduct Behaviors required by a group; established benchmarks that clarify or enhance a group's code of ethics.

Standing limit orders A limit order at a price below market and which therefore is waiting to trade.

State actors Typically national governments, political organizations, or country leaders that exert authority over a country's national security and resources. The South African President, Sultan of Brunei, Malaysia's Parliament, and the British Prime Minister are all examples of state actors.

Statement of cash flows A financial statement that details the movement of cash over a period. The statement is classified into operating, investing, and financing activities.

Static trade-off theory of capital structure A theory pertaining to a company's optimal capital structure; the optimal level of debt is found at the point where additional debt would cause the costs of financial distress to increase by a greater amount than the benefit of the additional tax shield.

Statistically significant A result indicating that the null hypothesis can be rejected; with reference to an estimated regression coefficient, frequently understood to mean a result indicating that the corresponding population regression coefficient is different from zero.

Status quo bias An emotional bias in which people do nothing (i.e., maintain the status quo) instead of making a change.

Statutory voting A common method of voting where each share represents one vote.

Step-up bonds Bonds for which the coupon, be it fixed or floating, increases by specified margins at specified dates.

Stock dividend A type of dividend in which a company distributes additional shares of its common stock to shareholders instead of cash.

Stock exchange An exchange in which equity securities are traded. See *exchanges*.

Stock split An increase in the number of shares outstanding with a consequent decrease in share price, but no change to the company's underlying fundamentals.

Stockholder overhang The downward pressure on the share price of stock as large blocks of shares are being sold on the open market.

Stop order An order in which a trader has specified a stop price condition. Also called *stop-loss order*.

Stop-loss order See *stop order*.

Stranded assets A resource that is no longer economically valuable owing to changes in demand, regulations, or availability of substitutes—for example, a newly discovered oil well that will not be brought into production.

Strategic asset allocation A long-term strategy that establishes target allocations for various asset classes and aims to optimize the balance between risk and reward by diversifying investments.

Stratified random sampling A procedure that first divides a population into subpopulations (strata) based on classification criteria and then randomly draws samples from each stratum in sizes proportional to that of each stratum in the population.

Street convention For yield measures on fixed-income instruments that assume payments are made on scheduled dates and ignore weekends and holidays.

Stress testing A specific type of scenario analysis that estimates losses in rare and extremely unfavorable combinations of events or scenarios.

Strong-form efficient market A market in which security prices reflect all public and private information.

Structural budget deficit Also known as the cyclically adjusted budget deficit. The deficit that would exist if the economy was at full employment (or full potential output).

Structural subordination Arises in a holding company structure when the debt of operating subsidiaries is serviced by the cash flow and assets of the subsidiaries before funds can be passed to the holding company to service debt at the parent level.

Structured notes A broad category of securities that incorporate the features of debt instruments and one or more embedded derivatives designed to achieve a particular issuer or investor objective.

Subordinated debt A class of unsecured debt that ranks below a firm's senior unsecured obligations.

Subordination A form of internal credit enhancement that relies on creating more than one bond tranche and ordering the claim priorities for ownership or interest in an asset between the tranches. The ordering of the claim priorities is called a senior/subordinated structure, where the tranches of highest seniority are called senior, followed by subordinated or junior tranches. Also called **credit tranching**.

Subprime loans Lending to borrowers with lower credit quality, high DTI, and/or are loans with higher LTV, and include loans that are secured by second liens otherwise subordinated to other loans.

Sum of squares error (SSE) A measure of the total deviation between observed and estimated values of the dependent variable. It is calculated by subtracting each estimated value $\hat{Y}_i$ from its corresponding observed value Y_i, squaring each of these differences, and then summing all of these squared differences.

Sum of squares regression (SSR) A measure of the explained variation in the dependent variable, calculated as the sum of the squared differences between the predicted value of the dependent variable, $\hat{Y}_i$, based on the estimated regression line, and the mean of the dependent variable, $\overline{Y}$.

Sum of squares total (SST) A measure of the total variation in the dependent variable in a simple linear regression. It is calculated by subtracting the mean of the observed values $\overline{Y}$ from each of the observed values Y_i, squaring each of these differences, and then summing all of these squared differences.

Sunk costs A cost that has already been incurred.

Supervised learning A type of machine learning in which the system attempts to learn to model relationships based on labeled training data.

Supervisory board In some jurisdictions, a corporation's board of directors is formally composed of a supervisory board and a management board. The supervisory board appoints and oversees the management board and often includes representatives of employees and other non-shareholder stakeholders.

Supply chain The sequence of processes involved in the creation and delivery of a physical product to the end customer, both within and external to a firm, regardless of whether those steps are performed by a single firm.

Supply shock A typically unexpected disturbance to supply.

Survivorship bias Relates to the inclusion of only current investment funds in a database. As such, the returns of funds that are no longer available in the marketplace (have been liquidated) are excluded from the database. Also see *backfill bias*.

Swap A firm commitment involving a periodic exchange of cash flows.

Swap contract An agreement between two parties to exchange a series of future cash flows.

Swap execution facility (SEF) A swap trading platform accessed by multiple **dealers**.

Swap rate The fixed rate to be paid by the fixed-rate payer specified in a swap contract.

Syndicate A group of lenders, typically made up of banks.

Synthetic protective put The combination of a synthetic long underlying position (i.e., a long forward and risk-free borrowing) and a purchased put on the underlying.

Systematic risk The risk of severe damage to the real economy caused by the impairment of (parts of) the financial system.

Systematic sampling A procedure of selecting every kth member until reaching a sample of the desired size. The sample that results from this procedure should be approximately random.

Systemic risk Refers to risks supervisory authorities believe are likely to have broad impact across the financial market infrastructure and affect a wide swath of market participants.

Tactical asset allocation A proactive strategy that adjusts asset class allocations within a portfolio based on short-term market trends, economic conditions, or valuation changes to capitalize on temporary market inefficiencies or opportunities to improve returns or manage risk more effectively.

Target capital structure Management's desired proportions of debt and equity financing, usually stated on a book value basis or indirectly using a financial leverage metric, such as net or gross debt to EBITDA or credit rating.

Target independent A bank's ability to determine the definition of inflation that they target, the rate of inflation that they target, and the horizon over which the target is to be achieved.

Target semideviation A measure of downside risk, calculated as the square root of the average of the squared deviations of observations below the target (also called target downside deviation).

Tariffs Taxes that a government levies on imported goods.

Tax base The amount at which an asset or liability is valued for tax purposes.

Tax expense An aggregate of an entity's income tax payable (or recoverable in the case of a tax benefit) and any changes in deferred tax assets and liabilities. It is essentially the income tax payable or recoverable if these had been determined based on accounting profit rather than taxable income.

Glossary

Taxable income The portion of an entity's income that is subject to income taxes under the tax laws of its jurisdiction.

Taxable temporary differences Temporary differences that result in a taxable amount in a future period when determining the taxable profit as the balance sheet item is recovered or settled.

Technical analysis A form of security analysis that uses price and volume data, often displayed graphically, in decision making.

Tender offer A solicitation by a current or prospective shareholder to other shareholders to acquire a substantial percentage, including 100%, of shares at a specified price. This action is usually undertaken by a potential acquirer whose bid was rejected by the issuer's board of directors, prompting the potential acquirer to appeal directly to shareholders.

Tenor The remaining time to maturity for a bond or derivative contract. Also called term to maturity.

Term repos Repos with a maturity longer than one day.

Term structure of interest rates Also known as the maturity structure of interest rates, refers to the difference in interest rates or benchmark yields by time-to-maturity.

Terminal stock value The expected value of a share at the end of the investment horizon—in effect, the expected selling price. Also called *terminal value*.

Terminal value The expected value of a share at the end of the investment horizon—in effect, the expected selling price.

Test of the mean of the differences A statistical test for differences based on paired observations drawn from samples that are dependent on each other.

Text analytics Involves the use of computer programs to analyze and derive meaning typically from large, unstructured text- or voice-based datasets, such as company filings, written reports, quarterly earnings calls, social media, email, internet postings, and surveys.

Thematic risks Known risks that evolve and expand over a period of time. Climate change, pattern migration, the rise of populist forces, and the ongoing threat of terrorism fall into this category.

Thin-tailed Describes a distribution that has relatively less weight in the tails than the normal distribution (also called platykurtic).

Tiered pricing A pricing approach that charges different prices to different buyers, commonly based on volume purchased.

Timberland investment management organizations Entities that support institutional investors by managing their investments in timberland by analyzing and acquiring suitable timberland holdings.

Time tranching Structure of a securitization that allows for the redistribution of "prepayment risk" among bond classes by creating bond classes of different expected maturities.

Time value The difference between an option's premium and its intrinsic value.

Time value decay The process by which the time value of an option declines toward zero as the option's expiration date is approached.

Time-weighted rate of return The compound rate of growth of one unit of currency invested in a portfolio during a stated measurement period; a measure of investment performance that is not sensitive to the timing and amount of withdrawals or additions to the portfolio.

Tokenization The process of representing ownership rights to physical assets on a blockchain or distributed ledger.

Top-down analysis An investment selection approach that begins with consideration of macroeconomic conditions and then evaluates markets and industries based upon such conditions.

Total probability rule for expected value A rule explaining the expected value of a random variable in terms of expected values of the random variable conditional on mutually exclusive and exhaustive scenarios.

Total return Measures the price appreciation, or percentage change in price of the securities in an index or portfolio, plus any income received over the period.

Total return index An index that reflects the price appreciation or percentage change in price of the constituent securities plus any income received since inception.

Total working capital The difference between current assets and current liabilities.

Tracking error The standard deviation of the differences between a portfolio's returns and its benchmark's returns; a synonym of active risk. Also called *tracking risk*.

Tracking risk The standard deviation of the differences between a portfolio's returns and its benchmark's returns. Also called *tracking error* and *active risk*.

Trade creation When regional integration results in the replacement of higher cost domestic production by lower cost imports from other members.

Trade diversion When regional integration results in lower-cost imports from non-member countries being replaced with higher-cost imports from members.

Trade sale A portion or division of a private company sold via either direct sale or auction to a strategic buyer interested in increasing the scale and scope of an existing business.

Trade settlement date The date when the buyer and seller transfer consideration and securities.

Traditional investment markets Markets for traditional investments, which include all publicly traded debts and equities and shares in pooled investment vehicles that hold publicly traded debts and/or equities.

Tranches A grouping of securities within an issue with characteristics that vary from other tranches, such as different credit quality and seniority.

Transfer payments Welfare payments made through the social security system that exist to provide a basic minimum level of income for low-income households.

Transition risks Economic and financial losses from the transition to a lower-carbon economy in response to climate change—for example, the abandonment of an oil well that is no longer economical.

Treasury Inflation-Protected Securities (TIPS) US Treasury bonds with a principal that is adjusted for changes in the Consumer Price Index. TIPS are issued in 5-, 10-, and 30-year maturities.

Treynor ratio A measure of risk-adjusted performance that relates a portfolio's returns in excess of the risk-free rate to a portfolio's beta.

Trimmed mean A mean computed after excluding a stated small percentage of the lowest and highest observations.

Triparty repo A repurchase agreement in which the transacting parties agree to use a third-party agent that provides access to a larger collateral pool and multiple counterparties, as well as valuation and safekeeping of assets.

True yield Measures on fixed-income instruments use actual payment dates, accounting for weekends and holidays. The true yield on an instrument is always lower than the street convention yield.

Turn-of-the-year effect Calendar anomaly that stock market returns in January are significantly higher compared to the rest of the months of the year, with most of the abnormal returns reported during the first five trading days in January.

Two-fund separation theorem The theory that all investors regardless of taste, risk preferences, and initial wealth will hold a combination of two portfolios or funds: a risk-free asset and an optimal portfolio of risky assets.

Two-way table A table of the frequency distribution of observations classified on the basis of two discrete variables. Also known as *Contingency table*.

Two-week repo rate The interest rate on a two-week repurchase agreement; may be used as a policy rate by a central bank.

Type I error The error of rejecting a true null hypothesis; a false positive.

Type II error The error of not rejecting a false null hypothesis; false negative.

Uncommitted lines of credit Sources of bank credit that a bank can refuse to honor. Uncommitted credit lines are made up to a certain principal amount for a pre-determined maximum maturity, charging a market reference rate plus an issuer-specific spread on only the principal outstanding for the period of use.

Underfitted When a machine learning model treats true parameters as if they are noise and is unable to recognize relationships in the training data, making the model more likely to fail to fully discover patterns that underlie the data.

Underlying The asset referred to in a **derivative contract**.

Underwritten offering A type of securities issue mechanism in which the investment bank guarantees the sale of the securities at an offering price that is negotiated with the issuer. Also known as *firm commitment offering*.

Unearned revenue A liability account for money that has been collected for goods or services that have not yet been delivered; payment received in advance of providing a good or service. Also called *deferred revenue* or *deferred income*.

Unimodal A distribution with a single value that is most frequently occurring.

Unit economics The expression of revenues and costs on a per-unit basis.

Unitranche debt A hybrid or blended loan structure combining different tranches of secured and unsecured debt into a single loan with a single, blended interest rate.

Unsecured Without collateral; unsecured debt is backed only by cash flows of the issuer.

Unsponsored A type of depository receipt in which the foreign company whose shares are held by the depository has no involvement in the issuance of the receipts.

Unsupervised learning A type of machine learning in which the system tries to learn the structure of unlabeled data.

Utility tokens Tokens that provide services within a network, such as paying for services and network fees.

Validity instructions Instructions which indicate when the order may be filled.

Value added resellers Businesses that distribute a product and also handle more complex aspects of product installation, customization, service, or support.

Value at risk A money measure of the minimum value of losses expected during a specified time period at a given level of probability.

Value chain The systems and processes in a firm that create value for its customers.

Value proposition The product or service attributes valued by a firm's target customer that lead those customers to prefer that firm's offering.

Value-add real estate strategies Strategies that involve larger-scale redevelopment and repositioning of existing assets and that may allow the investor to earn a higher return compared with core-plus real estate strategies.

Value-based pricing Pricing set primarily by reference to the value of the product or service to customers.

VaR See *value at risk*.

Variance The expected value (the probability-weighted average) of squared deviations from a random variable's expected value.

Variance of a random variable The expected value (the probability-weighted average) of squared deviations from a random variable's expected value.

Variation margin The difference between current margin required and the current collateral price in a repurchase agreement.

Vega The change in a given derivative instrument for a given small change in volatility, holding everything else constant. A sensitivity measure for options that reflects the effect of volatility.

Velocity The pace at which geopolitical risk impacts an investor portfolio.

Venture capital Private equity investment in a startup or early-stage company involving high risk and a high rate of failure.

Venture capital fund A hedge fund that seeks to buy, optimize, and ultimately sell portfolio companies to generate profits. See *private equity fund*.

Venture debt Private debt funding that provides venture capital backing to start-up or early-stage companies that may be generating little or negative cash flow.

Vest To become unconditionally entitled to.

Vesting date The day that an employee becomes unconditionally entitled to compensation.

Vintage year The year in which a private capital fund makes its first investment.

Volatility The standard deviation of the continuously compounded returns on the underlying asset.

Vote by proxy A mechanism that allows a designated party—such as another shareholder, a shareholder representative, or management—to vote on the shareholder's behalf.

Voting rights The power of shareholders to cast votes in corporate elections for directors and other matters submitted to a shareholder vote.

Warrant An attached option that gives its holder the right to buy the underlying stock of the issuing company at a fixed exercise price until the expiration date.

Waterfall structures These represent the distribution order for cash flows and risk to different tranches in a financing structure.

Weak-form efficient market hypothesis The belief that security prices fully reflect all past market data, which refers to all historical price and volume trading information.

Weighted average cost of capital (WACC) The expected cost of debt and equity weighted by the proportion of each used in a company's capital structure.

Weighted average coupon rate (WAC) Rate calculated for a mortgage pass-through security by weighting the mortgage rate of each mortgage in the pool by the percentage of the outstanding mortgage balance relative to the outstanding amount of all the mortgages in the pool.

Weighted average maturity (WAM) Calculated for a mortgage pass-through security by weighting the remaining number of months to maturity of each mortgage in the pool by the outstanding mortgage balance relative to the outstanding amount of all the mortgages in the pool.

Winsorized mean A mean computed after assigning a stated percentage of the lowest values equal to one specified low value and a stated percentage of the highest values equal to one specified high value.

Write-off/liquidation Refers to a transaction that has not gone well, and the investment is likely to lose value. The private equity firm revises the value of its investment downward or liquidates the portfolio company.

Yield curve A graphical depiction of yields-to-maturity of bonds from the same issuer across maturities.

Yield spread The difference in yield-to-maturity between a bond and that of a another bond.

Yield-to-call An internal rate of return on a fixed-income instrument's cash flows assuming cash flows are received on scheduled dates and the bond is called at a certain call price and date.

Yield-to-maturity The internal rate of return that an investor earns on a bond assuming no default, the bond is held to maturity, and periodic cash flows are reinvested at the yield-to-maturity. Also called yield-to-redemption or redemption yield.

Yield-to-worst The lowest among a fixed-income instrument's yields-to-call and yield-to-maturity. A commonly cited yield measure for fixed-rate callable bonds.

Z-spread or zero-volatility spread is a constant yield spread for a bond over a government or swap curve.

Zero-coupon bond A bond that does not pay a coupon but is priced at a discount and pays its full face value at maturity.

Zero-coupon bonds Bonds that do not pay interest during their life. They are issued at a discount to par value and redeemed at par. Also called pure discount bond.